Innocence
Abroad

Innocence Abroad

Adventuring Through Europe At 64 On $100 Per Week

ൟ

with 20 original sketches by author

IRV THOMAS

Library of Congress Number: 2001117165
ISBN #:   Hardcover   1-4010-1099-7
                     Softcover   1-4010-1098-9

Cover photo by Joy Cutting

This book was printed in the United States of America.

To order additional copies of this book, contact:
Xlibris Corporation
1-888-795-4274
www.Xlibris.com
Orders@Xlibris.com

Contents

Dedication

This edition is gratefully dedicated to all the wonderful people of Servas, who contributed more to the joys of my journey, and to its very possibility, than any other material element involved

Prague . . . a thousand years
of European architecture
in a single grand city

...and I'm down there in the crowd!

Preface to the First Edition

The opening chapter of this book will plunge you right into an adventure tale. Abruptly, with no preliminaries as to what you are about to read. This, I am told, is good technique, to clutch the reader unawares in an unbreakable hold. So be it, but I have need to say a few things first, about this work that has taken me three years in the writing, on top of a year earlier lived. There is more to this than meets the eye; and for you who like to know such things in preparation for a read, I don't intend to leave you wondering.

Innocence Abroad is written to stand alone as a free-wheeling adventure story – absolutely true, just as it happened, except for a few altered names, and a rare bit of fudging where developments had to be simplified for the sake of clarity. But nothing is intentionally mis-stated; no part of it has been stretched for the sake of a good yarn.

The real story, however – the full story – is both broader and deeper than an adventure tale. The year abroad that the book details is the tip of a twenty-year iceberg – the crowning celebration of a long apprenticeship in a way of life as remote from the common as that of astronauts going off into space. My lifestyle and technique, of course, do not have that same high-visibility . . . in fact, it's hard to see any difference between me and one of society's derelict failures, until you look a little more closely at the details of the life being lived and consider the terms of argument.

It all hinges on that word, Innocence, a simple term with a diversity of usage. Even in the limited range of its meaning that has to do with simplicity and artlessness – which is the range I am concerned with – it lends itself to interpretive differences that may be entirely in the eye of the beholder. The Oxford English Dictionary itself refuses to pin it down, as indicated in this quotable definition of the substantive noun, a rambling effort that takes it all the way from sublimity to insanity:

Innocent . . . 3. A guileless, simple, or unsuspecting person; one devoid of cunning or artifice; hence, one wanting in ordinary knowledge or intelligence; a simpleton, a silly fellow; a half-wit, an idiot.

A slippery slope, that! Hardly encouraging to anyone who would pursue Innocence as a serious lifestyle. But that is exactly what I have done for the past couple decades, and I feel the need to elaborate a bit on where the Messrs. Oxford and English might have missed their boat . . . or lost the compass setting of their honorable intentions.

Innocence is contrary to everything in contemporary life. *Everything.* Not a single phase of life in today's world has not its protocol, scenario, schedule, routine, agenda, plan, or otherwise tied-down predictability. From shopping lists to insurance policies, from theater schedules to recipe books to weather forecasts, the world must be secured in advance of any venture into its fearsome wilderness. Control is the byword of life. Security, the only guarantee for peace of mind. It is so reflexive as to have lost significance in our daily considerations; we do it by rote.

Strangely, we allow a single exception and we maintain the sanctity of it with such reverence as to throw the entire passion for certainty into high-profile suspicion. *Children* have not only the right, but the virtual duty to cling to Innocence as long as possible. There has been little deliberation on what the eventual reversal might do to their adult psyches, and none whatever on what the passion for childhood Innocence may say about the nature of human life, *vis á vis* this whole issue.

I will not get into those questions, but would hope they linger in your mind awhile, to be nourished by what you find in these pages.

Along with another seldom attended fact, on which I shall rest my case against the big dictionary. For hundreds of thousands of years, humanity somehow thrived in a chaotic and uncertain universe. All the while, of course, we employed the best knowledge and cunning we had, which would seem to validate the stricture against Innocence . . . *except that*: the mechanical clock is only a few hundred years old; the calendar, just a few thousand; locomotion, other than by foot, is hardly older than that; medical know-how can variously be dated from the last century to perhaps as far back as Hippocrates . . . well, the point is that the cunning and knowledge of just a few millennia ago would pass for absolute Innocence today and it suggests that humanity has *always* made its way on some small portion of trust and some very large portion of Providence. We've just forgotten those terms of living and come to think that we are responsible for everything that happens to us.

I don't claim to have returned, by any stretch, to a state of Innocence. I have simply learned the wisdom and desirability of *approaching it*. I have come to trust it and am more able than ever before to put that trust into action. Nor even do I claim any special derring-do in this respect, for I know of others who have traveled with far more evident trust in the Universe than I've ever been able to touch. It is important to see trust as a path that one enters on – timidly and hesitantly at first, but gradually gaining a feeling for it. It is important, at this very time in our history, to step out on that path and begin to feel the real security of it.

The paths of trust and Innocence, while not identical, are closely linked. One cannot experience the reality of trust before letting go of certitude; and letting go of certitude is the very definition of the sort of Innocence of which I write. From the start of this adventure, I was pretty much 'flying blind,' letting events determine my course, sure of nothing except that I had my return fare in my pocket. That was the practical limit of my trust; everything else, including any certainty of continuing funds, was up for grabs. Even the matter of having a place to live when I came home.

Beneath the adventure tale, then, this book is an account of trust and Providence, and living in their aura. There is a second and somewhat more subtle theme that I can only lightly define here. The story, while it spans about a year and a half to cover the preliminaries, is essentially of a solid year, from September to September. The framework of this year, though reflecting circumstances integral to the journey itself, fulfills a certain sense of the year as an archetypal ripening cycle. I observe this, and many of the 'stations' of that cycle, throughout the book – though I never get around to detailing the archetypal format nor giving it more background than a bit at the very end. It's not an oversight; the subject is too extensive for explication in this book and will have to await another. But it's a system that I live by, so it had to have its place in this text.

You may also find yourself curious as to how I came to such a lifestyle, which only receives sketchy annotation here and there in the book. That, too, must be put off to a future writing. If this begins to suggest a series of books, you are not far off the mark. The present effort, in fact, has been visualized from the very start as the first book of a trilogy. A trilogy that will go fully into this matter of reclaiming Innocence as I've experienced it in my own life.

I know ... the 'crowning celebration' of it, as this tale purports to be, might logically seem the last part of a trilogy, not the very first. But consider it from another perspective: this book shows what a high experience it is to travel – or to live a life – with little idea of what's coming next ... and that it's actually feasible. The next book in the series will challenge the notions that goals must be set, plans well laid in order to live an effective life, and that you're at risk of failure or worse if you ever leave the track – the myths that make people so fearful of reclaiming Innocence. That book will also concern a 'journey' in a sense – a seven-year apprenticeship trail following life's cues and prompts as they came along. Innocence, not as a singular adventure, but as an ongoing adventurous path in daily and ordinary life. In the last of the series, I'll try to account for how I got from that old world of unfulfilling certainties, to this one where I know nothing, have hardly much more than that, and enjoy almost everything. After all, if I didn't first give you some idea of what the trail was like, you'd hardly be interested in how I found it.

Fall equinox, 1994
Seattle, Washington

Preface to this edition

It's a bit awkward, seven years removed from the earlier preface, to see all those confident promises of books never written. But in a life lived on the edge, it is ever thus – I have simply been busy with other things. Writing among them, to be sure, but not the work I had then in mind.

Had the gods seen fit to put this book into wider distribution at the time, my life might well have moved in that direction, but I am not into imposing my will on the Universe. Much.

A full cycle (7 years) of time has turned since then, however, and brought me the reasonable opportunity to give this book, in a new edition, the wider circulation I think it merits. It doesn't necessarily mean those promised works will be forthcoming, but it certainly brings that possibility up for consideration. Life is a doorway process: some of them open, some do not. And I, by long habit, follow the path of least resistance.

This edition is different, in a few respects, from the earlier. A new size and binding, of course, which puts a bit of constraint on the contents. The maps of travel have been omitted except for a single overall representation of the entire journey, where chapter 2 begins. The other illustrations have been winnowed to a prime choice of 20-best pen and ink renderings – my own, of course – and a couple other items new to the book. For those who may have encountered the tale on my web site, *all* of the illustrations here will be new.

The text, with minor corrections and refinement, is essentially the same but for two significant differences. Chapter 23 – the final chapter in the first edition – has been shorn of its old closure, and a new final chapter has been added. It is an epilogue, detailing a reprise journey made in 1997 over some of the same ground, with comparative and afterthought reflections.

That's about all that should be put in your way of an immediate plunge, except to acknowledge the critical help, for this edition, of my techno-savvy friend, David Blatner, who is always there for me in any computer urgency.

Enjoy the read...

Spring equinox, 2001

Seattle, Washington

Three Mutineers and a Warden's wrath

Delphi, Greece: October 5, 1991...

Let me begin by explaining how a respectable 64-year-old (that's me) got thrown out of the Delphi Hostel in the middle of the night.

Well, it wasn't quite the middle of the night. And I wasn't exactly thrown out. But for practical purposes it amounted to the same thing.

For that matter, I may not have been all that respectable, having just rambled through five months of a European summer season on nothing more substantial than a hundred dollars a week, like a footloose hippie of other times – an image hardly denied by the curly ponytail trailing from the crumpled brim of a blue cotton hat that had been through too many launderings. Still, age should be accorded some deference.

But never mind all that. The three of us were huddled that night on the small balcony outside my dorm, talking tactics in the sultry evening air. Far below, the lights of Itea, on the Corinthean coast, twinked on like faint first stars in the deepening dusk, while beyond them the soft serrate edge of a distant ridge was still visible against the last thin pastel of a brilliant scarlet sunset.

It was Matt who kept prodding us with his insistent emphasis on

"...*hostages*, that's what we are. Hostages to a woman who won't get her damn butt out of bed before seven in the morning to let us out of here."

He was talking about the warden's wife – the warden of a youth hostel, not a prison, though it would seem to apply either way in our case. His anger was both real and mock. Just as this situation of being imprisoned in a Greek hostel, high on Mount Parnassus, was both absurd and serious to each of us: Matt, Dave and me.

We weren't yet prisoners, but in less than an hour the doors would be bolted for the night. We had just that long to decide whether to stay with this 'hospitality' that would deny us an early morning bus back to Athens, or to chance finding our night's shelter elsewhere in this already tucked-in town of Delphi.

"Dammit." Matt again, "Get the White House on the pipeline . . . have 'em send in an air strike!"

From Seattle, like me, Matt was the quintessential Young American Abroad. His every movement radiated the cocky, 'don't mess with Americans' assurance proclaimed by his fantasies. In anyone older than his twenty-odd years, the rank jingoism would have appalled me. But below his shock of black hair was only Innocent Truth gazing from strong, clear blue eyes, and I recognized my own youthful patriotic pride of once-upon-a-time.

Dave was not much older, but of a background with a good deal more reserve. From Manchester, England, he was a rugby player, though his tall and lanky form seemed unlikely for the sport. An easy good humor tempered most of what he said and did, but Matt's heroics had been goading his competitive spirit. He countered, now, with an idea of his own: that we should draw the police into the dispute.

It made a bit of sense. Technically, our passports and not ourselves were being held hostage. Hostel practice is to hold passports under lock and key overnight, for simple safe-keeping. It effectively barred us from an early morning breakout, which had been Matt's first adventurous plan. Our passports were now in the warden's private quarters, taken there with a certain finality which even suggested that they'd had to deal with this issue before.

I had gone down to speak with him, as had the fellows before me, thinking that perhaps my grey-bearded maturity might pull a little more weight. But it was no use. The warden's resistance was impregnable. Referring to his wife, the T-shirted swarthy who stood inches short of my 5'11" in the doorway, shook his head sadly, "...she work a long and hard day..." – which may have been true, but I hadn't noticed that he gave her much help – "...and she need a big sleep."

His English carried the wrong suggestion, but his point came across. I pleaded with him that I'd never make the day's boat back to Lesbos unless I could get the early morning bus into Athens. It would mean another night's layover there for me.

He rose an inch, at least. "Hostel run by hostel time, not boat time!" And that was fairly well the end of it.

In this last narrowing hour before lock-up, Dave's idea that the passport issue would bring the police to intervene finally won Matt over. But I hung back, and let the pair of them tackle it on their own. I had some reservations about the whole business. After several weeks in Greece, I was already used to the casual way in which matters of seeming urgency are handled. But more than that, it wasn't my style to force issues and make things happen. It was very clear how the cards had fallen, here, and it made more sense to me to dampen my own agenda and let things develop as they would.

The three of us had separately arrived in Delphi on the day before to see the nearby site of Apollo's fabled temple, and the first night's imprisonment had been no problem for us. But we each intended to return on a 9:30 morning bus – only to learn that it didn't run on Sunday. Our only morning option was the 6:30 bus, now blocked by the intransigent warden, and we'd become instant compatriots in rebellion.

The easiest solution, of course, would be to check out and get lodging elsewhere. But we were all on tight budgets and the $5 hostel rate was the cheapest night's shelter to be found in this tourist town. We couldn't even be sure we'd get a refund if we left at this late hour. But it went beyond that, now. For both Matt and Dave, an issue of principle was at stake: whether they'd sit still for this high-handed, buckle-or-get-out choice the warden had laid down.

But would the police actually intervene in such a silly dispute? I didn't really think so, and was surprised a short while later when Dave suddenly popped into the dorm room wearing the smug grin of a winner.

"Get your stuff ready to leave at six in the morning!"

"You're kidding! What happened?"

"All it took was the sight of an officer, and they backed down."

Matt now crowded in behind and wouldn't let Dave tell his own tale. "Boy, she caved right in! Her husband didn't even show his face when the police came in with us. He let her do all the talking."

They were triumphant. Righteousness had won the day, and I had to admit I was impressed by their easy success. They went over every detail of the interaction and it certainly looked as though Dave had been the best tactician of the three of us. Until the warden appeared in the doorway, tight-lipped and visibly shaking with contained rage.

"The Englishman!" He hardly waited for Dave to acknowledge the call. "Get your bags. I'm checking you out."

A silence hung in the air as Matt and I, suddenly sober, waited to see what Dave's reaction would be. He met the thrust with the cool of a good rugby player, head-on and assertively. "Sir, your wife made an agreement with the police..."

"Police!" sputtered the warden, "...*I am police in this hostel.*"

There was really nothing further Dave could say to that. He shrugged and grimly set to the task of pulling his effects together as the warden stood glowering. Matt, in a moment of uncommon prudence, uttered not a word and turned toward his own dorm room down the hall.

I don't know if the warden had picked Dave as the instigator or simply the easiest to deal with, but it looked as though he meant to limit the night's loss to a single paying guest. However, Matt was back in a few moments with his hastily collected gear and I realized that my own moment of truth had arrived. The flow of events had left me a clear choice: to stay with a cheap night's sleep and settle for a late bus, or cast my lot with these out-maneuvered mutineers.

It didn't take much thought. I couldn't resist the spirit of the happening, the gusto and camaraderie of it all.

So there we were, tramping together down a deserted late-night street in Delphi, packs on our backs: two incorrigibly independent young bucks and an old graybeard unwilling to close the book on the adventures of a summer. It somehow epitomized, in a single, exquisite *mise en scene,* all of what the summer had been for me. The perfect postscript to a journey of fantasy dimensions.

Fantasy certainly says it. A pocketful of dreams carried for a lifetime, finally traded-in for a backpack full of memories, all the sweeter for my age and the crazy, innocent kind of travel that can only be done by the financially forlorn.

We found a place to sleep that night, thanks to Matt's recollection of a pension he had stumbled across, and a landlady's willingness to get out of bed and rent us a tiny room for $20 – though it had only two beds. Dave and I tossed for the privilege of sleeping on the floor, and I won, earning as well the slightly cheaper portion of our three-way split.

Sleepy-eyed the next morning, munching a pick-up breakfast of pears plucked from Delphian trees – the last of the season – we got our bus on schedule and made the five-hour journey to Athens without a great deal of further excitement. Once arrived there, we clasped in a three-sided handshake, shared one last, knowing grin, and turned our separate ways – not vowing to stay in touch, for the life of the road is a very transient high that can only be renewed on the road itself.

Dave was headed for Cyprus and Matt wanted to see more of mainland Greece. I made my own way back to the fabled isle of Lesbos, an overnight boat ride on bucking waves in a washing rainstorm, to claim the sweet little apartment I'd already arranged to rent for the winter: a congenial place for a quiet season of writing, in an ambience of seaside leisure and minimal distraction.

The ways of life are unbelievably provident – if you let them take their course. I could no more have imagined myself footloose in Greece, after sixty years of unbroken fidelity to American soil, than I would have thought myself to the moon. Yes, I'd had my dreams of vagabonding, a lifetime ago when the future was a wide-open, endless horizon. I grew up under the spell of Richard Halliburton who made far-away places sing with mystery and rugged adventure. But then came the narrowing, the choices made, one by one, that foreclose dreams as we pursue our real lives. My own held no promise of the kind of money such adventuring is supposed to call for.

My last twenty years, in fact, could be called hard-scrabble. I dropped out of the career world before it had fully captured me, forsaking a dependable income in favor of living as I wished. That meant growth and self-discovery, and a life of stimulus and challenge . . . but it also meant a steady flirtation with insolvency that locked my hopes for foreign travel as tightly in the box of old fantasies as ever they'd once been dreams to live by.

Nothing had much changed, in that respect, by the time I reached my sixties. I had less than $3500 at my disposal when I left the States, more than a year before this end-of-summer adventure in Delphi; and my income – not enough to quite reach the poverty line – came entirely from Social Security. Somehow, from this shallow base of travel funds, I managed to weather the international tide of recession through eight months of residence in London and five more on the road; and I was yet to add another six months before finally returning to American soil.

There was no guidebook to follow in doing this, and none could be written. It had more to do with a way of living, a certain consciousness that had worked for me for many years at home. Frugality has been an accustomed part of it. But then there is the element of raw chance: learning to live with the hazard of never knowing what comes next, only the inner assurance that whatever it may be will be okay. This was an outlook I had honed to perfection. The wonder of it – which I could not know before I got to Europe – was that it would work for me in this utterly unfamiliar world where I was entirely on my own, everywhere a stranger to language and custom.

Part of the secret, certainly, is the realization, beyond any shred of doubt, that life is provident if you follow its lead. Without this perspective, I would never have even dared such a journey. I was drawn into it by a set of events that only a fool would consider auspicious ... or someone who could see in such things the least providential path.

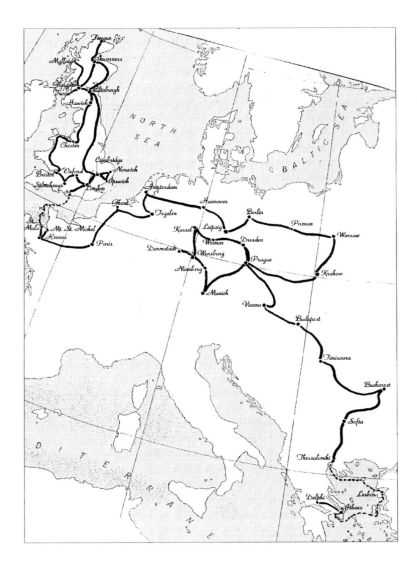

Delphi was the far end of a magical trail, highlighted by this nation-
less map. Countries are always bad news (they make wars and
regularly restrict people's lives), but cities are bountiful gifts of
friendship and culture.

Everything Sprouts in February

Seattle, Washington: February 1990...

People in other lives took journeys abroad; it was not the way of mine. I hadn't even a sense that it was within my realm of choice. My style in recent years had been to follow life's trail as it opened for me – which might seem a haphazard way to live, but the logic behind it is as solid as that of an oarsman moving with the current, or a cyclist with the wind at her back. I could make a long list of all the ways it clarified my life; but the ease of passage, for one of limited means, would easily claim the top spot.

The spring of 1990 found me at a trail closure from which I might have taken any direction. I was ending two years at the University of Washington, finally completing a Bachelor of Arts pursuit aborted when the world was young. Returning to school at sixty was a trail-inspired thing, too, but that's another story. Part of trail philosophy is that each new segment should follow naturally from what has gone before. This was the filter through which I viewed my world as time took me toward springtime and graduation. I was alert for cues as the event approached. But even more pertinent to the moment's heightened significance was the arrival of February, in and of itself.

February has become a magical month for me. As surely as it brings out the first green, the earliest blossoms, it sprouts my year's primary activity. Sometimes it's in a theme that seems to run through the month, but more often there is an actual turn of events, quite suddenly emergent as if roused from winter dormancy by the warming sun. February's happenings command attention like the lifting swells of a turbid sea beckon the calculating eyes of a bobbing surfer. The comparison is limited, though, for the usual February sprout is a surprise, and it rarely leaves anything up to choice.

For the first time at such a trail juncture, finances were not a critical consideration – in my own accustomed terms, at least. In the year just past I had turned the corner, from a reliance on education funding to the receipt of Social Security benefits, which assured me, now, a continuity of means. True, my monthly pittance, hovering below the $400 line, was hardly extravagant enough to live on; but it was close enough to my meager needs that the gap could be easily bridged. I had, in fact, the perfect bridge: a very part-time post as newsletter editor for the *Earthstewards Network,* demanding of me perhaps a week of focused attention out of each eight or ten.

This was the setting, then, with Europe only the dimmest gleam of a 'someday...' dream, when the February sprouts of 1990 popped up in my world.

Shortly before the day of valentines, I happened across an article in the university's student press about the *Council for International Education Exchange.* The CIEE is a quasi-official service organization facilitating student opportunities for travel and study overseas. Not that I felt study abroad was an affordable option, but it tweaked the old dream, and with my horizon about to open I had to give curiosity its due. But so light was its touch, in the moment's scheme of things, that two weeks went by before I finally checked it out.

I was more absorbed, at the time, by the prospect of giving a summer workshop at a California Unitarian retreat, an offer imprudently responded to weeks earlier, in the impatience of January. During these two weeks before my visit to CIEE the workshop was confirmed: I was committed to an August retreat on the Monterey peninsula.

The CIEE proved to be little more than a travel agency, to all appearances. I picked up a handful of literature there, a single piece of which survived that evening's quick survey. This was a booklet that described a work-exchange program with several other countries. A program enabling students to work and live abroad. No study involved, and ...

It suddenly dawned on me that there might be *no real cost involved!*

The program would provide a six-month work permit, which seemed to mean I could earn my way through a half-year's residence in some exotic foreign city. I knew my choice at once. London! I could live there, work there, make local friends, actually experience British life for awhile, not just be there and back, in a bit of tourist fluff. The thought of it, once I realized the cost-free potential, would simply not let go of me.

Bursting with the idea, I couldn't keep it from Terry the next evening, as she shared cookies and tea with me in the compact attic quarters of her Wallingford District house. Terry was also in pursuit of a late-life degree, though at 49 a mere youngster – but several times my rank, going for her doctorate. We had almost become housemates, a couple of years before; but the fates had intervened and sent me elsewhere when she bought this rambling monster of a building, clearly in its third or fourth incarnation if judged by the complexity of its jumbled architecture. She was partly in my own world of rebellious selfhood, but kept a solid foot in the real world of down-to-earth practicality and was thereby a good reality-check for me.

She caught my excitement at once, over the thought of spending six months in London. Neither of us had ever been abroad, and I detected a shade of envy in her blue eyes, but it was overwhelmed by the sparkle of support – until it came to the question of how I was going to manage all of this on my $400 a month.

"That's the whole point, Terry. They'll give me a work permit, and provide the job leads and whatever other assistance I need."

"Now, wait a minute ... " An eyebrow arched up toward the coal black bangs of a classic page-boy haircut that heightened, by contrast, the light complexion of her oval face. "Let me get this straight. You're going to get a job in London?"

"Why not, for six months?"

"You're going to get a *six-month job* in London . . . on a student permit? YOU?"

My reality check wasn't going exactly as I had hoped. "Look, I've got good skills. Writing, editing, Pagemaker . . . "

"Yeah, and you're over sixty, with no work references for the past twenty years. What kind of résumé are you planning to work-up?

"For students they won't expect a résumé."

"For a sixty-year old student, they will!"

"C'mon, Terry, don't be a downer." But I knew she was giving me `real world' arguments, and I had nothing to counter them with.

I brooded half the way home, and then slipped back into my own reality, hardly aware of the shift except for the fact I was suddenly feeling lighter. It was just too good an opportunity to pass up. The timing of its appearance was exquisitely perfect. How could I expect Terry to understand this as I did? It had taken years of journaling to see how each year's path opened for me in February – and then years more to confirm it, to learn how reliable it was. Without the experience, itself, Terry couldn't relate to this, no matter how well I was able to explain it.

But she was right, too, about the obstacles. In practical terms I had become a Rip van Winkle in the world of work. And I'd be talking to employers on their terms, not mine. Having a work permit might provide a legal basis for employment, but it gave me no particular edge in getting a job. The program, itself, was geared to youngsters, and I'd be in direct competition with them. Would I be crazy, to venture such a gamble on the way my reality worked? London is one of the world's expensive cities; just in case I *didn't* get a job, how far would my $400 go?

There were all sorts of logistic problems, too. I had six months after graduation to join the program, and it would surely take that long to prepare for it – but it was not as much my time as I would've liked. I had already promised to lead a workshop in August, which would take preparation time and also crowd my departure date with a trip to California. This, itself, was crowded by an unfinished thesis for my major, the Comparative History of Ideas, that required an extension of post-graduate time to complete. How would I find the time, in between those two demands, to take care of the hundreds of details that an extended journey abroad would surely entail? It would have to include the storage of all my belongings, for I certainly couldn't afford to continue a rental while gone, and that would be a last minute thing . . . between my return from California and the takeoff for England.

I wasn't at all sure it was worth the upheaval it promised, along with the further hassle of an entire resettlement process when I re turned. But try as I might, I couldn't disengage from the enchantment of the vision: a solid half year in London, with the potential of extension into a summer of European travel.

Terry still looked dubious when I told her that I had to do it. After all, I had been a closet Anglophile all my life and was sure I'd never again, at my age, have such an opportunity. I could either go for it and take my chances, or worry myself into staying safe . . . and unfulfilled for the rest of my days.

But she no longer responded with dire prophecies. "Spoken like a true Aries, Irv! Tell me what I can do to support you."

A quick glance at her tomboy-trim figure brought a thing or two to mind, but I stayed with the subject at hand. "What I need most of all, Terry, is somebody to be my stateside `manager.' Somebody to handle my affairs while I'm gone: money transfers, mail forwarding, dealing with the Social Security people if anything comes up . . . that sort of thing."

Terry accepted the job, and I solidified the arrangement by giving her a power of attorney, with the clearance to sign checks for me and receive my mail. Through March, we worked at refining those details, and looked into the various ways of money transfer, for I was not ready to rely entirely on the trust that was prodding me out on such a scary limb of adventure.

By the time we understood the cumbersome, medieval process of transferring stateside funds without a handy plastic card, I was beginning to regret the earlier indulgences of my life that had robbed me of my onetime good credit standing. Living without credit had been no problem at all, up to now, for the American Way of Debt is no foundation for a simple lifestyle – but it became increasingly clear that a credit card overseas could be a tool of inestimable convenience.

Up to my mid-April 63rd birthday, I was still operating from an 'as if' framework – living *as if* I was going to England, come September. The possibility was too remote from my world to simply accept it as a reality. But then my confirmation was received from the work-exchange program's New York headquarters – along with the detailed small-print of a contract giving me until the end of June to reach London. *The end of June* . . . quite a different time than the September date I had been pointing toward!

The problem was the half-year semester system they operated under, which gave no recognition to the quarter-year system under which I was graduating. It proved to be only a minor issue that I was able to settle by a phone call; but it was major enough to confront me with the possibility, for a few brief hours, that I might have to choose between keeping my August commitment in California, or abandoning it for a June flight to London. In that moment, as spring was about to move into summer, I knew for the first time that I was actually, *really,* going to England.

The credit card issue took care of itself, in the normal course of becoming a college graduate. As time moved into May, I was besieged with unwelcome solicitations for my "very first" credit card, as they often put it – the offers arriving almost daily by letter and phone call. They didn't know, of course, that my credit had foundered, years before, on the rocks of youthful extravagance. Without thinking twice about it, I'd routinely toss their entreaties in the basket or politely tell the callers I wasn't interested.

But one young fellow had a strangely hypnotic kind of persistence. His voice on the phone had a rolling beat, thick with laid-back boredom, like a molasses flow. "Aww, why not gi-i i-ve it a try-y-y? Wha-a-a-t's to lose?"

I told him it was a sheer waste of time, that I'd never pass a routine credit check.

"Hey, ma-a-a-n, you're a gra-a-ad. There ai-i-i-n't any credit check." This possibility hadn't occurred to me. In a sudden flash, I realized that he was offering exactly what I needed. So I gave in to his three-question application; and for good measure I sent in the very next mail solicitation that arrived, too.

The proximate result, six weeks later, was that I had two Visa cards. One, with a $700 credit limit, came from an old line California bank. The other, from a dinky bank I'd never heard of, gave me a $2000 limit and in the same envelope with the card was a ready-to-cash check in my name for $1000. I had a momentary flash of going to England and never returning, but then I sent this second card (and their check) right back to where it came from. I wanted nothing to do with any outfit that played that loosely with money and people's heads.

I can't remember which card came through the telephone solicitor with the lazy singsong, but he was my first angel for the journey, turning up before I even knew I needed him. Without his unwanted and persistent intrusion, my European money hassles would have been entirely beyond my coping ability.

I cleared the hurdle of my incomplete thesis early in June, thanks to an insistent deadline from an intractable professor who couldn't very well know he was actually doing me a favor. Summer's gathering intensity, then, found me with a reasonably clarified agenda: the nitty-gritty preparation for two challenges, one in California, one in England, and the barest gap of sufficient time between their demands.

For the rest of June, on into July, I worked at turning up job leads and employer possibilities, gathering names from the London directories: specialist hiring agencies, data processing services, anything that seemed like it might fit my qualifications. Despite Terry's doubts, I worked up a résumé that accounted reasonably – I thought – for my extended leave from the job market, with reference to study and freelance writing. I sent dozens of them off to London, hoping they'd provide me a running-start when I got there.

The problem that nagged me, however, and continued to grow as time brought it closer to reality, was what to do on my arrival in London. With not a solitary personal contact in that immense patchwork of a city, I was faced with several weeks of demand and disorientation. Where would I start? A hotel room, the normal answer, was out of the question for me. Even youth hostels in London were beyond my reach, at their senior rate of $17 per night. I'd be out there on the furthest limb of my life, clinging to the edge of an uncertain future ... but where was even that edge that I could cling to?

I turned to a resource that I'd known about for years, but had never the occasion to use: an international network of host families and travelers connected with the peace movement, that has existed for some fifty years. I'll call them *Good Neighbors,* or GN for short. I can't reveal the true name, and I must explain why.

The real name is not secret, but I don't want my writing to put any burden on the organization. Good Neighbors exists entirely, and rather delicately, on the goodwill of the host families, who will ordinarily provide travelers with two nights of hospitality in the furtherance of international friendship. It is a gesture of citizen diplomacy that could too easily be over-burdened with people seeking nothing more than a means of cheap travel. Curiously, not many people seem to know about them, though there is no concerted effort to limit publicity. But I'd rather you find GN on your own, than to be, myself, the cause of an overload. In a world almost entirely lost to commercialism, personal hospitality is a rare flower, and should be nurtured with care.

I paid the $45 to join, with an additional deposit for their British host list, and sent off letters to three hosts when it came. It wasn't entirely the measure of my optimism, that I sought only six nights of assured shelter; London is a favorite of travelers, and three hosts was the requested limit.

Step by step, item by item, the necessary preliminaries were taken care of, in those all-too-busy summertime months. I received my first-ever passport; I bought my $299 (student rate) one-way flight to London – who could know when I'd be coming back? I took out a youth hostel membership, a backstop of lodgings security; I arranged with another Seattle friend to store my household belongings in unused garage space, and I found someone to handle the Earthstewards News-letter while I'd be gone.

Even before summer's trip to California, returns from my resumés began coming in. They arrived in numbers that surprised me, consider-ing the transatlantic postage – just to say "thanks; but no, thanks," which is what most of them had to say. Some offered heartening en-couragement. A few actually invited me to stop by: a publisher and a couple of the computer placement agencies. The most exciting response came in late July, while I was on my way to fulfill the workshop com-mitment. Someone from a placement agency that specialized in Macintosh computer people had *telephoned me from London!*

I travel in the old style – no beepers, no numbers whereat I can be reached – and it was weeks until I was back from California, too late to attempt a return call. But it made little difference to me, for it seemed to mean I didn't have to worry at all about finding a placement, once I got there.

I wasn't worrying, though. With the assurance of fools and little children – the very models of Innocence – I had lost all doubt, by now, that I was going to succeed in London. The way the timing had worked for me and everything had fallen into place cleanly, without hassle, it was clearly an ordained trail. Anyway, I was having too much fun on the road to California for any further worrisome thought.

My *carte blanche* for six months of residence and work in Britain. Seriously, now, couldn't this fellow pass as a college kid? Wouldn't you give him a hire?

The Bearer of this card is a member of BUNAC.

The exchange employment programme of the British Universities North America Club and the Council on International Educational Exchange is designed to promote an educational and cultural exchange between students in the United Kingdom and in North America.

Students are expected to take employment for most of their stay. BUNAC is at all times ready to assist students who have difficulty in finding employment or accommodation.

Should students have any problems or difficulties, they should get in touch with their sponsors in Great Britain:—

British Universities North America Club
16 Bowling Green Lane
London EC1R OBD
Telephone: 01-251-3472

This is to certify that

IRV THOMAS

of UNIVERSITY OF WASHINGTON whose details appear below, is travelling to the United Kingdom under the exchange student arrangements approved by the Home Office and Department of Employment.

GARTH HORN

for British Universities North America Club

Date 10 APRIL 1990

TO BE COMPLETED BY THE HOLDER

Name THOMAS (last)
(IN BLOCK LETTERS)
IRV (first) (middle)

Nationality U.S.A.

Passport No. 072038082

Signature

(Photograph of holder)

Whilst the period of his leave to enter the United Kingdom the holder of this card may take employment at any skill level in Great Britain subject to approval of the local office of the Manpower Services Commission.

UNDER NO CIRCUMSTANCES MAY THIS CARD BE TRANSFERRED

No. 90 — 1378

THE LOCAL OFFICE OF THE MANPOWER SERVICES COMMISSION MUST APPROVE EACH JOB YOU UNDERTAKE, PAID OR UNPAID APPROVAL IS SIGNIFIED BY A RUBBER STAMP WHICH WILL BE PLACED ON THE REAR OF THIS BLUE CARD.

California Vagabonding

Seattle, Washington: midsummer, 1990...

Seattle is really my second home. I came here from Berkeley in the summer of 1985 – in September, as a matter of fact, almost five years to the very date before my scheduled flight to London. Just as February is my opening moment, September has often been the time of passage, of starting fresh in terms of new settlement. Or of closure, for the two are often the same event.

It had been that way when I came north. I hardly realized a major closure was taking place, but friendships were fractured and many aspects of my world up to then faded back from immediate concern. In California, my life revolved around a small alternative newsletter, published sporadically in the wax and wane of incentive. But life in the northwest braced me with different demands and a shift of focus was inevitable.

This September of 1990, too, was shaping-up as a watershed. I couldn't know the extent of it but I was radically expanding the size of my world, at the very least, and that was sure to bring change in its wake. Summer took on the feeling of a moment between worlds. It seemed a proper time to take stock of where I had been, and reconnect on that basis with all who had been important to me, everywhere. They numbered in the hundreds, after years of newslettering.

Most of June went into the effort – a 12-page opus recounting my five years since leaving California – desktopped at home and multiplied at a local print shop. Reflecting on the uncertain course of those years, and of my life in general, I called it *Derelict Days in the Northwest.* In space to spare, I invited all to a farewell party on the day before my departure. The quarter page that yet remained blank prompted a last-minute note that the newsletter and its mailing would set me back about $250, and I added that I was open to donations to offset the cost and help me on my way.

The August workshop commitment, summer's final hurdle, had at first seemed only a troublesome complication to what had become the year's main thrust. But it eventually turned out to have a perfect place in the scheme of things, providing an opportunity to pull myself into shape for the sort of adventure I was heading into. I had not tasted the rugged life of the open road since coming to Seattle. I mean "open road" in the most literal sense – as a hitch-hiker, my cross-country travel style whenever time and the season have permitted it. Five years rusty, now, and critically older, I wanted to make sure I could still handle it . . . just in case I should encounter the challenge abroad.

Long distance hitch-hiking is a late-life passion of mine. I did a bit of it in my youth, when it was quite acceptable for off-duty soldiery to travel that way – even though I was not in uniform myself. And then thirty years later, when I gave up my own automobile, hitch-hiking became an occasional necessity. It wasn't easy to do at 45, even though it had come into vogue again with the youngsters. I had to deal with the fact that my self-image had changed considerably. But within another year or two I was comfortable with it again – even beginning to enjoy it as a down-to-earth way of experiencing both countryside and people.

Maybe it's the maverick in me that likes it, for it certainly isn't an easy way to travel. Even though I enjoy it, it begins always with dis-comfort – the sheer shock of standing out on the road, a public spec-tacle, absorbing the puzzled or judgemental gaze of every passing mo-torist. An exercise in humility, confronting my pretensions . . . as well as the parade of them coming by. And then there is impatience to deal with, the vexatiously recurrent fear that no one will ever stop. It vanishes in an instant, of course, when someone does … and someone always does.

So I knew what to expect, as I positioned myself at a southbound freeway access on a mid-July morning, in Seattle's University District. I propped my pack in a clearly visible spot and held up a "Portland" sign, taking center-stage in a drama about to open, playing a role that was only momentarily uncomfortable. The day was as bright as July can be; and the excitement, the pregnant tension of the open road, provided the adrenalin to pull me quickly into the spirit of adventure. Hitching out of a large city means putting up with a thundering parade of mainly local traffic. Many hitch-hikers will sit tight, waiting for the long one even if it takes all morning. But riding is better than waiting, and I tend to trust the rightness of whatever comes along. It took about forty-five minutes for my ride to arrive, a mobile plumbing-repair shop that was hardly going anywhere near Portland, but the driver flashed a broad grin and just said, "Hop in!"

We were barely underway, moving into the stream of traffic, when my sign caught his eye again. "Oh, Oregon!" he exclaimed, "...Damn, what was I thinking of?"

He never quite explained that, but I gathered that he meant to go some other direction. Instead, he continued on down the freeway, telling me that he'd get me to another good hitching spot even though it took him far out of his way – like ten miles! It was a strange but seemingly auspicious start.

Where he let me off, another car pulled over so quickly that I had to grab my gear and run for it. This was a young fellow on his way to work, who took me another ten miles down the freeway. I was actually making progress – fitfully, like a sputtering engine that hadn't been run in a long while.

It was a lightly used access road I had to settle for, this time, and a much longer wait. It took about an hour before a classy Buick pulled over, driven by a tawny young airline stewardess. It's a bit unusual for me to be picked up by a good-looking woman driving alone, though it happens now and then. But climbing in, I spotted a substantial trickle of water running out from under the front of the car, which suggested a radiator problem.

Sure enough, it was boiling over, and we carefully released the pressure. But it was only a temporary fix, and there were no service facilities at hand. We limped into the freeway flow, rolling slowly along to the next exit, where we came directly upon a radiator repair shop as if it had been part of a planned scenario.

The thermostat had gone out, so it hadn't triggered either the cooling fan or the dashboard signal – that was the entire problem. A hurried patch was made to keep the fan going and let my anxious driver finish her trip; she could take care of it properly later on. In much easier spirits, now, she talked about her job and her hopes of going back to school, and I learned a bit about what the world of an airline stewardess is like. She dropped me off at a small town near Olympia, where the traffic was slow but sufficient, and the surroundings decidedly more peaceful than where my day began.

I reflected on the satisfying ride as I waited there for another. Hitch-hiking makes instant friendships – Christina was her name, a full-blooded Skykomish Indian – but it ends them just as quickly. Still, it left me with a warm glow, for had I not alerted Chris to her problem, she might have had a far more serious one on the freeway. It was her decision to stop and pick me up that protected her from it. Yet, there was something more to it. I wouldn't have been there had not the previous events on my journey been just as they were: the happenings we call 'pure chance' taking me precisely to where she would find me!

I've watched that sort of thing so many times on the road: chance events linking in an undeniably fruitful way. Maybe it is happening all the time, but hitch-hiking highlights it, for it is one of the few activities – indeed, they are rare today – that deliberately court the world of chance in daily life. To let go of control is not an easy thing to do, but it seems the most effective way for bringing Providence into view.

By four in the afternoon, two further rides had taken me into Portland and it seemed enough distance for a day's travel: 175 miles in six hours. I had friends in this city and could be sure of a night's shelter somewhere. First, however, I had to find someplace to freshen-up and get my bearings. Portland is the west coast city I am least familiar with. The journey thus far had given me little reason to doubt my readiness for it. I was tired, yes, but the day had turned hot and I had a larger pack than I was used to. Not at all large by back-packing standards, only about thirty pounds, but my highway travel was once done with little more than a daypack and sleeping bag.

I was also wearing heavier shoes than I liked – a pair of Rockports I was still breaking in. Pack and shoes suddenly teamed-up to topple me as I trudged wearily through Portland's riverfront section. My foot caught the edge of a curb, and down I went, the momentum of the pack pitching me into a full sprawl. It was more embarrassing than damaging, but I had a gash in my pants leg and a bad bruise under it. I wondered, as I band-aided the knee, if I was too far past my prime for this sort of thing. But a cup of tea lifted my spirits while I sorted over the prospects for Portland hospitality.

It was perhaps ten years since I had last seen Joan Lorenz – when I lived briefly near Monterey, where she and husband Roger partnered at a local alternative paper unforgettably called *The Nose*. She greeted me now with enthusiasm, and not the least surprise at my road-weary condition, for Joan knew the ways of my life. A hot shower was offered for my aches and exhaustion, and for my hunger a cold summer meal; and then we had lots of catching-up to do – as much as could be done in one evening, for I wanted to be on my way again, next morning, to maintain the pace.

The second day was a punishing one. It got hot early, and I was stuck at an inner-city freeway access until just before noon. The ride that finally came took me barely out beyond the city limit. I was grateful. But this spot proved even worse! After two more useless hours, I started walking up the freeway – partly in disgusted need for a change of scenery, and partly to reach a more promising location. The walk was a mixed experience: sweaty in the blazing afternoon sun, but peaceful in the surround of Chopin and Vivaldi coming in on my radio, all else shut out by ear plugs. Three long miles I walked up the highway, ignoring the mad traffic alongside of me.

Walking into the sun, I switched from my usual narrow-brim hat to a visored one, which just happened to have military-style camouflage coloring, and I suspect it may have flagged my next ride. The fellow who pulled over for me as I was nearing the crest of a hill was a gung-ho patriot sort, a rancher from Idaho in a big whining pickup with a rifle slung against its back window. He said he was headed for Eugene, a good hundred miles down the state, and it looked like the fates had finally clicked-in for me. As we hummed along the highway, he told me how he had started his ranch from scratch and made it on his own, in the best American tradition. He began it as a personal tale, but I had the distinct impression it turned into a sermon. He all but spelled the message out, "Lift yourself up, man, set your sights as I did..."

About twenty miles along our way, he turned to me with a 'good buddy' look and suggested we stop for a drink; and that was my undoing. Without thinking of the implications, I innocently allowed as how I could certainly go for a cold Coke in this heat. He looked at me rather oddly, at that, and when we pulled into the next town he suddenly remembered some business he had there. He left me at a refreshment stand . . . after first buying me a Coke, and nothing at all for himself.

So there I was, well into a scorching afternoon, five hours on the road and not yet forty miles out of Portland. It was shaping up as a true test of my taste for this sort of adventure. Yet, there was nothing for me to do but go on with it.

It was a rather sad looking rural access road, this time – I wondered if it had any traffic at all, or if I'd only be walking in the hot sun again. But just as I started into it a freeway-bound pickup came flying by, and I barely had time to fling my thumb up, to make my needs known. A cloud of dust practically hid its sudden stop. But there was no room for me. Three Spanish-speaking crop hands filled every inch of cab space; all I could understand was their waving motion toward the open truck. They barely gave me time to clamber in, and lurched away at the same breakneck speed.

Except for the circumstance that I found myself nestled among big duffel bags, which proved to be comfortable riding cushions, I had every reason to suppose it was another short ride that would turn off at some local farm road. But it didn't. On they went . . . and on, and on. It was a wonderful ride, the finest sort that a hitch-hiker can get: I was stretched full length, feet forward, my head against those duffels, the wind rushing my hair and offsetting the sun's heat, and miles were going by as swiftly as the trees at roadside that rose sheer into the blue, from my truckbed perspective. We went past Eugene, past Cottage Grove, past Roseburg, on into the mountains hardly pausing to shift gears. I began to wonder if they were going clear to Mexico!

Deep in the mountains somewhere between Roseburg and Grants Pass, they turned off on a barren minor road, making some wild motions at me through the cab's rear window. Since they hardly slowed for it, I had no choice but to go along. We soon reached a tiny store and gas pump, where I could see they had arrived among friends. It was like a way-station on some covert underground railway; or more to the point, a pit-stop in a high-rolling trucker's derby. They gassed-up, sat down to talk and eat awhile with other swarthy bracero-types, and I found a moment to get in some largely finger-pointing map talk with one of them – to discover that they were headed for Redding, halfway into northern California!

Well, an open pickup and the wind in your hair can be great sport in the sunshine, but it's miserable at night. And right now, the sun was about to be nibbled by the crest of the surrounding high line of hills. I had friends on either side of the state line, and I figured I'd just see how far daylight would take me.

They slowed a bit when the journey resumed. But evening came on rapidly and I was beginning to wonder if I'd be able to see where to hop off; and whether they'd stop the truck within walking distance, for me to do it. We came to the little town of Phoenix, where my Oregon friends lived, but it was behind us before I could even decide if I wanted to get off there. Hornbrook was now the place to look for, just across the state line; but my only memory of the place was a barren crossroad – long before the time of freeways. And it would soon be too dark to make out anything at all.

While I was turning these imponderables over, huddled against the now chill headwind, we suddenly slowed. I looked ahead to see the bright and blinking lights of California's agricultural inspection station, an enforced brief halt that I had forgotten all about. I realized instantly that it was exactly what I wanted.

"*Adios amigos! Muchas gracias,*" I tossed off my entire grasp of the vernacular, waving them on their way as I let out a deep sigh of satisfaction ... with the ride, with myself, with the whole day's irregular course of events. California, here I was! – in the sort of turnaround finale that's only possible in hitch-hiking, where chance lurks with every next car coming down the pike, and things somehow always work out.

Louis Durham, in his country seclusion at Hornbrook, was only a phone call away – and quite surprised that I was at the other end of it and close enough to be picked up. Once more I was closing a gap of many years. Lou had been an administrative minister at San Francisco's Glide Memorial Church during their wild and wooly '60s, and the prime organizing energy behind a pioneering middle-age, middle-class shared living situation, as well as other alternative developments of those years.

Again, it was only a one-night stay. I was feeling stronger, thanks no doubt to the day's fast finish, and wanted to get right on with it. I had no way of knowing it yet, but my instincts were right on target ... I was tracking a piece of good fortune that had yet to show itself and I couldn't afford to be late.

I knew exactly where I was going the next day: to Red Bluff, 170 miles downstate. It called for just one good ride, and I got it quite easily at the border inspection station, where all southbound cars have to stop. I even scored an air-conditioned vehicle, a stroke of first-rate luck since we were headed into California's hot Central Valley, where the day's temperature was going to crest above 1000.

My driver, this time, was a real estate appraiser from the Seattle area going to Sacramento for a family funeral. We had some stimulating conversation on a variety of topics for most of the two and a half hours that it took to reach Red Bluff, and he stopped there for a bite of lunch with me before resuming the journey alone. But I almost had second thoughts about letting him go on without me, when we stepped out of the car into a virtual furnace. I have friends with well-cooled homes in Sacramento. But I knew I had to reconnect, here in Red Bluff, with Hal Howard. We had been housemates for three years in Berkeley, and had known and worked with each other since the early 1970s. I hadn't seen Hal since I settled in Seattle, and it was too long overdue.

This time, I would have stayed longer than one night . . . but here, it turned out, was the one place that I couldn't. Hal happened to be the only one along the route who knew I was coming, though he didn't know exactly when I'd show up. The day before I got there, he received a call from a mutual Berkeley friend, Yana Parker, who asked if he'd care to house-sit for a couple weeks. He didn't want to, himself, but he was quite sure that I would! I phoned Yana at once to confirm the arrangement, and it was so close to her departure time that I couldn't even hitch the rest of the way, but had to grab a bus into the city the next morning.

Yana's two weeks away were perfect for my own purposes. I hadn't made any prior plans for where I'd stay, in that period, simply because there are so many Bay Area friends to see when I am there, that I just assume I'll find a new host every few days. But this was perfection, for it gave me a central 'home' while I was there. The gift also included use of Yana's small Honda, providing all the mobility I might want. Even more, it gave me a telephone-response machine, a Macintosh with laser printer on which to finish the prep for my workshop, and a shy little cat to look after me when the day's activity was done.

Sometimes, in those twilight moments before drifting off to sleep, I find myself counting not sheep, nor blessings, but the amazing string of 'if's that have to fall into proper place for such impossible instances of Providence to materialize. If, in that last moment of my last ride, I had decided to go on to Sacramento . . . If I hadn't soured that Idaho rancher exactly in time to catch those three California-bound braceros . . . If I had neglected to let Hal know I was coming, or if he just hadn't thought of me when Yana called . . . It is truly mind-boggling.

Yana Parker, in the days when we saw more of each other, used to put out a lively little communal newsletter that circulated like a grapevine – which is what it was called – among a good many of the collective-living houses in the Bay Area. The timing of her two weeks away meshed so perfectly with my own that on the very day she returned I was off and away to the south, toward Monterey and the Unitarian retreat at Asilomar.

There's really not much to say about the workshop that belongs in this book. The subject of it was a fascination of mine that has deepened over the years: the seasonal cycle and its influence on consciousness and our reality. It was well-received, and shortly afterward I made my swift way back to Seattle by an inexpensive overnight bus called the Green Tortoise. I could not afford to dally, for only two weeks remained in which to finalize every last detail before taking off on the greatest adventure of my not-exactly-humdrum life.

On the whole, I was quite satisfied with the roadtrip. People who should know had told me that hitch-hiking is no longer as easy as it used to be, but the magic of my own had been quite as good as ever. I was gratified that I still had the energy for that sort of travel, and my stamina seemed remarkable for 63 years of a non-athletic life. If I pay attention to where I plant my big feet, I should have no future trouble at all.

The journey had a fringe-benefit that I only realized as I was packing my recent world into cartons and crates: it softened the edge of the separation blues that always accompany the closing-down of a residence – for this departure was a future move, as well as the start of a present adventure. My several weeks away, together with a sense of settlement at Yana's, had already made the break. Packing and storing my belongings seemed now only a formality, not the saddening experience it so often can be.

It somehow all got done by the night before the farewell party. The upper-floor room that had been mine, in this Ravenna group house, for two fun and busy student years, was now bare but for the backpack and two small satchels I'd be taking with me, each stuffed to its limit.

My world, by this time, was very spacy, for I had devised a routine to neutralize jet-lag. Every third day, since my return from California, I had been turning-in an hour earlier, edging myself at the same time into an earlier wake-up. On this night before party-day I was in bed by six, and up at two a.m. – the longer to prepare my potato salad contribution for the afternoon potluck.

The first party guests to arrive were a couple from California's north coast whom I never expected to see in Seattle. I had hardly absorbed this surprise, before there were others: correspondents from Illinois and from Florida whom I had never even met before! I couldn't believe it. It made no difference that they "just happened to be in the area," these were testimonials to friendship that would many times warm me during the cold winter that lay ahead.

For all the competition that a mid-September Saturday afternoon presents, some forty people came that day, including several of my recent professors at the university. And folks brought more than pot-luck contributions: they swelled the pot of funding donations that had already reached $750, pushing it up past the next hundred-mark.

Altogether, it was the sweetest tribute that an old derelict, just five years in town, could hope to have. I was still dizzy with it twenty-four hours later when I boarded the Pan Am flight that would take me direct to London. The lingering spell of it remained as I gazed down at the sunset-glowing rooftops of a fast-fading Seattle, with the roaring thrum of jets providing background music for an adventure at last underway.

Replingham Road in Southfields, from a 1910 postcard – but it's
hardly different today. I lived right around the bend down the street.

London High

Airborne, over arctic seas: September 10, 1990...

I was wide awake at the first hint of dawn. The earthline was sharp against a soft glow that soon turned brilliant scarlet, and as daylight filtered in I could make out a deep blue world, below, of endless sea pocked by specks of pure white. Hundreds of them. Huge floating icebergs, looking insignificant from this altitude.

The rest of that stratospheric morning between worlds was an immersion in formless white haze, opening now and then to a glimpse of countryside that had to be northern Britain; and then, with the quickness of a dream sequence, we were descending. All at once the unmistakable city of London materialized on a steeply banked turn toward Heathrow airport.

There it was: magical London in a panorama below me, going by so swiftly that I didn't dare rest my eyes on a single one of its multitude of spectacles: Westminster Cathedral . . Big Ben . . the river Thames . . the stately, one-of-its-kind, Tower Bridge – architectural Pomp and Circumstance to greet my arrival, as if it had been arranged from on high. Well, it had, of course!

I went with the herd through the airport routine – waiting for baggage, waiting for customs, getting stamped and certified at immigration – wide-eyed like a kid at everything suddenly British all around me: the billboards, the candy racks, the very looks of people . . . but most of all the strangely elegant way that everyone spoke, even tod dlers talking to one another. There was a vast unreality to it, as if I had walked right off the plane into a Masterpiece Theater presentation.

Quickly enough, I was done with the formalities and had next to find my way out to a suburb called Eastcote. I knew not enough, yet, to take the underground – the subway system – which would have been the fastest, smoothest way out. Instead, I went for a big red double-decker, nearly getting run over before I reached it. Loaded with baggage, I looked the wrong way at a crossing. It would be weeks before I'd be able to cross a street without a conscious halt to break a lifetime's orientation. And I never would get used to the echo effect at mid-street – the encore 'wrong way' glance to catch traffic coming the other way.

But my closest brush with disaster on that first day was when I nearly left half my valuables on the red double-decker. I was simply carrying too much. Not only in baggage, but in my head. Things were happening too fast for me to classify and absorb. My focus was on everything at once, and spread far too thin.

I had a map and knew where I was going, and was fairly sure I had the right bus. But I had no idea of its route or how I'd know where to get off, other than what I could learn as I went. Naturally, I had asked the driver to let me know when we reached Eastcote.

"No trouble, lad, it's a station."

"Oh. Will you tell me when we arrive?"

He gave me a narrowing look, at that. *"It's a station!"*

That obviously was supposed to tell me something about it, but all it did was intimidate me. I sat down. The only thing to do was pay attention at every stop we made. A 'station' – what did he mean by that? A rail station? A police station? A gas station? How was I supposed to recognize it?

I took up a whole seat with my pack and bags, which was just as well for I could watch both sides. London buses have bins for luggage, but I was too fuzzy in the excitement of it all to see that. I didn't dare climb to the upper deck, for I had to be near the door. The bus had no springs and the driver seemed to relish shaking us to bits, but I was too busy trying to track our progress on the map to care – a detailed book of street maps I'd had the sense to pick up before leaving the airport.

We must have gone through half of London's outskirts before I spotted Eastcote Lane and lugged my stuff heavily toward the exit. But the driver stopped me before I could get off.

"This ain't Eastcote, *I told y'it was a STATION!*"

He fairly yelled it, before he saw my stupefied expression and finally realized I just didn't understand. "Si'down, lad. I'll tell y'when we're there."

It was all I had wanted in the first place. And I wished he'd stop calling me 'lad.' He was twenty years younger than me.

I suppose I expected something fairly magnificent after all the fuss, but it was just a modest little brick structure, a station on the underground line. This was where I very nearly left my jacket behind, with passport and money-belt in an inside pocket. Nobody nearby said a word when I got up and left it on the seat. I was spared by just the barest flicker of a feeling, as I was almost out the door, that something was wrong.

In due time, I reached the home of my first Good Neighbors host and was able to unburden myself of baggage for awhile. Lynne was a momentary anchor point, an engaging young woman who invited me to join her in a night out with a friend, and we saw the film *Cinema Paradiso.* I was living a dream: out with two women on my first night in London, in the flashing, splashing carnival center called Picadilly Circus. But it was quickly clear that I'd better get some London income in a hurry if I expected to sustain any such nightlife. The £4.50 theater price converted to $8.50 – for a single feature film.

I got my bearings at Lynne's, but it was hardly more than a breathing space; two nights, and then off to another host in another part of town. The three hosts I had arranged for in advance were woefully insufficient. I would be at large in London for the rest of September – three long weeks – lugging a load that somehow kept increasing as I migrated from host to host. Before the ordeal was done, I was listing and lunging along like some hybrid cross between a bird of passage and a lumbering beast of burden.

I had no time to relax. Three concurrent agendas chased each other in ever-tightening circles through my weary head: to find some affordable and decent quarters; to get a job; and to stay at least one host ahead of the two-night limit on GN hospitality. There was also the social requirement of being a proper guest at each household that took me in. It was so maddening that only a vague impression remains, of those earliest of my London hosts.

But it would be difficult to overstate the blessing of having what amounted to friends I could stay with, even if only friends of a brief and shifting moment. The hotel or hostel alternative, had it even been affordable, would have left me lonely and isolated just when the stabilizing effect of a supportive friend was most needed. The GN households ran the gamut from elegant to barely adequate, but I usually had a room to myself, and always congenial hosts.

My days were a steady round of employment agencies, which became a routine of keyboard tests and advice on the British job scene – no referrals. I was quickly disabused of any thought that I could get by on casual charm; it would have to be neckties and a suit, the 'uniform of servitude' long since expunged from my wardrobe. And quite beyond my bracket of affordability at this point. In grim determination I canvassed the Oxfam shops, Britain's charity thrift stores, until I found a grey pinstripe that was good enough. It buttoned tight but didn't look half bad, and set me back less than six dollars – plus the cost of a couple pockets sewn in by a cheap and handy immigrant seamstress.

Coloring every aspect of my activity was the impact of London prices and the alarming rate at which my money seemed to be draining away. Somehow, $150 had gone out in *the first three days*. It included one-time costs, to be sure, like the $68 for police registration, a toll exacted of visitors staying longer than three months. But the pace of outlay hardly slackened. At the ten-day mark, my funds were down $260 – double my stateside income for the same period, and a scary 15% of the $1870 I had brought with me, to last until I landed a job.

Remarkably, in my fluid state of affairs, I actually connected with a bit of work toward the end of my second homeless week. One of the agencies sent me on a two-day desktop publishing assignment – exactly what I had hoped to find. I had to cope with an IBM/DOS computer, instead of the Macintosh I'm familiar with, which was a bit unsettling, but I carried it off well enough and earned a quick $215, less $65 taken out for British with-holding tax.

The brief but heady taste of success demonstrated a take-home potential that might easily exceed $1500 per month, and set all kinds of winter possibilities dancing in my head. Everything appeared to be happening just as it was supposed to. The truth of it, however, was that I had lucked into a last-gasp bit of employment in an economy that was, at that very moment, turning cold and blue. It served to buoy my spirits – not to be taken lightly – but was no indicator of what lay ahead.

Meanwhile, by the end of that week that saw my finances enhanced, a shelter crisis was taking shape. Everything seemed to converge at once, in a way that left me too little time, with too many threads to keep track of. On the evening of my first day of work, I turned up a short-term rental, for perhaps a month or two, but it wouldn't be available until the first of October – a week away. It wasn't nearly what I wanted, but it seemed the perfect answer for my tentative midstream situation. I was lucky, in fact, in London's highly competitive housing market, to find anything at all that someone else hadn't already beaten me to. But in my preoccupation with the house hunt and my temp job, I had not taken the time to find a weekend host.

Now, it was late Friday afternoon and I was up against it, using a pay phone for all I was worth. I mean it literally: British phone calls are timed, even locally (even from home phones!), and I was running out of coins. Not to mention hosts. Some already had guests, some required more than a single day's notice, some were just indisposed . . . no one would have me.

In the last few minutes before five o'clock, my desperation finally registered somewhere with the gods. I connected with a fellow just as he was closing his art supplies shop for the weekend. Another trudge across town, but it gave me a haven until Monday with a young couple in a crowded attic – so tight and tiny, that it could barely accommodate another body.

In the course of that weekend I joined my hosts in attendance at a small, private Sunday worship service, which favored me with two interesting encounters. One of them was a brief conversation with John Lahr, a writer and the son of Bert Lahr, who played the cowardly lion in that vintage film, *The Wizard of Oz*. But the day's truly providential encounter was with a wonderfully articulate British gentleman of exactly my vintage, who said he could put me up at his bachelor flat for most of the following week, while I awaited the readiness of my new quarters.

It was instant congeniality. Clark was a retired geologist with still a lot of zest for life, embarking on a second career in homeopathy. More than merely articulate, he had a raconteur's flair for the well-turned phrase. Dining together at a pub, on his generous treat, we seemed to spark each other to a rich recollection or a fresh insight at every turn of the conversation. It was somewhat like having a "Dinner with Andre."

Though charmingly British, with all of the conventions it suggests, Clark didn't fit the generational mold any more than I. On a motor-scooter, he'd buzz me out to a bookshop, or up along Hampstead Heath, the great park-like area behind his home, jockeying through traffic like an unruly kid. When I discovered his passion for Dixieland jazz, matching my own, I knew I'd found a real gem – the first person since my arrival in England with whom I felt a genuine rapport.

I stayed with Clark to the end of the week, when he had other guests due; and I left anticipating a lot of later time together once I got settled. He drove me across town to my final GN host, for the last of my homeless days. This was Marjory, an earlier host, of whom I had asked the privilege of a return visit since she lived just up the hill from where I was about to rent. It meant I'd have a friend as a neighbor, in this suburban section of London called Southfields, which added a further touch of good feeling to the prospect ahead of me.

Marjory, like Clark, seemed also an epitome of British style – though in its more reserved aspect, which set our friendship on a keel of restraint. But as I came to know her better I found a whimsical wit beneath the surface of propriety, along with a very generous spirit. Marjory's home was a kind of boarding house for visiting language students from other cultures, which assured a diversity of interesting dinner guests. She happened also to have a superb library of London and British lore that tempted me to hours of browsing – more, by far, than I ever found time for. Our friendship would grow, and continue to be fruitful even after I left the British Isles. But strangely, I was not to see Clark again at all, though my episode with him was not entirely done.

Southfields, a pleasant little bedroom community south of the Thames, on the underground line to Wimbledon, is one of the literally hundreds of satellite villages that compose greater London, in a patch-work blend that no longer has any visible divisions. They string together along endless heartlines of commerce, often called the High Street, like daisies on a chain – but not like American suburbs, for each has a distinctive spirit, perhaps reflecting its onetime unique townhood in the far, far past. Their community identity, in many cases, goes back a thousand years and more.

The small and cheery cluster of shops that create the Southfields ambience radiates from a century-old underground station hardly a block's distance, down several streets. It caters to a mid-day trade of housewives – a social phenomenon that persists in England – imparting a settled, leisurely quality that instantly overwhelms the mundane, dreary aspect of returning from town after a day's work ... or, as in my case, after a day of seeking it. Old photographs show that the neighborhood's physical appearance has hardly changed from horse-drawn carriage days, though of course today's street scene has not the same quiet charm. But the old style is not entirely gone. Occasionally, the clip-clop of horse's hooves still echoes up the street, and a quick look reveals a mounted bobby on patrol, or a prim horsewoman on an early morning trot.

The house that would be my home for awhile was a narrow, two-story private dwelling, one of the sardine-packed brick and rococo family units of which there must be a million in greater London, all built just before the century's turn in a building boom of inconceivable energy. For the most part, there are no two exactly alike, which has to say something for the creative Victorian imagination since they are all so very similar.

The one I lived in took sunlight into practically every room ... except the ground floor one I occupied. For it, there was a narrow north view of sky and yard through tall, glass-paned doors. They opened outward, but not very invitingly in October's chill air. It was a darkside room, not meant to be anything but a place to sleep and dress. I made more of it, though, with a few well-placed lamps and a writing desk.

Being a shared house (more or less) it also provided a decently appointed kitchen, a washing machine and telephone for my use, and a TV set in a miniature living-room just off the vestibule. But the sharing extended only as far as space and costs. Socially, the place turned out to be rather barren. My housemates were two charming young women of whom I saw very little and one man of indeterminate charm who elected to keep entirely to himself.

But it was reasonably priced, by London standards, at £45 per week. I was starting to think in these terms, and preferred not to dwell on the fact of it being $85 – or $365 per month, a price within penny-pitching distance of my entire Social Security income. It was a place to be for awhile, and that was of paramount importance. In a month or two we'd all be ousted so the owner could begin some refurbishing, and at that time I should certainly be able to afford something more suitable for the winter.

Or so I told myself.

October was as fine a month in London as it is in Seattle – crispness in the air, a lot of clear blue skies and an avalanche of color along London's streets and in its commons, as trees gradually shed their leaves. Job-hunting was enjoyable in that aspect, if less so for its lack of encouragement. The agencies generally blamed the shallows on the turn in the economy; but rampant age discrimination also played a part. It wasn't subtle at all. In one instance, I was told point-blank by a young agency interviewer that there was no use even opening my portfolio, as they had no client who'd hire anyone of my age. At another agency, my résumé prompted a surprised question clearly related to age: What ever "had possessed" me to return to school?The British attitude toward their elderly can be seen in the term by which they are generally referenced. Not seniors, which conveys a positive sense of rank; not elders, which could suggest a level of attainment; they are called *pensioners,* a term reflecting the sad image of older folks as used-up, burned-out, has-beens. They seem not to realize or care that people generally fulfill the roles in which they are cast.

I suppose the same could be said about roles people cast for themselves, and it had been many years since I last regarded myself as a career-style job seeker. I had become, instead, a forager, and learned to utilize somewhat different kinds of instincts in pursuit of my needs. Eventually, these instincts set me onto a London trail – not a very gainful one, but maybe as good as this dreary winter could offer. It began at a so-called Job Fair that I visited on one of my daily forays in October – a sort of employment lottery sponsored by a temporary consortium of high-profile firms. Long lines of hopefuls, with long faces of career-style seriousness, stood patiently in queue waiting for a few minutes of hopeful interview with glad-handing personnel reps. It was obviously no place for me, and I didn't remain long – but long enough to collect a handful of literature.

Giving it a cursory look-through on my underground way home, I flashed on something that rang bells of recall from many years back: *New Ways to Work,* a name too distinctive to have been accidentally duplicated. It had been used in California twenty years before, by a pair of women with the unlikely names of Barney and Sidney, whom I had once known. The local address was not far out of my way, and it was still early enough to check it out. If nothing else, the adventure could lift my spirits from the drag of the day's sorry business.

I found the office up a double flight of stairs, a few blocks from Islington station. My guess was immediately verified: they had a solid connection with the California group. The idea of job-sharing had spread from the west coast to the east, and then leaped across to London. It was like running into an old friend, even though I didn't know anyone in this British outpost. But conversational access was what I wanted.

OM

The London office was managed by a fellow named Charlie, an easy-going sort who had received his 'commission' from Barney, herself, in New York. After sharing my memories of how the whole thing began, back in Palo Alto, I asked Charlie if he had any ideas for my job quest. He thought I should try the volunteer organizations. They always had trouble with the going pay scale, he said, for such skills as desktop publishing, and were therefore often in need. He advised me to put an ad in the monthly newsletter of the *London Volunteer Services Center* (LVSC), which went out to more than a thousand such groups.

So I went the next day to LVSC and met Sean, their slim, soft-spoken newsletter editor, only to learn that even a small ad would cost more than I could afford. But Sean introduced me to Massimo, who handled the computer training for volunteer groups, thinking he might have some ideas for me. Massimo, his dark Italian hair bobbing around as we talked, took a sudden interest in my Pagemaker expertise, wondering if I could impart some of it to their training crew . . . in trade for an ad! He checked with Sean, who agreed that it would be a fair bit of barter.

I didn't see myself as an instructor. I hadn't that level of skill, and certainly not on their IBM-type system. But the entire mood was informal and they were willing to make allowances for my lack of instructional experience; and after all, hadn't I just done a couple days' work using IBM hardware? Besides, this wasn't a hire-for-pay, in the strictest sense. So I agreed to it. I came in on the following Saturday and did a passable job, gaining a bit of teaching experience in the process. My ad would be in their next issue – unfortunately, almost a month down the line.

But Massimo came up with another idea for me. He said I should register with a certain alternative employment agency that I had not heard of before. They were far out of the central area, across the river in a part of greater London called 'Elephant and Castle.' By now, I could see that this was a developing trail and knew enough to stay with it, alert to every nuance of information and possibility it might reveal.

I found the place buried in a security-locked building, which seemed an unlikely location for a job agency. Fatemah, a dark-haired, cheerful and lively young woman of middle-Eastern lineage, was running the small office. There was none of the usual artifice or formality, here, the facade that typically distances agency from client. She soon had me in shirtsleeves helping her with some computer problem as if I belonged there. The afternoon went swiftly by, and then Fatemah and her office cohort, Jay, dragged me off to a free Friday evening jazz concert at the South Bank, an art center on the Thames. Anything can turn up when following a trail.

When I returned, the following week, Fatemah asked if I was ready to learn Ventura Publisher, another kind of desktop publishing software – learn it well enough to teach it to someone, a particular client of hers, for pay! I knew immediately I'd be stepping in well over my head. The program works on a principle quite different from Pagemaker.

"I don't even know how Ventura Publisher works, Fatemah!"

"I have all the manuals for it. You can do it."

"Come on, now, manuals can't teach you to teach something. And I'm not that familiar with your computer system."

"You can work with it here, as long as you need to. You can do it."

"Fatemah . . . it's crazy!"

"You can do it, Irv, I know you can do it."

I hadn't tried to fool Fatemah, and she was not dull about computers – perhaps a bit too innocent, but not dull. And yet, she was prevailing on me to practically lay myself on a stone altar.

I shook my head once again. "Naaa, it's too scary. I'd just . . . "

But my argument faltered as it came back to me that this was, after all, part of a trail. It was totally unthinkable, it was utter madness, but . . . how could I argue with the progression that had already drawn me, step by step, into areas of computer expertise I considered beyond me? This next step, though, was a quantum jump – as foolhardy, from my perspective, as walking into NASA thinking I could program the launch of a space shuttle. But yet, how could I argue with it? This was clearly *my Trail!*

Within the week, I began putting in the time I could manage, a few hours every day or so, learning to work with Ventura, and taking its manuals home for study. I never became very proficient with it, but I learned enough to get by . . . if no one who really knew the software were looking over my shoulder. I wrote a summary of what I was learning, carefully skirting the area that was still a mystery to me, and then we worked this into a printable format, with the software, so that we were able to produce a 'manual' – (this is so outrageous, I can't even believe I let myself get talked into it) – with the agency's own name on it. This all took place within a few weeks, and then I somehow found the nerve to spend most of a day 'teaching it' to the fellow Fatemah had in mind.

It was almost my complete undoing. He was sharp enough, I'm sure, to see through the whole sham – certainly to see my sweaty nervousness and uncertainty at the slightest glitch. But he was a good sport about it and seemed genuinely pleased to have someone 'helping him' to learn this package. I received $150 for the ordeal – and regardless of whether I taught him anything or not, I earned every penny of it!

After that episode, I didn't even flinch when asked, by the person whose small ad I next ventured a response to, if I were a qualified Pagemaker instructor – making no distinction as to the kind of computer involved. "Yes, sir," I gave it all the confidence I had in me. *"Qualified and experienced!"*

He operated a small independent computer instruction business, contracting as a broker with all sorts of computer people to offer their instructional services to firms and government agencies with short-term urgencies. He was in need of a Pagemaker pro for occasional assignment. A month before, I wouldn't have dared respond to his ad. Aside from my limited skills, I wasn't supposed to earn any money in Britain outside of regular employment. Contract work was strictly out, on penalty of having my work permit revoked. But times had changed. The trail had led to this, and I was now in a survival mode.

This new connection didn't bring much in, but it kept the winter wolf from chewing on my toes, and my spirits from going completely down the tube. My first assignment was at the DTI, the *British Department of Trade and Industry,* at a mid-city location near Victoria Station, where I was given a security escort into the bowels of the building. With my somewhat specious credentials, I felt like a hacker breaking into the government computer system. I gave two days of instruction to two very young fellows, who were so subdued through it that I began to think I really was qualified. I got $245 for it – no deductions taken out, but the figure has to be adjusted for the cost of a pair of new shoes ($37.50) that I had to groan into, and wear at the constant risk of callouses, to be business-like presentable or else lose the assignment.

Later instructional episodes, many weeks apart, took me to the *British Naval History Museum* at Greenwich, and to an insurance company on the south coast, at Bournemouth. All together, they brought in about $650, not very much when spread over the deep three months of winter. But a lifesaver, on the same terms, for I'm not sure my spirits would have held up without that bit of distance from disaster's edge. It certainly validated the wisdom of tracking trails, however irrational they sometimes seem.

There was another trail, too, of an entirely different character. It started back in Seattle with my early round of letters, several of which had been sent to magazine publishers. It might seem that writing would be a natural employment possibility for me, but I don't have an occupational background in it. I did, however, write to a few retirement-age magazines, British and American, suggesting the possibility of an article or two on what I was doing. Only one, in England, responded with any interest at all and it was slight, merely suggesting that I stop in when I get to London.

It was a month after my arrival before I got around to it. I found the offices of *Choice* situated in a colorful little corner of the city, by St. John's Gate, a remnant bit of ancient London. Editor Wendy James seemed a bit dubious about me at first, but our conversation warmed quickly and she suggested we continue it over a pub lunch that extended for two full hours. Unaccountably, I was in fine form for the occasion, and happily rambled on about the range of my ideas and past projects. And she, being interested in my generation, of course, though in her own youthful forties, was a good and encouraging listener.

Wendy was definitely interested in an article or two; but I, in the moment's uncharacteristic exuberance – probably the lingering afterglow of my first two days of paid hire – was all for doing an entire series of articles! I envisioned a half-dozen segments, starting with my return to college and detailing each stage of the job-search, to finally end with my eventual success (according to the script). Wendy was cautious about it. The magazine had never run a series before. But she was willing to think it over. Afterwards, I was surprised at my own brashness that day; it was as if some hidden spirit had taken possession of me.

I began the writing almost immediately, for I was determined to produce a series and let it speak for itself. On completing each of the first few segments, I'd rush off to the office by St. John's Gate, type it into one of their computers and give it immediately to Wendy. She seemed to like what I was doing with it, but wanted the whole batch in hand before making any commitment. I couldn't finish it, of course, until I actually landed a job – which, as the days moved toward November, was starting to look more and more like less and less of a likelihood.

November was also the month I'd have to start looking for another place to live. My landlord, however, a chunky Irishman, had said nothing of it when he took my rent. At least I didn't think he had. His brogue was so thick I could seldom be sure of what he said without having it repeated. Had he had a change of heart? But the following week, my two charming housemates put a deposit on larger quarters for themselves and announced a move at November's end. This triggered the landlord into action, and I received three weeks notice that I must be out by then, too.

Despite his earlier forewarning, it hit hard, for I was in no position to pay for better quarters and dreaded a return to the dreary search – which was still too fresh in memory. London house-hunting is strictly an evening task, as most landlords work in the daytime; and having no car at my disposal meant a reliance on the phone, and then scurrying to check out perhaps one or two while time enough remained for it. Most of the time, someone had already staked their claim with hard cash by the time I found my way to the offering. It was entirely useless to say, "please wait until I get there."

It came as quite a surprise, then, to hit paydirt this time on the second place I looked at. It was not far away from Southfields, perhaps an hour's sturdy walk, located in a more down-to-earth community called Balham. It lacked the pleasant village ambience that I had enjoyed for six weeks, even seemed rather grim at first look. But Balham's lengthy High Street and its offshoots had a certain nitty-gritty realism about them that I could get into, as a London experience, and it turned out far more appropriate than South fields, to the sort of winter I was heading into.

The landlady, Mrs. Firfirey – the only name I ever knew her by – was a small and wonderfully sweet Indian woman who lived there with her two sons, Rahim and Fahim, one a bit over twenty and the other a bit under. They occupied the two lower floors and rented out a small top-floor apartment, self-contained except for the sharing of a mid-level bathroom, for the same £45 per week I had been paying. In Londonese it's called a bed-sitter, a sitting/sleeping room of micro dimensions with a kitchen even tinier. But for me, it was a perfect size; I've lived in small quarters and know how to make the most of them.

North-facing windows, one for each room, offered an expansive view that soared skyward over distant rooftops. A perfect antidote to any possibility of claustrophobia. In the foreground, long and narrow backyards abutted the grounds of a great old brick school building, with trees everywhere. A huge television set was also in the bargain, my pacifier for a cloistered winter. The window in the daytime, the TV at night.

My writing desk looked out on a world of billowing cumulus or somber overcast. Anything at all close to clear skies presented a steady procession of aircraft on the flight path into Heathrow, bearing airline insignia from every country in the world. Once each day, if I could catch the moment, the French Concorde skimmed by on delta wings, a graceful sight never to be seen back home. I was happy as a robin working there (when I wasn't worried as a worm, over what would become of me).

Renting the place put an immediate crunch on me. I had to take it at once or lose it, but the chunky Irishman would not budge a farthing for any rebate on the month's rent I had just given him. It meant a total loss of two weeks rent; almost $200 spent for nothing.

My starting bankroll of $1870 was already down to $720, after two months in Britain – even with earnings added in. The payment to Mrs. Firfirey now cut that by more than half, and red lights were flashing. I could hold out through November, but by then I would need a transfusion from home. Even the exchange rate had been shifting against me in recent weeks, so that my 'same price rent' would actually be $20 more each month, after the new cash came in.

The move to Balham proved to be the Great Divide for me. I finally had to come to terms with the insistent realization that I was not going to get a regular job at all. Several things forced it on me. For one, I no longer had a home telephone. The LVSC ad, just now coming out, referred inquiries to my Southfields phone number, which was about to be disconnected. I also knew, from many years past, that December is the worst time for job-hunting. And with January's arrival only two and a half months would be left, that I could still offer to a potential employer.

It should have been obvious before the move, but I hadn't wanted to see it. I was too intent on the agenda to read the clear signals. Everything – outside of those brief teaching gigs – had gone wrong, the results often mocking my very efforts, as if they were demanding some recognition that it was a dead-end trail.

There was the interview Lauren had gotten for me, the only real job interview in two months of search. Lauren was my ally in the agencies, the one who had phoned me in Seattle while I was in California, calling because she had come from Seattle, herself, before she married an Englishman and moved to London to start her own computer placement service. Young, blond, refreshingly American in this remote world, Lauren was on my side and I didn't have to play any job-applicant games with her. In mid-November, she managed to set up an interview for a short-term job with a top advertising agency that seemed exactly right . . . and I somehow blew it.

Then there was the wrenching, if also humorous, *Que sera* incident. On a Friday in October, one of the agencies had called me to come in immediately and pick up a temp assignment for three weeks of clerical work, to begin the following Monday. I raced into town as fast as I could and breathlessly up several flights of stairs ... only to be told that the job order had been canceled after I was already on my way. It was a crushing blow, considering how my anticipations had soared. I sagged back down the stairs, seeking something, anything, that could explain this meaningless 'joke' of the Universe, and as I opened the outer door I heard melody above the street rumble. Along the sidewalk came a dignified old fellow in full tuxedo, crested by a magnificent sombrero. He was pumping an absurdly small accordion to accompany the lyric that came forth in a thin, wavering voice ... *"Que sera, sera...whatever will be, will be..."*

The message was at once personal and sensible: things are just the way they are, regardless of what I imagine they should be. I put a couple coins in the fellow's cup and blessed him, and really meant it. I just had forgotten one of the cardinal rules of following trail: the doors have to be open. When they're closed, it's the wrong trail.

Now that the picture had finally come into clear focus, I cursed and laughed at myself for having been blind to it for so long. Then I spent the better part of a week trying to assess what was really going on. The surface aspect was obvious, but what did it all mean? I needed some understanding, to know how to proceed. If I was wrong about the job, was I wrong in coming to London? After all, I wouldn't have made the journey had I any idea that I was not to find a job. So I had to know, now, if it was a bad move – in which case, I should consider dropping the whole thing and getting out as quickly as possible. Or was there something more to it than I could see?

I reviewed the chain of circumstances that had set me on this course to begin with – the meaningful February events, etc. – and saw no reason to change my first assessment. I looked back at the unique London trails that had actually opened for me, and saw them as clear messages of encouragement to hang in and not lose hope; and the same could be said of the brief September work that had come along. Despite the financial shallows, nothing seemed to suggest that I had made a mistake. Then I took a thoughtful look at the two weird things – seemingly impossible things – that had happened to me, just before the move to Balham.

The first of these involved a suburban woman I met through a personals ad in a local paper. Before actually meeting, Jolene and I exchanged letters. This was during the time I was using the computer at Fatemah's agency, and one afternoon as I was absorbed in that work, a woman had come in for an interview. Fatemah had few clients, which was probably the only reason I could even recall it later, for there was no interaction between us, and I remembered nothing very singular about the woman: middle-aged, tall, in an overcoat, typically British in her voice and manner. But this woman *happened to be Jolene,* as we only realized later by reflection, after the chance discovery that we both knew Fatemah. In that brief time before we actually knew each other but were in contact by mail, fate had brought us to the very same room, in all of London, at the same moment!

The other strange instance involved my erstwhile friend, Clark. Shortly before my move from Southfields I received a phone call – a vaguely familiar voice checking matter-of-factly who I was, then asking for a mailing address, and then hanging up after thanking me. Not immediately realizing it was Clark's voice, I assumed it had something to do with one of my employment applications. But a couple of days later I received a packet containing more than a dozen pieces of un-opened mail that were addressed to Thomas Irvin – *the exact reversal of my own name* – mail that had been forwarded to Clark's address! These were wrapped with a rather curt note from Clark saying he was tired of holding mail for me and more than a bit upset that I had used his address to receive forwarded mail, without ever having asked his permission.

It was not my mail, of course, and it took a bit of investigative work to unravel the mystery. Clark lived on the ground floor of a six-plex and saw little of the other tenants. Apparently, on the first of October, just days after I had left his hospitality, a young fellow named Thomas Irvin moved into an upper-floor unit. Clark, the first to see each morning's mail, had started plucking the poor fellow's letters whenever he spotted one, assuming quite naturally that they were for me. From his lingering irritation, when I called afterward with the explanation, I suspect that some part of him could not quite believe that I wasn't somehow the cause of it all.

And maybe, at some level, I was! I suppose some would consign these strange, synchronous events to chance, with a calculation of staggering odds. But it doesn't really wash, for the odds insist on extreme rarity and I have experienced too many such happenings. This pair, in fact – the incident with Jolene and the other with Clark – occurred within days of each other, which constitutes yet a third 'chance pairing' in time. I find it easier to believe in a world of purposeful pathways behind the agendas we pursue, invisible but for the occasional surfacing of some oddity that clearly speaks of another sort of order, with meaning that only intuition can surmise.

Whatever deeper meaning such a synchronicity may hold, its mere occurrence is a trail marker for me, from a very easy line of reasoning: In order for it to happen, I must be at the right place at precisely the right moment, and therefore it tells me that I am exactly where I should be. This being the case, London was clearly the right place for me; and being there without a job – for that was just as certainly now part of the trail – had to be right, too. With this recognition I was committed to staying, and ready to take on anything a London winter might throw at me.

The St. Pancras rail station, a Victorian relic either loved or despised by Londoners for its ornate excess. I rather liked it.

London Lowdown

London: December 1990...

When I finally decided to end the whole charade of looking for a job, two things became critical. One was a very careful structuring of budget and money process, for I had to be absolutely sure I could make it through the winter if I was going to hang in. Trust is fine, but there is also peace of mind to be considered.

The other matter was my half-finished series of articles. The theme of the series, after all, was an older job-seeker successfully navigating the hazards in a strange land. What now, if success was out of the picture?

I put the articles on hold for the time being. Something could yet develop. The now-and-then computer instruction might solidify into something more steady; and there was always a chance that Fatemah or Lauren might come through with a job. I wasn't deciding not to work, just quitting this fatuous pursuit of employment. Anyway, three of the articles were already written and the project could mark time for awhile.

As things now stood, I had $3000 back home, and $300 in local funds. My costs, outside of rent, were averaging $110 per week – much too high. But three of my last five weeks had come in below $85 and I felt I could take it down much further, now that I had accepted the idea of a survival winter. I set $70 as a weekly ceiling, with a Visa draw for it every third week. To prevent a solvency bottleneck, I'd pay the rent from my Westminster account, after fattening it with a transfer of $1000 from Seattle. This would assure sixteen weeks of rent without need of another major cash transfer. And my Visa would remain reasonably clear for emergency options.

In many ways Balham was perfectly suited to this exercise in frugality. In hard contrast with Southfields' semi-urban gentility, where mothers navigated infants in prams along sunny sidewalks and little old ladies took time from their morning shopping for bits of street-corner tattle, Balham was a sudden splash of basic-survival reality – a no-nonsense, gritty world of weather-beaten old men and bargain-sharp housewives. It was the proper fit for my prospect of a crusty winter.

Just off the High Street, I found a block-long street market – an earthy institution seen everywhere in Europe but virtually lost in America, to our sanitizing March of Progress. I remember a vestige in the San Francisco of my youth: the Crystal Palace Market near city hall, a cavernous indoor enclosure that sheltered sacks and stacks of every imaginable kind of bulk food. Dried fruits and dates from exotic lands, peanut butter being churned in huge vats, arm-thick salamis that hung in pendulous rows from overhead hooks, bushels of unwrapped breads radiating a bakery-fresh aroma that trapped anyone within nostril's distance . . . a vast bazaar of smells and sights, now only a sensual memory. Seattle's Pike Place Market remains with us; but like so much else of our earthy past it has become primarily a tourist function, a kind of caricature of the real thing.

Balham's street market became my produce resource. Housewares, too, and a variety of local seafood, much cheaper than in the shops. Lines were shorter than in the supermarkets, and those that queued up were a sure indication of good prices or better selection. I'd be saying, "three of those and one of these, and a half pound of . . . " while the fast-moving stall-keeper toted prices in his head. With food fully a third of my non-rent expense, the street market played a vital part in my budget. I even found affordable treats there, like freshly marinated herring; I could get a whole fish for only $1.60. I was a kid, the last time I'd had herring sold in bulk – in San Francisco's old Jewish district, where

Mr. Shenson used to pull one out of a barrel and wrap it in newspaper, throwing marinated onion into the 25¢ bargain.

Balham's High Street, in fact, reminded me of nothing so much as my old San Francisco in its Depression decade. It was one of the sweeter aspects of wintering in Balham, especially under economic strains appropriate to the memories it stirred. Here was the same dismal looking architecture – not precisely in style, but certainly in mood – and the same streetside ambience: dreary little eateries with hunched-over locals taking their day's news or working a crossword, over slowly sipped mugs of brew. Sitting over my own, every so often in the gray and wet of that winter, I'd watch the parade of thickly clad people trudge by with sack and hand-cart, at their day's shopping, and it was as good as being back in the Fillmore district of my boyhood. It might seem a strange kind of memory for a sweet glow, but hard times were often good times, in retrospect . . . in deeper ways.

What the street market didn't produce in reasonably priced housewares, I could seek at weekend recycling occasions variously called jumble sales or car boot sales. Londoners come together in a kind of mini-flea market instead of doing it individually, as we do with garage sales. A church would sponsor it, charging an entrance fee of ten pence, and any sort of treasure could turn up. I found a perfectly usable typewriter for five and a half dollars. A practically new crockpot cost me a bit more, almost $15, but I figured it would pay its way in coaxing me to home-cooked meals.

Having my own kitchen made all the difference in the world. In Southfields, the kitchen always felt like someone else's, and I'd just as often go up the street for a takeout serving of fish and chips, letting it go at that. I never tired of British fish and chips – but a single piece over the counter cost about four dollars, close to half of my daily allowance. My new kitchen had only a two-burner hotplate, so the crockpot, or slow-cooker as it's called there, was given a lot of use. I cooked up a weekly batch of what one Seattle housemate used to refer to as my 'stewp' – a stew-thick soup consisting of all the vegies I could cram in, slow-cooked in a tomato-base brew with a generous helping of mussels to jazz-up the flavor. Here in London, though, it was cockles, a cheap and tasty variety of local shellfish.

Living poor is actually a lot of fun once one gets into the spirit of it, because of the creative ingenuity it inspires. There is a satisfying thrill in finding useful things in unexpected places, converting the discard to the triumphant discovery. I could neither afford nor stitch drapes, for example, for the window of my bedroom. I didn't need them for privacy, for the room was situated high and away from curious eyes, but I favor a bit of darkness in the morning so I can ease into daylight as I'm ready for it. I found what had been the flat container of a large framed picture, and when I opened the cardboard to its full size it was a perfect fit for my drapeless window frame. Every night, each time I put this 'shutter' into place, I felt a glow of satisfaction simply because it had come to me with such serendipity.

A similar find was the daily afternoon trove in the trash bins outside the Balham station. The hordes of returning commuters deposited not only newspapers but a great variety of reading matter as they emerged from the station – riches far beyond what I ever had when I could afford to buy a paper or two of my own. London must be the world's greatest newspaper city, with a dozen or more dailies, several of which rank with the best journalism to be found anywhere.

I had to laugh, when the realization hit me that I had travelled halfway around the world to become a street-person, rummaging through garbage bins in neighborhood London. Oh, if my friends could see me now! But they would understand, for I have always been a good forager. Foraging must someday come into its own as a domestic art, making of daily life an adventure in creative recycling – which it once was, before we became captive consumers in the thrall of advertising and obsolescence. Foraging is healthy for the spirit, as it is for the pocketbook; and not less significantly, for the environment as well.

Foraging took me to the libraries, of course; there were several of them in easy reach – book-lovers' delights, to begin with, offering a sudden immersion in a whole range of books seldom found on shelves in America. A free library card gave me access to a half dozen borough branches, whose bulletin boards told me of other local resources. That's how I discovered the *Balham Skills Exchange,* a community institution nearby that may have been unique in all of London. For the mere price of listing myself as a willing instructor in desktop publishing (services for which I was never called upon), I had free access to the Exchange's word-processing equipment on a bank of a dozen computer terminals. They even had Pagemaker software. Everything at my disposal, for any level of writing that I wanted to do.

I seldom had to leave Balham that winter, but the temptations of greater London were naturally hard to resist. It was the easiest of journeys – a brief rail ride from a station only a short walk from where I lived. I could be in Victoria Station, or Waterloo on the south bank, in just fifteen minutes from home. It is now, and was then, hard to believe that trains came through Balham on a ten-minute schedule all day long!

But the winter fact of it was that I couldn't afford to go into town more often than once, or twice at most, each week. At job-hunting, I'd done it almost every day. My senior discount gave me a full day's transit, on rail, bus and underground, at just a bit over $2. But the screws had since tightened ... and tightened again at the turn of the year, when the full-day fare for seniors was actually doubled! At four dollars, I reserved the occasion of a London visit for day-long excursions once or twice a week, cramming as much as possible into them – and was thankful that the weather usually made it easy to stay home.

I never got enough of London – but then I'm not sure that I ever could. The streets, an eclectic mix of style and content from all of London's yesterdays, could be wandered endlessly for their endless visual feast: Georgian rows, all white and stately, sturdy Empire classicism, Victorian turreting and filigree, old and silent churches surrounded by their little graveyards, walls still standing from Roman times, wonderfully castellated Medieval gates and towers, quaint pubs of every age and style, even the most ordinary buildings posted with reminders – often several to the block – that here lived or died some notable of British letters or science. And always to be encountered, the tight-turning alley, the unlikely stairway or portico, the unsuspected opening into another vista, another time-warp.

Window shopping, alone, was a whole world of adventure – an ethnic world in miniature, with shops ranging from the tawdry to the untouchably elegant. A world, for me, where all was free to see, nothing free to grasp; an entertainment, an exercise in resisting temptation. But there were ways to ease the pangs of poverty: from streetcorner stands, an apple was a cheap and pacifying chew, or a couple of carrots. Sometimes I'd get a paper cone full of chips, hot from the deep-fry for a dollar or so, and leave the fish for the more affluent. Tea or coffee was only a third-choice alternative, for they don't know the custom of a free refill in Britain.

But any deprivation on that level was more than offset by the great variety of mostly free museums, too rich to be taken in concentrated doses of more than a few hours per visit. I could easily lose myself in the British Museum, the queen of them all, dreaming my way through halls filled with inspiring marble sculpture from the Parthenon, or handwritten documents from all the greats of England's history, or the Rosetta Stone – the very original! London's free museums helped to square the four dollar fee for getting into town.

Other free offerings could be found with a bit of attentive search. There was music at South Bank and also at the Barbican, another multicultural center, or at St. James Church, a community center in the very heart of town. I watched the Lord Mayor's Annual Parade from a choice spot right near the grandstand – a tradition of British Pomp and Circumstance, with medieval-clad horsemen and other traditional costumes totally unlike anything ever seen back home. And I had come to London just in time for the half-century celebration of the Battle of Britain, to watch ancient aircraft soaring overhead. I never thought I'd ever see a Spitfire in the air!

While most of these exploratory wanderings were done in cheerful solitude, I also had a surprisingly active social life for someone in my circumstances. One of London's less literate journals was a weekly tabloid called *Loot,* devoted to classified ads of every variety – including free-listed personals. While still in Southfields, I had placed a small bit of personal poesy announcing my availability for amorous adventure, and was rewarded with more response than I had expected. Most of what eventuated were one-time encounters over tea and scones, which was all my budget could handle, but one or two friendships lingered on through the winter. Jolene, who was part of that strange October synchronicity in Fatemah's office, was a real sparkler who briefly brought me into her family circle. She knew the countryside and had a wagon in which to explore it, should a rarely sunny Saturday happen to come along.

A special section for message-ads, in the *Loot* pages, had become a bulletin board for pseudonym-disguised participants whose curious and tantalizing dialogues went on endlessly. They called themselves Looters, and every so often came together for a celebratory evening in some local pub. I met a strange woman whom I only knew as Witches Cat, through this exchange, and got invited to a Looter evening of 'plonk' at the nearby St. George Inn. About thirty people came, a young artsy and literate crowd with Looter names I was already familiar with: Pink Flamingo, Innocentia, Doctor Q, and others I no longer recall. It was a cheap but special bit of London life, not to have been missed.

For the most part, though, my winter was passed in the sometimes boring, sometimes relaxed ambience of my small quarters in Balham, in comfortable retreat from weather for which a single word will suffice: dismal. Television has never been a habit of mine, but I got hooked on it this winter in London. I became a qualified, card-carrying couch potato. The card was my pocket list of not-to-forget programs, which included among other shameless things a soap opera. Yes, I got hooked on an Australian soap called *Neighbors*. But my favorite was a free-wheeling weekly current-affairs discussion simply called Questions. A four-sided panel representing all shades of British politics took questions from a participating studio audience, and the display of rapier needling and downright slashing sarcasm was marvelous to observe. It was a ringside seat on British verbal joust, on all the issues of the day.

Considering that my London stay coincided with the entire development of Maggie Thatcher's fall from grace, and her replacement by John Major, it was as good a moment for seeing British politics in action as one could ask. That, and the Gulf War following closely upon it, made for a media circus that was a match for anything the U.S. has to offer. As to the war, of course, the British all along felt it was America's private oil battle, shared generously with the rest of the west. But when the glories were being toted, England had no problem claiming her portion.

The ultimate test of a winter in poverty is how one weathers the holiday season, with its chancey play on the emotions at every level. Thanks considerably to friends – on both sides of the Atlantic, now – I did all right on that score. I had primed the pump, stateside, by drawing up an interim progress report (so to speak), and sending Terry a copy she could duplicate and mail, at domestic postal rates, to all who had sponsored my journey. The mail in return brought a further sprinkling of donations, though none had been requested. One sweet friend in California thought I ought to have a steady angel and began sending me monthly tithings.

Among my London friends, I was invited to several seasonal celebrations and had Christmas dinner at Marjory's – a traditional turkey dinner, of course, finishing with that old English standard: brandied pudding with hard sauce. Taking the severe weather into account, as well as the suspended local transit for the holiday, Marjory even let me stay over that night in one of her guest rooms.

Earlier in the month, I had been invited to an office party at *Choice*. It wasn't the time for any extended discussion of my dormant article series, but I had the feeling that Wendy wanted to know where I stood with it. And I, likewise, needed to sound her out on the shift in direction. I came away with nothing very clear on the matter except that Wendy was working with tighter space constraints and could give me no more than a page for each article of the series. This called for sharp cuts in what I had already submitted. Though of course, I wasn't yet sure that I could even continue with the start I had made. Her interest seemed undiminished, but there was a kind of 'party gloss' around her energy and cheer that left me still uncertain as to where everything stood.

It turned me once again toward the writing, however. I could see now that the only honest way to work with it was to swing the series around at midpoint – just as I had, myself, been swung around by the course of developments. It gave the project a new twist, with a fresh challenge: to open a series on one enthusiastic course, stumble into its failure midway, and then shift the agenda . . . without diminishing the validity of what had gone before. But I still hadn't a clue as to what the last-half direction should be. The model was me, and I didn't know where my own life was going.

I began at once, tightening what I had already written. I would cut it to size myself, rather than leave it to an editor. I kept the high, confident tone, pointing it ever so slightly toward a change of pace. A new version of segment three would cover the turnaround: my deepening confusion over the consistent failure to find a job, and then a flash of insight – that my work-permit had simply been a 'bridge of confidence' enabling me to come to Britain on trust alone (having no other reason to suppose I could afford it). Part four, then, would pick up the tale with what it means – in practical terms, and in dealing with issues of age and isolation – to approach a winter of dedicated poverty as a positive adventure instead of an unfolding disaster. The writing challenge was not the turnaround itself, but how to make an upbeat experience of it, for Wendy would want no tale of distress and defeat.

My rewrite of the first two parts went out to *Choice* early in January. Segment three was not nearly as easy. I struggled with it for several weeks, sure almost every evening that I finally had it – even starting, at one point, on part four – only to come crashing down with a re-reading the next morning. When I once or twice found myself suddenly soaring, the 800-word limit brought me down like a popped bag of wind. I began to doubt it could even be done in such brevity.

January has always been the bleakest, most self-doubting month of my year. I am sustained only by the continual reminder that it's the last hurdle before February. But it's not a hurdle, it's a mire, a morass of sluggish headway that forbearance alone must cope with. My dwindling resources had already put the idea of footloose travel on the continent, at the close of my London commitment, under a shroud of doubt. It would be a pity to waste such a close approach to Europe, but there was nothing happening to indicate that the fates were favorably disposed. And now, in January, the ebb tide of time edged into my energy like a scythe cutting into a field of wheat. The tide of the year, and of my life as well.

Those (usually the under-fifty) who glibly assert that age is in the mind are only right up to a point. Even the best-maintained bodies – and mine is not that – lose their flexibility as the years stack up. Limitations set in, and one never knows when they will next strike. Or how. Slipping on an icy Seattle street, a couple years before, had already cost me half the use of my right shoulder. A crotchety-stiff back was now the first challenge of each day. I slept on hard floors just to ease the morning's creaking pain, but there were still days when I could hardly reach my feet to pull my socks on.

Not to mention various internal things, intestinal and otherwise, that didn't always function as they used to. Or the occasional bout of tachycardia that suddenly set my heart racing at three or four times its normal rate, like it had to get to the end of its run as quickly as possible. I've learned to manage this by quickly slipping into a biofeedback mode, but it has to be done within the first few seconds of onset.

One evening, while leaving a London friend's house after dinner, the heart speedup struck just as I was saying my goodnight. Rather than make a fuss over it at the door, I simply hastened my departure. But that brief delay allowed it to get away from me. I tried every way I knew, then, to bring my pulse back down, but nothing worked. In the daytime, I would have gone to a doctor's office – a surgery, as they call it – or directly to a hospital. I had done it for lesser problems. Treatment received from the British health care system is as good, and quite as prompt, as in similar stateside facilities, notwithstanding the cautionary stories we are told; and the costs, even for a resident alien, are virtually nothing. But this was a weekend evening, a cold night; and in the grip of this condition I hadn't the energy to make such an effort.

It was all I could do to walk to the rail station a few blocks away, and drag myself finally up the double flight of stairs, at home, to my bed. Drained of any further survival concern, I left a brief note on my desk: "In case anyone finds this..." – actually thinking I might not wake up in the morning! I did, of course, wake up – everything was fine and normal the next day. But it's a scary situation, and not one I'd want to confront on the open road in a strange land.

Jolene came up with an idea, around mid-January, for a springtime drive down through France and Spain to visit her aging father, and before long I was seeing it as a fair compromise with my fading fantasy of a more extensive circuit of Europe. The fantasy – once a mere flirtation with such possibilities – had come to assume the proportions of a Grand Tour that would take me all the way into a second and more carefree winter on the Iberian coast of Spain. All through the fall, I had stopped in at consulate offices in central London, spinning dreams. But that was before The Fall. And now I was willing to settle for a couple weeks of safely sterile motor camping with Jolene, in humble recognition of 'reality.'

But it was premature. What could I know of reality, before February's arrival?

When February finally did arrive, it came in with a cold spell said to be Britain's worst in four years, bringing snow nearly a foot deep and great icicles that grew, Jack Frost-like, down the overhang of my windows. The view from my aerie was a lovely fugue in white, and even more beautiful in the haunting pink glow that came with night. It made little difference to my activity, for I was still locked in mortal combat with series piece number three, determined to make it work as I wanted, or see the whole project in ruin at the walls of its resistance.

I hadn't been in touch with Wendy at all, during those weeks of my agony and self-doubt, and rather anxiously tore open the envelope that arrived from her by post, on the 6th of the month. I was on the very edge of success with the tormenting article, and this new input – whatever it could be – sent sudden tremors of dread through me.

The brief letter inside said not a word about the series; it asked if I'd write a short article – a one-pager, again – on something we had talked about at our very first meeting in September. At that lunch, I told Wendy how I'd once spent a full year teaching myself to do left-hand portrait sketching as a likely way of getting in touch with my right-hemisphere potential. She was impressed and thought it had article possibilities, but we had never pursued it further. Here, now, was a solid offer for the article: £100!

Everything about the letter was a surprise. Rate of pay had never before been brought up, by either of us. I was elated, of course; but just as much puzzled by her lack of comment about the series. Was this perhaps intended to soften the blow of a change in plans – like a 'consolation prize'? I was so close to a finish, however, on the troublesome third article that I set the letter aside and turned back to my work.

I finished it that afternoon – finally certain that I had a successful version within the required parameters. It sent me high enough, with the added impact of the letter, to soar right on into part four, which fell into place within the next few days. Whether spurred by Wendy's hard-cash offer, or in the natural seasonal course of things, I had broken through the winter doldrums and the energy was rolling.

Not wanting to chance an interruption in its flow, I continued to hold off on the requested article, and started on the fifth piece in the series. Part four prompted the theme of it: following trails and staying solvent. It rolled out like it had been waiting in my head for the gate to open. I astounded myself by producing a ready-to-go draft in one day! It was the 10th of February, and on the following day, I sat down and encored the accomplishment with an inspired one-draft article on my left-hand artwork.

True to form, February had brought in energy and change. The next few days revealed that it went far beyond the writing, as my whole life suddenly lurched into forward motion. Wendy was now willing, on the strength of what she had in hand, to set a publication schedule for all seven articles, fixing a price for the lot at £700. The dollar's sudden rise during the Gulf War had cheapened that to $1300 in stateside value, but it was a figure hardly worth complaining about.

The next surprise came when I drew a rough balance on my entire five months of London living, adding a projection for the sixth that yet remained. Here's how it came out:

6-Month Outlay	Amount	Income	Amount
cost of rent	$ 2200	computer income	$ 900
all other expense	$ 2300	article earnings	$ 1300
		Social Security	$ 2400
TOTALS	$ 4500		$ 4600

I was actually out of the red! – as had seemed hardly possible all winter long. It came so close to a perfect balance that one might suppose some hidden orchestrator had arranged it just so . . . almost as if to constitute a trail sign.

Was this my green light to pursue the fantasy-journey on the continent? I was as well-funded, now, as at the point of my arrival in England. True, there was no longer the prospect of enhancing it with employment income, but I knew I could get by on the road much more cheaply than I had been able to live in London. I wasn't entirely sure the old body could handle a European road trip, but the answer to that could be found by a few weeks on the road in Britain, which I wanted to do anyhow.

I knew, now, how to close the series for Wendy. The theme of the sixth segment would be the importance of accepting whatever life brings, even if it isn't what you planned . . . even if it seems the pits. I might have turned around and gone home in November, to cut my losses – it would have been the prudent thing to do. But I hung in, letting fate play out its full hand, and found my trail validated, along with every one of the risks taken and choices made that enabled me to follow it.

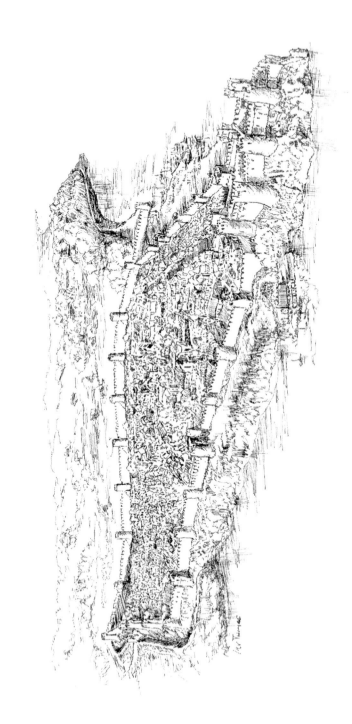

Conwy, an existing walled town in north Wales, though it now spreads beyond the walls. This view taken from an artist's reconstruction of how it was.

Footloose, foolhardy and freezing in Britain

London: end of April, 1991...

The Journey with Jolene never did happen. Her plans were for later, and mine had to be earlier if I were to see the rest of Britain. The Home Office, in charge of immigration, had given me until the 7th of June to be out of the country. With little enthusiasm for the cold countryside of a British spring I didn't want to attempt a road trip before the end of April, so it left me only five weeks in which to accomplish it.

Though small by American scale, Britain is packed with places worth seeing and I quickly realized the inadequacy of five weeks. Wanting to maintain, as well as I could, a leisurely pace I made the hard choice to stay with the main island and forget about its partner across the Irish Sea. I mapped five regions, and wrote to secure weekend Good Neighbors hosts to pace my progress. For weeknights, I would take whatever was handy and affordable wherever I should find myself. That was the plan, and it looked good on paper; but the road sets its own agenda for footloose travel. Only one of my intended hosts ever materialized, and when the time came I almost wished he hadn't.

The one thing I could hardly afford to be loose about was my money supply. I wanted to use my Social Security income as a budget basis, taking it in a weekly Visa draw of $95. But the whole thing had come under a haze of uncertainty because of a foolhardy thing I did in February. My card was due for a July renewal with an increase in its limit, from $700 to $1200. But knowing I might be anywhere in the midst of Europe by then, unable to get the new card and suddenly without any money access at all, I had sent Visa a request to advance my renewal time to May, even if it meant holding my limit at $700, and asked them to send the new card direct to me in London rather than routing it through Terry in Seattle.

It was innocence in its worst aspect. I full well knew the risk of interfering in a computer process, especially with such a complex request. I was courting the full power of Murphy's Law. But all I could see at the time was the equally Murphy-prone risk of a Visa card chasing me around through Europe.

The net result of my effort was nothing at all: I heard not a word from Visa up to the moment of my departure. It would seem the gentlest retort that Murphy could come up with, but it left me in a complete fog of uncertainty as to what would develop in the matter. Westminster Bank came to my rescue, for the moment, providing me with an ATM card that I could use in cash machines around the country, so long as I kept funds on deposit. A backup that would end, once I left England.

The rest of my trip prep consisted of a hitch-hiker's guide to Britain's motorway system, a stripped-down road atlas annotated with every shred of locational information on hosts, hostels and sightseeing that I could cram into it, and a Vibram renewal of my Rockport walking shoes. I would take no tent or camping gear, just my sleeping bag and ground cloth with a thin, back-length piece of padding, plus an easily rigged overhead mosquito cover. I had a full-size rain poncho that could serve as an over-all tarp in case of emergency. The only new gear I bought was a super-light water-resistant windbreaker that rolled tightly into a belt-pack. At $50 it was my biggest expense, but it allowed me to leave behind a much heavier all-weather Gore-Tex jacket. My final carrying weight was only 25 lbs. I was gambling weight against weather, of course, and it could backfire on me.

Marjory had consented to be my London base, as Terry was my Seattle anchor. I left my excess belongings with her and planned my return for the few days before June 7th, when I'd make the final arrangements for either going on into Europe or heading for home.

The adventure would begin by rail. I wanted none of the hassle of trying to hitch out of the world's largest city. Marjory once more offered a transition zone for me, as she had when I first settled in Southfields. I vacated my Balham residence with Mrs. Fufirey at April's end for a final weekend of Marjory's 'bed and board' comfort, balanced on the knife-edge of uneasy tension between anticipation and apprehension.

Monday's grey overcast was no energizer. I lingered through the morning at last minute stuff, almost hoping that rain would provide an excuse to wait another day. But by noon it was still dry so I shouldered my pack and headed for London's Paddington Station, from where Oxford was only forty-five minutes away. Even as the train pulled out, the sky was still trying to decide whether to lighten-up or unload.

By the time we got to Oxford the decision was in. Water came down with pluvial abandon, confirming the most insistent of my pre-trip fears. I later learned it was the heaviest single day's rainfall in six months. But there is something singularly liberating in such a beginning. When the worst happens right at the start, all you can do is laugh at how pointedly the Universe responds to your sense of limits.

I found myself, in fact, revelling in the downpour, as I walked through Oxford town taking it full blast. I had placed just one call at the station, to a friend of a friend back home who'd sent me the name. Relief at Martin's spur-of-the-moment welcome was part of my cheer, but mostly it was the cathartic lift of being at last on the open road, done with winter's long wait and all the pre-trip anxieties. The rain was a baptism. I could have taken a bus, but I walked the weather-ravaged mile joyously getting soaked.

Martin was involved with right-livelihood issues and alternative economics. I knew that already, but I had forgotten my further information that he had been a Labour Party city councilman, and I plunged into instant quicksand with a comment on Britain's recent election that could be construed as a positive assessment of the Conservatives. What I thought was a cold glare, however, turned out to be Martin's normally serious way of pursuing political discussion. I angled out of it with some discomfort, and after that stayed carefully away from politics. Reminiscing about our mutual friend took up the slack, with small talk on what might be seen in Oxford on a rainy day. Martin's russet-haired wife, Mandy, was an easier conversationalist, if just a bit intimidating by her straightforward way of nursing an infant as we talked.

I almost hadn't come here at all. For uncertain reasons, Cambridge has always held a greater fascination for me than Oxford and I thought I'd have to choose one or the other at the very end of my route. This first week was for the southwest corner of Britain: Devon and Cornwall, with Oxford far off to the side of my course. But when one of Marjory's friends said I shouldn't want to miss it, I patched it in as my first stop.

She was right, I loved Oxford. Somehow, this rainy-day gray was a perfect complement for the yellow-tan tint of its college stonework, quarried in sufficient volume to cast the character of the entire town. I explored a few of the college quads, but with spring exams underway most of them were off-limits to visitors. It made little difference, for there was enough else to see in the crosswork of shopping streets and passageway alleys that interweave among them. For me, they radiated the charm of a Dickens lithograph, though they weren't really that quaint. But they seemed to typify a vision of 'olde England' carried for years somewhere in my head.

I found the Ashmolean Museum, an archeological repository that had been a legendary name to me since pre-teen days of intellectual foray, when I romanticized over the discovery of Egyptian royal tombs, and the pioneer dinosaur-digs of explorer Roy Chapman Andrews in outer Mongolia.

I had only intended to spend one night here, but the continuing storm and the sheer pleasure of walking Oxford's rainy-day streets made me receptive when Martin's welcome was extended for another night. I spent most of that next day browsing bookstores, flirting with my most dangerous passion. I was hard put to resist their pull in London; and now, free of survival constraints, I could contain the impulse no longer.

Secondhand bookshops have been a hazard to my budget since nearly as far back as memory can take me. In a university setting, I find them almost impossible to resist. In Britain, especially, they were full of unexpected gems that seldom surface in stateside shops. But I handled myself nicely, here, purchasing only one slight find – for Terry, as it happened – and had the shop post it back to Marjory rather than add its weight to my pack.

The weather hadn't much improved by Wednesday. But I could delay no longer – though I had to stretch for the willpower to cast myself out, suddenly on my own once more, in the frigid countryside. I wanted to head south, directly to Salisbury Plain and Stonehenge, for the week was half gone already. But there were no prospective hosts in that area and the weather had me intimidated. I decided on Swindon, half the distance and somewhat west of the course, but progress of a sort.

Though cold, it was tentatively dry that morning, and seemed a fair time to try my luck at hitch-hiking. A local bus took me to the edge of Oxford town, where I picked a likely spot and stood braced against icy winds, feeling awkward as usual. Facing left lane traffic was a unique experience, but otherwise it was the same old game. After three-quarters of an hour, with an occasional few raindrops to keep me aware that there was no shelter should it get serious, my ride came along, a young fellow in a big blue truck – or lorry, to be proper about it. He took me the full thirty miles to Swindon, clearly pleased to discover that he was giving an American his first ride in Britain. In Swindon, I reached a GN host couple in nearby Wootton Bassett, a village named for some ancient feudal lord, if I remember right. British place names quite often sound as though they were arrived at by mischievous elves playing word games.

I was immediately welcomed with hot tea and biscuits, prepared by a flaxen-haired young Scottish matron named Ann, whose husband,

Jon, was off at work – which turned out to be downstairs in a basement veterinary surgery (that's a clinic, remember?). He fascinated me that evening with a discourse on the increasing use of acupuncture and homeopathy in treating animals – proof, it seemed to me, that such healing is not merely psychological. But it was Ann's thoughtful reflections on the challenge of keeping a country family in good balance that made the deeper impression on me that evening. Thanks to the absence of one of their two teen-agers, away at school, I had a room to myself . . . but chose to make my bed that night – as I would many times in the coming weeks – on the rug-cushioned floor.

Morning brought the surprise of sunshine! Ann had her own surprise – a suggestion that I might like to pedal the twelve miles down to Avebury on the family's spare bicycle and see the great stone circles there. So off I went, with a small lunch she packed for me, along a bumpy, narrow country road, glorying in the sun like any carefree school kid . . . for two and a half miles until the rear tire began to fade. So much for teen-age joys at 64. I found a phone about a mile further along, and waited there for her to come and get me in the family wagon. We went on to Avebury in a more seemly fashion.

Avebury's fame centers on an assortment of giant hewn stones patterned in impressive circles whose age and exact purpose has been lost in Celtic antiquity. They are widely regarded as evidence of the very earliest human efforts at understanding and relating to the Universe. I spent a half hour among those great brooding stones. The complex almost overwhelms the small village that has grown around them. It is a large enough arrangement, and the visitors were few enough on this sunny but chill weekday morn, that I could quietly walk among the stones, feel them, lean against them and try to conjure scenes that might have taken place here, thousands of years ago.

The next morning I was off to Stonehenge, spurred to an early departure by the continuing sunshine, this time via county bus at a cheap rate ($5.75) for the entire day. It didn't go direct, but down to Amesbury, a couple miles from the site, where a transfer bus comes through every two hours. I somehow managed, despite good enough timing, to miss this second bus – which proved to be the day's blessing.

Rather than wait two hours for the next, I shouldered my pack and set out on the two-mile walk, which has got to be the only way to properly approach Stonehenge.

I'd been told by several people, including my recent host, Ann, that Stonehenge is not as impressive as its fame would suggest. Since becoming a major tourist attraction it has been protectively roped off from full access. The visitor is allowed only within a hundred feet or so, which deprives one of the entire experience of being within the setting. This is like barring visitors from the interior of a great cathedral. It makes a spectacle of Stonehenge instead of an experience – a prove-you've-been-here camera target for the thousands who weekly come by bus and auto.

But by the pure accident of hiking to the site, Stonehenge became for me a uniquely memorable experience. The walk begins as an easy rise, curving up from Amesbury toward the main highway which crests in a shallow dome at just about where the two roads join. At this point, still a mile distant, the henge comes into view, lonely in the rolling green meadow, not impressively large except in contrast to the ant-like figures that cluster around. It was this contrast, and the invisibility of all tourist trappings as the stones loomed slowly larger on my approach, that gave them dignity and put the human element in proper perspective. Coming to the monument at a measured pace, with earplugs in place so that the roar of traffic going by was only a gentle hum, my walk became a meditative pilgrimage.

I've often wondered if a hearing handicap might not be a blessing in today's high decibel world. I regularly use earplugs to cut the blare, just as dark glasses are used by others to moderate glare. I've discovered, in fact, a curious relationship between hearing and vision. A change in one can affect the subjective experience of the other. I found this out, one day, while walking the open roadside with a snugly set pair of earplugs. Beyond all credibility, it *visually slows down the traffic* by a substantial margin!

When I finally reached the site it was practically an anticlimax. The huge stones had gotten small, in the surround of those tourist-ants now grown to full size. Any sense of awe, or even respect, was impossible in their midst. I chose not to pay the $2.75 asked for a slightly closer view. I'd already had the view I wanted, and was satisfied to be on my way.

It was Friday, now, and I realized, as the departure bus took me back to Amesbury and on toward Salisbury, that my week's moment of truth had arrived. The patched-in trip to Oxford, with my weather-wary lingering there and at Swindon, had used up most of the time meant for Devon and Cornwall on the coast. Prudently, I decided to abandon that agenda . . . to gracefully accept its loss and head directly west toward Bristol rather than force a catch-up pace on myself for the rest of the journey. I'd get a good weekend rest, and be in place for next week's intended passage through Wales. But Salisbury gave me a taste of just how arbitrary my choices had to be. The town begged for exploration – one of the most picturesque spots I had yet come to. But I had just a half hour between buses, or else get caught by darkness midway along the next leg.

Heading west, trying to decide whether I should lay over in Bath or go directly on to Bristol, I was suddenly inspired by the day's lingering sunshine. Who needed the hassle of seeking a host in either place, when I could just as easily spend a night under the stars? The two towns were only twelve miles apart, and I targeted a point midway between them, figuring I could go either way in the morning, as fancy should suggest.

Alighting from the bus at a village called Saltford, I headed down a ravine road to get away from the highway and soon struck a hiking trail alongside a rail line. I followed it west toward Bristol, and within a half mile encountered a hideaway spot completely off the trail and out of its sight, the perfect place. There was hardly an hour left, now, before dark – just time enough to lay out my gear and get comfortable.

Sleeping in the rough, as they call it in Britain, was an adventure indulgence harking back to many trips made in earlier years. It never occurred to me that I hadn't done it in awhile, and might not have quite the same physical resiliency for it as I once did. I was pleased with the choice, however, and lay there happily nibbling on crackers and an apple until I saw what was happening to the sky. The shallow light of sunset on the west horizon had darkened to a colorless haze, of the sort that all too often in my experience has signaled the approach of stormy weather.

I was too committed, now, for any second thoughts. I quickly spread the poncho taut above my sleeping-bag, thankful for the presence of a few hardy scrub trees to which I could secure it with nylon cord and the further assist of two or three stakes. I hoped it would all be unnecessary. But it was quite necessary.

The rain began shortly after dark, and while never very heavy it did not let up before morning. My protective measures did amazingly well, allowing me a decent length of warm sleep, though not entirely a dry sleep. In fact, midway through the night I had to improvise a further bracing of the poncho/tarp to forestall a disaster that threatened from the water that was accumulating above me. But it had already encroached, giving my warm cocoon the icky feeling of nocturnal incontinence.

I was up with the grey dawn, miserably damp and stiff but in reasonably good spirits, all things considered – quite possibly because the ordeal was over, or at least the passive part of it. In seeming contrition, the rain paused for just the time it took to get into some dry clothing (relatively speaking), collect my gear and move on out toward Bristol, following the tracks. It was mushy walking, skirting puddles, hassled by wind-driven moisture that collected on my brow and dribbled down into my eyes. According to my map, a rail station should be nearby. It somehow never struck me, that no train had gone by since I first came upon the tracks, the evening before.

About two miles out from my rain-soaked night's bivouac the station materialized out of the foggy murk, just up ahead . . . but something was extraordinarily wrong about the place. It was totally deserted and silent. Yet, trains stood ready to depart. Trains that . . . were not of this time! Powerful old steam engines with great black drive-wheels as tall as me, and coaches of a similar ancient vintage. I was momentarily sure I had been thrust back into the last century, in this eerie gray mist – until a clatter broke the spell, and I swung around to see a trash man by the corner of the station, dumping a garbage canister.

He seemed as surprised as I, at the sight of my own surprise. "Ye'll find no one there, Mate. Museum's still shut down fer winter."

"Museum?"

"Sur-r-e." He had a bit of brogue. "Were y'maybe lookin' fer the Dooblin Limited?"

I told him I only wanted to get to Bristol, and he came back with a hearty laugh, informing me that these were old, abandoned tracks. But he proved to be an angel, for he was driving off toward the real station, a mile to the north, and said he'd take me along.

In the due course of a short train ride I reached Bristol Station, still wet and cold, and found a heating vent to sit by while I surveyed the possibilities for a weekend host, over hot tea and a crumpet. It was midmorning, and my fourth phone call connected with a young mother named Debbie. She had three uproarious kids, all under eight, and just the barest space to put me in: a spare cot in their dining room; but by this time any shelter at all looked extremely good. It wasn't just "any at all," though, for I found Debbie to be a serene and spiritual woman strongly motivated by an inner call to the Anglican priesthood, and I liked her right from the start.

I had no particular reason to want to see Bristol. I went there for its proximity to both Wales and Bath. Everyone had said Bath was the one place in Britain I should not miss. But I found Bristol much more to my liking. It might simply have been that I have no great feeling for Georgian architecture, which is entirely what Bath is. Or maybe because I'd hoped there might be some hot baths there. No one seemed to think it odd that there are no longer any hot baths in Bath – which is what the place historically was all about.

I took that side-trip on Sunday. On the Saturday of my wet arrival at Debbie's I set right out in search of a laundromat where I could dry my sleeping bag, and was at once drawn along Bristol's interesting alleyways and avenues. Debbie lived among the hills and hangouts of a college district – the gallery and bookshop sort that are such fun to explore. But this was also an old-time and long lived-in district which, in its hillside way, had a strong San Francisco flavor that felt instantly congenial. All day long I roamed: browsing shops, walking to the high overlook above the Avon River where it flows into the Severn, marvelling at the grand old suspension bridge that crosses the gorge, here. It was designed 150 years ago by a young man of thirty named Isambard Kingdom Brunel, and he died twenty-six years later – before it was completed! My walk then took me to the city's free museum where I found a unique collection of ship models illustrating the entire history of sea-going vessels – from the primitive multi-oared Phoenician sort to the grand luxury liners of just awhile ago – all built to the same scale, so that endless interesting comparisons could be made.

Bristol's secondhand bookshops, some of the cheapest I would find in England, yielded five small items, all for about $13, including a hard-to-find volume of personal philosophy by John Cowper Powys, whose writing had begun to interest me, and a small, nicely bound edition of W. H. Hudson's earliest work, *The Purple Land.* One proprietor would mail the lot to London for me, for another few pounds (seven dollars!). It was an extravagant indulgence, the whole business, but I had to be good to myself after a night out in the rain. That evening, Debbie served a meal of cooked duck for the occasion of my visit, and the kids were on their best behavior – albeit with unrestrained curiosity about their grey-bearded guest.

My first week's travel expenses, even with Saturday's book binge, came in quite handily at $89.39. $25.53 of that had gone on books and their postage, a category amount exceeded only by the $28.46 that went for transportation.

The Road from Bristol to Wales crosses the Severn River, a mile-and-a-half wide cleavage at this point in its stretch toward the sea. I hitched a ride that took me several miles further, up to Chepstow, and my first opportunity to explore the remains of a real castle. It wasn't all that large, as castles go, but at the $2.25 entry fee it was more affordable than most of those I would later encounter. There wasn't all that much to actually see, but I was so charmed by it that I spent two full hours among the ruins, teasing my imagination with scenes probably gleaned from old movies. The great old banquet hall was nothing but a great old opening to the sky ... but there were holes in the stonework for great old crossbeams that once girded its great old timbered floor. Anyway, it was my first real castle and I could have spent another hour there; but the road toward further adventure called.

Onward, for a mile-long walk up a tree-bordered, sun-spackled country road, to the highway going north, where I was picked up in hardly any time at all by an elderly couple who had actually doubled back after first passing me by. Age, at times, can be a distinct advantage in hitch-hiking. They were quite fascinated to find someone of their own generation from America, at the humble and unlikely task of thumbing a ride in the countryside.

Just a few miles along our way they stopped at Tintern Abbey for a rest break, allowing me to linger at one of the most beautiful ruins in all of Britain without even losing my ride. Tintern's gaunt, towering facade was a lacework filigree of delicate stonework etched against this day's bluest of blue skies. The spring-green meadow grass carpeting its open interior presented a rare vision of nature within the church – a church that all too often rejects nature. I momentarily regretted not having a camera with me.

By the time my driver let me off at Monmouth, a further few miles up the road, clouds were gathering and the day's high energy was on the wane. No GN hosts were nearby, but one of Britain's few affordable youth hostels was, at nine dollars, and I found it in a classic Tudor style structure that had once been a boy's school. It was nearly empty and I was given an entire dorm room to myself. Having no social responsibilities here, and no good reason for seclusion, I spent the last few hours of daylight exploring the town.

I found an archaeology dig happening right in the heart of Monmouth. A crew at work inside an old shop-front had cut away the ground just a few feet, to expose the old Roman street pattern as it crossed this point. Two-thousand-year old building foundations were clearly visible. From what I could gather, the locale is a hive of such sites, with a strong community commitment to investigate and preserve them whenever a turnover in local property offers the opportunity.

Monday's thirty-five miles was not a large stride for a week that had to see me all the way through Wales, but it had been an easy, straightforward passage with no sense of urgency. Tuesday was something else again – all around. It began with a failure of my Visa card, the ATM machine informing me that I had drawn my limit, which simply didn't make any sense to me. But this, at least, was no immediate problem; the Westminster Bank card came through for me with the week's cash.

My day's objective was to head directly west, avoiding the industrial south coast of Wales so I could more quickly reach its rural and west coastal regions. The atlas indicated a routing by secondary roads that could accomplish this, with a little hitch-hiking luck, by way of a midway town called Merthyr Tydfil – which is only important to this tale in the way it eventually skewed my day's journey. The skies warned me, from the very start, that the day could be troublesome.

My first ride took me an uneventful seven miles. Then I was picked up by a cheerful fellow in a big meat truck hauling whole carcasses and cuts to butcher shops, up one road and down another. He talked a non-stop monologue that went this way and that, like his routing, and I lost track of where we were until we got to Pontypool, which was well south of my intended course. But it was raining by this time, and I had no inclination to be back out at the roadside.

He loved his job, he kept telling me, though I couldn't imagine why, the more he told me about it. He started each day at 3 a.m. and worked ten to twelve hours, six days a week, during which he was responsible for the meat-cutting as well as delivery and accounts, and he received no overtime pay, it was a flat salary . . . but he loved it! Every so often I'd wait in the truck while he hauled carcass, looking more bloody and exhausted at each return – but quick to resume his testimonial eloquence, until I wondered if it was a rare form of compensatory sarcasm to keep his own spirits up.

From Pontypool we kept right on south to Newport, on the coast, where he knew the cheapest place in all of Britain, he said, for fish and chips. It was true, they only cost $1.90. We touched into Cardiff, further along the coast, then north again past Castle Coch and up to Pontypridd, the end of his run – and pretty much nowhere, as far as I was concerned, but nothing had encouraged me to get off anywhere along the way. By this time, a full sleet storm was pounding us, and I had to run for cover when he announced the journey's end. He pointed out a footpath through the brush, leading to a raging stream crossed by a foot-bridge to the other side, where I'd find a rail station from which to further my day's rather dubious progress. It was a narrow, cable-hung boardwalk that swayed in the wind over the torrent below, like I was crossing a gorge in the high Andes. The day's very substance had begun to disintegrate into the surreal.

Pontypridd is a rail junction that offers three choices, like a Y. The two northern directions dead-end at about equal distances and the south-bound one eventually turns near the coast, to head westward into the Welsh sunset – were there a sunset. I should have waited for that one, but one of the northbound forks went to Merthyr Tydfil, on my once-intended route, and without thinking it all the way through I hopped aboard a train ready to leave. It was a labored half-hour uphill grind. The conductor seemed completely oblivious of me as he paraded several times through the car collecting fares, so I simply didn't pay.

At Merthyr Tydfil it was dry again, but so darkening that I had visions of imminent deluge. In these circumstances it made little sense to hitch-hike without knowing I'd find a host. The only one in the area was twenty miles beyond Merthyr Tydfil, and I placed a phone call . . . only to learn that he was not prepared to receive a guest without prior notice. That settled it. The train – the same one I had just come up on – was ready to head south now, and back on it I went, this time paying my fare, determined to stay on board. Past Pontypridd, past Cardiff, until we came to someplace where GN hosts were more plentiful.

I hung in for a hundred miles of twisting train ride to Carmarthen, so absorbed with weather and host concerns that I hardly gave attention to our passage through the heart of the Welsh coal-mining district. It was sunset time and quite cold now. Remarkably, I was under clearing skies, for the moment, but the day's highly volatile weather guaranteed nothing and I knew I must find quick and easy shelter – hopefully with one of the half dozen potential hosts in the area. Given the nature of this day, though, I was alert to anything in the environment that might offer a place to crawl into and hide from the night sky. Not again would I take my chances with a roofless bivouac.

I had no cause for concern. My second phone call found the welcome I sought, a woman who said apologetically that she could offer only one night of shelter. It was all I needed, and lovely to hear. Celia, who drove to the station to pick me up, was slim and attractive in jeans and had auburn hair of the deepest hue I have ever seen. It recalled to me, from somewhere long ago, a richly polished Brazilian mahogany with a similar lush, dark luster. I couldn't keep my eyes from it – to the point where I was afraid my attention would become conspicuous.

She and lawyer husband Mike lived in a rambling old streamside house several miles out of town, along with three youngsters – in one of whom, Robyn, I glimpsed myself as a precocious pre-teen, a half century back in time. There were other people around, too, whose status – neighbors, friends, lodgers? – was not quite clear to me. But they all joined in preparing the evening meal, and I helped a bit, myself, with the salad. It was a completely casual affair, with conversation to match, and ordinary local gossip. I remembered little of it, for I still could not keep my eyes from that auburn hair.

Carmarthen was my southwest corner-point in Wales. Celia drove me, the next morning, to a tiny village called Cynwyl Elfed – a picture-postcard bit of rural Wales, on the road to the crescent coastline of Cardigan Bay. And the best spot to hitch from, she said, though virtually no traffic seemed to be coming through. But the day had dawned crystal clear, nature at its best, and it made little difference to me to linger here under brilliant blue skies. Eventually, a couple who looked like they had come straight out of Berkeley in the 1960s came along in a small car and picked me up. They said they'd never been there; but we were clearly cut from the same pattern, and conversation came so easily that they went some distance out of their way to get me right out on the coast, at a place called Aberaeron.

If the day itself was perfect, this was the place where perfection was complete. The sight of those cobalt-blue waters, sparkles of sunlight rippling across their surface to the crystal-sharp line where a cloudless cerulean sky took over, was a vision of timeless paradise. I looked for an excuse to linger in this Elysium, and found it in a shop with homemade blackberry pie. The slice I was served towered like a small mountain, but it vanished much too quickly while I wrote a few post-cards.

Once in awhile, it is actually too lovely to be hitch-hiking. I wanted the feel of the road under my feet for awhile and walked out of Aberaeron, on up the highway along the coast. It had become the sort of day, with its morning vitality at full tide, the scene and weather incomparable, that can, in one brilliant sweep, wipe out an entire dreary winter – or perhaps a lifetime of them. The very contrast between these two days – yesterday's insanity and today's grace – and the realization of how readily one can follow the other, seemed to put all anxieties and doubts into a proper relationship with life's essential goodness. Walking up this road, centered between earth and sky, past and future, I needed nothing in the world that wasn't just around the next turn.

A ride was around one of those turns, and then another, and then I was in the market town of Machynlleth, tucked back ten miles along the river Dovey, from the waters of Cardigan Bay. The town's name looks relatively simple but it is a real tongue-twister in Welsh. I found a GN host here named Martin, a partner in a bicycle repair business, also affiliated with an alternative energy demonstration project in the nearby hills that is known all over Britain. Tall, with the agile moves of an athlete, Martin wasn't quite sure at first that he could host me, as he was going to spend the night elsewhere himself. But then he decided there was no reason I couldn't stay in his quarters alone, if I didn't mind.

Mind? It might not have occurred to many hosts, but a night free of socializing responsibility – a night just to lay back and fall apart – is the finest sort of hospitality a host can provide. Not often, perhaps, for getting to know each other is a critical part of what Good Neighbors is all about. But the occasional offer of a place to myself was one of the rare treats I encountered on the hospitality trail.

Martin took me to where he lived, a quaint little house that had been converted from a tiny onetime chapel that stood at a crossroads some distance from town. He showed me everything I needed to know, about lights and stove and whatever, and then left me there to spend the evening as I pleased. It actually had the feel of an old chapel – a certain quality of quiet reverence – but had been marvelously refitted for split-level living.

Outside, a few thatch-topped stone cottages, and some ancient barns in tumbled condition beneath tangles of ivy, presented a rural Welsh scene straight out of the last century. There was hardly a soul to be seen anywhere. The quiet was so pure, it felt ... it felt like cut crystal. Inside, a fireplace to be stoked and lit, a hot shower to be indulged, and stereo equipment with classical records on the rack. I caught up on my journal that evening, with lights low and the soft strains of Debussy, interpolated by an occasional muffled bleat of a lamb somewhere, to match my mood. I was in no hurry to end this perfect day.

It was short-sighted of me to turn down Martin's next-day offer of a second night at his place, but it was already Thursday and I was hardly halfway through Wales. But I was moving much too fast for my own good, though not yet aware of it. After a brief visit to the *Centre for Alternative Technology,* Martin's particular pride, I hastened on up the coast. The day was a mix of hitching and rails, keeping to the coast for the best scenery. But I went a rail station too far, at the upper end of Cardigan Bay, and was faced with a four-mile hike up grade, to intercept the highway that had gotten away from me. At the top, a young fellow and his girl took me the remaining twelve miles to Caernarfon, the day's destination, situated on the strait that separates the great isle of Anglesey from the Welsh mainland.

I had written to a communal group near Caernarfon that seemed interesting enough to visit – not leastwise because they were supposed to have a hot-tub, surely the most therapeutic invention ever devised, and one sorely missed ever since I had left California (and after my four-mile, laboring climb, "sorely missed" was exactly the term for it). They had never replied to my inquiry. But that wasn't the same as a rejection, so I phoned them now. Whoever answered recalled my letter immediately and gave me directions to find their place, which was some distance out of town via local bus and a good deal of walking. I wrote it down as best I could, a complexity of obscure landmarks with unspecified distances along country roads – instructions that looked rather formidable at this near-sunset hour.

In fact, daylight was waning when I reached the road on which they lived. Here, houses were named and not numbered, and I couldn't tell how far along it I'd have to walk. I was sure I had found the place, at one point, and pressed through a scourge of barking dogs to knock on the back door. I greeted the woman who opened it with a weary, self-satisfied grin – only to learn I was at the wrong place. English is not very well spoken, this deep in Wales, which didn't help matters. Just as darkness was making it impossible to follow the trail any further, I made out the name of the house I was looking for on an open driveway gate.

It turned out they were no longer a communal group. Francesca and Abraham were all who remained from that collective effort of a dozen people, along with an assortment of children who could not all have been theirs. But it appeared they were all, for the moment, in residence. I was welcomed and fed with what remained of a good dinner that was served before my late arrival. The loaf of fresh bread I brought with me went into the breadbox. I often brought an offering, and it felt really necessary here since this was not a GN host and I was there by the pure grace of their hospitality for a complete stranger – in the mistaken notion, yet, that I was visiting a communal group.

I felt, in fact, a bit awkward in the circumstances. Yet, it's only the inhibiting effect of a culture entirely contexted in enterprise and profit that walls us off from such rewarding human contact. I was made to feel entirely welcome, and was soon taking my own 'seconds' from the pot on the stove. Happily, the children managed their post-dinner wild-ness without once crashing into me, and then I was shown to a small trailer outside that was to be all mine for two nights. The only thing that could have improved the situation would be the hot-tub . . . of which nobody ever said a word.

Beyond the ordinary weariness from a day's travel, I seemed to be in greater need of rest and should have taken it as a warning signal – though what I might have done in consequence, I'm not sure. But I latched on to that little trailer like it was a haven in a storm, and slept well into the morning. Then I went into town, intending to explore Caernarfon Castle, an impressively large old fortress. But I balked at the $3.75 admission charge. Instead, I climbed a hill in town to look at the excavated remains of an old Roman fort and its museum, for free. And in a bookshop, I put out $5.50 for a study of sun worship down through the ages, by archaeologist Jacquetta Hawkes – the very heart of calendar origins, and a work I had never run across in the States. Such is the way of habit and priority. In the evening, back at the non-commune, I played a card game with the kids and again turned in early.

Saturday brought clear and sparkling air once again, springtime cool and filled with puffball white clouds. A lovely start for this, my last day in Wales, as I headed for Conwy on the north coast, about twenty-five miles distant. I wanted to explore one more castle, and I lucked out on this one: it cost no more than the Chepstow castle, where my week in Wales began. This one was larger and better preserved, as well. But the real treat was the town of Conwy itself, a medieval walled city with most of its ancient battlement, gates and all, intact – yet, a town fully alive in today's world. From the castle parapet, I could see the whole enclosure, perhaps a half-mile square or greater, with post towers rising in minor majesty every few hundred yards along its rampart – twenty-one of them in all. I could squint, and for an instant see a full-scale medieval setting.

I walked out of Conwy across one of the twin bridges that span the Afon River, and a half mile onward to a vehicle roundabout – a traffic circle hub for several intersecting roads. It held such a tight weave of Saturday traffic that the inner ring wasn't moving at all, the outer ring not much better. I found the spinoff that went east toward England and stood there – more conspicuous than I wanted to be in the circumstances. A hitch-hiker can't very well be retreative about his activity, but being the only new thing for several hundred stalled drivers to put their eyeballs on was not what I needed.

But my rescue was not long in coming: two of the most attractive young women, I daresay, that I have ever received a ride with, and we were into almost instant conversation – about my journey, my way of life, and some of their perspectives on life that reflected a good deal of depth. It was a half hour of thorough enjoyment, until they stopped at a roadside restaurant for a bit of lunch. I was invited to join, but I could see at once that it was beyond my means so I simply said I'd rather not delay my travels, and would hitch on from there. They said they'd pick me up again if I should still be there after lunch.

I must have stood there with my thumb out, ineffectually, for nearly an hour. Just as they emerged and got into their car, with a look and a wave in my direction, some damn fool driver coming out of the parking lot ahead of them stopped for me! It was one of those awful slow-motion, fast-action moments: he opening his side-door, me standing there in momentary indecision about how to handle it, and the young women cheerfully waving as they went around the whole tableau and out onto the highway. I think it was the only time in my hitch-hiking life that I ever experienced deep disappointment on getting a ride after an hour's wait.

I wasn't much for conversation with the poor fellow, and he didn't take me very far, perhaps fifteen miles. I didn't even give him a very cheery farewell. He surely thought me the most ungrateful wretch he'd ever picked up – never knowing why.

I got over it by the time my next ride came along, a middle-aged couple who said they stopped because of the American flag pinned to my pack. I often wondered at the ratio of people who picked me up because of it, to those who let me stand because of it. This driver went out of his way to take me into Chester, the region's largest town and my day's target. Chester would be my springboard toward Scotland. But the place was a surprise I hadn't expected: a remarkably picturesque town center with a wonderful array of half-timbered old structures, their upper stories over-hanging the sidewalks in a cozy, sheltering way, projecting a perfect traditional image of Elizabethan England.

But here, alas, I hit a roadblock on the Good Neighbors list. With a dozen numbers to call, I couldn't make a good connection with anyone. I waited a half-hour and made a second round of calls to those who simply hadn't answered, and – bingo! I turned up a host in the neighboring town of Mickle Trafford. It took nearly another hour, in the deepening twilight, to get out there, and once more I found myself provided with an unusually restful situation, my third such in a row. The gods were taking better care of me than I was of myself.

David and Vanessa were a compelling mid-50s couple in many respects. He was, by persuasion, a former Tory councilman for the region. And by profession, a dairy farmer herding 125 head of cattle – though one would never suspect it from the secluded appearance of his country property, nestled behind rows of screening hedge in an area that seemed more suburban than rural. He was also one of the most challenging and wily – I am tempted to say deadly – conversationalists I have ever encountered. David loved the verbal duel and he was a master at it. I had to be really on my toes to stay abreast of him in a joust, let alone to best him at it, which I never succeeded in doing. I could hardly help but gain some respect for his conservative positions.

Vanessa, for her part, was a more companionable sort of conversationalist, with empathy the keynote of her style, able to convey instant while yet sincere friendship – a difficult combination. She also baked a thief-tempting nut bread. Their home was expansive, though not ostentatious, but the upstairs room they put me in seemed the combined size of every bedroom I'd had, all week long. The great double bed hardly made a dent in its generous space. Sunday morning in that room was like a moment of eternity, and I spent an hour in bed browsing a century-old copy of *Mrs. Beeton's Household Hints*, a staple of Victorian Britain, with everything from recipes to advice for the lovelorn. One memorable passage described the best, or maybe the oldest, method for tenderizing a flank of beef: place it under the saddle of your trotter before his morning run.

I had every good reason to idle all of Sunday away, there, but my travels had acquired a momentum of their own. I was obsessed with making the most of every day, and Liverpool was close enough for a sidetrip from Mickle Trafford. I did it on Sunday – to find nothing there worth the effort – in disregard of the exhaustion slowly piling up in me. But I wasn't really aware of that yet. I had now come through two weeks on the road, with no evident problem except the on-again/off-again Visa card – and it had just worked for me in Chester. My expenses were slightly over budget, but not enough to worry about. Everything seemed to indicate that I was doing fine.

Vanessa packed some nutbread and a banana for me on Monday, and then I went north like a shot: took a bus out beyond the Liverpool-Manchester axis, to a motorway entrance, and very quickly got a ride with a Scottish businessman who drove me clear through to Carlisle, 200 miles and just shy of the border. He offered to take me all the way to Glasgow, but I was intent on a certain mission now, a quest that would take me instead on a slant toward Edinburgh.

I had, in fact, intended Carlisle as the day's destination, never imagining I would make it by noon. It was perfect, though; we had come through a violent storm that was behind me now, and the day invited a continuance right on toward Hawick, the village I wanted next to reach. But it was on a secondary road, and instead of resuming the hitch-hike it seemed wise to consider regional transit from Carlisle.

Walking the mile from the motorway into town with that in mind, I encountered a wonderful old Scot with a r-r-r-rich Harry Lauder voice (does anyone still remember Harry Lauder's Scotch burr?), who seemed absolutely delighted at the sight of me, near to bursting with uncontainable joy. He caught me poring over my map at a street corner and made a one-man welcoming committee of himself. I thought, later, I might easily have cajoled a night's shelter of him had I been inclined to stay in Carlisle, but the mid-day urge to move on was too strong.

I had known I was headed for Hawick – which is pronounced 'Hoyick' – long before I knew I'd even make the journey. It was the first of three unique quests that would provide a periodic bit of investigative focus to my otherwise haphazard travels. Detective adventures of the 'needle in a haystack' sort – although I didn't yet realize that the one in Hawick was anything more than the simple fulfillment of a promise to a friend, with no anticipated complications.

Jim Hall is an elderly fellow I came to know during my first year of settlement in Seattle. He's something of a recluse, gifted with a sharp and perceptive mind that nourishes a critical irascibility toward the foibles of society, which probably accounts for the ageless inner vitality that belies his now ninety years. He grew up in Liverpool and came to America in his youth, leaving behind a sister who for many years had been living in Hawick. I had given Jim my assurance that if I went anywhere near there I would pay her a visit for him. That was the mere extent of it ... until I got to Hawick.

The bus from Carlisle went through some of the most idyllic meadow country I had yet encountered: rich green rolling hills with just the right measure of scattered oak, an occasional stream, yet hardly any sign of habitation, and all of it gleaming in the freshness of recent rainfall. The countryside was so entrancing, so pristine, that it was almost a shock to burst suddenly into the rather substantial town of Hawick. The address that Jim had given me for Jean Hyslop had led me to expect a small village, for it was only the name of a road, Buccleuch, with no house number. I was surprised and dismayed, then, to learn that Buccleuch was a long and prominent street in town with numbered housing to its outer extremity.

So it became a quest. But not before I had first checked the telephone directory to discover more than a dozen Hyslops listed, none of them Jean or J, and none of them on Buccleuch. The clock said 4:30 and I figured a quick check with some county office would be the most productive course of action. But when I reached the Town Hall it had already shut down for the day. With no other bright idea, I asked an available cleaning woman if she had any thoughts of how to pursue this search. She suggested I check with the post office up the street.

On my way to it, rushing lest I get there also too late, I went past a window that said Town Council, and someone was just emerging and locking the door. I put my problem immediately to him, and he said I should not go to the main post office but to the branch of it that was right at the head of Buccleuch, back in the other direction. I turned back immediately and headed for it, almost at a trot, pack and all. It was still open when I got there ... but the clerk was not at all familiar with Jean's name. She suggested I try the music store about halfway down the first block of Buccleuch, saying the proprietor had been on the street a long time and probably knew everybody on it.

The music shop man, after thinking a bit, couldn't recall any Jean Hyslop, either. I prodded him with the possibility that she might be in the care of younger folk, and he recalled an elderly woman with a young couple at "that house over there with the stairs jutting out," a bit further down the road. But when I asked the young couple there, they just shook their heads and suggested I try at the antique shop, a few doors back. This was becoming absurd, by now, but having no other trail I continued with it.

The folks in the antique shop thought they'd seen several elderly people living in an adjoining courtyard. I went in there and at once ran into a fellow in overalls who wanted to know what I was looking for. I put the story to him, in its accumulating detail, and he pondered awhile and wondered if it might be an elderly woman he knew as Mrs. Jean Lennox, who used to live there and whose name had been changed by a recent marriage. She now lived up the hill, he told me, off to the side of Buccleuch Road, at a place called *St. Margaret's Retirement Home.* It all seemed unlikely but I went off up the hill to check it out.

The attendant who answered the door didn't know a Jean by either name, but thought I should try across the way, at the *Buccleuch Retirement House.* This seemed immediately promising, for it could account for Jim's failure to provide a number – even if it wasn't actually on Buccleuch Road. But the names brought no flash of recognition here, either. Then the woman at the door had a sudden thought and asked me to wait a minute. She returned a few moments later with a gleam in her eye, saying she'd found what I was looking for. One of her chair-bound tenants, it seemed, had a visitor that very afternoon, who turned out to be . . . Jean Hyslop! I was given an address for the *Balgownie Retirement House,* some distance out on Buccleuch Road.

I went out there immediately – and sure enough, it was Jim's sister. A frail wisp of a woman for whom I had to keep the conversation narrowly focused, she was quite amazed and charmed, that a friend of brother Jim from faraway Seattle should seek her out, here. And I, of course, was still dizzy from the trail of serendipity that had made absolutely no rational sense, yet had put me on Jean's doorstep within 90 minutes of when the search was started. We had an hour-long visit over tea and cookies, before I took my leave for fear of exhausting her.

I don't know how many angels were involved in that run of referrals. Any one of them could have stopped the trail cold by not sending me on to the next. But one, at least, was certainly an angel: the man in the overalls, for he was not anyone I was specifically referred to, and he was the one who intervened to direct me off Buccleuch Road, and toward – for all I could know – perhaps Jean's only friend in town.

But it was time for the journey's reckoning to begin.

I had harbored the hope that in locating Jean I might also find a place of lodging for the night, for there was neither a host nor hostel anywhere near Hawick. It was clear, though, that I'd receive no invitation to pass the night in a retirement home. The sensible choice at this point would have been a B & B, and I could have stretched for the $20 that one would have cost me here. Even though the skies were clear, it was cold, cold, cold … and I was weary, weary, weary. But I was fixated on budged concerns, and I had already overspent, this day, with bus rides at both ends of my run. Weary and cold, or not, it was going to be a night spent out in the rough.

In the lingering daylight of this northern latitude, I had time enough to survey the town, to find the most likely spot that would keep me dry, warm, and unseen. So I put away my victorious quest and got down to the nitty-gritty of trudging from one end of town to the other. Staggering would be more like it, for I took another one of those stumbling falls on a raised bit of sidewalk, just as I had – in another lifetime, it seemed – in Portland. I was up before a count of ten, but I was clearly on my last legs. Clear to me now, not then.

I found my spot in the shelter of a grandstand on an open, accessible athletic field – so open that I had to wait until full darkness to be sure no one would spot me. One can never be too careful about bedding down in the midst of a town. Even at 10:30, I felt the need to take an evasive route to avoid people in parked cars – perhaps only young lovers who wouldn't have noticed, but a lurking stranger is the target of every suspicion. It must have been near midnight before I was securely settled, and warm enough in my down bag to drift off to that sweet harbor of rejuvenation.

And then some internal devil snapped me out of my sleep shortly after four in the morning, and I couldn't reclaim it. I lay there until daybreak watching the bright morning stars, and then worked as fast as possible to get my gear together in order to stay warm. But it was at least another shivering hour before any place in town serving hot coffee was open.

By the time I was underway again, beneath a mercifully warm sun in a cloudless sky, I knew I wasn't feeling my usual morning charge of energy. I primed the pump again with a full breakfast at a roadside cafe, but that didn't help either. It was nothing I could put my finger on, just 'the blahs.' Two rides took me the forty miles to Edinburgh, a city that would have cheered and fascinated me on any other day, but not this one. I moped around a park in the heart of town, not even feeling like calling a host, but I knew I must. It would mean I'd have to be sociable, and certainly no burden, and the prospect had all the appeal of a ride on a roller coaster.

But sitting in the park offered no relief, either. The city seemed intolerably noisy. By mid-afternoon the sunlight, challenged by a growing swarm of clouds, had decided to quit its job and the air was turning chill again. I hadn't even any interest in a giant booksale underway near the park – which verified that I was in pretty bad shape.

So I went to the phone, only to encounter the ultimate disaster: a solid wall of rejection. Even calling the unanswered numbers an hour later, as in Chester, brought no result. It was after 6:30 now, and I considered my options. I could take a train for Glasgow and another cluster of possible hosts, an hour away – but that was a gamble, and the time and energy drain of it didn't appeal to me. Or I could try the Edinburgh youth hostel – and pay eleven dollars for a dorm bed. Or try the two suburban hosts on the list, which I had avoided up to now. I called one in the town of Dunfermline, fifteen miles north, and she answered! I had a bit of difficulty with her thick Scotch burr, but I was fairly sure I heard her say that she was no longer a Good Neighbors host. And then, perhaps sensing my agony, she said I could come over anyway.

It was quite exactly the place I needed in that moment. Kathleen, a soft-spoken redhead with an easy smile that resided more in her eyes than anywhere else on her features, was an independent computer analyst, and as easy-going on social protocol as any host I'd had. She understood my situation immediately and prepared an instantly therapeutic bowl of hot soup, and then told me that I could remain there the entire next day by myself while she took care of business elsewhere. I curled up shortly afterward and slept about ten hours that night.

In the morning I was completely useless. Not a grain of energy, and my whole body ached. The prospect of only a day here was frightening when I let myself dwell on it. I knew better, of course – Kathleen would let me stay on if I had to. But I was faced with a real concern that I could not dodge. If this is what happens to me after two weeks on the road, what is it telling me about the rest of my journey? Never mind Europe, what about the remaining three weeks in Britain?

In the purest turn of fate, or let us say by the gift of the gods, Kathleen happened to have a copy of the *I Ching* among the books on her shelves. I'm not entirely sure, but it could well have been the first copy I had seen since I arrived in Britain. For those not familiar with the book, it's an ancient Chinese oracle system. It's much more than that, but this is not the place for a detailing. The *I Ching* had been my chief source of guidance for many years in California, and while I don't fully understand the working of it (no one really does), I have seen enough of its potency and reliability to have the highest respect for it.

The question that confronted me now, about the wisdom of continuing this journey, was precisely the sort of question for which the *I Ching* is best used. Which is to say, merely, that I was on the fence with it. I was teetering between yes and no, and could accept either determination – but needed some sureness of making the best choice. By some strange and marvelous alchemy in-credible to our rational ways, the *I Ching* is somehow able to reflect back to us what we already know at some level, but don't know that we know, because of all the static thrown up by the reasoning mind. It's as simple, and as complex, as that.

I covered both sides of the matter, asking the question in a format that is only for those with a well-honed feeling for the *I Ching:* Should I persevere, or call it off? Its response, in the form of a text reading, affirmed my journey and provided some perspective on why I had been tripped-up by this sudden physical agony. For the first time, I saw how insistently and insensitively I had been pushing myself to the limit of physical endurance. It was a healthy corrective, and I resolved to listen more closely thereafter to the cues I had been virtually ignoring.

It was a critical moment for the summer that was taking shape for me. On the turn of a coin – the method employed in consulting the *I Ching* – I would have called off the whole adventure. But the moment was magical, along with my 'chance fortune' of having reached Kathleen's, where the trusty oracle was available. And Kathleen, of course, ranks as a full-fledged angel, for me. The crisis was successfully navigated.

The Scottish highlands, a wonderful rail ride. This view adapted from an old British Railways poster, the original watercolor by Terence Cuneo.

From Tongue to Nose,
to close the circuit

Dunfermline, Scotland: May 16, 1991...

I knew I'd be traveling the Continent, now. The experience at Kathleen's was transformative. All my earlier uncertainties about the summer ahead were gone – and with them, momentarily, much of my enthusiasm for the rest of this preliminary journey. I wanted to cross the channel and take on the year's real challenge.

But why waste opportunity? I still had three precious weeks on British soil, and far too much of village and countryside, right here, that I might never again have the chance to see. Scotland, especially, for I'd been too occupied by quest and qualm to give it any fair attention. I wanted to reach its wild northern shore and get a taste of the highland country.

Scotland's rail system offered the best solution for covering territory too thinly populated to support hitch-hiking. A Rail Rover Pass, at the relatively reasonable cost of $55, would allow me unlimited travel north of the border, on any four of the eight days after its purchase. Scotland was so vast – very nearly as great in length as England below it – that I should have little trouble getting my money's worth of mileage; and eight days were just about all I could devote to it, at this midway point in my journey. In fact, I'd have to forego any further time for exploring Edinburgh – for the moment, at least.

I had a last and hurried look at the city as I was taken to the rail station by a young associate of Kathleen's, a Canadian-American named Sarah who had come to Scotland as a GN traveler, herself, and decided to stay and work awhile when Kathleen offered the opportunity. In the brief conversation as we drove in, I found out that she had also stayed with David and Vanessa, in Mickle Trafford. It was fun to compare our impressions, and I had a sudden sense of being part of a grand world-wide network. A lingering, almost plaintive look in Sarah's young eyes, peering up at me as I said a hasty farewell in the underground drive-in zone of the railway station, left me regretting the rush of my schedule.

She had driven me south across one of the two great bridges that span the Firth of Forth, to reach the city, and now the train took me north across the other bridge, toward Aberdeen. I expected to find my night's host there, with the option of going on to Inverness, the last northward outpost of populous settlement. At high speed we clicked along the rails, first to Dundee and then up a crystal clear coastline, reaching Aberdeen about four in the afternoon. Of five possible hosts there, not a single one materialized for me. I took the six o'clock train for the further hundred miles to Inverness – a commuter run making every stop. But the oak and gently rolling hills of an increasingly barren countryside shortly took over.

It was table-seating in this coach car, and for most of the way I sat opposite a stunning young woman apparently headed home from a day at work, the two of us alone at this particular window, each absorbed in our private reflections – my own largely on her. The perfect picture of cool, flaxen-haired Scottish beauty, well-dressed to a level of simple elegance, she studiously avoided any eye contact, in the proper fashion of British train travel. I was so intimidated by the energy of that avoidance, and the very weight of this 'protocol of reserve,' that I found it easier to contain the urge than try some small talk which might have opened a conversation. I could hardly help but reflect on the irony that hitch-hiking, which bears such a heavy stigma of societal distrust, is so much more fluidly friendly and gregarious than rail travel – in a world that suffers all too much alienation. She got off the train at a village called Huntly, and the sense of futility in me was so strong that it came out in a short bit of doggerel scribbled on a blank page of my GN host list.

> To the lady from Huntly I wanted to say,
> "Might we casually pass the time of day?"
> But the lady from Huntly would not have replied
> with anything more than a turn to her side.
> It's the way, don't you know, of a British train ride.

We passed within a few miles of Findhorn just as dusk was closing in. I had already given some thought to the possibility of seeking my night's shelter there, but I suspected – rightly or wrongly – that after many years of fame they probably ask a fee too stiff for me. Inverness, however, sitting astride the river that links Loch Ness to the sea, was a sufficiently satisfying alternative. Its charm quite surprised me. I had somehow anticipated a primitively simple community this far north . . . very likely because of a thoughtless association with just such a village in California that bears the same name.

I quickly exhausted the host possibilities in Inverness, which were slim to start with. Scotland's Good Neighbors, like the Lady from Huntly, were not proving at all hospitable to me. I'd have to start relying on youth hostels, which would put a further strain on my already 'rail-roaded' budget. The hostel in Inverness cost almost ten dollars for the night. But, filled with young folks, this one had at least a more cheerful atmosphere than the hostel back in Monmouth. High on a hill, it also provided a magnificent view of the river Ness, festooned by street lamps like Christmas ornaments, as it twisted through town, and reflecting the light of a perfectly placed moon.

The next day's plan was for hitching – such as the rarified traffic would support. It was a much longer wait than I had become used to, but eventually a ride came along – a courier driver who took me some 35 winding miles into timber country, to a village alongside a rushing, foam-flecked stream. It was a whistle-stop sort of place – on the rail line, in fact – with plenty of roadside space to wait for my next ride, but little else. I needed only fifteen more miles to reach Lairg, from where a postal-service bus made scheduled daily runs up to the coast. But I might more quickly have walked it, for the scarcity of traffic at that place. After a useless hour standing in the sunny but chill noon air, my options were clear and simple. A train would soon arrive that could get me to Lairg in time for the bus, or I could remain the night in this tiny village, with likely nothing but the same pair of choices on the morrow.

I really hated to take the train, at this point, and throw away one of my four days of use for just fifteen miles, but it was the only sure way to reach the coast that night. Once aboard, however, I made a brilliant discovery. The Rail Rover pass carried its days-of-use information *on the back side,* and not all conductors (not this one, at any rate) bothered to turn it over and check the dates. The passenger was expected to honorably enter each date of use into one of four boxes on the back. I took full advantage of this windfall gift and didn't bother to enter the date.

In my rule book, anything one can get away with is fair game, so long as no one is hurt in the process. Life is full of streetwise opportunities affording one a bit of extra economic leverage, and quite often at no displaced cost to anyone at all. In this situation, for instance, I was using a ticket already paid for – merely neglecting the rigid fixture of its four-day limit, for which no one would ever suffer. Perhaps a bookkeeper in some hidden cubbyhole of the rail system, concerned about *per capita* accountability. But loopholes are there for the needy and bold; and the gods, alone, are the provenance of such happenstance gifts. Or angels wearing railroad uniforms.

The post bus is something of a quiet secret in Britain, a way of back-country travel that reflects the rather quaint old idea that government should serve people's needs in every way possible. Dorothy, back in London, first alerted me to it. Mail is delivered to outlying areas by small vans with room for several passengers who pay a modest fee for passage. Routes are run to a timetable, usually once each weekday. I was the sole passenger on the 45-mile run from Lairg to the coast and it cost me four dollars.

The bumpy road, one lane with passing space every few hundred yards, sloped down out of the barren hills to the coastal village of Tongue. I had no difficulty spotting the hostel there: a lonely sentinel on a tidewater inlet, in earshot of the surf ... a two-story Victorian, looking as incongruous in its solitary situation as the civilized strip of paved road beside which it stood ... both intruders in this setting of pure, wild nature. The village, almost a mile back from the shore, was only a bit less intrusive: a loose cluster of shops and barns huddled over a sleepy junction of country roads. Seaside mountains stretched to the very end of visibility; and the silence, except for surf and gull screech, was simply immense. I dropped my pack at the hostel door and set out toward a hill beyond the village with stone ruins at its crest. I never reached them because the trail bogged into marsh from recent rains, but the few hours given to the attempt, in that surround of unsullied nature, were some of the most peacefully satisfying of my entire journey.

Choosing hostels over the possibility of sleeping out was another part of that resolve to take better care of myself. I had to be a little more flexible and willing to accept their cost, at least until the weather became more supportive. This old frame house, the onetime manse of some reclusive Scot, was large enough for fifty travelers, though only a few besides myself were there so early in the year. Emptiness gave the entire structure a cavernous quality that matched the vastness of space outdoors and made for an unusually quiet and restful stay.

In fact, I hardly saw any of the others. Sunrise on Saturday morning streamed into my private dorm room, splashing the wall with unreal color. I had my fruit and tea in the dining room in utter solitude, and took a morning stroll on a cove shore that was all mine. I might even have stayed another night, but for the fact that a layover would require an additional third night – there being no Sunday post bus – and my 8-day rail pass was ticking away. Tourist conveniences invariably prove to be tourist fetters.

The long journey back to London began with a quick circuit, by post bus, of the outermost settlement on this desolate but beautiful tip of country: primitive cottages at the seaside's very edge, linked by yapping dogs and wide-eyed children – like some half-forgotten *National Geographic* image – with the wild, tumbling surf nearby sending acres of mist into the air. We picked up two young Canadian fellows on the way, whose vocal enthusiasm shattered the morning's reverent mood. Like a discordant voice in a choir, it proclaimed their lack of attunement to the land's character.

At the Lairg terminus, I waited the hour and a half to train time in a frontier-type cafe, savoring a hot bowl of tomato soup that cut through the morning's frigid chill, and smiling dubiously at the red-bearded, leather-booted mountain climber across from me as he commented on the newly arrived "warm weather." Considering that our latitude was something north of the Aleutian Islands, he may not have been kidding! We talked a bit about the highland region to the west, and next on my agenda.

Getting there from Lairg, however, was a roundabout journey, and I don't think I could have managed it without the remaining five days of my four-day rail privilege. I had to go all the way back into central Scotland to get a train out of Glasgow, which meant a night's stay down there, somewhere . . . and it turned into three nights, before I finally got to the northwestern coast.

All the rest of Saturday I was on the train from Lairg, watching the countryside unfold . . . from the barrens of the north, up into the Grampian Mountains, rocking along beside tree-sheltered streams and sheep that gazed at us with passive disdain, to the rolling, farm-spattered hills of Scotland's rich heartland. Other Americans came aboard and I found myself in an unlikely conversation with a North Carolinian on a golf circuit – hearing of courses compared, and why Scottish greens are the very best, and nodding in vague appreciation of golfing glories that concerned me not at all. Along the way, we paused briefly at a town decked out in holiday style, with marching bands and kilted paraders who were celebrating something, I never knew what. The whole day's journey, from its start on the wild north shore, was a potluck of visual overload – right up to and including our arrival at Stirling.

I meant to go all the way into Glasgow, but in the day's waning light, yet thirty miles out, we came to the fanciful, fairytale architecture of Stirling. At least it looked that way in the glint of a setting sun, and on pure impulse I left the train, figuring I could always phone for a Glasgow host from there, if it came to that. I had no real concern about finding a host in the region, for the bulk of Scotland's population is concentrated here in the axis between Glasgow and Edinburgh. But the mysterious Scottish curse would not turn loose of me and I met with the same old failure as before. Hosts were not at home, or could not take me at such short notice. There was another youth hostel in Stirling and it seemed again the easiest way out.

I found it up a steep avenue lined with wonderful medieval stone architecture: a great old multi-tiered structure with central courtyard, itself a vestige of ancient times and former use as a nunnery, with passageways and dead-end nooks that a first-time visitor could easily get lost among if not careful. At $7.35, it was as cheap as the one at Tongue. But my week had already soared beyond the budget.

The place was full of guests, yet I felt more isolated here than I had at Tongue. The case of a solitary traveler among cheerful groups of people who already seem to know each other. I was in a crowded dorm, this time, and weary enough to doze late into Sunday. But not as late as a fellow in the corner, who slept through all the noise of morning cleanup. He sat up with a start, as I was about ready to leave, and wanted to know where he was. With that opener, I got into a friendly conversation with a young Turk, in Britain to learn English, and before I left I had his address in Istanbul with a promise of hospitality if I ever got there.

I took the train into Glasgow, not exactly sure what my Sunday course would be. It's not my favorite day for travel, or for much at all. Stirred by the morning's conversation, perhaps, I suddenly wanted to 'be someplace' and not on the road. I wanted to find a host. So I got busy on the phone once again. But once more – as ever, in Scotland, it seemed – I drew a blank. I turned to the outlying area, and finally connected with a retired librarian down the coast in a beach town named Troon, which is Gaelic for 'nose,' a reference to the spit of land on which the town sits.

Vera lived by herself in a duplex apartment just a block from the sea. The beach was rimmed by a quiet neighborhood street of homes, as though it hadn't occurred to anyone that sea-front property might be especially valuable. The boardwalk mentality had somehow bypassed this little town.

Vera hadn't received many travelers and was so delighted with my arrival that she insisted I stay the preferred two nights – would have encouraged a third and a fourth, I'm sure, had I been willing. So I lingered, soaking in the somewhat rare warmth of sun and good conversation – realizing, after three nights without a host, that the conversation of intentional hospitality cannot be matched by casual encounter. As to the peaceful ambience of Troon, nothing could portray it so well as the Monday incident when I lost my glasses while walking along the beach front to get a bus into Glasgow for some sight-seeing. I found them seven hours later, on my return, exactly where I had dropped them on the sidewalk.

Tuesday's train north from Glasgow took me into the western highlands. It felt like being on top of the world: great humps of lumpy mountain, mostly barren but with some superb overlooks as we'd slant down the side of one 'lump' to cross a trestle and slowly angle up the next. It was still the Grampian range – at one point, less than twenty miles distant from the parallel section of Saturday's train ride, but no tracks crossed the rugged gap between the two. When we reached the rocky Atlantic shore, close to the end of the run at Mallaig, the scenery became spectacular.

I intended to catch a ferry at Mallaig to Skye Island, where I was somehow going to make it to a hostel somewhere on the other side. But the train, while exactly on schedule, reached Mallaig five minutes after the last ferry for the day had left. I can only assume it was a schedule 'coordinated' to the convenience of the local lodging trade. It left me once more out in the cold, quite literally. There was no hostel here in Mallaig, and nothing but tourist prices at the nearby inns. I could take the train immediately back forty miles to Fort William, where there was a hostel, or else submit myself once again to wind and stars – and hopefully nothing worse.

It really wasn't such a bad evening for sleeping out: cold, but quite clear. I'd need some shelter from the wind and prying eyes, but that usually turns up with a bit of search and I had several hours before darkness to find it.

It wasn't so easy, as it turned out. But I had committed myself, with the departure of the last train for Fort William. Mallaig is essentially a fishing village with a good deal of round-the-clock dock activity going on. Around every corner, it seemed, and in every cranny I sought, rusting equipment of one kind or another took up every bit of space. I tried to look inconspicuous, probing casually from place to place, and ultimately found my way to some dockside processing buildings that seemed fairly well deserted for the day. One among them had a recessed corner sheltered by an overhang at the top, with enough lightweight gear strewn around that a rude protective screen could be set up, and even a bed of netting to cushion my sleep.

But as careful as I had been, I hooked the curiosity of some of the town's kids in my wandering search. I caught a few furtive looks directed my way, and words in hushed whisper as I went by. They were pre-teens for the most part, so it didn't really worry me, but I had no intention of letting them see me head back to my chosen campsite. I took, instead, another casual direction and returned around the water side of the building, fairly sure I had eluded them. I put a sweater on and sat down at the dock's edge for the hour of chill sunlight that remained, to enjoy the marvelous view. Skye Island was a black silhouette that lay like a crumpled shroud on the shimmering dark blue water. The sky itself, clear and deepening in hue, outlined the hover and dip of gulls, while an occasional fishing craft made its distant throaty way toward the sea. I couldn't have picked a better spot or found a better moment for it.

Then, with every bit of affected innocence, three young girls that I recognized at once as part of the curiosity crowd came around the corner of the building to gaze at the sea ... and sidewise, at me. The only way to deal with it was to break the ice, and I said a cheery "Hi."

Once they learned I was American, all their shyness dissolved and they chatted with me like we were old friends. I was perfectly honest about intending to sleep out "somewhere nearby," and they became very solicitous about my welfare, but I assured them I'd be okay. The most talkative of the trio kept telling me I must be sure to visit Borra Island, where "...all the MacNeills are." I made the surprisingly correct guess that she was a MacNeill. Eventually, a few of the boys came by and joined in, but they never overcame their shyness as readily as the girls. And after that, they all left me entirely alone.

By any standard, it was a successful campout, even though I could hear the noise of work crews, not too far away, during the night. I was up at daybreak to catch the six a.m. train. It would mean another night out here, somewhere, to see Skye Island now, and I wanted to get back to Edinburgh for my last night in Scotland, with a chance to see the city this time. And perhaps to see Sarah again. I had two more days to use the rail pass – if I could manage to preserve the last remaining open box on the back of it.

But that possibility seemed to vanish as the train picked up momentum down the coastline. A very conscientious conductor stood over me while I carefully penned "May 22" into the final box on the back of my pass.

Edinburgh fulfilled all my expectations the second time around. Kathleen was happy to have me for another night in that now familiar Dunfermline apartment, and thanks to the very early train out of Mallaig, I had most of that afternoon to enjoy the ambience of the big city. Edinburgh has a nice cosmopolitan flavor, lively and easy at once, rather light-hearted for a great urban center ... a sense, almost, of music in the air. The heart of the city is actually an open area, a space of parkland and mall, with its south flank rising suddenly in a great embankment surmounted by the old Edinburgh Castle. To the north of that central area, along any cross street, is a view of the Firth of Forth, Edinburgh's inlet from the North Sea. Looking across to its far shore, I was instantly back in San Francisco, gazing at the hilly shoreline of Marin from Pacific Heights – a view that was once an everyday part of my life. I think it was this, more than anything else, that put me completely at home in Edinburgh.

Sarah was there for me, too, validating the intimation of a possible friendship between us that had lingered after my hurried earlier departure. Mature friendship across the double generation gap has only been possible for me within the past decade or so, and I consider it a rare blessing. Not easily attained, I might add, for there is so much 'preconceptional baggage' to be overcome – particularly with respect to cross-gender friendship. But the unique interactions that evolve – when they do – are worth the effort.

There was one more thing to do before leaving Scotland – one last reason for my return to Edinburgh. Eighty miles up the coast toward Aberdeen, standing alone on a cliff by the sea, a few miles from the town of Stonehaven, was ancient Dunnottar Castle. It presented the perfect combination of easy accessibility and isolated grandeur. Ever since I passed it by, on the earlier run toward Aberdeen, in the rush of that day's agenda, it had been on my mind to come back if I could. And this last day in Scotland was perfect for it in every respect. I timed it so that I could spend three hours hiking out to it and back, and then get the southbound express that would return me all the way to the border.

It was a magically perfect finale. The trail went cliffside above the sea, across fence stiles and through sheep pasture, under the bluest skies imaginable. The castle itself, an unreconstructed ruin, stark and magnificent in this isolated setting, could have been a film-set for Hamlet with lifelike realism. It was a delicious last taste of Scotland. I even had time, back in Stonehaven, for tea and shortbread at a sidewalk cafe before my 2:11 express came through.

And all of this at no extra transportation cost! For I hadn't yet exhausted my survivor's bag of tricks when I signed-off the last box on the rail pass under the eagle-eye scrutiny of that dutiful conductor out of Mallaig, one day shy of the full eight. In writing *May 22*, I had carefully shortened the final '2.' Using the same pen this morning, I neatly made a '3' of it.

It should only have carried me to the border – that's as far as I could legally get with the pass – but I squeezed an extra bonus out of it:

the express made no border stop. I was supposed to change trains at Edinburgh and taken a local. Instead, I stayed with the London-bound express, ready to pay a surcharge if required. But nobody asked to see my ticket before we reached Newcastle, sixty miles further down the coast. All in all, I guess I got about three times the transportation value out of that $55 rail pass.

Back in England again, I had little difficulty locating a Newcastle host, but walked into a rather odd situation. The person on my GN list was not actually there. It was the home of his mother . . . who wasn't even the one to invite me in. I had spoken on the phone with another woman entirely, who was conducting a residential growth workshop there, on the weekend that was about to begin. I never quite sorted all of this out – though I did finally meet the mother – but it was a pleasant lodging of two nights, with no reason to complain. Except that on the final morning I felt a bit out of place taking toast and tea among the assembled weekend workshop guests.

The part of Newcastle I saw felt like a midwestern American town. I was mostly occupied, there, by a resumption of Visa card problems, trying to find an ATM bank machine that would give me more than £10 – another strangeness that I couldn't account for. I wouldn't get very far on $17. In the course of this travail, I was accosted by a young couple of clearly uncertain means who asked if I could sponsor them to some gas money. I am ordinarily at least sympathetic to such requests, but I wasn't in a mood for it and brushed aside their entreaties, at which the woman caustically suggested that I might someday find *myself* without funds. With only £4.20 in my pocket, I felt like barking back at her that the day had just arrived. But I was sure she'd never believe it. My good old Westminster Bank account finally came to the rescue. But I knew I'd have to do something about that inscrutable Visa card sometime in the remaining ten days before I took the plunge into Europe.

Just out of Newcastle, I took to the highway again and knew immediately that I was back in hitch-hiking country. Three rapid-fire lifts got me to York, some 75 miles, a town famous, and justly so, for its abundance of quaint historic architecture, along with one of Britain's most impressive cathedrals. Here, though, I drew a complete blank, in the search for a host. But the cold latitudes of Scotland were behind me now, and the evening air of York seemed almost balmy.

I roamed through the parks and among ancient Roman ruins in the heart of town, spotting several fair prospects for a night's comfort. I finally settled on a secluded parking area enclosed by a small complex of school buildings. While it was essentially a parking lot, there were trees, shrubs, and a kind of long-forgotten garden, overgrown and flush with all the camouflage I would need, even though it afforded no structural screen. But the area itself was entirely separate from the outer streets. It was so remote from the summer evening throngs that I laid out my gear at once and just relaxed with an hour of good music coming in on my battery radio. A few cars drifted in just before dusk – something was going on in one of the near buildings, and I took care to stay out of sight.

At twilight, after I was snug in my sleeping bag, a fellow strolled by within fifteen feet of me singing to himself, on a path from which I was clearly visible if he had just turned his head a bit. But he didn't see me at all, for there was no break in his melody. I felt as if I had a cloak of invisibility. Another gentleman, grey-haired and rather dignified, came out of the building momentarily and relieved himself when he was quite sure there was no one around to see him. I drifted off, soon after that, and it was one of the most pleasant of all my nights out.

On Sunday morning the town of York, so busy the evening before, was as empty as if every soul had followed a pied piper – and the town's physical character matched the theme to perfection: narrow, crooked alleys lined with leaning buildings, their half-timbered upper floors jutting out almost far enough to hug each other across the gap. I walked south until the town thinned out and traffic began to thicken, and then I found a good spot to wait for a ride. Before long it arrived: a congenial fellow in a small pickup truck who said he'd help me find Sherwood Forest, if it was there. He had simply asked where I should like to be dropped, and I told him.

It had been a fanciful dream of mine to spend a night in Sherwood Forest, maybe to encounter a ghost or two clad in Lincoln green. But my map wasn't quite good enough, or the right road eluded us, or whatever is left of Sherwood is too small to be noticed. My driver did the next best thing, taking me to the outskirts of Nottingham. On the four-mile walk from there into town, over hill and dale that felt proper to the image, I came upon a woodsy detour that seemed to be right out of a fairytale, and I decided to be satisfied that I had found a Sherwood Forest remnant, after all. But it was a little too close to town to spend the night there – I wasn't looking for an encounter with the ghost of the Sheriff of Nottinghamshire.

I wanted to linger a bit in Nottingham and look for any more of that romantic imagery that might be discoverable. But the town was unexceptional except for a marvelously original statue of Robin Hood. It was chunky and bold, nothing at all like the Errol Flynn version, yet somehow quite all right. I found GN hospitality in the upscale suburb of Gotham, with a young couple, Lewis and Heather, for whom I was their very first Good Neighbors guest. For the occasion, they took me on a country drive to see some nearby stone villages, and a Pagan-vestige celebration called 'Well-dressing Day.' It featured a competition in art created from entirely natural materials: seeds, flowers, bark, grasses, etc., complete with a marching band at the head of the award procession.

From Nottingham, still hitch-hiking south, I stopped at Northampton, where Visa is handled in Britain, to see if anything could be learned or done about my fitful and fickle card. I was directed to Barclaycard headquarters, the British agent for Visa – a black fortress of a building so protectively paranoid with security measures that I had to use a telephone in the lobby to get nothing more redeeming than the advice of a toll-free California number to call. I postponed it for London and took a bus on to Cambridge.

As loose and easy as I had tried to keep my travels, the arrival in Cambridge was timed to coincide with one of their periodic antiquarian bookmarkets that was set for the following day. Its importance hinged on the mere fact that I hadn't yet been to one of these affairs in Britain. I wanted to see Cambridge, itself, of course, and had made my one advance reservation with a GN host, there, for the final weekend of the journey. But that was yet several days away, and I had hoped to bridge the gap with one or two other hosts in the area. But I found myself disappointed with Cambridge, right from the start.

Its streets felt less hospitable than Oxford's, and the colleges somehow colder, less inviting – which surprised me after a lifelong mindset that favored Cambridge, of the two. It felt doubly unfriendly when I tried to locate a host. Not one, among a fair-sized list, was available to me. I was used to this, by now, and recognized that I had no justification for being critical of it since the rules of the game were to make advance arrangements. But my way of travel could not easily handle that. As a last resort, I called my upcoming Sunday host to ask if he could possibly take me in earlier. But no, he insisted on the arrangement we had made many weeks before. The youth hostel was too expensive for me, and I was down to the last recourse: another night out in the rough.

I found my spot within some shrubbery, in a well-used park right next to Christ's College, at the very heart of town. It was fairly well hidden from every side, though close enough to several park benches that I was almost inside conversations. I heard fragments of an exuberant exchange, with even snatches of song, among several old and younger footloose types, making light of the very sort of outcast life I was engaged in. They might easily have been rehearsing for a parkside showing of *Oliver!* It all settled down with the approach of evening and I got a good night's sleep there.

Daybreak's problem was being wide awake, up and about, with absolutely nothing to do – not for a couple hours, until a coffee shop opened, and then a couple more before the booksale got underway. It was expectably out of my price range, but I found a pair of items on a £2 'throwaway shelf,' one of them by Dorothy L. Sayers who, despite her greater renown as a mystery writer, did her most enduring work on metaphysical and social themes. This small volume, *The Mind of the Maker*, may have been overpriced, even at $3.50, but her serious work had always eluded me in the States.

There was little use remaining in Cambridge after that, and I decided to head for East Anglia, almost sorry, now, that my weekend arrangement compelled a return. I'd have much preferred going straight to London, to relax and prepare for the channel crossing, than linger further on this all but completed circuit of Britain. It pointed up the pitfalls of a predetermined itinerary. Sure, I could simply have abandoned it and sent my regrets, but the other half of the problem was the schedule with Marjory for my return on the following Monday. The only thing to do was bear with it and see what the journey's extension offered.

The first thing it offered was a hair-raising ride across the East Anglia countryside in a hot red Porsche, the speedometer trembling up at 130 mph – and that's miles, not kilometers. I was riding with a would-be jet pilot in the guise of a regional Kirby distributor, who seemed to be trying to crack my cool. But I've been driven by crazier fools ... though never at that speed. Needless to say, it didn't take long for the sixty-mile drive to Norwich.

I had no trouble discovering my next hosts, there: Pam and Pete, a young couple trying to make a go of a green-oriented sales agency for personal and home products. They lived in a lower duplex unit, small rooms crowded with shelving that held plastic containers of every sort and further disarrayed by all that goes with the nurture of a small child. Pam, it developed, was a doctrinaire Liberal, and I tripped over my own feet once again – which strangely seemed to happen to me more often with Labourites than Conservatives. I merely said something about finding it a stimulating challenge, to make this sort of journey on poverty resources.

"Stimulating?" She looked at me rather dubiously.

"Well, sort of proving it can be done, you know."

"Just because it can be done doesn't mean it ought to be that way."

I should have realized that she was focused on poverty as a handicap of inequality, while I was hailing its adventurous aspects. "I mean, it's so threatening to most people. But traveling poor is a real discovery process, just seeing what comes of it. Crazy as it seems, things always seem to happen for the best."

"Don't forget, you're white and American, but what about ... "

and she was off into a litany of the dispossessed poor ... here, there, and all over.

I tried to explain that I had said nothing in favor of poverty, and went on with the point I was really trying to make: that our personal reality is determined at least as much by our attitude toward circumstance as by circumstance itself. But it was like throwing gasoline on a small fire.

"There are too many people in this world," she went on, hardly pausing to think about what I'd said, "whose `attitude' is determined by a poverty reality much more severe than your hundred dollars a week for traveling around, and you don't help their struggle by suggesting that they've got an attitude problem."

It was a discussion turning swiftly into a disaster, and I had to back off entirely with some humble contrition, allowing her point. But the damage to our relations had been done, and most of my further conversation was with Pete.

When it came time to move on I decided to visit Ipswich, forty miles to the south, and both of them told me it was hardly a place worth seeing. It turned out that Pam, whose scorn for Ipswich was as great as Pete's, had never once been there in all her 35-odd years! I realized, then, that the poor woman had not an adventurous bone in her body.

The two towns were actually not much different, Norwich having perhaps an edge in historic interest, but Ipswich was close to the sea, which reasonably made up for it. I was quite journey-weary, by this time, and found the large, immaculate home of my Ipswich hosts, Jill and Patrick, a very welcome change of venue. They, too, were political liberals, but of a less fractious sort: reserved, intellectual – more likely, I suspect, to fund their causes than march for them. They took me out on a wonderful dusk-of-day nature walk in a nearby reserve, hoping to provide me a hearing of the nightingale. It never showed up for us, though.

I returned to Cambridge on a direct Sunday morning bus, facilitated by the sudden appearance of another angel – a stranger who popped up from nowhere to advise me that the bus I wanted was leaving, in a very few minutes, from another gate than the one I was waiting at. I have no idea, to this day, how he ever knew where I was going. He butted into a conversation I was having with someone else, over whether the exact fare was required on these buses, and Cambridge had never been mentioned.

But I was little better off making it early than late. The weather on both ends was dreary, and I already knew my evening's hosts were out for the day. I passed the afternoon of this forgettable Sunday in a Cambridge free museum of the uninspired kind, feeling like a sad-faced basset hound tied-up and waiting for someone's return. Finally, I walked out to their home, getting there in time to hide under the eaves from rainfall just begun – for they were not yet there. Our arrangement, made back in March, had been for seven p.m., and at precisely that time their car pulled into the driveway. Dinner was soon underway, pre-planned with as much precision; and I learned as we dined that Alan and Toni were both mathematicians teaching at Cambridge. If it didn't actually explain their precisional lives, it left me feeling as though it had.

The motorway was within sight of my upstairs bedroom window. I expected the short fifty-mile hop from Cambridge to London would be a snap, and there was never any question but that I'd do it on the road, weather permitting. The weather on that Monday morning was as clear, and quite as cold, as a pitcher of ice water. But that was not going to stop me. I was out there in the frigid sunlight as early as I could be. There was just one thing wrong with it all. I was at a north-of-town motorway juncture trying to hitch south – probably the dumbest mistake a hitch-hiker can make. No, there's a dumber mistake: I was stubborn about it.

None of the options seemed very attractive, once I realized my error. I didn't feel like hiking all the way back through this sizable town again, and it seemed a foolhardy risk to tempt the constabulary by walking down the motorway (three miles) to the south-end access. I couldn't bring myself to try the radical alternative that was probably the best: hitching north, to reach a more likely spot from which to hitch south. Instead, I stood there and nearly froze, for a full five quarters of an hour – the longest wait of my entire British journey – until a big truck and trailer rig finally stopped for me, a rare lift in any situation. Happily, he was going all the way in to Heathrow airport.

It took over two hours to get there, in London's traffic maze, and seemed more like a half-day, for I was in a half-world of rumbling comfort and drowsy exhaustion . . . luxuriating in the double-dosed euphoria of respite from the morning's biting cold and the last-leg completion of my five-week adventure/ordeal. I was in a blissful nowhere-land that kept fading in and out of reality, and I've no doubt the driver was absolutely sure I was stoned.

He dropped me at a point close to the Underground, and I was soon knocking on Marjory's great old hardwood door in Southfields, quite ready to call it a journey.

Great old Westminster Tower and Big Ben, from a perspective originally put to canvas by Claude Monet in 1871.

Weak knees
at the pit stop

London: June 3, 1991...

I had until the seventh to be out of the country. That meant a jam-packed four days for me, leaving little time for leisure, for losing my momentum . . . or for letting anxiety get the better of me. It was a moment of extremely high vulnerability, weary as I was from the rigors behind me, yet knowing they could hardly be more than a tepid prelude for the plunge I was about to take. But I had enough to take care of, in these four days, to keep the fears buffered for awhile.

Thankfully, Marjory's ever-generous hospitality gave me the quiet and private space that the transition required. From the panelled vestibule of her well-appointed home, to the five bedrooms upstairs, to the breakfast readiness of her morning table, it was like being in an inn; and with her full evening dinner service it was even more. After the briefest of greetings, I was out of there to get the mail that awaited me at my old Balham address. On my return, I pulled the blinds in the small room with a narrow-slice view of St. Paul's dome in the London distance, that Marjory had provided for me, and let myself crash for the rest of the afternoon. It was the moment I had been waiting for, all day.

At dinner, for house-guests from Italy, Spain and Japan, as well as

Marjory herself, I offered a brief report on the journey. Three thousand miles in 35 days, nine hundred of them by hitch-hiking. I'd stayed with fifteen hosts for 26 nights, lodged in four hostels for one night each, adding up to $34, and I'd slept out five times, dry all but once. My further journey costs came to: $166 for transportation, $144 for food, $45 for eleven books and their shipment to London, and $98 for all else. A grand total of $487, or $97.40 per week.

Finances for the road ahead were Tuesday's first order of business. I closed out the Westminster Bank account, taking in exchange £750 in American Express travelers checks. Equating, at the moment's trade rate, to $1275, it was essentially the income from my *Choice* articles, and would be my backstop, held in reserve until its use was absolutely necessary. It assured me a flight home from anywhere, as long as I could hold on to at least half of it. Overcoming my habitual reluctance for long-distance telephoning – even though it was toll-free – I made the call to Visa in California and took the time to explain all my concerns to them. They promised to rush my new card immediately. Through Terry, that meant I'd get it either in Paris or Amsterdam – IF I got it – and I had until the end of July to continue using my old card ... IF it continued to work for me.

Then there were friends to see, one more visit to the Balham Skills Exchange to get out a brief stateside newsletter, and a bit of shopping to do. More than a bit, costwise. I wanted to replace my winter-heavy sleeping bag with something more appropriate to a lightweight summer, and found a fine two-and-a-half pounder in the youth hostel shop for $100. Still worried about the hassle of being a language orphan everywhere I went, coping with a different culture every other week, I picked up a particularly good quick-reference volume called the *Traveller's Survival Guide*, along with a hitch-hiker's guide to Europe. I also paid an easy $8.50 for a Senior Euro-rail card, providing discounts of 30% to 50% off rail rates for the entire year – for bonafide British residents. My still valid London senior rail card turned the trick for me.

There was finally a lot of packaging to be done. I had to ship, or arrange with Marjory for later shipment of, a half dozen cartons. Some of my belongings were going directly back to the States, and some would be held for later shipment when, and where, I should end up – for the idea of a second winter of settlement somewhere had already become part of the loose plan. And yet a third group of materials were to be sent by Marjory in a series of monthly mail drops in care of *poste restante,* or general delivery. That way, I was able to break my assortment of maps and host lists, along with relevant pages torn from a copy of *Let's Go: Europe,* into month-by-month packets to keep my load light.

The Plan, much as I wanted to avoid pre-planning, had to accommodate such mail drops, which meant I had to have a skeletal framework of timing, and stick to it. I didn't want it any more elaborate than that. Unfortunately, it had already taken on more elaboration, and I had to wrestle with some hard choices while I was still in Britain. The original fantasy had been a grand clockwise circuit of Europe, ending in Spain, with hope of finding a place of winter settlement there. In the deep of my London winter, I roamed among the consular and national travel offices of the various countries in search of maps and literature. But the Spanish consulate was closed for remodeling, so I sent a letter, which idly included a question on the funds required of a traveler, on entry. I seldom asked this of any other consular office, but it seemed wise considering my thoughts of settling awhile in Spain. I didn't want to hazard a last-minute refusal of entry.

I was jolted by their response: the visitor had to bring in eighty dollars for each intended day of the stay. I wrote back, supposing that a six-month residence might make a difference, but it merely got worse on those terms. So I crossed Spain off my path and looked instead at a winter in Greece, where no such strictures applied. The "circuit" was now looking more like a crescent, with Italy, as well, chopped from the plan. In fact, it was a rather crumbling crescent, because I was having second thoughts about east Europe. Those countries had been open to visitors for less than a year, and some were still restrictive. Czechoslovakia, for one, had a minimum-cash requirement. It was not so high as Spain's – I could have handled it – but I was put off, and had even sent a letter of rebuke to Vaclav Havel. I had visions of authoritarian border inspections, in which anything might go wrong.

The end result was that I decided to avoid the former Soviet states, even to the extent of chopping Berlin from the crescent because it required travel through recently east territory to get there. The single exception in my plan, and the one that preserved any semblance of a crescent to it, was Hungary. I wanted to reach there if I possibly could, because I had a longtime correspondence friend, an attorney, in Budapest. I couldn't pass up this chance to meet him in person.

All of that juggling had taken place before I took off on my round of Britain. Now, things were jostled again. A letter was there in Balham from old friends now living in Berlin, who would love to see me if I could get there by early July. I also had word that the group I was affiliated with in Seattle, the *Earthstewards,* were holding their first European Gathering in the southeast corner of Holland during the last week of June. And it got more tangled: just as I had tried to set up weekend hosts in Britain – a great idea that went sour – I did it also for my first few weeks on the Continent. The results that greeted my London return were a mixed bag if ever there was: conditional acceptances, outright rejections, and entirely missing responses. "Can you come two days later?" "If you could be a week earlier..." Try as I might, to tie these loose threads into a pattern, they only tied me in knots.

It was a microcosm of life, itself. Something has always come along to throw me off balance, however much I attempt to assure the predictability, or at least the safety, of my world. It wasn't as if I didn't already know this; but the awesome prospect of going, now, into a land entirely remote from my life's reality . . . going there as a total innocent, with no real idea of what I was letting myself in for, had generated these desperate efforts to be sure of something – anything – that was likely to become of me, once I left the shores of language understood.

I finally had no choice but to write each of these potential hosts a letter, thanking them for their generosity and saying that I might be in touch as I came through, but I could keep no agreement. All except for a Paris host whose invitation I kept, in the sure prospect of a city so large and threatening that any small claim on security was too precious to let go.

Thinking about my budget constraint, alone, was enough to give me spasms of anxiety. Sure, I could handle it on the road in Britain, where every sign was readable, any question askable ... where I could spot the last-minute notices, take full advantage of the small print, and find my loophole in the words that spelled it all out. How was I to contain costs where none of these cues were working for me? And the distance – every day would take me farther and farther beyond an easy retreat to British soil. How could I even use the telephone when I had to?

It was a thin and fragile prospect, the whole business: travelers checks I'd rather not use, a Visa card with built-in uncertainties, and the long gamble that I'd be able to contain expenses at $100 per week. Even students, given every discount and traditionally the most impoverished of travelers, do not attempt it that cheaply. *Europe by Train,* a guidebook especially addressed to students, advises that lodging and food alone (without transport) should be figured at one of three basic levels: for expensive countries, $47 per day; for medium-cost countries, $25 per day, and for the cheapest countries, $21 per day. I was shooting for ALL expenses, in ALL countries, all summer long, at $14 per day.

Thursday evening after dinner I was alone with all these misgivings, knowing it was too late to back down – even if there was still time to do so. It's an odd conflict, when you're scared but committed. I felt suddenly more lonely than I had ever been in my entire life – as if I was getting ready for my own execution. I turned in, with all those goblins on my mind, for such sleep I could get in the circumstances.

The following morning, June 7, 1991, I made a long journal entry just before departure, in an effort to stay on top of my insecurities...

" ...Well, yes, I'm fearful, in a sense. That's what this feeling of imminent and highly personal doom is all about. But the bird out my window, as Francis would point out, is burdened by no sense of concern for what the day might bring. And he is very lightweight! Would that I could approach it. I should keep it in mind, tho – and, as well, the always-right things that happened to me on my just completed journey.

Let my burdens be only on my back, and not the constraintive pressures of having to get to a certain place by a certain time, or the fear that I'll otherwise be among devils. For I know in my heart it isn't so – tho my left-brain refuses to listen.

"I've got about six hours to deal with all that remains here. And then I'll be self-contained once more, ready for anything, and almost as free as that bird. I'm just going to navigate toward clusters of [Good Neighbors] possibilities – first at Rennes, then in Paris, taking my pleasure (or fate) in the open countryside as it comes. With much more freedom than in Britain, even, for there are hardly any advance impressions of what I may encounter, good or bad. And maybe that's the way to avoid being a tourist, when all is said and done."

Found on a postcard, this is the very barge I stayed on/in for a couple days, with Roland and Armelle, on the Vilaine River in Rennes.

All the way out
on the limb

St. Malo, France: June 8, 1991...

I don't know about the other channel crossings to France, but the overnight ferry from Portsmouth to St. Malo is the perfect adventure opener. The sea-going vessel stands off the French coast until the earliest light of dawn and then moves at quarter speed, silent as a raider, through the dense gray-white of a morning fog – heedless, it seems, of jagged rocks and tiny islands that loom suddenly into visibility at what appear to be perilously close distances.

I was alone on deck, roused by daylight from five hours of fitful sleep there, after choosing open air over the crowded interior where everyone else without a stateroom spent the night. Captivated, now, by this eerie dream-like waterscape, I was suddenly aware of another passenger alongside, a woman I'd already met on the Portsmouth bus from Victoria Station and had not seen since boarding the ferry.

Together, we watched the rampart walls of a great fortress materialize from the grey mist as we edged into the harbor, and I found out she knew more about St. Malo and the Brittany coast than I could have learned from any guidebook. She had grown up here right after the war and then married a Welshman, moved away, and become so thoroughly anglicized that only her name – Reneé – revealed her roots. I had stumbled upon a bilingual guide to ease my entry into France. Could the gods have any better responded to my uncertain confidence in this venture?

Grey-blue eyes glimmering in a field of freckles that softened features firmed by middle-age, Reneé was clearly excited about her first return in more than a decade. The demands of a high-skill trade – restoring oriental ivory carvings – had kept her too busy, she said. It had grown from a hobby and there were too few good practitioners to fill the call for it. Even with clients in Paris she never had time for the slow, easy ferry to St. Malo, which accounted for the early-morning enthusiasm she was sharing.

I followed along to meet her brother when we docked, and they took me to a brasserie in the old harbor section just opening for the day's trade, where we talked awhile longer over morning-fresh croissants. All of my remaining British coin and paper had been converted to francs back in London, but I hadn't yet any sense of value for the coinage. Reneé insisted on paying as I awkwardly dallied over it – a native's welcome, as she put it. Croissant with coffee, 11 francs ... $1.80.

Most of St. Malo, they told me, had been rebuilt after the war. The ancient fortress town had come through the first four years of conflict intact, but it was ripped apart by American bombers clearing the way for Ike's invasion of the Normandy coastline, quite some distance away – an aspect of the war we never hear about when its exploits are told. The rebuilding was done as nearly as possible to original form, but one can easily tell the new from the old by the textural difference in the stone. Still, it had stylistic integrity, and strolling the streets of the old walled-in section provided a charming image of Medieval France.

I parted from my briefly met friends soon after that shoreside bit of breakfast, later wondering if I should have been so hasty. I might have had a first-night host had I stayed with the conviviality. But I was too excited to remain in one place on this first day in France. I knew, furthermore, that the longer I should cling to such easy security, the harder a full plunge would become.

Marjory had loaned me excellent maps of the area, and my plan was to head for Rennes, forty-five miles to the south, a commercial hub with Brittany's largest cluster of Good Neighbors hosts – in fact, the largest selection of them in any one place this side of Paris. A walk out of St. Malo for several miles would bring me to the village of St. Servan, where rail and road took different paths to Rennes, and I could take my choice.

In London, of course, everything looked crystal clear on the map. Reality was not quite so clear. Here I was, walking down a road that seemed much like any other, except I couldn't read a thing   neither road signs or billboards, nor anything in the shop windows. I ambled along as though I knew exactly where I was, and where I was going, when every step took me deeper into a world where I could no longer communicate. It all felt very unreal.

I recalled a strange fellow I once met named Henry Seventy-seven. Henry had just ended a voice-fast, as he called it – five years of 'unspeakability,' during which he had said not a word to anyone. He told me how easy it had been to relate to everyone, and thus get by: he would just smile, point to his mouth and shrug his shoulders.

I was in the midst of these musings, and hardly beyond the port area of St. Malo, when a big stylish car pulled alongside driven by a fellow who spoke to me in Italian, as near as I could tell. I thought at first he was offering a ride, but it seemed he was instead trying to give me an expensive-looking leather jacket that went to nearly knee-length. In severely broken English he let me know that it was fresh from the Milan factory for which he was a sales rep, and he had pulled over just to give it to me . . . free!

I stood there laughing at the complete absurdity of such an intro-duction to the French countryside. I had no idea what the scam was, but the very thought of adding such a heavy piece of wear to the already sufficient burden on my back brought on further waves of laughter. He kept insisting it was a free gift, but then there was some-thing about giving me a ride all the way to Italy . . . if he could only get the gas to make the journey. It finally emerged that he wanted me to sell a second jacket, somehow, somewhere, for the gas money – the very thought of which sent me into another round of hilarity. He finally drove off, with a sorry smile at my rejection of his offer ... and with my free jacket as well.

A further distance along, I spotted a laundromat and took time out to dry my damp sleeping bag, managing, with a feckless mix of polyglot and finger-pointing, to learn from a woman and her son how the dryer operated. After I had gone on, her teen-ager caught up with me to return the map I absentmindedly left on a table – probably in a flash of subconscious resentment over its seeming uselessness. Nothing I had come to, after leaving the old walled town, had any apparent relationship to what was on the map. I used it, finally, to show a shopkeeper where I was trying to go, and he assured me I was on the road to Rennes. St. Servan had apparently grown into this endless stretch of shops and services. But the railroad was nowhere to be seen.

Somewhere along the way, under a steadily clouding sky and convinced that I was never going to get into real countryside, I lost my enthusiasm for the walk. Picking a likely spot, I made a roughly-lettered destination sign and started doing my thumb thing. It was nice to be facing traffic on the proper side of the road again.

I stood there a full frustrating hour. Plenty of traffic went by, and people were curious and interested in me but nobody would stop. The boy from the laundromat zipped by on the back of a motorbike, and then again, flashing a hand-wave each time with a wide grin. The natives were definitely friendly, but ...

Then a car pulled over, so deliberately that I suspect he might have doubled back for me. He was a school teacher who spoke a very little English and seemed to be saying that he taught French – which made no immediate sense to me, since we were in France. Until I sheepishly realized that we have English teachers at home. When we reached Rennes, I said I had to find a phone. He promptly insisted on taking me to meet his sister, who apparently spoke English and also had a phone I could use.

It was her husband, Raphael, however, who spoke English and spoke it quite well. A doctor, with an air of quiet authority and seriousness about him, he looked to be well into his forties. But what I learned in conversation suggested a somewhat younger age. We talked as he was trying to help me find a local GN host.

He had taken the list of names right out of my hands, once he understood how the system worked, and begun calling people on it, despite my insistence – possibly half-hearted – that I could handle it myself. I stood there helplessly listening to a pair of intense conversations, with not the vaguest idea of what was transpiring, before he gave it up and returned the list to me. I called the next one myself. It was a French response, of course, which I quickly converted to a thickly Gallic English by saying I was a GN traveler looking for lodging. The fellow hesitantly told me he'd consult with his wife and call me back.

It was during this wait, perhaps fifteen or twenty minutes, that Raphael began to reminisce about having hitch hiked himself, when much younger, around the United States and Canada before he entered medical school. He spoke wistfully of it, as though he hadn't given it any thought in years – yet he instantly located his old road-journal and a few souvenirs from then. I was struck by the circumstance that he had been on his journey, in 1971, at the very time that I broke free of my old world. We found the precise date in his journal when I quit my last job in San Francisco, and Raphael had been in Santa Fe on that day heading for California.

The journey so deeply affected him that he'd had a hard time returning to a routine of study; and ever so slightly there was a sadness, even a hint of regret, in his reflection on that – though he denied it when I asked. By now, the host I had called was phoning back to tell me it was perfectly all right and I should come by at once. Before driving me there, Raphael gave me a small French tricolor, the very flag that had been his backpack emblem on that journey of twenty years earlier. It was the perfect ritual welcome to Europe, as if that hour's roadside wait for a ride in St. Servan had been necessary, on this first day, for just the right one to come along.

My GN host was not to be found on a street, but on a canal, a branch of the Vilaine River that runs through the heart of this sizeable town. And quite literally on the canal: it was an old haulage barge, a huge hundred-footer by fifteen feet of width rocking gently at its moorage. Roland, the host I had spoken with, had been fifteen years at the slow job of making it livable, as he could find the time from his main preoccupation with film production. It was cozy and spacious at once like an old country cabin, complete with wood-stove and vintage furniture. Portholes were just above water level, louvre windows a bit higher, and the headroom was sufficient as long as one took care to sway down a bit at the gangway entrance – over which hung a turn-of-the-century photograph of this very same barge in its former incarnation.

Roland and Armelle were having an informal party that evening – the reason he'd been hesitant about inviting me to stay. Before long, friends began to gather in the large central section of this homey barge, perhaps six or seven adults and as many youngsters, who looked after themselves as the party got underway. There was not much I could understand, so I remained – in the style of Henry Seventy-seven – a smiling, silent guest, nibbling at pizza and various cheeses as an endless flow of wine gradually made language less and less of a barrier.

Roland did fairly well with English, though I needed his frequent reminders to speak more slowly. Armelle had a much slimmer grasp. One guest, Phillipe, turned out to be fluently bilingual and gifted as well with a fine sense of humor, and he became a catalyst for me as the evening got merrier, so that I finally felt I was really 'there.' At least until I'd had more wine than I could handle, which was impossible to avoid in that setting. The bottle wasn't just passed, it was poured, and nobody, not even Phillipe, understood me when I said, "enough!"

The kids, the older ones, seemed a bit in awe of me and wouldn't engage with my efforts at exchange. Until it was time for their departure, when I got shy farewells – salutes to an image of hippie adventure that I suppose I conveyed. One young fellow, the very picture of Sean Connery's youthful apprentice, Adso, in the film version of Umberto Eco's *Name of the Rose,* proudly tossed at me, "Peace and Love," in perfect English from the gangway, and then fled quickly into the night.

From Reneé, to Raphael, to Roland – three 'R's to match the alliteration of Halliburton's *Royal Road to Romance,* and to initiate my own on this incredible opening day of it. I was given a bunk bed, and the soft bobbing of the barge worked nicely with my woozy condition to send me gently and swiftly into my first night of Continental dreaming.

Next morning, I went with the family – Roland, Armelle, and their perfectly impish little girl – for a Sunday excursion to visit Armelle's parents in a rural setting about twenty miles west of Rennes. We left the highway at that point and journeyed south another few miles on a narrow road, passing cottages that begged for artist and canvas, until we came to a smaller trail and finally the secluded hermitage we were seeking, almost invisible from the roadside so shrouded was it by vines and shrubbery.

Armelle's father, Emile, was an old *Maquis* guerilla, the resistance group that fought Hitler's four-year occupation of France – and I suppose I regarded him with the same awe that the kids, the night before, had for me. Marie, his wife, was a robust, classically Gallic woman, in striking contrast to the svelte Armelle. Her particular pride that day was a great table overflowing with country-style foods for us: salads, pastas, all sorts of vegetable dishes – artichokes much larger than any I had ever seen! And bottles of wine, of course, made right there on the farm. It was becoming clear that I might not get out of France with any sobriety left. I relied on Roland for translation, but Marie was an absolute wonder at communicating her rich sense of humor without benefit of language. She used her eyes, with head and body movements, and I swear some of it had to be pure telepathy.

Eventually, I went off with Roland and Emile on a drive along back roads to the north, past the sleepy villages of Paimpont and Concoret, to take in tow an old Rover that Roland meant to cannibalize for one that he was refitting. I didn't realize what I was getting into. The Rover had no brakes. They lashed the two vehicles as closely together as possible, but had to leave some slack for a turning radius, which meant that the Rover – in which I rode with Roland – became a battering ram. It didn't seem to bother Emile, and we went lurching and zig-zagging with the abandon of an old Keystone comedy, pounding Emile every time he hit the brakes. I was a bit surprised that we actually made it back.

The day ended with Roland and I and the little imp taking a walk in the rural countryside, in the gathering dusk. Around us were old stone cottages cloaked in vines and distant treescapes in silhouette, timeless like a framed Monet. The little one sat atop Roland's shoulders part of the way, clearly no burden in his regard for her. This was the quintessential easy-going, casually charming Breton. He wore the traditional loose scarf around his neck, could not sit in a chair without lounging in it, and attended to conversation with slightly raised eyebrows whatever the topic – suggesting a bored competence rather than skepticism. Roland was instantly likable, and as fine an introduction to French style and sensibility as I might have found.

I wanted to stay awhile in Rennes and get grounded, before charging off toward Paris. It was 225 miles, from here to there, and I wasn't yet sure I could handle such a distance so sparsely settled with hosts. But I didn't want to overstay my welcome on the barge, so I phoned and found another host couple in Rennes. Roland tried to dissuade me when he found out, but the deed was done and he was kind enough to drive me over – I think he really wanted to check them out, in a protective concern for my well-being.

Eric and Marie occupied an austerely furnished, immaculately kept duplex, a complete contrast to the bubbling disorder of life on the barge. I had misgivings about the change, at first, but these were charming and attentive hosts. Living simply was a major focus of their lives, which included growing much of their own food. Eric, quite fluent in his English, was a computer engineer with a passion for solitary sailing voyages. Marie, whose English was a halting, uncertain affair, was a medical librarian who spent part of each week in Paris at her job – a half-day commute by train.

Now I took the time to explore Rennes, an ancient city of captivating charm. In the old section at its heart were two and three story buildings so old that they had lost their absolute respect for gravity and its demands. They seemed to lean casually on one another . . . sort of like Roland lounged on chairs. But none were in danger of collapse: they were too tightly packed to allow it. Here, for the first time, my budget was seriously threatened by food temptations. Cheeses were remarkably cheap, and breads, baked fresh twice daily in the small bakeries, were quite impossible to resist.

It was all too tempting, in my dread of the open countryside, to cling to the least bit of security. Eric easily persuaded me to return from a side trip to Mont St. Michel and stay with them an extra night. That became, for me, a first venture all over again, for it required a train ride, forcing me to cope with the language issue. Eric softened the blow by taking me to the station – the *gare*, they call it. The morning's only train was about due, as I fumbled for the right amount in francs. Eric came to my rescue, paying the $9 fare for me in the tight-schedule rush. A new twist, perhaps, on Henry Seventy-seven's method of 'getting by.' I tried later to pay it back, but Eric wouldn't hear of it. As a last contribution to my welfare, before hurrying off to his own affairs, he made sure I was waiting on the right platform.

The railroad, however, pulled a track switch at the last minute, diverting the train to another platform. I would have missed my journey entirely, but out of the smoky haze where I waited at the railside came another angel, right on schedule, to hustle me off toward a further platform. He was a young law student from Tunisia who had apparently heard my final exchange with Eric, about which train I was supposed to get. I was almost ready to take these rescues as a matter of course.

Visiting Mont St. Michel checked off a lifelong dream. Marie had managed to convey that it would be filled with tourists, so I was prepared for that aspect. The rainy day reduced the throng and lent more atmosphere to the visit. A $2.75 senior fee took me all the way up into the cathedral area, where I was just in time for the day's noon mass, an impressive experience in that setting, beneath stained-glass that towered to an incredible height. A choir of visiting school children enhanced the effect, and at just the right moment the overcast sun burst across hundreds of colored panes high up in the vaulted interior, as if some Hollywood production manager had a hand in it. I silently blessed all the Michaels who have enriched my world in recent years. Then, to balance accounts with the more heathenly spirits that motivate me, I found a nicely secluded spot in an outer yard and took my relief there. In a Pantheist's world, all things natural are sacred.

Back again in Rennes, Thursday dawned with a bit of threat in the weather, but not enough to delay my departure. I bused to the outskirts, bought a fresh croissant in a nearby bakery for 23 cents and found my hitching spot. I waited only twenty-five minutes, this time, for a ride with a teacher of English. Once underway, he told me he was headed for the town of Vitré, and I remembered that I had intended to reject any ride going there. Vitré was several miles off the main route and I was concerned that I might get stranded there. As usual, however, my mind had gone completely blank the moment a car stopped for me.

Looking at the map as we rode along, I saw that I could yet avoid Vitré. I showed my driver how he could help me by continuing on the main highway until we reached a 'T' crossing that could take him into Vitré and leave me in a good position for my next ride. It seemed clear enough; but my map didn't indicate the entire situation. There was also a 'Y' avenue, several miles short of the cross traffic I was hoping to tap into. And sure enough, that was where he dropped me. It only dawned on me as I watched him speed away on the 'Y' road, toward Vitré. There was virtually no eastbound traffic coming onto the highway here – the same sort of situation I had blundered into on leaving Cambridge. Compounding it, there happened to be road repair going on at this point, bottlenecking the highway traffic into a one lane flow. Slim chance, here, that anyone would stop for me. But my more immediate concern was that the clouds had now become ominous ... dark, lumbering masses obviously getting ready to disgorge.

I had to get out of here, and that meant I had to walk out, the threat of a downpour giving me no time to linger over the issue. Rather than walk the five miles into Vitré that I might so easily have ridden, it made more sense to stay with the main highway. I couldn't be much more than three miles from the 'T'. I took off at a forced-march tempo, hoping at least to reach some cover before the heavens let loose. There was none at all, anywhere nearby.

Road markers every hundred meters, sixteen to the mile, paced my progress as I raced the clouds. But it was no good. Thirty-four markers out, I lost the game. My poncho was out as fast as I could manage it – for what little good it did in the stormy rage that came down on me. There was nothing in sight, absolutely nothing, for a moment's cover. I could only carry-on and take the soaking. And reflect on how easily I might have been comfortably dry in Vitré.

By the time the crossing came into view the rain had passed. I was so wet that it made little difference anymore; but it was good to be done with it – done with the walk, and at a place where I could resume my hitching. And then I saw the fellow who was already there.

He was a black from Martinique – as I could barely make out, for he only spoke French. He pointed on a pocket watch how many hours he had been waiting for a ride. I knew, from his obvious down-and-out condition, that he could be there for many more hours, and I knew I had not the patience to wait with him. The situation, for me, had become hopeless. After giving the fellow a ten franc piece ($1.60) in place of the cigarette he begged, I set out on the only course now left: walking down the 'T' into Vitré – but not so low in spirit, after all. There comes a time when one has to bow gracefully to the sovereign will of the Universe. Once that occurs, the burden of purpose is lifted and everything feels pretty good again. In the hour's walk, I turned the whole business over in my mind, considering it from every side, and decided that the lesson it held for me was to take the ride as it comes. The trail always goes to the right place, according to trail philosophy, and no good will ever come of second-guessing or trying to manipulate it.

In Vitré I headed for *le gare*, the rail station. An English-speaking ticket agent told me I could make it to Chartres that night, most of the way to Paris, by a complicated three-part passage, changing trains at Laval and Le Mans. Should I dare it? The four hour journey would put me there at 10:45 p.m. But what to do in Chartres at that hour?

In a park across from the station I pored over my resource material. My options boiled down to a GN host in Le Mans or a hostel in Chartres, and I could hardly make the choice without placing a phone call to assure it. With two hours before departure time, I set out in search of a pay phone; and in that timespan, I found out why Vitré was worth all the trouble I had come through to get there.

Seemingly hidden behind a maze of narrow streets close-packed with ancient half-timbered structures was easily the most enchanting castle of all that I had come across. A chateau it was, here in France. Up high on the hill, a massive wall of dark stone surmounted by turreted towers of the same murky hue in a fairy tale arrangement – the whole of it a stunning blend of Medieval power and French temperament. Seen from below, its dark mass hovering over the village structures with a fearsome, brooding dominance undisturbed by any evidence of modernity, it was a sudden peek into the long, long ago, and I halfway expected to see the glint of flashing armor on its battlement, or a maiden's surreptitious look from one of the high turret windows. Nothing in the entire scene, down to the very street I stood on, suggested the twentieth century.

In the time I had, I couldn't find an entrance to it, though I very nearly circled its perimeter. But that first view, the complete surprise of it, was all I really needed and it left my impression of the chateau entirely untarnished by touristic debasement.

When I finally found the pay phone, I had circled right back to the rail station. Had I merely gone the other way, to begin with, I would have found my phone and never have glimpsed the wonderful chateau at all. I called the Chartres hostel and they did have room for me – and alerted me that the doors would be locked at 11 p.m., fifteen minutes from train arrival time. A further element of tension added to the already tight schedule of connections. As I bought my ticket, some strange fellow was babbling to any and all in the vicinity – and of course, I could understand nothing of it. Nobody paid him any attention, but I did, simply in order to stay out of his way. For no reason that I could tell, he suddenly insisted on giving me a ten-franc piece. The very amount that I had earlier given the black fellow from Martinique, out on the highway.

The train connections marvelously came off without a hitch and I arrived in Chartres right on schedule. The hostel was a mile away, leaving me no choice but to take a taxi. It set me back $5, and the hostel another $9, both of which added up to my day's allowance – yet it was only half of what I spent on this strangely mixed day. But in later looking back on the whole adventure of miscalculation, I realized that it had brought me through the barrier of all my fears about traveling Europe. I was doing a lot of singing out there in the rain, once it had begun, and hadn't been at all concerned for what might eventuate in that wild situation. Just taking each development as it came. So the price of passage was hardly exorbitant.

The Cathedral at Chartres, standing on a rise, lords it over the entire town, as much as any chateau possibly could. This was evident when the morning mist and rain gradually cleared, to reveal the cathedral's impressive stature about a mile from the hostel. It would not take much of a detour to reach on my way out of town.

Quite by accident, I took a route that led me to an ancient Roman church by a quiet stream at the foot of the cathedral hill. Nobody was around, but it appeared to be open for entry and I wandered in. There was not a bit of furnishing or decoration, just an immense open space dominated by several huge stone columns. Something unavoidably imposing and serene about this great, solemn emptiness moved me to an unintended bit of meditation before I continued on toward the Cathedral. The place was called the Abbey of Sainte André.

Mont St. Michel's cathedral had stirred hope that the French retained a more reverential attitude for their great church structures, than the tourist focus I encountered in Britain. But I found there really wasn't much difference at Chartres. Among other disabusing impressions was the sight of a priest sitting in a brightly lit confessional, waiting for penitents to drop by, almost like a concessionaire at a street fair. All it lacked was a sign, "Lighten your burden for twenty francs." In the end, I valued my moments in Sainte André's Abbey more than my experience of the Chartres Cathedral – though it is certainly a magnificent structure.

I walked from there to the Paris motorway, perhaps another mile or so, and soon had a ride with a pair of fairly young German fellows on their way home from a channel crossing, both of whom spoke good English. They were going to bypass Paris, and offered to drop me at Etampes, for a straight shot into the underside of the city on a lesser highway. But then they asked if I'd rather be dropped at the motorway turnoff, about twenty miles short of Etampes. Faced with a choice, and having no better guidance than the lesson of the Vitré episode, I decided to stay with the original suggestion.

It had become a sparkling day by the time we sided off the motorway toward Etampes – the whitest of puffball clouds drifting lazily through a brilliant blue sky, reminiscent of idyllic days when I hitch-hiked as a youth in long-ago California, before the advent of freeways or smog. (Yes, Virginia, there was a time before smog in California, when traffic was gentle and the Open Road was a refreshing two-lane adventure . . . and I am lucky enough to have been there.)

Etampes was a pleasant but unexceptional little town, by the growing extent of my French countryside standards. It was on a rail line into Paris, but the day was too bright to consider that, even though the highway at this 25-mile distance was a roaring mass of juggernauts. I made the brief mistake of trying it full-strength, and then backed off to the access road, where I waited hardly fifteen minutes for a young woman going right in to Paris. A golden-haired angel, I should add, for even though she spoke almost no English she managed to insist that I give her the exact address of my Paris host, the one I had written to from London, and then drove me right to it!

I had been chauffeured to all three hosts for my first week in Europe (not to mention the taxi in Chartres). Not at all bad, for a stranger in a strange land . . . a 'pennyless' innocent who doesn't know the territory and can't *parler* the language.

And rather amazingly – even with Thursday's transportation expense ($21.75) and the $9 hostel night – I managed to hold my week's costs very near the budget line, at $101.31. It was a good fiscal omen for the journey and enabled me to approach a week in Paris with an open attitude as to its possibilities.

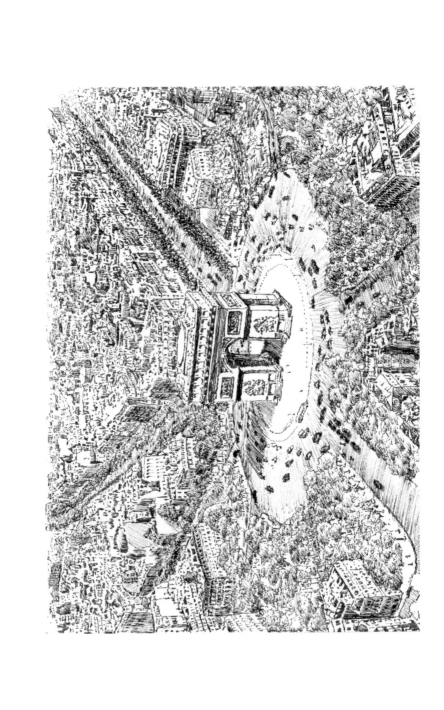

Parisian dalliance

Paris: June 14, 1991...

I never knew how sterile my winter in London had been until I saw Paris. Not to deny the stimulation of London – but if London is a stimulant, then Paris is an *excitement!* If London be captivating (as it certainly was for me), Paris, for contrast, can only be called intoxicating. The pity of it all – nay, the tragedy – is that I could spare only a week for it in the momentum of my roll through Europe.

Evelyne, the host I had fortunately kept, from my original GN contacts, lived in Montrouge on Paris' south fringe in a block-long concrete apartment building of typically dreary postwar design. I had phoned ahead from Rennes on Eric's generous insistence. Now I called from a nearby booth and she said I could come right up.

Tall, slim and angular almost to the point of being ungainly, she greeted me at the door. Beneath an uneasy bun coiled from shoulder-length dark brown hair, her quick smile made instant sunshine of features otherwise sober...disdainful of cosmetic foolery. The lack of artifice imparted a certain ageless quality; I couldn't have guessed Evelyne was in her forties. Our conversation was off and running at once, but it took me awhile to get used to her accent. Like starting a race without the handicap lead I should have been entitled to.

I was given a back room furnished with little more than some of Evelyne's own sculpture, and a great mattress that took up half the floor space. The sculpture, stark white and spare, one piece clearly a self-portrait, was her pastime and private passion. Professionally, Evelyne was a translator, self-employed, with a busy schedule of commissions. She was fluent in both German and English, and able to make her way with Spanish and Dutch, as well.

She shopped for supper an hour after my arrival, while I stayed behind and took a nap to restore my energy for the evening. I woke to the sizzling sound and smell of kitchen activity. An aromatic ratatouille almost ready to eat, served with steak – something I hadn't tasted in a few years. While I'm nominally a vegetarian, there are other things to consider when on the road. First of all, the obligation to be a good guest, appreciative of whatever a host chooses to share; and then there is the principle of accepting what the Universe brings – a Universe less rigid in its provision than we in our demands of it. We dined and talked, and wined . . . and talked on, long into the evening. Here I was in Paris, perhaps the most magical city in the world, with no urge at all to go out and explore. But the magic was right here in Evelyne's apartment: the warmth and delight of a Parisian's friendship.

But the next day was a different story. I first took advantage of the telephone Evelyne offered, to arrange for two other Paris hosts during the latter part of my week. Then, furnished with a street map and transit advice, I set out on a long walk that took me right into the heart of the city, to the Seine River. And what a delight! A city of incredible vitality blended with gentility and charm. At every hand, the most magnificent building facades I had ever seen, harmonized by tributes, in an endless array of statuary, to feminine form and features – regal figures dominating the boulevards with their imperious hauteur . . . or softer goddesses gazing down from lintel and arch, in that radiant earthy innocence of la belle epoque, the age of Mucha and Toulouse-Lautrec. A feast of seductive imagery in stone. One could hardly live in such a city as this and not be sensitized to art and beauty.

Feast for the palate was there, too, hardly to be ignored – but not for mine. Paris could easily be the ruin of my budget if I gave in to its edible temptations. Mine was the cheapo tour, and I got by on my usual mid-day apple and an 80-cent almost-pastry from a street vendor

– some strange baked thing coated with cinnamon. But my comestible restraint posed no hardship . . . gluttony was fully served by the visual feast underway.

Any hunger I had to stifle, that day, was offset in the evening when I joined Evelyne at a pre-arranged rendezvous for an Italian dinner. We were a party of four, with two earlier guests of hers who happened to be back in Paris staying with other hosts. They were from Seattle, too; and quite incredibly, one of them had been in the same program as I, at the University of Washington, and even remembered having seen me there! She took this 'small world' phenomenon quite easily in stride, as though it happened regularly, and the four of us squeezed into the tightest seating imaginable for a clam and rigatone feast. At something close to $11, my most expensive meal thus far, it completely trashed the day's austerity.

All the next day I went walking again, mainly along the river and on the *Ile de la Cité,* the island in the Seine where stands the Cathedral of Notre Dame. The breathlessly monumental and inexhaustible extent of classic Beaux Arts architecture one sees from the bridge over the Seine – for it isn't just here and there, or even in clusters, but literally everywhere – simply cannot be compared with anything in the States. Or, really, with anything less than nature's own impressive sweep of magnificence.

I didn't go inside the Notre Dame Cathedral, discouraged by a $3.25 entry fee. I did, however, stand there to watch the tourists stream out, and watch them walk by the scatter of people begging alms there. The crippled and deformed, whose very presence at this tourist locus puts a double counterpoint into play: on the one hand, with the Cathedral – spirit expressed as priceless spectacle – and with sight-seeing pilgrims, on the other, who pay to grace themselves by viewing the shrine, yet remain predictably blind to the plight of these woeful who gather in the shadow of this monument to the patron of charity, itself. I played this back and forth in my mind, like a discordant bit of blues, until I could puzzle it no longer. I was ashamed enough to give a coin to a sightless man before walking on.

It was my turn to treat, for the third and final night at Evelyne's, and we went for a late pizza dinner at a quiet little place near her apartment. It felt like some closeness had developed between us, and for the first time I experienced a real regret at moving on to another host. But it had already been arranged. Evelyne said she'd be in Munich on a contract job, sometime in August. If I could manage to be there during those few weeks, we might be able to arrange a rendezvous. She even broached the idea of a possible visit with me if I should find a wintering place in Greece.

The second of my Paris hosts lived on the north side, up near Montmartre and the famous old *Moulin Rouge* Theater. This was a young couple, Josette and Jean-Pierre, occupying an expansive old-style apartment on an upper floor. Their door opened into an amenity I had forgotten I ever once lived with: a long central hallway branching to each of their several rooms. We have undergone such a steady 'upgrade' of residential style, in America, that it's been easy to forget the spaciousness, and the ways of space, that were once a part of ordinary living. Here was a reminder – the first of many I was to have – of what we've lost along the way to better living standards, so-called, in the urban 'space wars' of America commonly called progress.

For all of that, their kitchen was tiny and cramped, an indication that the original apartment was even larger and had been split in two. Josette led me on beyond, to the dining room, its table set almost formally for dinner, down to linen napkins in silver rings. They had been waiting my arrival – intent, it seemed, on being perfect hosts, and I felt awkward at being late. But they radiated only that idyllic happiness of a marriage not yet beyond its first year – though I never confirmed my impression.

I blamed my tardiness (not quite truthfully) on a scary encounter that occurred in the Metro – the Paris subway. On the platform of my exit, I had to get by a pair of fellows engaged in something serious. The one I had to pass had a knife in his hand. The other was taunting him from a subway car whose door remained open, as if to let the drama proceed. He, too, may have had a knife; my attention was locked on the mean-looking one standing in my way, waving his in the air. He had wrapped a blue jacket around his other arm, ready for close quarter fighting. Whatever they were yelling at each other, it sounded like a challenge to tangle, and I couldn't be sure it wouldn't explode before I got by.

I suppose I didn't really have to walk by him, but he blocked my way to an exit and my impulse was to get out of there as fast as I could. A quick, unhesitant pace took me around and past him, and I didn't look back. The few other people nearby stood and watched, with that morbid curiosity that is often stronger than prudence or fear; but I just wanted to get out. Only later did it occur to me that I was close enough to have been grabbed as a shield or a buffer, had the action suddenly ignited.

But that event hastened me, if anything, to Josette and Jean-Pierre's. The reason for my delay had been a lingering late-afternoon tea with Evelyne, the last I'd see of her before leaving Paris. It was hard to quit our endless flow of conversation, though it was seldom of more than incidental consequence.

"Where deed you go, zees aftair noon?"

"To the Louvre. Nobody does Paris without it, right?"

" . . . Duz Paree weethout eet?"

"Oh, you know, Evelyne. A visit wouldn't be complete without the Louvre."

"And what you think of eet?"

"To be honest, it's the most confusing museum I've ever been in. I was lost almost as soon as I left the lobby, going through one room after another, trying to find what I wanted to see. The rooms link like rail cars, and if you 'get off the train' there's no way to find your way back to where you began."

"But evairthing ees marked, weeth signs all ovair."

"Sure. In French. There's nothing in English beyond the lobby."

"Well, what you expect? You een France."

I couldn't argue with her logic. I went on to tell her how it finally got so frustrating that I just wanted to get out of there. But finding an exit was no easier than anything else I had been looking for.

"What was eet you were looking for?"

"Oh, there were four or five things I had hoped to see, but I only managed to find one of them, the *Venus de Milo*. And it didn't even have any arms!"

Her brown eyes told me what she thought of my humor.

She did, however, suggest that I try the *Museé d'Orsay,* and that was my next day's direction. It turned out to be everything that the Louvre wasn't. Recycled from an old railway station in the heart of town, the *d'Orsay* was blessed with a great open interior, like a cathedral, and took every artful advantage of it. A central display of sculpture, with emphasis on 19th century stone and bronze work, ranged upward along gently stepped levels open to the high ceiling. It was one exquisite piece after another, a really amazing collection, culminating at the topmost level with a copy of Rodin's massive portal called *The Gates of Hell.* Inspired by *Dante's Inferno,* Rodin had worked at this for almost forty years to create a masterpiece so compelling it is hard to turn away from. The portal is solid, yet … seemingly fluid, engorged with figures partial and complete, each in ceaseless struggle, straining against its containment in that solidified nothingness.

Exhibit spaces to the sides of the central corridor were filled with 19th century oils, much better illuminated than is usually the case in art museums. Off in a far corner, the only spot with sufficient wall space for it, hung a monster-sized, unusually detailed painting of Paris as seen from the vantage of a balloon in 1855. Painted by Victor Navlet, it was done with such realism I was quite certain, coming upon it, that it must be a photograph.

I paid for a second, and even a third entry to the *d'Orsay* (at $2.40 per), returning on subsequent days, in penalty for my ambling, 'potluck' way of seeing the sights of Paris. Walking was far more fun than taking the Metro, but I would find myself drawn down one side street after another and by the time I reached the museum, each afternoon, I was shocked at how much of the day had drifted away.

I made sure of an early return to my host, for the second night's dinner. Josette had promised a Paris Special, and she served a perfectly cooked soufflé followed by a flambé dessert! It reflected their tasteful, elegant lifestyle – which she, however, insistently referred to as 'simple living' because it included no automobile or television. Josette seemed always 'on stage,' with an engaging, positive personality. I thought, at first, it was an occupational facade, for she ran a local guide and greeter service from their home. But before these two brief days had gone by, I could see she was really that way – a charming person, never flustered by any situation, though at times she was clearly under pressure, trying to blend home and business worlds. John-Pierre, who worked as a customs inspector, was congenial too, certainly, but not in the same ever-gracious, outgoing way as Josette.

Next morning, I strolled the Montmartre area, but far too early to see any of its bohemian life. I went off, then, to find the Arc de Triomphe and walk from there back toward the d'Orsay, along that great avenue called the Champs Elysées. But I was stopped in my tracks, at the great arch, by sheer fascination with the traffic circle around it – surely the finest spectacle in all of Paris. The craziest, anyway. Like spokes on a wheel, no fewer than twelve major boulevards feed into this one grand circle: three to five concentric lanes of rolling, rushing vehicles, with no traffic control that amounts to anything. A lone gendarme clad in grey and blue tried to regulate the flow from the Champs Elysées, but he was mostly reduced to dodging it. I stood rooted there for more than an hour waiting for an accident to happen, unable to imagine that it wouldn't.

The swirling maelstrom only paused when some driver, finding no ready egress from the inner churn, would pull up short and wait for a break, halting the flow behind him. In a chain reaction, the entire wheel took the cue until nothing at all moved and the orchestrator who had started it all – or stopped it all – would slip through the frozen melée, grandly exercising his moment of power. Then it would all resume as before. No accidents! Almost as marvelous to behold was the occasional bicyclist who'd casually pedal into this onrushing whirlpool and make it through without a scratch, and seemingly without a concern.

I finally, with some difficulty, disengaged from the fascination and made my way down the Champs Elysées. I suppose I expected to see elegant carriages and arrogant boulevardiers, the image I still carry from the film, Gigi, but it was just another park-lined avenue, with nobody there but me. I got as far as the sight of banners proclaiming an Art Nouveau exhibit, a personal passion that can sway me in any direction, anytime. Locating it, however, was another matter. I found the door to an art museum, paid the entry fee of $3.85, and discovered I had bought a thorough-going exhibit of Georges Seurat with bi-lingual courtesies. I would not have known how to ask for my money back, so I stayed, and learned more about Seurat and his work than I ever wanted to know.

That evening, I had to move along to my third Paris host located in a quaint neighborhood south of the Seine, not too far from the Eiffel Tower. The crosstown routine was beginning to feel like London in September, though it had none of the earlier anxiety. Marielle was expecting me, of course. She lived in a second-floor apartment, which at first struck me as modest but then turned out to have enormous rooms, almost large enough for her enormous collection of books and ephemera. She was a lifelong student of people and cultures, with an insatiable urge to collect. An Italian dinner awaited my arrival, with the usual wine, and – as we ate – the usual getting-to-know-you of GN hospitality. Her English was good, almost without accent.

On the high side of her forties, Marielle felt mired in a daily office grind, a job that limited the pursuit of her intellectual leanings. Her life, in fact, seemed an uneasy truce between its practical demands and her personal commitments. I could feel the resentment, and I could certainly identify with it. I hoped I might find a good opening for some positive input from my own background.

She was off to work very early in the morning, leaving a key with me so that I could sleep as late as I wished and come and go at will. A place to myself for awhile offered a relaxing break from both sightseeing and sociability, and I idled my morning time almost entirely away. It was my last full day in Paris, though, and there were a couple must-see items on my agenda. I took the closest one first – the Rodin Museum – and set out for it, walking, despite the wet day. Something between a heavy mist and a light drift of rain was being teased and played with by breezes that were starting to get serious.

The museum is at Rodin's old estate and workshop and holds the largest collection of his work, along with that of his increasingly recognized protegé, Camille Claudel. It was an impressive collection, and I spent two or three hours browsing there. Strangely, the work of his I liked most wasn't done in the massive, brooding style we associate with Rodin. It was a very early work, while he was yet a student: the study of a young woman in a spring hat – a light-hearted effort, radiant and lovely, that perfectly captured the freshness of her youth – and as surely expressed his own.

The day, weatherwise, had become a disaster. Regrettable, but there was no way that I was going to miss the final item on my agenda. After all, the Eiffel Tower, 102 years old, has to be the most singular attraction in all of Europe, a devotional pilgrimage, at least once, for even the most jaded tourist. Well, okay . . . a necessary lapse for the most devout anti-tourist.

By the time I got there, all I could see was the base of it: four great tower legs squaring an entire city block. Above, they faded into an impenetrable mist. A day like this was for the truly devoted – a surprisingly large crowd, as it turned out. We clustered around various bits of shelter waiting for the tilted elevator that inches up the tower leg at an angle. Four such elevators, one for each leg, are on hand, but only one runs on weekdays. I bought a middle level ticket for $5.15 – a bad choice, but I couldn't know it until my options were gone. Another $2.75 would have taken me clear to the top. But it was perfectly obvious there'd be no decent view at any level, this day. In the circumstances, I figured I had the day's best price for being able to say, "I was up the Eiffel Tower." Never mind the near-zero visibility of it.

And then I discovered the true cost of a poor man's bargain: the crowd that stood waiting for the elevator to take them back down. Twice as many people as the creeping thing had room for, standing out in the wet – a jet-stream at this altitude – so as not to lose their place in line. Fifteen minutes in the wind-driven drizzle, and then the agony of seeing the elevator door shut before I could reach it. I didn't dare go back into the sheltered part of the platform lest I miss the next one, too. 'The next one,' of course, would be the same one – after it had gone all the way down, then back to the top, and finally returned on its way down again. Twenty minutes more, and no choice but to stand in this crowd, in a whipping spray that had already soaked through my rain gear. The $2.75 differential, I now understood, was for a useless trip dry, instead of a useless trip wet and miserable.

For my last Paris dinner with Marielle, I brought back two huge artichokes, and as she prepared them along with a pot of pasta we fell into some rather serious discussion on the purposes and meaning of Good Neighbors hospitality. It began quite innocently with my idle observation that it was possible to travel on far less money than the travel industry would have one suppose. I was quick to add that this was due in no small part to the blessing of Good Neighbors. And Marielle was equally quick to point out that GN was a friendship and exchange network, not just a device for cheap travel.

Suddenly, I found myself uncomfortably on the defensive. I could hardly deny that cheap travel was a large part of my purpose, and for me a necessity. But admitting this seemed to tar me with a stain of 'irresponsibility,' in Marielle's perspective.

It was an old challenge in new clothes. Having dropped out from the career world in mid-stream, I had many times, over the years, been charged with pursuing a wayward life; and I'd certainly had my own doubts to deal with, over it. Nobody grew up in mid-century America without receiving a ramrod-strong dose of what it means to live responsibly. Thoreau, my inspiration in such matters, might have been a voice of conscience for us, but no one ever took seriously his spare version of the simple life.

It was a far wider issue for me than Marielle's immediate concerns, however, and I wasn't at all sure I could respond without bringing in a lot of old baggage.

"Well, the way I see it," I began, uneasily, "I am involved more fully with my hosts than merely by an exchange of viewpoints. I make them partners in my journey, in a very real fashion . . . I bring them a sense of truly helping me."

"Yes, like the – how you call it? – the pan-handler, the alms-seeker, brings a sense of goodness to refresh those burdened with wealth?" She smiled as she said it, but it was clearly intended to cut through my self-justification.

"You could see it that way, I suppose, but it's more than a `sense of goodness.' Friendship is caring, and caring grows from more meaningful connections than just a polite and distant hospitality."

"That may be true," she came back, thoughtfully, "but it has to go two ways; it cannot happen when one has all the giving, and the other all the receiving."

"But that's not a fair measure, Marielle. The traveler, by his very nature, is on the receiving end, always. You are suggesting that it is somehow more so if he travels in actual need of what the host provides. I say it makes the transaction more real, the generosity more meaningful."

"And also more of a charity," she shot back. "It can make the host feel like she has no choice but to help, which upsets all the good work being done."

The artichokes came out of the boiling water, now, and as she drained them over the sink I took a moment to clarify my thinking on this whole thing. She was making a critical issue of the exchange that takes place between host and guest, and it became the only avenue for any legitimacy I could seek. What was it, after all, that I offered, as my end of the transaction?

"Actually, Marielle, a traveler like me brings a very unique gift to the host. A gift that could hardly be conveyed except by the way I travel." A sudden shift of her eyes toward me registered either interest or resistance, I wasn't sure. "I'm a living example that it can be safe to move outside the boundaries of security and certainty, and live a more free and fulfilling life."

It was a risky claim, to walk out on the limb of this argument with, and I knew it the minute she began her response. "Oh, so easy to say," and she let a slight pause precede the rest, "but it's just a rationalization. In America you can make such choices, but the daily reality here, and in most of the world, doesn't permit living by whim. You bring a gift nobody here can use." And then her final observation, a gratuitous *coup de grace,* "You are just an American who could not travel without using our hospitality."

Yes, I thought to myself, this is the ultimate rejoinder, in one form or another. To Americans, I can live this way because I'm single and without 'responsibilities' (our self-serving euphemism for confining commitments). To a European, I'm able to do it *because* I'm an American – white and male, as is often further added. There was no way to put my sense of it across to her without pulling all the stops.

"Look, Marielle . . ." I searched for the words, "I wouldn't have come to Europe if no path had opened for me. I would simply have accepted that it was not my trail."

"You see? You admit it couldn't be done without taking advantage of these hospitality offerings."

"No, you don't hear me. Whether a path opens for me, or not, doesn't matter. Either way, it's my cue; the trail goes one way, or it goes another. Only on the surface does it look like I live by whim. I follow the cues of Providence. When I didn't get a job in London, that was as much a gift of Providence as if I had found one."

"That's crazy! We can't live that way here. We have to go through rejection after rejection until we finally get a job, in order to pay the bills. There isn't any other choice . . . except for those on public charity."

I was sorry I let myself get drawn into it. But committed, now, and feeling the anger rise, at her failure to hear me, I took a deep breath and went on. "Public charity, pan-handling, hospitality, income . . . why do we put these labels on what Providence brings? They only cloud the fact that our necessities are provided. And look what the cloud does to us: good money and bad money, decent ways to get it and indecent ways. Staying pure becomes obsessive. It turns life into a struggle. But life is a gift, Marielle, a daily blessing. Why make a struggle of it?"

"So how do you get around it," she asked, with more pain than exasperation in her rising voice . "How do you get around what you have to struggle with every day?"

"By taking whatever comes. Taking whatever comes, and considering it your proper portion, your gift . . . your message, perhaps, if it doesn't feel like a gift, or your directional signal. *I'm* your gift, Marielle, just as you're mine. The only problem anyone has ever had with Providence is that we think we're entitled to more, or better – and so we struggle to obtain it."

There was nothing further said by either one of us for a long while, and then the subject was entirely different. It had felt more like a stalemate, than any shift in her point of view. Then late that night, drifting toward sleep, I wondered about my own point of view. Marielle, after all, *was my gift*. Should I be looking at something in that discussion? Perhaps at how I had let her push my buttons?

She had, in fact, sensitized me to the delicacy of the host/traveler relationship, a realization that ultimately led to my decision to cloak the name of this hospitality network with the pseudonym of Good Neighbors.

My Friday departure had been planned at midweek while I was staying with Josette and Jean-Pierre. I would take the train north to Lille, my last stop in France, where a host awaited, already confirmed by telephone. Since I knew the schedule, and everything was arranged, I saw no need to hurry. I lingered for a final leisurely taste of Parisian neighborhood flavor – not realizing that my rail discount went off at noon. I had read all about how the French railway system gives no discounts during the 24-hour period that begins at noon on Friday. I read it on my first day in Paris, in my valuable *Traveller's Survival Guide*. And then I promptly forgot about it. I got to the *Gare du Nord* an hour past noon, and had to pay $23.20 for my ticket instead of the $11.60 my Europ Senior Rail Card entitled me to.

The pointless waste accounted for nearly all of what I overspent, that week in Paris. My expenses came to $115.37, and the two-week average now stood at $108.34. It was hardly a tragedy, but I was infuriated at myself for the stupid lapse responsible for it, and sank into a foul mood for the afternoon's journey. The funk lasted until we were about an hour out of Paris, when it was interrupted by the small, mocking voice from somewhere inside me. It sounded remarkably like me:

"Marielle," it cooed softly, "don't you realize that Providence is *everything that happens to us* . . . !"

A scene on the Ghent canal, from a postcard purchased at the little shop in the foreground.

Navigating between disgrace and disaster

en route to Lille, France: June 21, 1991...

Other than my foul mood and the weather that matched, I recall little else of that Friday afternoon train ride through northern France. I was preoccupied with a deeper aggravation than the pique triggered by that train fare incident: the haste of my journey. I could easily have spent a week longer in Paris and still felt short-changed. But circumstances had crowded me out of it. Even heading for Lille, the most direct route to Belgium, was a compromise with an earlier intent to go by way of the coast.

If there had been an overriding journey image when I set out on this European summer, it was the carefree, footloose wanderer with no claim on his time or direction. I had, for two weeks, preserved the illusion ... lingering in Brittany, hitch-hiking to Paris – part of the way, at least – but then the overwhelming profusion of Parisian attractions had caught up with me, a richness of possibilities that words can't even contain. Time vanished and the carefree image along with it, and here I was: the typical agenda-bound tourist racing heedlessly to his next destination.

There was no way out of it, however. Not for the next few weeks, at any rate. The news of an Earthstewards Gathering in The Netherlands had pretty well settled it. That, and my need to reach Berlin by early July if I wanted to connect with old friends there. It meant a rush through the Lowlands and a fragmentary experience of places like Amsterdam and Ghent, locales worthy of whole weeks in their own right. Quite likely, as well, a derby dash across all of northern Germany. Carefree travel, indeed!

I shouldn't have really been surprised, though. Summer has its way of speeding up all of life, and it makes no difference how we would *choose* to have it. The imperative is as much beyond our will as the emotionally unstable torpor of wintertime and the sudden, predictably compelling sprouts that follow, a month or so into each new year. That we are creatures of self-motivation with reasoning capabilities has no great bearing at all on the equally sure proposition that we live our lives in the fundamental flow of natural cycle. How could it be otherwise? Every life form on the planet has evolved within the same natural order.

I would have had to abandon any sense of order at all, in my travels, if I were to evade the press of developing events. And even then, how is one to avoid the effect of 'what is happening' in the very moment? If the world in its entire ambience intensifies as summer progresses, there is simply no way to escape the push and pull of it. The only salvation, as I learned long ago, is to let go and roll with it, through all its craziness, like a downstream whitewater run on a raft.

I couldn't possibly pass up the Earthstewards Gathering, anyway. The timing and locale of it were impossibly provident – made to my order. I had been at the very first Earthstewards Gathering in California, in 1985. My affiliation, in fact, went back years before that ... before the organization had even found its formal identity in 1983. This opportunity to see it taking root in Europe, was a privileged gift, certainly worth the price of a fragmented journey. Even if I must do it as a gate-crashing outsider – for no one had invited me, and I wasn't at all sure I could manage to afford it.

The five-day Gathering was already underway, even as I hurtled along beneath overcast skies toward one last French host in the small border city of Lille. I intended to slice it both ways: to squeeze as much of Belgium into the weekend as I could, and try to reach Tegelen, Holland, by Monday afternoon.

It was raining when the train pulled into Lille, and I immediately called my host-intended, Eric, at the furniture store where he worked as a buyer. It would be an hour before he could pick me up. We arranged it for a bistro across from the station, where I could use the time to update my journal. The place was almost empty, allowing me a choice of tables – wet or dry. I picked a spot just inside the wide open front where I could be seen, a purchase of tea and croissant the price of my wait, along with an hour's worth of drafty wind. Right on schedule, a sedan double-parked and an energetic, clean-cut young fellow greeted me with that standardized affability of white-collar people everywhere. He grabbed my pack before I could, to heft it easily into the back seat.

Eric lived with his girlfriend, Marie, in a movie-modern apartment furnished in somewhat sterile up-scale taste, graced with the inevitable balcony – whose charm, however, was compromised by a view of the industrial side of town. In all, not a very relaxing environment and it was just as well that I could stay only a single night. But two things made the evening more memorable than it might otherwise have been: I happened to be Eric's very first GN houseguest; and I had arrived on the evening of the Summer-day Music Festival, a national observance only a few years established but already on its way to becoming a tradition. Everywhere in France, that evening, musicians of every kind were performing at free venues, in solo and in concert.

The rain was a bit of a damper on the event in Lille, but Eric took me to the town's recently refurbished opera house. It was opulence in miniature! There could not have been twenty rows of seats on the main floor, but the interior was decorated with the extravagance of a big city Met. Four banks of balconies, loges and box seats, and a magnificently ornate chandelier floating in dignity beneath a gathering of pastel cherubs. It was far more impressive than the evening's music, a performance of classics by an amateur group with more to be said for their energy than their style. We abandoned them, midway, for a drive through the town's older section and my first view of Flemish architecture with its step-like roof lines.

Back at the inglorious apartment, Marie had already prepared a four-course dinner but we had to wait the arrival of some friends driving out from Paris, who did not get there until an hour before midnight. And then we dined until one o'clock in the morning! Eric was the only one of the group who spoke any English at all, and I occupied myself, for the most part, with a recurrent fantasy that they were all talking gibberish and only pretending to understand each other. After all, wasn't I smiling along with them, and maintaining an attitude of interest?

I slept on a living room couch ... slept well into Saturday morning, but it made no difference since I couldn't use my rail pass before noon. Eric told me where I could find some cheap cassettes of French song – only $1.60 apiece – on my way to the station, and I shipped them home with the happy thought that long later I'd have the refreshing surprise of discovering what I actually bought, on that last day in France.

Saturday's train took me into Belgium toward a host I had called from Eric's, the previous evening. Being entirely on my own, on Europe's rail system, was still somewhat intimidating and I tried to hedge my risks. I figured I could define my route with a hop-scotch chain of hosts not too far apart. I'd go for those on a direct rail line and trust the fates to see me safely across the hops. Before the week was done, however, any illusions that I could maneuver myself clear of railroad chaos would be washed out.

A train change at Ghent gave me a three-hour layover – not time enough to see much, but I wasn't about to spend it sitting in the station ... not in this city whose charm is the stuff of legend. The scene outside the station, however, held no appeal – a drab section of closely-packed, uninspired structures. I wandered down a cross street, seeing nothing any different. But here were tracks, and up the street came a thing out of my past ... a trolley car! Shades of old San Francisco, where they used to rumble right past my home on McAllister Street.

It was worth riding just for old memories and so I hopped aboard, having no idea of where I was going, and let the conductor take what amounted to ninety-five cents from my open handful of coins. As if I'd said the magic word, I was taken to the colorful heart of Ghent – to a lovely canal bordered by a picturesque assortment of those step-facade buildings and a nearby market mall where I could taste the city's vitality. Its edibles, too. A street vendor's genuine Belgian waffle followed by marinated herring from a deli counter – not the proper epicure's combination, I suppose, but they were cheap and I could order by pointing. I also picked up a fine looking loaf of bread for my next host. The streetcar got me back in good time, and I was soon in Tielt, my host town, still savoring the taste of herring.

A phone call brought Kristien, a cheerful, vibrant woman driving an oversized blue van. She, and husband Geert, both of whom spoke excellent English, lived near enough for me to have walked, had I known where to go. Like Evelyne, these were hosts I had earlier contacted from London – of particular interest to me because the list told me that Geert shared my passion for the *I Ching*, that ancient oracle that had kept my journey alive when I fell sick, back in Scotland. He even had Dutch versions of several commentary texts that were favorites of mine.

Finding a companionate soul in this regard meant finding someone who also shared my sense of a rhythm, consciously acknowledged, by which life is most easily lived. For this is what the *I Ching* is essentially based on. We all ordinarily live in harmony with a daily rhythm and think nothing about it; and many of us are at least aware of some annual rhythmicity. But its elements are so commonplace that we give no thought to their deeper implications. One would hardly plant flowers in autumn, any more than start a project at midnight or go to bed with the rising sun (save those who foolishly work to such a schedule) – yet we never consider the pointlessness of other undertakings outside of their proper cyclic moment, or take advantage of the incredible boost of natural energy available to endeavors properly timed.

Geert had been a social worker until they started a business distributing health products, now eight years old and thriving. They lived and worked in a brand new house, and the room they put me in was stocked with herbals, cosmetics and homeopathic remedies – safely shelved, there, from the probing curiosity of three small children. Dinner that night was a simple but filling vegetable loaf, along with cheeses and breads, and we talked late into the night about the world and its many inner fascinations.

I wanted, also, to sample the old city of Bruges, and took a side-trip on Sunday. But aside from a museum with the craft of a local artist named Brangwyn, who had worked beautifully with design and natural materials, it didn't have the same impact on me as Ghent. It could also, however, have been a first touch of continental overload, for I was once again moving too fast and trying to see too much.

During Saturday's layover at Ghent, I had asked about the rail routing from there to Tegelen, and I had only to get the 9:30 Monday morning train from Tielt in order to reach the Earthstewards Gathering that afternoon. Kristien fed me a great breakfast and I was at the station a good twenty minutes before train time, everything smoothly in place for an easy, uncomplicated departure. Until I had the bright idea – with "Murphy" written all over it, had I paused to think about it – of buying the ticket for the full journey right here instead of getting it in Ghent, where the details had been laid out for me.

Tegelen, Holland, is situated north of Maastricht, above that toe of The Netherlands that sticks down into Belgium like a woodworker's joint, locking the pair of them together against the close-by border of Germany. The routing I had been given at Ghent went all the way east through Belgium before swinging up, at Liege, toward Maastricht.

But now, the ticket man in Tielt had to figure it all out for himself, and he took an entirely different approach, attempting to route me north before heading east. That, at least, was his intent; what he actually did was confuse himself, fumbling through one book and then another, while people on both sides of the counter were distracting him with other concerns, so that he continually lost track of where he was.

Train time edged closer, and I could see he was getting nowhere. I tried to urge him back to my original routing, but he wouldn't let go of his own.

Five minutes to go, and he was still flipping pages. He turned to ask someone else, then, and feverishly began all over – calculating, now, the route I had asked for to begin with.

People were crowding the counter, now, for passage on the arriving train . . . and suddenly it was pulling up to the platform, the bell tolling its urgency to get underway again – but he was still calculating! The fellow assisting him assured me the train wouldn't leave without me, though nobody made any effort to hold it. I had an all but irresistible urge to bolt for the train and take my chances with the conductor.

Finally, with as much ticket in hand as I could get – he couldn't book me, he said, beyond Maastricht – I went racing out the station door (as fast as one can race, with twenty-five pounds on his back), only to see the train door shutting in my face! Casting innocence and dignity to the wind, I sent up a frantic holler, with all the vocal energy I could raise . . . and the door yawned open again.

In Ghent, my composure somewhat regained, I had time to change coinage and lay in some food for the journey. At a sandwich bar, a sign said "English spoken," so I asked for a cheese and tomato sandwich with mustard only. When I opened it on the train, I discovered I had cheese, ham, and hard-boiled egg with pickle and onion – no mustard. But there were more important concerns, by then, than my taste buds.

The train was a half-hour late leaving Ghent, and I was worried that I might miss the connection I had to make at Maastricht. But we never even made it to Maastricht. At Liege, as I sat in the coach with my food and half my gear spread out, I suddenly realized I was the only one left on the train. And it wasn't going anywhere. Horrified, I hastily packed everything up, just about the time a conductor came through and tried to tell me something. His efforts became antic and then frantic, before he finally burst through the language barrier with, "End. End. Ozzer train come."

It was a full hour, however, before another train came along on the northbound track. I boarded without bothering to discover that it was an express, which I only learned when we roared right on through Maastricht – my intended transfer point. What now? I could hardly expect it to make a stop at the small town of Tegelen. Not to mention the fact that my ticket didn't even cover me any longer. But the real question was how far I'd have to ride this highball.

We rolled on through the flat countryside past one station after another, until finally, by some sweet grace, we were slowing for a stop. It was the junction town of Roermond, at the top of Holland's great toe and still south of my destination. I lost no time in getting off. Another train was loading passengers on the adjoining track, and a platform sign said Tegelen. Aware that I might lose it if I took the time to purchase a ticket, I threw propriety to the wind and just went on board. Nobody ever did ask to check my fare.

Finally at Tegelen, I wasn't sure of my next move. I was looking for a place called "de Voorde," but I didn't know if it was a village, an estate, a retreat center, or what. The stationmaster didn't speak a word of English. Some likely looking fellows just off the train spoke English, but they knew nothing. As I stood there wondering what next, along came a postal truck. The driver spoke no English, but he finally got what I was asking and motioned me into his truck and we took off. After no great distance at all, he pointed out a big old monastery structure, recently remodeled and gleaming in the late afternoon sun like a freshly washed babe. I told him he was an angel, knowing he couldn't understand, and headed up the front stairs.

It appeared, from the food being carted into a dining room, that I was just in time for dinner. But this Gathering was already two days underway, and I was not yet a part of it. I had to take care of whatever preliminaries were called for – very likely, some money to pay. I had worried about this, and had no idea what it would set me back. Similar events in the U.S. could go as high as $50 per day. I had usually gotten some concession, often by sleeping out in the open if there were camping areas, or sometimes just by pleading hardship and relying on the goodwill of a community that knew my contribution as newsletter editor. But that was in the States, where I was known to everyone. We'd had five years of Gatherings on the west coast and I was practically an original fixture.

Here, it was an entirely different ball game. The Earthstewards, now more than two thousand members strong, had finally a large enough

European contingent to begin doing Gatherings of its own: this was the first of what would probably become annual celebrations, parallel to those held in the States.

Earthstewards originated as a vehicle for self-empowerment in international citizen diplomacy. It was one of the earliest groups to establish home-to-home visits with Soviet citizens; and it pioneered the realization of a link between our Vietnam vets and those Soviets who had fought in Afghanistan. Rooting itself, now, directly in European soil was like coming into a birthright – a natural evolvement for the Earthstewards. But over here, I was simply a name in the staff box of a newsletter – and not even that, anymore, for I had vacated the post a full year before. So I didn't know what I'd have to face, as to cost. I only knew I had to be here.

At the registration desk I told them I had come for just the final two days and wanted the cheapest accommodation. And I asked if Danaan was anywhere around. Danaan Parry is the man who started Earthstewards, a big red-haired Irishman whose wonderful heart is even larger than his massive chest. Danaan and I went a long way back, and while I would hesitate to ask directly for his charitable interference in these dealings, I knew that any such hope would have to start from our connection.

They didn't know exactly where he was at the moment, but I could talk with Henke, who was handling the administration of the Gathering. Henke, as I already knew, was a prime mover of the European Earthstewards, and I had actually written to her long before I knew of the Gathering, to say I might eventually get to Holland, and wanted to meet her if I did – with the unspoken agenda of possibly finding a place of shelter for a night or two in Amsterdam. But her response had been a bit equivocal and I didn't look for any special favors from her now, so I passed by the suggestion and said I'd talk with her later.

At that juncture, one of the two at the desk suggested to the other that they get me settled somewhere so that I could eat dinner, and take care of the details later. They assigned me a space in a dorm room on the third floor, and on the way up I ran into Henke – who didn't know me, of course, but I recognized her from a picture that had been used in the newsletter – coming down the stairs with someone I instantly knew: Diane Gilman, one of the editors of the magazine, *In Context,* who whooped in surprise at seeing me and clasped me in a hug. She had been at my farewell party in Seattle, the prior summer. I introduced myself to Henke, then, and after a moment she remembered the letter and made the whole train of association with who I was and what I was doing in Europe. Her greeting nevertheless felt a bit cool. Henke is an imposing, energetic woman, but there is a Germanic reserve about her – or possibly it was my unexpected and somewhat unorthodox appearance.

Awhile later, after getting my gear off my back and cleaning up a bit for dinner, I passed by the registration desk on my way to the dining room and one of the heads there bobbed up to say, "Don't worry about the registration arrangements, Henke said she'd take care of it."

I nodded agreeably, not having the foggiest idea what was meant by that.

Thus did I enter another world for a span of very close to forty-eight hours. A kind of half-world that seemed to be taken out of time, for it was a world of sheltered seclusion, partly in the pattern of a return to stateside times, partly in the very real ambience of a reconstructed monastery, partly relaxing, partly exciting, partly agonizing – but definitely removed from the world of the traveler. I was fed, lodged, occupied and preoccupied in the assortment of small and large group activities that take place at such functions. Hardly the least of my preoccupations was what this was all going to finally cost me. And close upon it, whether I might find some easy way of getting from here to Amsterdam. Indeed, as the time grew progressively shorter, my feelers went out for whatever solution to that puzzle should present itself. But meanwhile, I was taking my pleasures – and my lumps – as I found them.

At dinner, I quickly spotted the few other Americans I knew: Robert and Diane, who jointly published *In Context;* Danaan, of course, who welcomed me with a great bear hug; and a California Earthsteward named Nancy, whom I recalled from earlier Gatherings. Seated near her was a rather attractive blond woman from the Seattle area named Roberta, a recent Earthstewards recruit with perpetually smiling eyes, whom I hadn't met before. The rest, perhaps thirty or forty others, were from various parts of Europe, mainly Scandinavia and this west-central region. Most of them spoke English fairly well and I was very easily at home among them, sharing tales of my journey.

On Tuesday, the accumulated tensions of two-and-a-half road weeks since my departure from England transformed into total physical exhaustion. I felt as useless that morning as a popped balloon. Sometimes when this happens, I become acutely, irrationally sensitive to my social environment, picking up slights where they never were, indulging in random bits of paranoia. I couldn't figure out, this day, why Roberta was avoiding me after seeming so responsive the evening before. Then there was Henke. I told her I wanted to find a ride to Amsterdam after the Gathering, knowing that she'd be driving there, herself. I made no headway at all, even seemed to put her off by my approach, and I assumed she was displeased with me for some reason.

After lunch I abandoned the group activity and went to cultivate my worms out by the wall bordering the west side of the grounds, where I could be quietly alone with the placid Maas River, a few hundred yards away, watching the small open-deck boat that ferried three or four vehicles at a time, along with foot traffic, back and forth, back and forth ... At least there were no new threats to my well-being there, and nobody to blame anything on. From the shallow rise on which de Voorde stood, the Lowland plain stretched endless across Holland toward the dipping sun, and it was as peaceful a spot for regeneration as one could ask.

Maybe I drifted off to sleep there. At any rate, I was suddenly aware that dinner was already underway, and then I felt cheated because no more salmon steak was left when I reached the table. I accepted my fate like gritty dirt, appropriate to the sort of the day I was having. But then someone else came in even later than I, after the food had been removed, and it catalyzed my anger. I strode righteously into the kitchen and filled a plate for her – asking permission of no one. The release felt good.

By evening-time I was beginning to pull out of my funk and the world around me lightened up. A fellow named Heeren, from Amsterdam, said that if nothing else should develop for me he'd be driving as far as Utrecht, which was most of the way. Then I joined a full-group exercise in which we each put our name into a passing hat. The hat went around again, and everyone pulled one name from it. We were informed, now, that each of us was an 'angel' for the 'mortal' whose name we held. Nothing was required of us, except that for the remainder of the Gathering time we send that person good energy. But we were not to reveal ourselves. Naturally, each of us immediately scanned the circle to find our 'mortal' – and, as instantly, tried to avoid being trapped by the gaze. The circle broke up in laughter.

Despite the lift in spirits, I was half-decided on an early Wednesday departure as I turned in that night, instead of remaining for the rest of the activities and the mid-afternoon closure that was scheduled. Whether legitimate or not, when my rejection buttons get pushed a streak of defensive independence rises in me. I could easily walk to the rail station and take care of my own journey to Amsterdam. I might even get by the front desk before anyone was on duty there . . . and avoid the other Big Question!

But I awakened to the patter of dripping rain in the morning, and my rebellious ardor was somewhat dampened. I decided to hang in for awhile – through breakfast, at least – and pulled the blankets over my head to avoid the day awhile longer.

At breakfast, Danaan, making the closing-day announcements, plugged my quest for a ride to Amsterdam. That might help, I thought. He also had another personal note: a sweet old white-bearded gent with dancing eyes wanted to announce his engagement to a young woman hardly half his age who had come to the Gathering with him. I thought that was just lovely, and after breakfast was done I made a point of presenting my congratulations – and envy. His name was Hans, and he told me that he had been wanting to know more about me, too. So we spent a half hour talking with each other. He was from a suburb of Amsterdam – and of course, I asked The Question, but he told me he had a packed car or he'd have already offered to take me.

Bit by bit, I whiled the morning away, finding one or another reason to stay a little longer, until it was already lunchtime. Roberta was congenial once more. Rides were being offered – though none to Amsterdam. I had Danaan to thank for that. He had ended his plug for me with, " . . . or anywhere else. Irv goes where the rides go." Other pleasant bits of conversation were cropping up, here and there, as folks came by for some closure with me. I made sure that Heeren was still in the vicinity, realizing I'd probably end up riding with him after all, to Utrecht. And periodically, I wondered whether I could somehow escape the final reckoning, which was sure to be the ruin of my budget. Strange that no one had approached me about it. Was it possible – that cryptic remark about Henke "taking care of it" – that she had actually covered me?

It was worth the wait, I realized in the end, just to be in the Gathering's closing exercise: we formed a single long line that doubled back on itself, so that each one of us could face everyone else, pausing for a moment to gaze directly into each pair of eyes passing, one-on-one (or is that two on two?), and share a blessing . . . the line moving slowly, slowly along. For all its simplicity, I think it is one of the most powerful exercises ever devised.

So here I am, down to the crux of it. The day has arrived at four o'clock, the Gathering's final hour. Danaan has already left to catch a flight. Time only for one more round of tea and cake, and the very-last-minute stuff to be said, before we scatter to the compass points.

Roberta wants me to be sure and write when I get settled in Greece. She'd like to travel again, one of these days.

"You mean . . . a visit?" I regard her with a wish-I-could-believe-it look.

"Oh, who knows," her eyes still registering that vague smile.

Hans winks at me from across the room.

A charming woman whose name I never did get is suddenly there asking how I can just "let whatever happens" decide my course for me. Danaan's exaggeration, again. Just as I begin to explain it, Heeren pushes in to say that he's awfully sorry, but he's staying for another night – *there is no ride to Utrecht!*

In my first flush of reaction (after an idiotic burst of laughter, at the irony of Heeren's timing), I wildly start looking around for whoever, at this late moment, I might yet ask for a ride – and then I get the full impact of the message: GIVE IT UP. Just let go of it.

The reality of the moment was that it was quite late, and I knew I had to leave immediately. I popped up from my cushion like a piece of burnt toast, said goodbye to nobody, and headed for the hallway where I'd left my shoes and baggage. I dragged it all toward the front porch, boldly past the registration desk, suddenly resolved that I was going to get out of there without hassling the question of money still due. In the splash of Heeren's cold water, I had been thrown back on my survival instincts.

As I sat outside pulling my shoes on, Hans came by to say that he was leaving – and right away caught the drift, in my attitude I suppose, that I had no ride at all. His question about it seemed academic, since he'd already told me he had no room for me. But seeing, now, that I was about to set out on foot, he started figuring how he could make room for me!

It was accomplished in a few minutes, by shifting some baggage to a second car in the party and squeezing his three passengers all into the rear seat, so that I could ride with him in the front.

Meanwhile, in the very midst of these arrangements, Henke had come out to sit on the front porch and watch the whole business in progress. She just sat there, quietly watching as we shifted baggage and people, with no discernable expression on her face. But I, of course, *knew.* In my mind's guilt, she was sitting there wondering whether, or how, to brace me about my unpaid debt. I couldn't look at her directly; I was in a miserable state of ambivalence about what to do.

We were down to the very end of delay, Hans at the wheel ready to leave, and I could hardly avoid some sort of goodbye to Henke, a gesture of appreciation – but for exactly what? And in what terms? How could I omit some expression of gratitude, if she had somehow covered me for the cost? But how could I reveal that assumption if she hadn't?

In cowardly confusion, I hugged her in a silent farewell. As I pulled back from it, she had an odd half-smile that gave me no clear meaning at all. The *Mona Lisa* was an open book, by contrast! It was a completely agonizing moment – and I lost it . . . I broke. Out came a stupid, all-purpose remark that really said nothing at all.

"Let me know," I mumbled weakly, "if you need anything from me."

She looked at me in genuine puzzlement, and I fumbled some further words about money perhaps still due, at which she shook her head in complete dismissal of the whole thing. "Oh, I don't handle that They take care of all those matters inside, at the desk."

No clearer on anything, now, than I was before, but having lodged my foot in the doorway to disaster, I realized I had to follow through . . . and go inside again. I yelled to Hans, waiting patiently in the car, that I'd just be another moment.

Inside, I tried to register a casual air as I asked the freighted question. The reply came back with a cheerful smile. "Nope, you're all clear, Irv . . . unless you know of anything still unpaid."

Well, I really didn't. I only knew that I hadn't paid anything myself. And in this crucial moment, with Henke still out on the porch and Hans waiting in the car, I decided it was better to leave this small detail out of the discussion.

When I finally got comfortable inside the car, though still dizzy from all that had transpired in the hardly twenty minutes since Heeren had tossed his bomb, I saw that Hans had apparently emptied a shirt pocket on the ledge above the dashboard. Sticking out from among the few cards was a small slip of paper with my name on it . . . *in my handwriting.* I pulled it out and looked inquisitively at Hans while he idled the motor at a red light.

He gave me a sly smile. "That's right," he said, his blue eyes doing their dance above that lovely white beard, "I'm your angel. Gotta take good care of my mortal."

I don't know, to this day, the whole story of what took place, there at de Voorde, and maybe I never will. All I can really be sure of is that my budget was out of the red, with a super-low figure of $51.50 for the week's costs, giving me a three-week average of $89.26. Where angelwork is concerned, it's often better to keep things just a little out of focus: the less you can explain, the more you can regard with wonder.

Amsterdam is made up of some 90 islands, with more than 300 bridges linking them, and this is a typical view of one.

Broken Dreams in Amsterdam

en route to Amsterdam: June 26, 1991...

The two-hour ride with my angel, Hans, and his companions across the flat face of that country known as The Nether Lands – for the fact that much of it is below sea level – turned out to be little more than a comforting bridge from one unnerving situation to another. By the time I arrived in Amsterdam, on a local train from Hans' suburban village of Muiden, it was 7:30 in the evening and I had no idea where I would stay the night. Compounding the problem I had let my pocket funds dwindle to practically nothing. In Dutch guilders, my cash on hand amounted to about $6.50.

Yet, to my amazement, I wasn't feeling edgy or desperate. This was my first arrival in a major European city in such uncertain circumstances and it surprised me with a rush of adrenalin ... I felt gloriously high as I left the railroad station and walked into an electric mix of inner city life: vendors, beggars, musicians, people moving at a jumbled pace, tumbling around and into one another – and bicycles, thousands of them. It could as well have been high noon from the carnival sense of action. But I knew it wasn't, and that I had better get busy on the telephone.

More than a dollar was slotted fruitlessly into phone calls before I fully realized that I had innocently picked the worst possible place and time for my "here I am" approach: an annual all-Europe meeting of Good Neighbors regional facilitators had just taken place here in Amsterdam, and every last local host had those visitors on their hands. None, at this point, could accommodate an ordinary traveler.

I turned to listings in the suburban area, starting with one in Haarlem who had been among those preliminary hosts that I earlier engaged and afterward canceled from London. She, too, had guests from the conference – two of them. But as we talked, she picked up the note of growing urgency in my voice – for it was now after eight p.m. – and finally decided she could somehow manage a third guest if I honestly didn't mind sleeping on the living room floor.

Getting out there took a train and bus fare, leaving me with just two dollars in ready funds. I had counted on finding a cash machine along the way, but no such luck. As I walked the last few blocks to her address in a pleasantly upscale apartment neighborhood, reflecting on how easy it had been to let my immediate solvency slide down to practically nothing, I was accosted by a pair of serious looking men in full-buttoned coats, who asked me darkly whether I was on my way to see a woman named Carty. I answered, with casual cheer, that I certainly was, and they braced me on either side, as an escort . . . like in a bad movie.

These were Carty's two guests, Georghe and Tom, having a bit of fun. Georghe, a chunky bear-like fellow with swept-back, greying hair and a twinkle in his eyes that he could hide at will, was from Romania and told me later that he was astounded by my breezy response to their intentionally menacing approach. Such inquisitorial intrusions back home, he said, were no laughing matter. Tom, whose own silvery hair had long ago abandoned the crest of his head for the creases of his countenance, lived no farther away than Amsterdam, but he and Carty had a personal relationship and regularly visited with one another. They were a surprising couple – he almost twice her age. But his vitality was such that a mere age comparison was meaningless.

Carty, herself, was a study in burnt orange: her short cut hair, her lipstick, a soft impression of freckles and the tones she chose to wear. Her small, compact frame made an attractive package of it all. She was a nurse, sharing with her teen-age son, Ruben, an upper-floor high-rise unit with a commanding view that stretched – as only in Holland – to infinity's horizon; half of it over a private balcony, seen through floor-to-ceiling glass, and half from the walkway that went by her kitchen window. Below and all around, arrayed like one of those diorama tableaux that museums love to display, the busy-work of a semi-rural countryside: delivery wagons scurrying up narrow roads alongside meandering canals, the rich green pasturage of dairy farms, pocked here and there with lazy grazing livestock … and even a classic Dutch windmill or two.

My first concern, after a reasonably comfortable night's sleep on Carty's living room floor, was a replenishment of cash. And almost as important, a trip to the Amsterdam post office, for this was my first scheduled mail drop. Carty provided me with transit scrip so I could be sure of getting into town and I found the ever elusive cash machine there without any further trouble. Then the mail, a fat little batch that I refused to open until I could find a table, with service of tea and toast, while I relished each piece of it. Along with the personal mail and the packet of next-stage maps and host lists, sent by Marjory from London, I found my new Visa card with its $1200 limit – presumably the end of my cash hassles. Presumably.

The rest of that first full day in Amsterdam was spent in search of some music tapes. Not just "anything cheap," as on my last morning in France, but a search for some very specific tapes I had reason to hope I might find here – recordings that I'd been tracking for many months. Indeed, it had assumed the proportions of a quest, like my Scotland search for Jim Hall's sister in Hawick.

This quest, too, started in Seattle. Before I ever imagined I'd be going abroad I happened across an album recorded in the mid-'80s by an Amsterdam group calling itself the *Broken Dreams Orchestra*. It was a mix of unusually appealing vocals on a selection of old American pop standards from the 1930s and 1940s with a central theme of loneliness and heartbreak – slow-tempo, melancholy songs like: *It's the Talk of the Town, I Cover the Waterfront* and the title piece, *Boulevard of Broken Dreams.* They were fresh arrangements yet they captured, as few reprise efforts ever do, the mood and idiom of those earlier times, with wailing sax refrains and the hauntingly sad accent of several young Dutch vocalists. I was charmed and fascinated, and I wondered if there were any other recordings by them.

At the time, I wrote to the New Jersey distributor, who thought there had been other albums but none were available in the U.S. I was given the name of a London distributor. I checked it out while I was there, but they had only the album I already possessed. They gave me a phone number, however, for the group's bassist and co-leader, Gert-Jan Blom, in Amsterdam. It was an old number – two years old, they said, and now two and a half. Still, it was enough to go on, plus the outside chance that the old recordings might yet be found in some Amsterdam shop. But that hope quietly died in an afternoon of roving and asking. I was told the group had broken up several years ago – like an old dream, perhaps. The phone number I'd been given just kept ringing; and the directory provided no further information.

Back again at Carty's, it was my last evening to get to know Georghe a bit better. He'd be returning on Friday to Timisoara, on Romania's west edge near the border of what was still called Yugoslavia. My intended routing from Budapest to Greece, through Yugoslavia, was looking riskier by the week, in the already simmering agony between Serbs and Muslims. The only travel-cheap alternative would be through Romania and Bulgaria, so I wanted to solidify this connection that had fallen into my lap by pure innocent magic. Georghe was Romania's GN coordinator, and he'd know all the hosts in the country.

He was wonderfully easy to know. He spoke English well and had a receptive attitude to everything under discussion, his bushy eyebrows rising with interest at each new idea. Tom and he kidded each other like they had been friends for years. But Georghe told me the situation in Romania, only a year earlier, had been so paranoid that he hadn't dared to let himself be known as a GN coordinator or host. GN travelers coming through were instructed to carry no lists with them. But that had all changed, he assured me, with the recent overthrow of Ceausescu and I'd have no problem going through the country. In fact, he insisted on a visit from me! I gave him a copy of my letter of introduction as a promise.

And then, after Georghe's departure, an unexpected blessing for a weary traveler. Carty was off to Amsterdam for the weekend with Tom – letting me remain there in the apartment entirely on my own. The time at de Voorde, earlier in the week, had taken the edge off my exhaustion, but the relaxation afforded by private quarters is a gift of the gods.

I spent most of Friday exploring Haarlem, an amazingly clean little town, riven and ribbed with canals just like its larger neighbor, Amsterdam. I found a museum devoted to one of my favorite Dutch painters, Frans Hals, located in the very building where the old master is thought by some to have passed his last years, when it was a home for the aged and indigent. Being somewhat 'aged and indigent' myself, I felt a sense of communion with the old fellow. Back at Carty's with some freshly purchased fish, I enjoyed the lately rare treat of cooking my own dinner.

That evening, trying Gert-Jan Blom's number again, I got a response. It was a voice in Dutch, of course, but no problem. Everyone in Holland, it seems, speaks English – but only if it is spoken to them, resulting in the odd effect of a language barrier that dissolves instantly with a word or two in English. It wasn't Gert-Jan Blom on the line, however. He no longer lived there, but I was given another number as a possibility. This one answered with a recorded message in Dutch; but the novel sound of a musical dog barking a tune in the background suggested that I had not lost the trail.

On Saturday, entirely enervated by the abundant luxury and this opportunity to live for awhile as if I actually lived somewhere, I didn't even take an intended trip to the nearby ocean beach. I spent the day answering mail. My sole interaction with the outside world was to secure a Monday host in Amsterdam proper so I'd be able to see more of the city and make a final effort to complete my musical quest – whatever could be done for it.

That evening, however, I got lucky. The melodious dog was re-placed by Gert-Jan Blom, himself, and we talked for a solid hour. He was the one responsible, he said, for those orchestrations that were such delicious echoes of my youth. He told me the entire history of the project, from its genesis in his fascination with America's Depression-era big bands, to the group's initial success in Amsterdam, to the annual *Festival of Broken Dreams* that they invented as a vehicle for taking their music on tour across Europe . . . to the final 1987 tour that made it all the way to Canada – though never into the States. And he com-miserated with me over the group's final dissolution. He was, himself, responsible for that, too. For Gert-Jan, the orchestra was a creative project, not a bid for commercial success; there were other things he wanted time to work on. I could easily relate to such priorities . . . though I wished he had only waited a few years.

The youth in his voice told me he had never lived in the times his music so richly evoked. Somehow, his sensitivity to the music itself had been sufficient for the re-creation of a mood and a reality long van-ished, and I found this incredible. For his part, Gert-Jan seemed im-pressed that anyone – especially of the generation that could recall 'the real thing' – should be so moved by his work as to undertake such a search for it.

There had been forty pieces in their repertoire. The album I al-ready had was the second of four, and Gert-Jan felt the group had improved for each session. But he had no idea where any of those albums might be found. Our conversation went so well, however, that he offered to make me tapes from his own copies if I would come by to get them. My cup was not only full, it was splashing all over the place! I might cautiously have been concerned about the cost, I guess – he had said earlier that someone from Texas actually offered him fifty dollars for one of the unobtainable tapes. But the flow of our talk was so mellow that I didn't want to bring anything that crass into it.

On Monday, as rested as I could ever hope to be, I lingered long enough for a farewell breakfast with Carty, took the short trip to Amsterdam and found my way to the well-hidden third-floor apart-ment of my next host, Hennie. She had tea and cake waiting for me, and the enthusiastic welcome of GN people everywhere. I saw at once, from the sort of books that filled every corner of her quarters, that Hennie had scholarly inclinations, though she worked as a bookkeeper. Just like Marielle in Paris, I thought. But Hennie had a much more upbeat view of life, and her laughter rippled as easily as her words. We had an hour's worth of getting to know each other before I hastened away to the other side of town to find Gert-Jan Blom's residence.

He lived in a walk-up second-floor flat with huge rooms and high ceilings, a marvelous space for study and work – and just the rudiments of domestic life, for he lived alone. As I expected, he was only half my age, tall and rangy like a basketball player and sparking with the same warm enthusiasm about my having contacted him as he'd shown on the telephone. In fact, we simply resumed our discussion of the earlier evening and continued it for two further hours. But this time it was on a more personal plane. He told me of a ruptured love affair with one of the vocalists, and how the circumstances around it had made the heart-break music a living reality for him at the very time the recordings were being made. He'd actually wept, he said, while some of those pieces were being recorded – and I could hardly help wondering if I had somehow picked up this subtlety in the music when I first heard it.

Then he gladdened my heart by refusing to take a single guilder for the tapes he had made for me. I had already come to terms with the likelihood of a price on them, and perhaps more than I could afford. I wanted this music! I walked the couple miles back to Hennie's apartment in a cloud of contentment, successful in this second quest beyond all my hopes . . . and made a point of giving $1.50 to the first down-and-outer who crossed my path, just to keep myself square with the gods.

That evening, just after dark and after Hennie had served world-class pancakes stuffed with bacon, such as none I had ever eaten in my life, she took me on a stroll of the canal paths. Cobbled walkways softly lit by the gentle yellow glow of street lamps took us along the quiet line of boats, of every size and vintage, bobbing an easy rhythm on the dark waters – the rising curvature of their uniquely Dutch hulls exquisitely suggestive of wooden shoes. Here and there, a waterside cafe, outdoor tables with couples talking softly as if the very quiet of such a setting had awed them into hushed respect.

These water-split avenues offer a sheltering effect at the same time as they feel expansive – a curious and unlikely blend of contraries. Leafy trees contribute to the effect, as does the seamless backdrop of Flemish architecture on either side. There is not a pause of space between these quaint old buildings. They lean tipsily forward, like sodden drinking companions playing loose with gravity, to provide hoisting clearance for the jibs that jut out from every high facade.

Up one of these shadowed avenues, Hennie took me by the Anne Frank house – now such a peaceful setting that it was hard to believe the desperate situation played out here a half-century ago, when a young girl was dragged from her attic seclusion of many months to become a martyr in the struggle with bigotry – a cause hardly less volatile today than it was then. The house has been turned into a museum. It was after hours; but the sight of a cash register inside this shrine seemed to tarnish it. I saw in that image a symbol of the subtle connection that has always existed between economics and bigotry.

I'd had the forethought while at Carty's, to arrange for my next on-the-road host in the border town of Oldenzaal. It practically reached out from the map and grabbed me – a rare gap of unfinished motorway on the high-speed route to Berlin, promising several miles of hitchhiker-friendly open roadway. Carty's Amsterdam friend, Tom, intrigued by my style of travel, said he'd pay my train fare to Oldenzaal if he could ride along with me.

Tom was a sweet old soul – though he'd have had some suitably acid reply if anyone ever said it within his earshot. He took his fold-up bicycle for the day's outing, to pedal back home afterward. He was in pretty good shape for seventy-odd years – an interesting counterpoint to his almost saintly features. That bearded visage was unforgettable . . . yet strangely familiar at the same time. I had seen it a score of times or more, on one or another Renaissance canvas – a Titian, or a Raphael perhaps. Tom would be that old one standing off to the side, a sheet draping his shoulders, his brow arched in wrinkles, his soft, world-weary eyes imploring the heavens for a sign of grace.

But off the canvas he was sharp and vital, ribald in his humor and trenchant in some of his opinions. He gave some trumped-up excuse for his surge of generosity, and then when I tried to pay my own way he stopped my protestations cold with a single piercing question.

"How is it, Man, that you talk so much about the gifts of Providence, and then you refuse them when they come along?"

He was a retired teacher of languages and had no problem with English, except for that insistent affectation of "Man," which figured in every other sentence. A remnant of the 1960s hip travel crowd, I suppose, it reflected his unquenchable affinity for younger people, which was demonstrated in another way before our rail journey was done. Without half trying, he somehow engaged a college co-ed across the aisle from us in easy conversation. I could hardly help but recall my own ineffectuality with `the lady from Huntly,' of an earlier train ride.

We had a two-hour layover in the town of Hengelo, hardly six miles from Oldenzaal. We could have walked as easily as waiting, but the day had gotten hot, so we strolled instead to a charmingly peaceful shaded park – which turned out to be a cemetery. But it afforded us a quiet bench in the cool of trees and may have suggested the turn of our conversation, for Tom wanted to talk about life and death and the absurd belief "of some people," as he pointedly put it, in reincarnation. He was a rationalist, through and through, and a potent debater. I was hard put to justify some of my irrationalities, and found myself trapped more than once in our hour's talk. But then I should not have taken `de bait' to debate with a rationalist, in the first place. It was like diving in the water to settle a dispute with an octopus.

I made my stand on the equivalence of beliefs. "The pure fact of it is that we know nothing, right? We simply *choose to believe* one thing or the other."

"That is certainly a fact, Man. But why should you choose to believe the thing which goes against everything your senses tell you?"

"Doesn't it occur to you, Tom, that it might be the other way around: that we translate sense perceptions according to the very way that our beliefs tell us to?"

"And that, Man, is exactly why you have to be careful about what you're going to believe!"

"Well, hey, belief isn't something I just decide to throw over me, like a coat. It comes in the slow accretion of experience. It's not even an IT ... a belief doesn't stand alone, it's part of a whole structure that involves all sides of my life and being."

"Still, you have to have a gate somewhere, where the line is drawn at what you leave in, and what stays out."

"Easier said than done, my friend. If you live with a truly open mind, the gate has no firm lock."

"Not true, Man. That is loose thinking, not an open mind."

He was cutting me to shreds. I had to get him looking at his own blind spots, not at mine. "Okay, Tom, okay. Admittedly, I keep my mind a little loose. I don't like a world limited by hard reality. My reality has soft edges and it lets me live in a lot more freedom by trusting what happens. Your insistent realism confines your adventurous spirit ... it serves you like a pair of leg irons."

His unusually long pause at that suggested I may have touched home – though I had exaggerated a bit. I'd be hard put to match Tom's adventurous instincts in some respects – his ease at making conversation with coeds, to name just one! But he proved perfectly capable of meeting my metaphor, and one-upping me in the process.

"A point, Man, a point. But I can get farther walking in leg irons than on slippery banana peels."

On the morning of July 4th – not a holiday in these parts – I took to the open road again, after spending just a night in Oldenzaal with Rob and Anneke, a pair of teachers. One night was all that any of us could spare. I had only a few days, myself, to reach Berlin, and they were ready to leave for Bavaria on a week-long bicycling vacation with their children. The day was about as nice as July can offer: crystal blue skies, as I set out on foot along the highway to reach the stretch that had arterial stop signs. It was a half-hour walk, but once there I had my ride in ten minutes with a very young woman in a tattered, fully-packed old van. Ashka was her name, Polish, and she was going all the way to Lodz, in her homeland.

A slight, waif-like creature whose solemn, pale features seemed to contradict her evident youth, Ashka neither smiled nor talked much, though her English was quite good. It required first a border stop to change money and then a rest stop where we shared our various store-bought foods in a makeshift lunch, for me to learn that she had come from London and a possibly finished marriage there – she wasn't sure, yet, how it would turn out. She had taken this opportunity of delivering someone's goods, for a return to Poland where she could be alone for awhile and sort things out.

She was entirely wrapped up in her problems; but there was an elfin sense of humor and a charming laugh when these qualities managed to surface. I could certainly have gone the distance to Berlin with her, and would have enjoyed it; but I had one more agenda item far short of Berlin – a side-trip from Hannover. Just a modest detour, I thought, but of such are life's surprises made.

Shortly after noon, Ashka dropped me at a service area outside of Hannover and I set off from there on foot toward town. A local bus came by and I clambered aboard, asking a single-word question . . . "Centrum?" The driver nodded, giving me a transfer and taking what he needed from my handful of coins. Where I was to transfer was a complete mystery that only deepened as we went on . . . and on. It was one residential section after another, looking for all the world like California suburbia. There were no cues from anything along the way.

Two elderly men across from me, one rather dour-looking, the other sporting a jaunty beret and infinitely lighter, were conversing in German. Presently, and quite unexpectedly, the cheerful one looked over and asked in perfectly good English about the lightweight sleeping-bag strapped to my pack. The ensuing conversation lasted all the way to a transit nexus, where everyone had to leave the bus. I knew, by now, this man with the beret and the easy manner was my angel. He guided me into a subway station and pointed me to the line that would take me right to the railway depot.

I emerged from the underground in the heart of town, to the rousing music of a big oompah-organ on wheels – marching music, so characteristically German that it seemed like a welcoming scenario, scripted for my arrival. I wanted to linger, but the morning was moving along and I had to reach a place called Steyerburg, 35 miles to the northwest. One of the Earthstewards at the Gathering had invited me to visit what may well be the largest collective community in Germany, a group of a hundred people who had been living together for five years. But to reach the tiny village called for three stages of transit: a train ride, a country bus, and then a further lift by someone I'd have to phone at the other end. By the time I learned all this at the ticket counter, I was having second thoughts. But Ashka was miles gone, and here I was.

I got the right train, to Nienburg, but missed the bus connection there in the confusion of trying to figure the German station pattern. I actually watched the bus as it boarded passengers and pulled out, without me – never realizing it was the one I wanted. Or that it was the last bus for the day. So much for trust versus banana peels.

Nienburg is smalltown Germany and I got nothing but blank stares when I tried to ask questions in English. I called the number I had for Steyerburg – after twenty minutes of fiddling with the telephone – and got someone who could understand me. He gave me directions for an alternative bus route, with a promise that I would be met at the other end of the line.

It turned out, naturally, after a half hour of bouncing through the countryside, that there was some ambiguity about where to get off the bus – and I found no one waiting where I alighted except three drunks who tried to entice me into their circle. I declined, of course, but could not make myself understood and finally had to walk away, to their cries of abandonment. I walked to find a telephone. Going into a place that looked vaguely like a country post office, I almost collided with a bearded young fellow ... who looked at me in sudden, questioning recognition, and said he hadn't seen me get off the bus. Hey, hey – score one for trust!

Christoph, my Earthsteward connection, was on hand when we reached Steyerburg, and obviously surprised that I had actually come on his invitation. But he recovered nicely, and secured for me a nearby attic sleeping-space before taking me on a grand tour. I was quite amazed at what they had put together here. Once, long ago, it had been a residential camp for workers in a nearby Nazi munitions factory. Several dozen frame and brick structures at the heart of it were sufficiently intact for residence when the group took over, and others were reconditioned as more joined. A large, multi-level central building became their all-purpose community center – for dining, offices, stores, a children's school and an assortment of meditation rooms reflecting the multiplicity of spiritual paths within the group. Out beyond the central complex was extensive open land for future development, now being used for perma-culture crops and recreation.

I had seen large collective groups before, like the Rajneeshpuram community in Oregon, but the singularity of this one was its freedom from ideological conformity. A full third of the group consisted of small children, and their welfare appeared to be the closest thing to a central focus. Christoph spoke of a steady stream of people seeking to join. But the community's prime concern, for now, was to achieve stability and cohesion before any further growth.

I was underway again the next day, after an extravagant breakfast put together by Christoph's friend, Katarina, who also drove me back to Nienburg on the rail line. But I saw no reason for going back into Hannover. It would simply delay the rest of my journey to Berlin, when the open road was the more direct route. I could be right on the autobahn in one easy ride (two, as it happened). In my haste, however, there was one small detail I disregarded: getting a sufficiency of cash.

It seemed unnecessary. I was sure I'd be in Berlin by mid-afternoon – only 140 miles, an easy shot on a major freeway. But early or late, it should make no difference. I had friends in Berlin and I'd be under no pressure for immediate funds. If anything went wrong . . . well, I had about eleven dollars in deutschemarks in my pocket, enough for almost any emergency. The week had gone well, thanks to Carty, and to Tom's assist on rail fare. It cashed-out at $85.04, notching my average down another full dollar, to $88.20 per week.

Maybe it had gone a little too well. The time to be wary is when you're most sure of things. After all, it was Friday . . . with banks about to close for the weekend. And the open road is a great joker.

This burned-out church, the Kaiser Wilhelm Gedachtnis, remains as an everlasting WWII memorial, in the very heart of Berlin.

The banana peel route to Berlin

outside Hannover, Germany: July 5, 1991...

I found the perfect spot for a freeway hitch – a final red stoplight, slowing the traffic as it entered the autobahn. They all had to pause, before going by my BERLIN sign. And they did. For almost an hour, until one pulled up for me. He wasn't headed for Berlin, however. In the tangle of our efforts to communicate, I finally made out that he was going to Magdeburg, about forty miles beyond the old East boundary – which was forty miles away itself. Balancing for only a moment on my hesitancy about the eastern zone, I quickly gave in. I was tired of watching that endless stream of cars go by. After all, Magdeburg was just off the autobahn; it wouldn't take me off course. I got in, and we sped off.

As we put fragments of conversation together, a word here and a flash there, I learned my driver was a displaced Afghan. His name was Conrad, and he had married an East German woman two years ago and come to live with her in Leipzig. He drove this commute every week, 140 miles each way to a factory job in Hannover, and considered himself lucky for having it, though he had been schooled as an economist.

Leipzig! I suddenly realized he was going on through Magdeburg, and another sixty miles south in the old East territory, to a prominent city – an old center of German culture. A chance, and possibly the only one I'd have, to experience the fullness of that recently socialist German world – if I dared. I hadn't even given a thought to doing anything like that, but it would provide a much better glimpse of what East Germany had been like than the limelight area near the Wall. The Good Neighbors list was handy in my pack, and I quickly checked. Sure enough, Leipzig was on it with more than a dozen host possibilities.

It was that crazy sort of idea that once given a toe-hold shoves every caution out of mind. I had put East Europe off limits right from the start. The prospect was still scary, fraught with more risk than I wanted. Somehow, with angel rescues and pure dumb luck, nothing had gone wrong for me – but how far could I push it, this innocence? Conrad might make it there before the banks close, but . . . what if he doesn't? Can I even use my Visa card in the old East? But none of these uncertainties could dislodge the adventurous impulse – not even the persistent specter of Tom chuckling, in the back of my head.

Halfway to Magdeburg we crossed the invisible line into the former territory of East Germany. Remnants of fencing and guard towers were still there, a year since the old order had collapsed, but no other indication of a different kind of country. Not until I glimpsed the looming, dark huddle of ancient Magdeburg, where we turned off the autobahn. We zoomed through an edge of the city on a bypass – brooding, grey stone walls of immense size, but few people in view and even less auto traffic. Streets were rutted, their shoulders overgrown by weeds and ragamuffin shrubs long ago lost to any gardener's attention. The contrast with Hannover was immense, the plunge so sudden – notwithstanding our eighty mile passage – as to jolt the senses.

I had a great urge to be let off, right there – partly in a last flash of diffuse insecurity over what I was letting myself in for, aware that I could easily get back to the autobahn. But partly from an uncontainable desire to see more of this fortress-like, Medieval city – more than our swift detour would allow. I tried, in fact, to convey to Conrad that I needed to find a bank, and that Magdeburg might be my last chance.

But it was too complex for our level of communication. His swarthy face broke into a grin as he nodded agreeably and continued on through.

On we went, along a two-lane highway with a fair amount of traffic, turning this way and that, as roads once did, through villages that looked – for all of my own world – like the towns in border Mexico: dusty, nondescript shacks leaning against shabby, nondescript buildings, with unkempt foliage growing everywhere. Barren, dreary living conditions. Yet, with a certain coarse charm, just as one finds in rural Mexico. The honest truth below the facade of modern urbanity. All the artifice, the sterile hygienic preoccupations of the western world, chrome-plate and plastic, finished concrete and tidy landscaping – all of it suddenly gone, flipped over in a time warp. Startling, ugly . . . but somehow, in its realness, almost refreshing.

We had to stop for gas – benzene, Conrad said. While we waited ten minutes in line, I bought a liter of apple juice, just over a quart, paying fifty-eight cents. But the delay was nothing compared to an hour-long roadblock farther along our way, which wiped out any last hope that I would find a bank open in Leipzig. I expected to see the remains of some horrid auto accident when the line started moving again, but we had simply been stalled for road work. An hour-long traffic tie-up for roadwork!

It was five o'clock when we reached Leipzig, and I asked Conrad to drop me at the rail station. Before anything else, I had to get a ticket to Berlin. And this evening's departure schedule, in case my host list should fail me.

But something more critical failed me at the ticket counter. If I hadn't bought the apple juice, I would have had enough for the fare.

All was not yet lost. I spotted an exchange booth in the station, still open, even though it was supposed to close at 5:00 – *geschlossen,* one of the first German words I picked up. But they couldn't deal with my Visa card. I was down to the last resource I had – the travelers checks . . . American Express . . . don't let me down!

It was the magic name that unlocked the cash box. But I just about blew it, at this point. I was so cautious about using travelers checks, my ultimate bottom line – my ticket home, if it came to that, or the reserve for next winter's settlement – that I cashed a single £10 check ... fourteen extravagant dollars. I immediately purchased the ticket to Berlin and stashed it safely away.

The next hurdle was the telephone – which, as I had already come to learn, is a game of wits in Europe, no two locales using the same sort of device. The range and diversity of their invention is marvelous to behold. These in Leipzig – once I found one in working condition – called for the coin to be deposited before the mechanism actually required it. At some point midway in the dialing the coin box sucks it in, and it had better be there in readiness. I got it by trial and error.

Not all the hosts on my list even had their own phone. But the first one I reached said I could come, and they lived fairly near the station. I was elated; but I told them I'd be awhile getting there. Realizing the economic situation of these hosts, I felt I should get some dinner for myself before I went, and possibly a loaf of bread for them. Besides, I was aching to have a footwalk look at this city and didn't want to wait.

When Conrad had pulled into the heart of the city, it seemed as lively as any other. But that impression quickly dissolved as I walked away from the depot. The few shop windows along my way displayed very little in their windows. Many were entirely bare, with backdrop curtains veiling the interior. Food stores had two or three items massed in a repetitive, uninspired display, often dusty as if they had been there for weeks. Those few shops I could peer into revealed a simple countertop layout with a thin and limited selection on the back-shelves. But most were already closed, even though it was not yet six p.m. Hardly any people walked the streets.

Aside from this lack of visible life, however, and the cheerless absence of decor, the buildings presented a massive, multi-story stone facade, characteristically European, like a faded old photograph from the past. It was as if I had stepped into an old film of Europe Before The Great War – allowing for the deterioration of time, for the facades were in need of a good cleaning. Perhaps even re-surfacing. But it was a patina of age, which only served to enhance the elsewhen-in-time effect.

I came at last to an open area created by the intersection of several streets, with quiet signs of vitality including a sidewalk cafe. I almost passed it by from pure habit, streetside dining being out of my budget range. But with choice so scarce here – and this being, after all, a tidepool economic area – I took a chance on it. I picked the least expensive á la carte entree, some kind of ragout as near as I could tell.

It was a quite picturesque spot – an old market square, I guessed. I sat in the sun, almost in the shadow of a lovely old tower, twenty stories high I'm sure, capped by a verdigris cupola that rested on several tiers of arched portals in a circular colonnade. My admiration was torn from it by the aroma of the plate set before me, a mini-casserole sizzling fresh from the oven, with a dark mix of meat and mushrooms in a piquant sauce topped by a taffy-thick melt of white cheese. And I plunged into my most indulgent dining since Paris. With extras and a tip, it took almost half of my remaining cash-on-hand, about $5.40. But with a ticket to Berlin in my pocket and a place to stay for the night, I didn't let it worry me.

I found my evening's hosts, Jeno and Renate, in a second-floor apartment in one of the massive, colorless buildings. The street entry took me into a vaulted outer hallway, dark and gloomy. Upstairs, I knocked at a pair of doors towering to twice my height, and when Jeno opened it narrowly I once more had that feeling of slipping into an old film. A movie of intrigue and espionage, this one. He moved softly and spoke with a kind of hush that blended nicely with the darkened vestibule he led me through. It was only a crossway area with a fan-spread of closed doors leading to various rooms – yet, the size of a room in its own right. I followed him into a huge study or library that had been given over to Renate's use. She was bed-ridden with a broken hip, and I had a flash memory of watching Katherine Cornell play Elizabeth Barrett Browning, many years ago, in just such a stage setting. Indeed, the room was easily as large as a theater stage.

When I expressed my amazement at the sheer sense of space, Renate told me that the original apartment had been split to make two. To her, it was crowded! She also apologized for its run-down condition, though I assured her that anything wanting in that respect was more than offset by the sense of gracious living her home bespoke. These were not well-to-do people by any measure of their own culture. Jeno was an engineer, and Renate a teacher of English. But they had lived here all their married life, and she before – going back about thirty years. I slowly took in the room as she talked . . . a grand piano, even diminished by the room's size; shelves of books that climbed toward the high ceiling; a generous assortment of cushion-back chairs and lounges; drapes that might have been museum tapestries on the tall windows – there was no reason to seek life outside this home, which is the constant provocation of the tight space Americans have come to accept.

For space, in some peculiar way, is not just space – it is *time*. I could instantly feel, here, a sense of leisure imparted by the generous dimensions. Or perhaps a sense of life's proper pace. Just as one is moved to speak softly in a cavernous interior, from some deep inner quieting, so is it that one moves with an ease – *lives* with an ease – in a large contained space, time becoming a part of the experience and not just a measurement of it. When we cramped ourselves into mean little enclosures for the necessary sake of cost (in our world of affluence!) we lost that gift. This was surely the point at which we created the true ratrace: a small enclosure that encourages one to run. We wonder, today, why 'the good life' ever eludes us. We left it behind by gambling with space . . . and forfeiting the sense of leisure that once enriched our lives.

Jeno and Renate were in their early fifties and desperately afraid, now, for the rush of changes that were suddenly complicating their world. A shallow platitude or two, on my part, revealed my ignorance about it and Renate gave me a recent issue of *Time Magazine* with a cover article on the disillusion that had set in after the first year of German unification. I was up late, that evening, getting a fast education. The two Germanies, for so very long denied their natural linkage, could not seem to stabilize with each other. My hosts had lived their entire lives under a system of guaranteed security, a platform suddenly falling away, and they were already feeling left behind in the struggling tumble of a newly competitive world, the pressure for change having grown to where it couldn't possibly be relieved in any smooth, painless transition.

Nothing I could say to them would ease their anxiety. I tried to encourage them to take a positive approach – to start 'inventing' their future by dealing with realities of opportunity, the way an American learns to do. But my efforts came across, I'm sure, as mere insensitivity. They were trapped in the lifetime they had lived.

As was I! For in *their* home I was suddenly in my grandparents' simple world, as if I were truly a traveler in time. Yet, I didn't dare try to express my sense of that – of what they were about to lose – lest it compound their anxieties. To me, their private world was a vanished time; but they were still in it. No ... Jeno and Renate were already racing through time toward my present, a journey they would have to complete – for good or worse – before they'd be able to see their present world as I did.

In the morning, I had a chance to see the positive side of the changes. After sharing a typical European breakfast of rolls and cheeses, Jeno took me to a huge Saturday street market not many blocks from their home. Neophyte capitalists by the score, selling what they had managed to grow or create at their workbench or kitchen stove. It was bubbling with vitality, like a London street market but more so. I wandered happily through it for more than an hour, gorging myself on the cheer and excitement, a complete reversal of the mood in the empty streets of the previous evening. I bought a few cheap things, mostly foodstuffs, and then headed for the railway station to get on toward Berlin. Enough remained of my detour funds for a bowl of surprisingly good onion and meat broth in a cafeteria.

I had very little coinage left by the time the pint-sized Gypsy panhandler accosted me at the station. She was impossible to satisfy, which is what one learns quickly about Gypsy children, and I narrowly escaped, as the entire family descended on me like pigeons flocking to someone dispensing crumbs. When I counted what was left, on the train, it came to exactly eleven *pfennig* – all of six cents! Skidding along on the banana peel again.

I shared a compartment with an engaging young *fraulein* from Dresden with streaming blond hair, on her way to attend a rock concert with her eastside Berlin boyfriend. I learned from her that the train would drop us at the *East Berlin Bahnhof* (station), and I'd still have to make my way across the city divide. Barriers were down but the cultural division remained, slicing the city in the old rutted split. She assured me it would be no problem, for the Berlin Metro system shares the rails there and would accept my train ticket to complete the trip. And in Berlin, I should once more have access to funds.

But when I arrived in downtown Berlin I discovered, with shattering dismay, that not a single change bureau was open. I found myself, for all appearances, on Wilshire Boulevard in Los Angeles. Here, it was called the Kurfurstendamm, but the traffic, the noise, the modernity, the rushing crowds – everything felt like Metropolis, U.S. I had completely overlooked the possibility of short hours on Saturday, and all financial resources were locked down for the weekend. I was stranded on Wilshire Boulevard with six cents – not even enough to phone my Berlin friends.

I finally found a small hotel willing to cash another £10 travelers check at a slightly worse rate than I had gotten in Leipzig. It was about 6:30 p.m. when I reached Uta on the phone, to announce my arrival and get directions to her place out in the Friedenau section, an area on the south side that had largely escaped the wartime damage responsible for central Berlin's descent into California urban intensity.

My visit with Uta was also, and maybe primarily, to reconnect with a longtime friend, Lowell, whom I had lost touch with some years before. In fact, I only knew Uta through Lowell. They had met in California in the early 1980's, traveled the States together in a small van for awhile, and then Lowell joined her when she returned to Berlin, just about the time I was leaving California for Seattle.

That was the way I remembered it all, but things had turned around since then. They were just good friends, now, no longer in a couple relationship. Uta now shared a large apartment with another woman and was better able to host me than Lowell – who happened to be between residences at the time I was there. For the moment, Uta was providing Lowell with living room space until he found new quarters. So he and I shared her living room that week. But space was no problem, for it was another one of those expansive old apartments of pre-war times.

Other than the brief couple of days I had spent at Carty's apartment in Haarlem and the mixed time at de Voorde, this was my first opportunity in a month of travel, since leaving London, to completely let down and release the tensions of being on the road. In a larger sense, it was the longest break in nine weeks of travel since my last secure residence in Balham. Collapse was in order, and I made the most of it. It was the ideal moment for it, too, with summer now at full blast. Days in the mid-nineties, sweaty like a sauna, and sudden afternoon thunder showers that sent down torrents. I could relish its intensity in my momentary sheltered immunity from it.

Best of all, though, was the rare company of old friends, a pleasure I had almost lost sight of. Uta – slim, tall and tanned, radiating an incredible youthfulness for her fifty-odd years, intriguing as much for the warm interest that her blue eyes invariably registered in even the most casual conversation, as for English skills so rich with accent I sometimes thought it was really German she was speaking. And Lowell, slim and tall himself, a few years younger than Uta, reserved and quiet almost to the point of self-effacement.

Lowell has pursued a life of continual transition, in constant search of something he has never been able to articulate. When I first knew him, he operated a Bay Area electronics repair business. He sold that and ventured into long-haul, big-rig truck driving. The next thing I knew, he had turned to flying and made his livelihood for several years as a courier. Wearying of that, he joined a collective at a country hot springs . . . but it proved no more the goal of his search than anything else had. It was there that he met Uta, who had come to study massage therapy. In Berlin he took up garden maintenance work and studied German language and culture.

But this, too, had apparently lost its edge and he was already talking of moving on. I've always been intrigued by the way Lowell can change his life so radically every few years. At the same time, the weariness suggested by a search that never ends is almost palpably painful to me – for I am an Aries, too, and know the feeling.

M

Lowell was my guide, of course, for what might be worth seeing in Berlin. The Wall, to begin with – and it was not nearly so impressive as I had imagined. Most of it had come down, but long stretches still stood, with art and graffiti in a running 'commentary' that celebrated its demise. I was more impressed by the brooding old Reichstag building on the east side, relic of the Hitler years and somehow more the emblem, to me, of Germany's twentieth century anguish.

But the most impressive sight of all was a towering, awesome remnant of World War II standing right in the heart of the city. The stark shell of a great church, the *Kaiser Wilhelm Gedachtnis,* a strangely beautiful monument to war, though it is nothing but a blackened, silent hulk that sits square in the midst of hyper-modern architecture and high-intensity activity – almost in rebuke. A mute counterpoint to the crashing disharmony around it. But more: a wordless sermon on the multiple tragedies of runaway nationalism . . . and the ethno-centrism that nationalist power ultimately reflects and thrives on.

It seems banal to highlight one of the world's great cities in a context of despair and destruction; but I found little in Berlin with anything better to say to me. The heart of the city had been entirely rebuilt as a result of the wartime damage, and my Wilshire Boulevard comparison just about says it all. I valued a museum display of turn-of-the-century *Jugendstil* art – the German counterpart to Art Nouveau. And I found my way to the westside suburb of Spandau, where an ancient castle called The Citadel stands on a peaceful riverbank among overgrown greenery, seemingly undisturbed by the ages. But other than these minor rewards, the only worthwhile thing I really got from Berlin was a much needed rest.

Lowell took me on a local jaunt eastward, outside of Berlin, to visit a friend in the countryside village of Friedrichshagen. It was a quite ordinary community; but the smalltown flavor of casual neighborhood, after the madness of Berlin's Kurfurstendamm, felt so charming that it fueled my growing interest in the East European experience. His friend, Astrid, was much more upbeat about it than my hosts in Leipzig, though she, too, spoke of the challenges – most currently, having to cope with a sudden 600% jump in rent, as a compensating offset for the recent conversion of marks that had suddenly made every East German six times wealthier. Astrid said that people had quickly gone out and bought automobiles before normalization raised those prices, too. The impulse led many to foolishly plunge more than they could afford.

Here in Friedrichshagen, we were halfway from Berlin to the Polish border. Every experience I'd had of the East and its people, starting with Ashka, was softening me to the prospect of taking a side trip into Poland. Berlin, itself, had been a side trip to begin with. I hadn't even wanted to venture through eastern Germany to reach it. My sole 'risk' into East territory was to be Budapest, where I had a friend; and then I added Georghe, in Romania, to that prospect. But it all felt different now. Leipzig, for all my fears, had come off easily. More than that, it was a particularly exciting experience and I wanted more of it. I had no GN host list for Poland, though, and wasn't at all sure I could get hold of one in a few short days.

I went with Lowell to the American Embassy to see what I could learn of the passage through Romania and Bulgaria, and was told there would be no problem. Romania might require a visa, but that could be had from their Budapest consulate just as easily as from Berlin. I learned also, to my surprise, that Czechoslovakia no longer required any minimum daily money exchange, and suddenly the speculative sidetrip to Poland seemed a perfect opportunity for a visit to Prague, too. Why not? I was even willing to risk it without host lists, though they would be immensely helpful if I could get them. I called the Berlin GN coordinator to see if there was any chance of it on such short notice. His only copies were in the hands of another traveler; but he might have them back by the weekend if I could possibly wait.

On Friday, in ninety-degree mid-day heat, buckets of rain suddenly poured down, and then a murderous assault of hailstones, some as large as an inch in diameter. I laid out a loose route, that day, for a weeklong swing into eastern country. It should give me time enough to see Warsaw and Prague, and come back into Germany through Dresden. The young woman on the train had stirred my interest in Dresden, but it was a place that seemed to have a magic pull on me anyway, though I couldn't say why. All I knew of it – or thought I knew – was that it had been shattered by one of the most concentrated, senseless incendiary bombings of the entire war. Hardly a reason to want to see what's there now, but who can explain wherefrom such obsessions arise?

Dresden, like Leipzig, was on my Germany host list and I selected what seemed a congenial and promising host on it, a young woman who spoke good English and had an interest in matters philosophical and spiritual. I sent her a letter of introduction noting my likely date of arrival. There was no time left for any confirming reply, but at least I was giving prior notice this time. (Never mind that it had always backfired on me, before.)

I made a serious effort to slim down my pack at this point, too. It had become paper-heavy with an accumulation of maps, souvenirs, journal-notes and such. I sent a packet home to Terry. But the real weight was in the hefty handbooks that had seemed so necessary when I planned the journey. They turned out to be 'worry books.' I hadn't made a bit of use of them. The realization of this was wonderfully liberating, and in a sudden surge of confidence I threw out the whole batch except for my international hostel directory and a small multilanguage dictionary. No more *Let's Go* ... no more *Hitch-Hiker's Manual* ... no more *Traveler's Survival Guide*. There was no further point in carrying the weight of old insecurities on my back, anymore than in my head.

On Sunday, the host lists came: two slim booklets, one for Poland and the other for Czechoslovakia, with hundreds of names. Considering the recency of open relations between east and west, the GN lists were surprisingly extensive. Without knowing the full history of it, I could only assume that these lists had been growing for many years.

On Monday morning I hit the road again, after nine well-sheltered days in Berlin. I took a train east through Friedrichshagen, and onward to Frankfurt-am-Oder – Germany's smaller Frankfurt on the Oder River. I wanted the experience, this time, of walking across the border into Poland. It was a sunny, cheerful morning and there were many making the crossing by foot, a walk of just a few hundred feet. The border guard could see at once that I was not one of the locals, but he waved me through at the flash of my passport without even looking inside to make sure it was mine.

The small town on the Polish side was called Slubice (the L has a slash through it and is pronounced more like a W). It had no charm whatsoever, a plain street bordered by plain buildings, around which hovered a plain-looking assortment of people engaged in their mid-morning affairs. One and two-story buildings indistinct from one another; not until I was up close could I tell that one of them housed a change bureau. With a week's worth of foresight, knowing I could not rely on my Visa card in eastern Europe, I had brought $100 in deut-schemarks with me. Now, I exchanged only a tenth of that for Polish zlotys – 125,000 of them – for there would be no way of turning them back into marks, or anything else. In this low-cost economy that might even be all I'd need, in the way of Polish funds.

My sheltered week in Berlin had taken only $76.75, and brought my five-week average all the way down to $85.91. But I had yet to discover what can happen in a land where everything is cheap and I have suddenly, by the simple effect of relativity, become 'wealthy.'

Warsaw's richly expressive monument to the Polish uprising, when they were overrun by the Soviets in a betrayal at the close of the war.

Bumming Poland with backpack and chauffeur

Slubice, Poland: July 15, 1991...

Everything gets distorted when the denominations on your paper money run to five figures. I cashed twenty deutschemarks in the little office doing an exchange business at the Polish border and received 125,000 zlotys. I had no idea, yet, what this sort of money would buy, but I was at once uncomfortable with such high-figure currency and fumbled for words to explain that I wanted smaller bills. The bemused woman took back one of the 10,000 zloty notes and gave me a handful of 500s. I'm sure she thought me simple-minded as I smiled my thank-you, for each one of these had less value than a nickel! I was just a little slow to connect the fact that my entire exchange didn't amount to $11.

I walked south out of town alongside the river levee on a quiet, tree-shaded road – an easy four-miles, hardly disturbed by vehicle traffic, to the Berlin-Warsaw highway. Couples and small family groups strolled by with buckets of berries from a small farmer's market and bazaar, just off the roadway in a grove of trees. I looked briefly in on it, and was boggled by prices like 15,000 zlotys per pound. I finally bought a big hunk of goat cheese for 7,875 zlotys (sixty-eight cents), to nibble on my way.

It must have been past noon when I reached the highway, a divided high-speed strip, two lanes on either side. I paused on the overpass to contemplate the idling line of huge trucks patiently waiting on their border clearance into Germany. In the other direction only an occasional car zipped by, and I could see the prospect of a long wait ahead of me. But the mid-day sun wasn't oppressive; I had only my own impatience to contend with.

I was merely standing there absorbed in these ruminations, gazing down at the scene, when suddenly a big gray sedan was alongside of me, its driver speaking English with a slight accent. He asked where I was going and if I wanted a ride! There are times when I can't quite believe my own life.

He was German, out to sample the Polish countryside, he said, for maybe a day or two, not even sure of where he'd be going. It was fine with me – neither was I. His name was Albert: mid-30's, short, bespectacled, with curly dark hair fringing a premature baldness – the entire aspect lending a cerebral appearance, which was not misleading. Albert had an inquiring mind interested in everything, though nothing very deeply. In fact, a dispassionate objectivity seemed to be his only passion. He evidenced remarkably little personal involvement with anything he talked about.

We discovered very quickly, though, something in common besides this perfect mutual timing for a visit into Poland. Albert was a semi-committed follower of Bhagwan Shree Rajneesh, who had recently died in Poona, India, after having outraged the good people of Oregon for several years and then been banished from further residence in the U.S. Albert had lived at the Poona Ashram for more than a year, until shortly before the charismatic Bhagwan's death. For my part, I had stayed a month or two at the Oregon community, Rajneeshpuram, as a visiting outsider in the early 1980s, before the place was convulsed and destroyed by scandal. That unfortunate finale overshadowed a remarkable instance of communal development, with much more to its credit than is generally allowed in the wake of what ultimately came of it.

But they set their own fate in motion. A defining characteristic of those who were deeply involved in the Rajneesh experience was their inner circle attitude, grown from a conviction that they were more in touch with life's mysterious depth than the common herd – an elitism that was bound to alienate them from the rest of humanity. Albert had this quality. He skimmed the countryside quite insulated from it in his high-profile BMW, almost godlike in a bubble of self-elevation. We sped through towns that cried out for closer inspection, hardly stopping long enough for personal urgencies. It was a top quality highway across level country with virtually no traffic to slow us, and Albert – fresh from Germany's congested autobahns – took it at speeds that were foolish, if not foolhardy. From years of hitch-hiking, I've learned to accept whatever comes and stay cool. But had Albert asked, I was not enjoying it nearly as much as he seemed to be. But then again, I hadn't even had to raise a thumb; I could hardly complain.

We reached Poznan, a third of the way to Warsaw and the only sizable city on the route, just before four in the afternoon. This was as far as Albert had intended to go. But it was such a fine road, beyond all his expectations, that he was tempted, he said, to drive all the way to Warsaw. Not without a night to sleep on the question, however. He found a hotel to suit his taste and pocketbook – on neither of which I could concur. So we parted at that point, agreeing to meet there for breakfast.

In the possibility of a morning ride to Warsaw, I decided not to seek a GN host and made my way instead to a youth hostel in a multi-use old school building. It was a hostel out of the Dark Ages. Sagging old cots with barely adequate bedding, shower stalls so filthy I decided against using one, no toilet paper . . . but it was cheap: $3.60 for the night. And private – an entire top-floor room to myself. Dormer windows looked out on a mid-city scene less imposing than that of Leipzig, but with the same sense of easy, quiet living – a simplicity sharply contrasting the haste and hustle of Berlin. Something about it, in fact – perhaps the entire lack of dazzle and show, and the streetcars down below – took me back again to the San Francisco of my youth. The narrow little trams, so crowded they appeared to have been built for children or pygmies, ran in tandem pairs and were tapered at each end, reminiscent of futuristic design in the 1930s.

Free of Albert, and with a few daylight hours left to explore my first Polish city, I set out walking and followed my instincts toward the center of town – a great market square. It was like stepping into a long-vanished age, for hardly a single visible structure could have been less than two-hundred years old. A turreted, vintage city hall, its pedigree indicated by an emblem and a date: 1555, occupied center stage in the square. Trailing to the rear of it, a string of marvelously narrow buildings of jumbled height and roof-line – a retinue, like an undisciplined line of soldiers following their leader in comic disarray. While around the perimeter, a phalanx of ancient structures stood in witness, like a sober gallery of judges, lending dignity to the jocular effect of the central scene.

Somewhere beyond the square I came to a massive, bulky church, clearly very old. It was plain and drab, huddled by equally unattractive buildings that had long ago crowded into its onetime grounds leaving no airspace whatever. I'd have gone on by, but the door was open and so I hazarded a quick look – and was struck, as if by an outpouring of choir song, by what I saw: an interior of carved and polished hardwood with sculpture everywhere, all in a color scheme of black with gold trim. My eyes went upward along massive marble pillars to artwork on the ceiling – pillars that appeared to be solid black marble all the way up, for I could detect no break in them, although their girth could not have been embraced by two men with outstretched arms. Interestingly, not a trace of stained glass could be seen. Yet, it took my breath away like no other cathedral I'd seen – and its drab exterior had given me not the slightest hint.

The next morning, slow in waking and unable to reach Albert by phone, I took a taxi for the several blocks to his hotel, unreasonably fearful of losing the possible ride to Warsaw. In my tourist-haste I got burned, paying more for that short ride than the night's lodging had cost. But I found Albert waiting, and my imprudent loss was offset when he bought me breakfast in the hotel. He even let me shower in his room before checking out.

We did some further local sightseeing before taking to the road again. I found a bookstore, and a beautifully illustrated volume on *Secesja* style, Poland's own version of France's Art Nouveau. It cost me $6.50, a fraction of its likely value in the States, were it even available there, and it suggested a fresh track for old pursuits that had been frustrated ever since I left England. Time and again on the continent I had walked into book shops from pure habit – pure useless habit, it had become, for all I saw was French, Belgian, Dutch and German texts. From now on, I would enjoy my old pastime in the universal language of art!

We made the 190-mile dash to Warsaw like Barney Oldfield wheeling it for a trophy. Such traffic as we encountered in this level farmland country moved at a snail's pace, probably set by the long, barrow-like horse-drawn wagons still in use here. More than once Albert had to brake sharply, exercising all the control he had, to avoid some vehicle changing lanes at thirty miles per hour – the poor peasant at the wheel hardly expecting anything like Albert on the road.

We got to Warsaw at three in the afternoon. Albert managed to find a tourist office where someone who spoke English was willing to make phone calls for us – to GN hosts for me, and hotel possibilities for Albert. It required six tries before I finally made a connection on mine with a possible host: they were waiting for another traveler who was already two days late in arrival, and I took the opening on that edge of uncertainty. Albert had several leads he was anxious to check out, so we followed that route first and he took a room at the second stop. All of a sudden, then, he tired of being my chauffeur. He was quite weary, he said, and just wanted to get some rest, and could I please find my own way to the host I was headed for.

It's strange, how easily one gets accustomed to the ever-present utility and ease of an automobile. I felt momentarily angry with Albert for wanting his own life back! But I contained it and bid him a cheerful farewell – after all, he had taken me clear across Poland.

It took me a few moments to return to the headspace of the solitary traveler and grasp the responsibility of finding my way in this huge city. I had a poor excuse for a city map, picked up at the tourist office.

It didn't even extend to where my host lived, which we had pin-pointed on Albert's larger map. But I knew that a bus along this boulevard went out there, and I knew the sort of intersection to watch for once I reached the vicinity.

Things, of course, never look like they're supposed to. I got off the bus too soon because I was afraid of getting off too late. But could I even be sure that I hadn't already done so? I was at a major intersection that was off my map, in an open area with good visibility, guessing that my destination should be not far ahead. I tried to make sure – if only I could find someone among the crowd at the bus stop who understood me. But one after another gave me an uncomprehending stare. This was the nightmare that had always haunted me: lost in Warsaw without a map, and nothing but blank looks for my every entreaty. I finally had to assume I must be right, and continue on down the main boulevard toward a row of condo-style high-rises in the middle distance.

I passed no one at all. It was very much like new suburban development areas at home, where nothing but automobiles are encountered. Finally, up ahead, a young woman came toward me. I paused as we passed, hesitantly asking whether she spoke any English.

"Sure do!" came the bright, smiling response. "Where y'from?"

An American! I could hardly trust my ears. It's not so rare to hear English spoken abroad, usually with German or Dutch accent, or else almost always British – but the distinctive sound of an American voice, in this remote Warsaw moment, was almost rapturous.

Not merely American, it turned out, but from my old San Francisco backyard: El Cerrito, California. She was in Warsaw on a student exchange for the summer. We stood and talked for awhile, and she confirmed that I was going in the right direction, probably to one of those very condos. Just as we turned toward our separate paths she tossed me a parting suggestion: "Go to Krakow – it's worth seeing."

My Warsaw hosts were Bogdan and Ewa, he an architect who worked at home, and she an English teacher, completely fluent. Their condo apartment was a bit on the crowded side with two small children and all of Bogdan's work materials, but I was frankly surprised at their well-provisioned life, after all I had thus far seen in eastern Europe. The only thing in the kitchen that harked back to earlier times in my life was a table-affixed, hand-turned meat grinder. For all else, I could as easily have been in a modern middle-class American apartment. Bogdan was a book collector and they had somehow crammed more shelving space into that apartment than I'd have thought possible. But then the clever, efficient use of space is something Europeans have a talent for – from their long historical development of conservative land use for a steadily expanding population.

I gave myself all of Wednesday to explore Warsaw. The city was extraordinarily alive, bursting with energy and street sounds, an incredible tumult of people and activity in all directions. It felt like I had walked into a mass re-birthing underway, with none of the jaded, slick feeling of Berlin's Kurfurstendamm, but the freshness of something seeking its own form and style. Sidewalk stands selling everything from cassette tapes to kitchenware lined the streets. The only negative note was a massive instance of bulk architecture called the Culture Tower, a brooding reminder of recent history that dominates the city by its sheer, singular size. I suspect it dates from the Communist years, but whether so or earlier, it radiates the cold linearity of life dominated by ideology, and I'm sure the city would be lovelier and happier, and probably flower with more grace, if they tore it down.

Beyond the central area I discovered the oldest part of town, by the river Wisla; and near there a monumental tribute to the Warsaw Uprising of 1945, when the city was tragically betrayed by Soviet forces they had counted on to help oust the Nazis. It was one of the most awesome sculptural groupings I have ever seen: a larger than life assemblage of desperate figures in torment and violence, practically vibrating in their realism and intensity.

Ewa had spoken of a museum devoted to Secesja art in the town of Plock, sixty miles to the northwest. I bought a rail ticket that afternoon, figuring that an early Thursday start should let me visit the museum and then take an afternoon train from there to Wroclaw, on a direct line toward Prague. But when Bogdan pulled out his railroad schedules that evening, it proved impossible to put together an itinerary that wouldn't involve an overnight stay in Plock, plus other complications.

So I dropped the whole idea, deciding instead to heed the advice of the young woman from El Cerrito. I'd take the Krakow express at 9:25 in the morning. Ewa wrote a note for me to present at the ticket counter requesting a ticket exchange.

At breakfast, Bogdan suddenly decided it was the moment to tell me all about the Warsaw Ghetto, the old Jewish quarter that the Nazis had flattened to rubble. It was 8:30 before I finally got on my way – time enough to *just miss the bus* that could have taken me to the train station in good time. I got the next bus . . . just in time to keep me on edge all the way into town. It took a route that was new to me. I lost sight of the landmark Culture Palace and lost my bearings in the maze of turns the bus took. It followed a long, roundabout route while time kept ticking away and I kept trying to figure out where I was. The whole plan seemed headed for disaster. I finally spotted the low, rectangular station facade just seven minutes before train time.

By then, it was too late to mess with the ticket counter line, so the problem assumed new dimensions. I had made a short hop in Holland without a ticket, but . . . a three-and-a-half hour express to Krakow? It was either take it without a ticket, or not at all. I got on and settled myself in a compartment with five others to await whatever should develop.

Mile after mile, no conductor appeared on the scene as we whizzed across the Polish flatlands and into rolling hills. I imagined the worst – getting thrown off the train – and figured I had better just act dumb . . . which wouldn't really be an act. We must have been halfway to Krakow before a conductor looked in and everyone reached for their ticket. Like some school kid with a note from home, I handed him the request that Ewa had written the night before. He studied it with a frown, then wrote something below and handed it back to me. Was that all? No. He brought forth a little book from an inner pocket and began making calculations, finally indicating that I must pay a 33,000 zloty fare plus a 5000 zloty penalty for boarding the train without a ticket. Total price for the 180-mile express to Krakow: $3.35.

Something about Krakow felt delightfully refreshing from the moment I arrived. The usual fruit stands and diverse entrepreneurs surrounded the depot, and I had to fend off taxi drivers, one of whom insistently wanted to drive me to Auschwitz. I brushed him away, remembering what I'd said to Albert when he spoke of wanting to see the Holocaust death camps: "not now, and not ever." None of these things seemed unusually refreshing, but a certain atmosphere hovered in the air like the breath of a late spring morning, though we were well into summer.

My second phone call turned up a host. Mindful of the six calls it required in Warsaw, I told him earnestly that I'd even be comfortable sleeping on a floor. His indignation at the very suggestion rang loud and clear. "No guest in my house sleeps on the floor!"

This was Greg (short for Grzegorz) who lived just an easy walk from the station, on the second floor of an old six-unit frame building – the very place he'd been born, he would later tell me, forty-four years ago. The whole building had once belonged to his family before Communism took their ownership away. Greg wasn't sure that he'd ever get title to it again, for the old records had long ago been destroyed. He lived there now with a child, who was away, and his wife, Gorza – secretary for the local theater company, a sometimes actress and would-love-to-be taxicab dispatcher, who could sit for hours listening to their radio dialogue. Greg was a journalist, interpreter and also a local disc jockey. Together, they made one of the warmest, most engaging pairs that I encountered on my entire trail.

Part of Krakow's instant charm was surely due to the circumstance that it had come cleanly through the war – one of the few major cities that hadn't been damaged at all. In consequence, it had continued to age in a graceful fashion, never forced into that dispiriting mix of old and new that reveals, by glaring prominence, what can no longer be decently maintained. Yes, buildings still fall into aged disuse here, but they blend with the rest of the old city in an overall image of harmony. A fascinating array of ancient architecture lined the quaint and narrow streets, continually surprising me with picture-postcard scenes at each fresh turn. At one such, I walked right into one of the grandest open squares, easily, in all of central Europe.

Krakow's market square is so immense that an Alhambra-like structure, huge itself, nestles within it like a jewel set into a ring. Called the *Cloth Hall,* it's a football field long, rising several stories, yet it doesn't compromise the open feeling of the square as a whole, which incorporates other structures as well.

The effect of a town or market square on the life of a community, as I saw it time and again in Europe, in small towns and large cities, is so invigorating and so graceful at the same time that I can't help feeling profoundly sad for its absence in the cities of America. People invariably gravitate to such areas, which certainly expresses an inner need for their social function. It is nothing like a shopping mall, where the emphasis is on trade and parking space, not community. The open square motif is to be found only one place in America: on its great University campuses; but in civic life, in this land of seemingly endless land, we are too overwhelmed by property values to indulge in anything so profitless as open space.

I managed to see a good deal of Krakow during my two days there, but – as with few other cities – it seemed impossible to get enough. On my second day, I joined Gorza at the end of her workday, and she took me on a tour of the 100-year-old theater and opera house, showing me parts of the building that few ever see. The onetime dressing room of their oldest and most revered actor, Ludwick Solski, has been kept intact, its walls covered by testimonials and mementos, since his death at age 99 in the mid-1950s.

Then I took Gorza to see a discovery I had made, myself, that day. In the dark corridor to an inner court, in one of the many old Krakow apartment buildings, I found a remnant of Secesja building art: a lovely panel of red poppies in stained and leaded glass, dirtied but intact above the interior portal. She had seen it before, but we stood and admired it for the time it took our eyes to adjust to the darkened passage. Going out, then, into the sudden bright light of the street, I blinked at what I was sure must be an apparition. Not thirty feet away, coming up the sidewalk ... *Albert!*

This was absolutely insane. We had parted company three days earlier, almost two hundred miles away, neither of us at that time having any thought of coming to Krakow. Yet, here we were, synchronistically converging at the same point in time and space.

Albert was as stunned as I – the only time I ever saw him lose his cool. Gorza understood nothing of our wide-eyed encounter until I was coherent enough to tell her, and then she looked at me as if I had performed a miracle – as if I'd had anything to do with it! But it turned out so perfectly for me that I could understand her awe. Albert was heading for Prague the next morning, and so was I! I would already have had my rail ticket, but for being short on zlotys that morning, when I went for it

. Before dark that evening, in a final gesture of hospitality, Greg and Gorza took me to a hilltop overlook, somewhat west of town, to see the entire city bathed in sunset. A score of church spires spiked upward, glinting gold like a troop of spear-bearing angels; and the fortress rampart of Wawel Castle marking the southern reach of ancient Krakow was once more aglow in Medieval glory, as only the brief image called forth by a sunset can reveal. The Wisla River flowed around the rocky rise on which the castle stood – the same Wisla that courses through Warsaw and on to the Baltic Sea.

We talked with some young fellows who had also come for the view, one of whom bore such an uncanny resemblance to my brother when he was young – even in his laugh and way of speaking, though he spoke no English at all – that I had a sudden flash my visit to Krakow had been no accident at all, but the likely urge of my mongrel roots to find their home. It had taken an assortment of happenings to overcome my resistance to traveling eastern Europe, to begin with, and then a further push by accidental events all along the way, to route me toward Krakow. The incredible encounter with Albert only served to confirm it – for that is the apparent point of synchronicities: to affirm hidden realities . . . to make them irrefutably obvious, unconditionally believable.

In Albert's immediate travel arrangements, my standing had slipped to that of 'fifth wheel' – or fourth wheel, anyhow. He had somehow latched onto two other travelers, both women, and I had to take a back seat. It was actually a blessing, for it somewhat shielded me from the worst effects of his driving. Poor Beverly was now in the hot seat, and more than once I could see her suddenly stiffen, or hear the slight catch in her voice as Albert continued to put his car through its paces. She was on her way home to San Francisco, flying from Prague. Our other companion, sharing the rear seat with me, was Stephanie, a young Canadian in temporary residence there. Albert, of course, was on his way back to Germany but wanted to cap his holiday with a couple days in Prague.

I had meant to spend a few days there, myself, but hadn't expected that I'd be putting five days into Poland. The scheduled date for Dresden was crowding me now; and I realized, further, that to remain in Prague over a weekend – for it was now Saturday – would simply crowd my visit into the worst two days for it. I decided, by the time we got there, just to stay the night, and make a point of returning later in my journey for a more substantial visit.

Albert was careful to stop for gas on the Polish side of the border, and for good reason. We had zlotys to dispose of and there was no better way. In fact, no *other* way at this point, for there was no place left to spend them. I was up to my neck in zlotys. After congratulating myself on having averted the purchase of a rail ticket to Prague, I realized that it saved me nothing at all, for I had already made the exchange – fifty deutschemarks – in anticipation of buying the ticket. I now had more than 300,000 zlotys with me and they were totally useless outside the country. So I became a major financier for this journey to Prague, putting 210,000 zlotys into it, or $18.50, which was more than the rail fare would have been. I consoled myself that it was the decent thing to do, for Albert had chauffeured me most of the way from Germany.

Saturday evening is not the time, in mid-summer, to be looking for hostel space in Prague. Beverly and Stephanie had already gone their separate ways; Albert lingered with me just long enough, at the accommodations desk in the central rail station, to secure himself a lead to a $25 room. I half expected he'd be sporting enough to let me share it, after what we'd come through together, but it never entered Albert's head. He wished me luck, and off he sped. So here I was, again, with the perennial problem. I hardly wanted to call a GN host just to pop in and out for the night. But the hostels were full and I wasn't quite up to seeking a spot under the stars for the night, either, which involves a whole other range of problems in a large city. I needed an angel again; but I haven't quite learned how to summon one.

I finally turned, in desperation, to the GN host list. But now I couldn't get the phone to work for me. I kept returning to the accommodations desk for advice on what I was doing wrong. Finally, the fellow offered to make the call for me, so I had to explain that this was a call to someone who didn't know me, for free lodging, which made no sense to him – so I started explaining Good Neighbors ... Well, something clicked in him (the angel button?) when he got the picture, and he said he could refer me to an 'alternative hostel' if I wasn't too particular about the accommodations.

He didn't give me an address, just a street name and a building description, and I could see why when I got there. It was an old section of industrial warehouses, huge structures that had no numbers. Somewhat uncertainly, I narrowed the choice to a solid old monster of stone, with a giant, locked-tight doorway and windows far too high to see into. I rang the buzzer and a voice came out of a little box. I said I wanted a room for the night, and the voice flatly said, "No rooms."

Well, that was it; I didn't like the looks of it anyway. I turned my back, without another word, and walked away. It was 7 p.m., no time for anything but to find myself a secluded spot somewhere. But I was hardly on my way before an old gent with a big white beard was out there on the street, hailing me back.

"Dorms," he told me, with an apologetic smile, "not rooms."

Okay. I let go a sigh of relief and followed him up to a large second-floor dorm room that looked surprisingly clean in the circumstances, and he opened a window to let some fresh air in. He wanted $3 for the night, which was more than half of what I had in Czech money. After that exchange fiasco in Krakow, and knowing I'd be out of Prague in the morning, I had changed just ten deutschemarks for Czech kronen. He told me of a place nearby where I could get a cheap but good meal, and assured me the hostel would remain open – though I'd have to ring the buzzer – until 11 p.m. He spoke English well enough that I was sure we had all our transactions straight.

I went and had a very satisfying broiled chicken dinner, with two cokes to slake my summer thirst and let me linger in the hardly busy cafe while I brought my journal up to date. I had now, in Czech money, just seven cents left – a level of currency risk that I was getting used to. It hadn't been an easy week on my budget, largely due to that last minute splurge for Albert's gasoline. I had spent $100.30, lifting my six-week average to a still respectable figure of $88.31. But that didn't include the 100,000 zloty note that remained in my pocket, though I'd never be able to make any use of it. I eventually sent it back to Greg and Gorza, for whom it had some value.

It was nine o'clock and getting dark when I went back to the hostel and rang the buzzer. No answer. I rang again, and no answer. I beat on the heavy door, but no one came. I rang and beat and yelled, to no avail. I was locked out, and the street was absolutely deserted. It was beginning to feel like some low-grade movie. Everything I owned, even my passport, was inside this building, and it was getting dark, and I was getting desperate. I imagined myself trying to explain all this to Czech police – if I could even find any police, with seven cents in my pocket.

Before my desperation could turn to panic, a young couple turned up who also wanted to get in. At least I had company, though they spoke no English. The young fellow was enterprising and agile, and did what I couldn't possibly do – he managed to clamber up a ledge to the open second-story window of my dorm, and disappeared into it. A few minutes later the fortress-like doors opened. I got a sorry apology from the old bearded fellow, who had been upstairs all the while listening to a radio.

What with all of that excitement and the day's long drive, all I wanted was a hot shower, down the hallway, and a long night's sleep in a cozy bed. I lay down to it in my private dorm room, finally, with that huddling glow that shuts out the rest of the world – all except the soothing melody coming in over my earphones. I seemed to drift between sleep and reverie, to musical cues, for a blissful eternity, finally laying the earphones aside and falling into total slumber.

At some pre-dawn hour, I have no idea when, I was aware that my blanket was being yanked away from the foot of my bed. In sleepiness, and by the light of the street lamp alone, I could only see what appeared to be an entangled mass of tattooed bodies writhing on a double bed near the window, with someone laughing at me – a young woman with hair as wild as a Melanesian native. It was entirely surreal, a dream or a vision, I wasn't sure.

The illusion slowly transformed, as my eyes and senses came back to reality. I could see that the 'tattooed bodies' were only the effect of yellowed street lamp on a flowered blanket design, and there were only two people there, fully clothed – one of them the dark-haired laughing woman, who could hardly have been twenty. Another young couple were relaxing on a lower bunk by the sidewall. The four seemed to be having a kind of Coca-Cola slumber party.

I was fascinated by it now that I was awake, and just lay there enjoying it all, pretending to have fallen back asleep. It reminded me of some of my own escapades at a similar age. I had no idea how they got in, but I imagine it was through that same window. The more active pair would occasionally turn their attention toward me again, tugging at the sheet I resolutely held on to, or once tickling my exposed foot, giggling all the while. But I figured they didn't need me. Their fun was in German and I couldn't have added anything. Finally, they drifted off to sleep, still entirely dressed except for shoes. The other young couple, a blanket over them, had been asleep in each others' arms for some time. The party was over.

I was suddenly aware – awakened again, for no particular reason – that dawn's shallow light had replaced the yellow glow. Then movement caught my eye. The quiet couple on the single bed – ever so gently and still beneath their blanket – were doing the slow, huddling movement of discrete love. It wasn't the first time in my life that voyeurism had been thrust on me, so to speak, but I think it was engagingly the sweetest.

M

The Dresden riverfront, on the Elbe. Her magnificent architecture, destroyed in a single night's WWII fire-bombing, is being painstakingly rebuilt.

I didn't know I hadn't been invited

Prague: July 21, 1991...

I had no time to explore any of Prague, before my 10:14 train to Dresden. But the visual impact of the railway station alone was enough to assure my return. A graceful orchestration of Art Nouveau design – those lovely flowing lines swirling to us from an age more given to gentle ways and beauty idealized than anything we can know at this end of the century. I did have time for a bit of breakfast, and just about enough left for it after cashing the last of my deutschemarks for the rail fare. I headed for the terminal's dining room in high anticipation of a setting to match the elegance of its graceful architecture.

What greeted me was a sorry old assortment of dining room furniture covered with table linen that might have been laundered the week before – one couldn't be sure. The menu offered a choice between ham and eggs, or cold ham with cheeses . . . that was it! I asked for eggs alone, but no deviation was allowed. So it was ham and eggs. But not recognizably; it more nearly approximated thin slices of Spam fried right in with the eggs, served on a plate garnished with pickled something. Salt and pepper were brought to my barren table and then shortly removed for another diner. Rolls without butter were there, if I wanted to pay extra. The service was just about as agreeable as the food.

But my attention was absorbed with the incredible contradiction that was evident the moment I walked into the dining room. It was a huge space that soared to theater height, and looking down on the scene with a suggestion of disdain were sixteen towering panels of ceramic tile that might have been styled by Alphonse Mucha, himself – an assortment of decorative scenes in Art Nouveau motif, each one dated 1903 . . . original works of art, every single piece! The contrast between what this room now was and what it clearly had once been fairly shrieked, like an Edvard Munch painting, the century's insanity and its insensible waste.

It was on this note, oddly appropriate, that I returned to Germany, headed for the city that remains a testament to insensible waste. The fire-bombing of Dresden near the war's end has become legendary in the annals of massive airborne destruction. The image that stays with me from some long ago documentary is a view of the night's blackness punctured everywhere with the bright flash of explosion and flame. Why on earth I wanted to visit there is still a puzzle to me, for I could only expect a sad mixture of eastern Europe's poverty with Socialism's dreary architecture.

I had chosen, at any rate, a magnificent approach. The three-and-a-half hour train ride from Prague along the Elbe River was picture-postcard scenery all the way: castles, wonderfully sculpted rock bluffs on the opposite bank and a fair amount of water traffic including great excursion boats coming up the river from Dresden. I claimed a walk-way window for myself for the best possible view of it all.

Hanging out a train window is the ultimate in railroading privacy – a bubble in which to think, dream and imagine while the countryside drifts by. European rail cars have passenger compartments on one side and a long walkway on the other, with no restriction against opening the windows on either side. But the walkway side is best, for it disturbs no one. Leaning out of a walkway window it's easy to lose oneself to the rest of the train . . . to the rest of the world! I was just another graybeard quietly acting my age, in a compartment with four or five others; but facing away from all that, with my hair flying in the breeze, I was beyond time or place ... ageless. I was Casey Jones at the throttle, or a soaring eagle with a vast view of the landscape ... or even that old outlaw, Black Bart, making his clickety-clack getaway after a highway robbery of the Wells Fargo stage.

Arriving in real life again at Dresden, it was 1:30 on a Sunday afternoon and I was very nearly flat of coin again. I was back in deutschemark country, but I couldn't do anything about it until the banks opened on Monday. In the meanwhile, I was counting on the host I'd had the foresight to arrange for from Berlin. But once again I was frustrated by the coin-telephone system and couldn't get through. In the face of this, it made easy sense to go directly out to the address by tram.

I must have spent close to an hour trying to relate street maps to posted transit schedules, all in German, to discover the right route. When I finally reached Simone's neighborhood, a quiet old residential section of wide streets and large tree-shaded lawns that certainly predated the war, I found the place without further difficulty – an old frame structure of several floors that looked like a onetime private residence, now divided into apartments. I was hardly through the garden gate, when a smiling young fellow popped out the front door and asked – first in German and then in good English when he got my garbled "No sprechen ze Deutsche" – he asked if I were Simone's guest. Hans was his name, and he seemed to think I was from Norway, but I corrected him on that point. He told me Simone was away on holiday and had left instructions that I should be given the key and could use her apartment for as long as I cared to stay!

After two days of hard travel and a night of dubious rest this was a blessing indeed. The lucky break of failing with the telephone had served me well – for had I simply got no answer to a ringing phone I'd probably have settled for looking up another host.

Hans took me to Simone's apartment in a separate rear unit. While not too large it had every convenience I could ask, even a stall shower, something of a rarity in east Europe. Fine old oak and walnut furniture and lush, oversized pillows suggested an indulgent, sybaritic taste for bygone eras. Homestyle relaxation was an instant temptation, here – but so was the beautiful day outside, in a Dresden that had hardly been destroyed and was now immensely compelling. I left my gear and went back out.

My transit map showed the Elbe River hardly a half-mile further along the way I'd come. A walk in dappled sunlight filtered through great old elms. The houses were gracious ladies of an earlier age, many on the shabby side but all of them aglow with an aura of charm. Or perhaps I was merely feeling the remarkable quiet that was every-where, as though Sunday in this place was truly regarded as a day of rest. These homes had large yards, veranda porches and endlessly var-ied wood construction details of a long vanished vogue.

At the river I came upon an intricately laced suspension bridge and a small cluster of neighborhood shops, all closed for Sunday. Drawn on, I crossed the bridge, a century-old structure referred to, I later learned, as the Blue Devil for its shade of paint. On the opposite shore the road curved up a steep hillside. But down along the river a bit was a funicular railway that climbed the hill straight up. They asked only fifty-five cents for the round trip, so I took it, and for a half hour at the top had a spectacular view of all Dresden nestled in a blanket of soft greenery. There was no visible relationship to that image of a black night except for some sections near its heart that seemed bare and still scarred. The Blue Devil, far below, looked like this picture on an old postcard I later found in one of the shops nearby.

When I got back to Simone's apartment, I could tell immediately, on opening the door with the key Hans had given me, that someone was inside – and then I saw her: a refreshingly attractive young woman busily occupied at the kitchen stove. All I could think of, despite her dark hair and complexion, was Hans' mistaken idea that I was from Norway. Had Simone been expecting a Norwegian guest, too, who had arrived while I was off exploring?

"Hello," I said rather hesitantly, to this vivacious young woman who glanced out from the kitchen like she owned the place. "I'm Irv Thomas, who's staying here."

"Hallo," she answered brightly, "I Simone who live here!"

She was a radiant smile from the moment she first saw me – in the captivating effect of which, the information took a moment to sink in as she went on.

"I come back from holiday now. And who you?"

I was finally getting the picture. "My name is Irv Thomas," I repeated. "I'm the Good Neighbors traveler who wrote from Berlin last week. I just got here a couple hours ago, and Hans let me in – it was very generous of you to leave the key for me."

"Oh, no," she said, the big welcome smile still lighting her up. "I leave key for Norway friend."

So it was true!

"But it line," she continued, "all right for you can stay tonight if you want. Where from?"

Her English was a bit fractured; but she was having a harder time with mine than I was having with hers, as I briefed her on how I came to be traveling in Europe. I figured she just hadn't been able to read the letter of introduction that I'd sent. But the full truth of the matter didn't dawn on me until Hans came by, a half hour later while we were having tea and cookies, to give her the handful of mail that had come while she was gone. And there, as she flipped through them . . . *was my letter!*

I had brazenly, if unknowingly, taken possession of a total stranger's apartment in her absence, and then let myself in with her keys, confronting her like *she* were the intruder and not I. Simone had been so cool about it all that I suspect Hans must have informed her before I came back, or else my backpack had cued her for my return.

Her entry on the GN host list indicated a facility with English, but I found I had to speak slowly and choose my words carefully. In the several days she let me stay – for her Norwegian friend never did show up – we'd sit at the big oak dining table, each with our own mini-dictionary, piecing together the more troublesome elements of conversation. The richness of Simone's bookshelves amazed me: Goethe, Rilke, Hesse, Heine, and other German literary figures I wasn't familiar with. She was everyman's image of a lively, attractive, on-the-make young woman of about 30, and yet there was this strong philosophical under-current to her world. Around Hans, she was effervescent, frivolous, but when she and I alone spoke the more serious side emerged – until she would embarrassedly put it away as being too deep to be talking about. I gathered it was a very private part of her life.

I wondered, however, if she was familiar with Taoist philosophy, which seemed easily congenial to her spirit. I had difficulty finding the right key-words for my inquiry. Finally, after her virtual insistence that she knew nothing of it, she took from the bookcase a small German text that I could instantly recognize as the *Tao Te Ching* from its for-mat. It delighted her (as it did me) that her collection held what I was inquiring about, and she insisted that I inscribe the fly-leaf with some-thing appropriate.

I felt a rapport between us stronger than with anyone since Evelyne in Paris – both rewarding and frustrating, since I knew our contact would be so brief. I correctly guessed Simone was a Scorpio, some-thing I can occasionally do when the connection is good. She worked as an optician – an "eye optikon" as she called it – in a neighborhood shop, but was unhappy at it. It hadn't been her own choice of career and was far too confining for her. And it was true, Simone's spirit needed room to soar.

On Monday I canvassed every bank in the center of town before I was willing to accept that my Visa card was as useless here as every-where else in the eastern zone. I fell back, once more, on the backstop travelers checks, cashing my first big one for £50 worth of deutsche-marks, thankful that I was no longer in 'spend it or lose it' territory. The rest of the day, and all day Tuesday, I roamed the city until I knew Simone would be home from work.

In sharp contrast to the hype-and-flash rebuilding of Berlin, Dresden is carefully laying out a new cityscape with an eye cast back to the grandeur of her past – working the space with a conscious awareness of its potential for magnificence. A remnant remains of the architec-tural extravagance of old Dresden in the heart of town, right at the river. They are reconstructing it as it once was, using old plans and photos. Saddening, to be sure, as a reminder of all that was lost – but at the same time, inspiring for what it lends to Dresden's future. This will oneday again be a Great City of Europe.

But large perimeter sections of old Dresden were never touched by the bombing and these were the areas I found the most enchanting. Here was a grace of style that is hard to put one's finger on . . . an atmospheric sort of thing – somewhat as with Krakow, but differently. Residential Dresden seems to luxuriate in an air of leisure. The subtle sense of another kind of city soul lingers here, in wide streets sheltered by great trees, in the oft-encountered bench that invites one to pause from the crush of whatever urgency is in the saddle. It's here in the long twilight of late July days, among folks relaxing at outdoor cafe tables in the very midst of comfortable old homes – cafes that never seem to be crowded, either with clientele or in that more intimidating way: the streams of people that surge by on the usual mid-town avenue, making gauntlets and obstacle courses of sidewalk service.

Simone took me, on our weekday evenings, to a couple of the cafes, and the mood I found there felt like places on a small college campus where students gather. The sense of leisure I experienced in Dresden wiped out any condescending pity I ever had for the sorry condition of life behind the iron curtain. Granted, their lot has not been an easy one; but it is the Western way of life that should be pitied, not theirs.

Wednesday morning I was on my way again, more than a bit sorry to be leaving both Dresden and Simone. But I had stretched my week in eastern Europe to the tenth day, and I was feeling the pressure of other promises. A third and final Quest awaited in a city called Kassel; and then visits with old friends in Wurzburg and Munich.

Simone had suggested one more stop in the old east zone on my rail route to Kassel: the historic city of Weimar. She had a friend there who might put me up for the night. It was mid-afternoon and raining when the train pulled into the Weimar station, and I trudged up wet streets to a midtown tourist office where I could get my locational bearings. Had it been a GN host, I'd have called from the station, but that felt awkward on a personal recommendation. Tourist map in hand,

I walked a half mile to a section of old frame flats – San Francisco style – where they lived, having no idea what kind of reception I'd find . . . but hardly able to imagine the one I got.

Two children answered the door, a boy about twelve and a girl maybe nine, neither of whom could speak any English. But they had an equally young friend upstairs who did speak a bit of it and he became our interpreter. Through him I explained that I was looking for their mother because I needed a place to stay for the night. They forthwith invited me in for a cup of tea, served with the grace of a hostess by the little girl, and to watch TV with them while they phoned their mother. But they never let me speak directly with her; my request went through the translator to the telephone go-between and thence to mother. I was advised, by return transmission, that they had no bed for me, but that I should come down to the music store they manage and they'd see what could be done. So when the TV cartoon had run its course the three kids and me, like some Disney crew of adventurers, trooped out mid-town to the music shop.

It was their Dad I met there (who, for all I knew, had been on the phone). His name was Andreas and his shop radiated refinement and high taste. It was entirely devoted to lovers of classical music, the connoisseur trade. He thought perhaps he could help me out, but I'd have to return at closing hour, 9 p.m. The process had become something of an uncertain intrigue by now, but it felt like things were flowing and I decided to trust it. I left my pack with Andreas, and – having only this single day's time for Weimar – set out to see what I could of the place.

The rain had settled down to an intermittent drizzle. My larger problem now was the sheer profusion of eye-catching attractions and tempting avenues down which to walk. Weimar has possibly the richest cultural history of any German town its size, east or west. Home of both Goethe and Schiller, the locale also figured prominently in the lives of Franz Lizst, J. S. Bach, Kafka, Rudolf Steiner, Richard Strauss, and Walter Gropius – to list merely the few names I recognized on building plaques.

I practically got lost, to begin with, in a great park that takes up much of the southeast quadrant of town, a place of seemingly endless paths and hidden stairways, with vine-encrusted stone ruins like etchings of a lost romantic age. Then I walked back toward Andreas' home and found myself in a trove of early-century Jugendstil architecture. Up one street and down another I went, and even into the outer hallways of a few apartment houses, in search of every hidden detail I could find.

High on a hillside slope the ambience quite suddenly shifted and I thought I was in the Berkeley hills of the Bay Area. All else of what I'd seen had the musty, age-weary look of systemic poverty – as I had come to expect in the old East territory; but here in these few blocks were tended lawns, painted fencing, even a backyard barbecue smoking away! These, I later learned, were the homes of the political elite. It brought to mind George Orwell's sly aside in *Animal Farm,* his parable of the Socialist state: "all animals are equal but some animals are more equal than others."

Returning, I happened upon the headquarter barracks of the small Soviet military contingent that remained in Weimar. I was fascinated to find it situated on Abraham Lincoln Strasse!

By 8 p.m. the thunder showers had resumed with a fervor, and I made my way back to the music shop, ducking from one doorway to another. After locking up, Andreas took me back to their home – perhaps his original intent. The young son had been sent to stay with a friend and I had his room for the night. I met Ulrike, Andreas' wife and the friend to whom Simone had actually sent me, and the three of us had a great evening of dinner and conversation that lasted well past midnight. So late, in fact, that Andreas overslept his usual departure time and I consequently missed the train that would have taken me directly to Kassel. I had to settle, instead, for a two-hour layover in the junction town of Erfurt, still in the old East territory – a place I'd never heard of, and a gift from Andreas that he never intended or knew about.

The historic range and preserved quality of Erfurt's architecture took me totally by surprise. Jugendstil building embellishment, alone, excelled that of Weimar; but it was only the iceberg tip of a veritable museum of architectural history going back to Medieval times. I even saw mud-and-wattle adobe structures on side streets – of heaven only knows what age. The prize was an 800-year-old stone bridge of five arches across the Gera River, overbuilt completely with small shops on both sides so that it presented just a narrow, lane-wide crossing. It couldn't even be seen as a bridge without going upstream a bit for the broadside view.

Rushing through all this in two hours between trains was tourist banality in the extreme. The amazing thing was that the time passed with a magical slowness, even permitting a degree of leisure: I lingered in a small cafe savoring a local pastry with tea. On the other hand, if I had been in less of a rush to get to Kassel, and waited for the next direct train out of Weimar, I would never even have known what I missed in Erfurt, for nothing had alerted me to the town's exciting display of architecture.

I was hardly prepared, by the time-warp experience of eastern Europe and in the immediate afterglow of Erfurt, itself, for the futuristic rail terminal at Kassel. Up along swift escalators, surrounded by gleaming aluminum and great curving panels of glass . . . I had seemingly gone too far forward in time, to find myself debarking at a Star Trek space station. The jarring disorientation was almost physically painful – the psychological equivalent of coming up from a deep-sea dive with the bends.

I worked my way through four potential hosts on the phone before finding one who could take me in. And when I saw the grab-bag blessing I had drawn, it was too late to back out of it. Michael and Hildegard were absolutely charming people – he, a long-haired computer aficionado, and she the perfect radiant picture of a doting mother and housefrau – but their household was a total disaster area. To begin with, it was undergoing major reconstruction, walls torn out everywhere and the disarray of unsorted possessions at every hand. But these folks were blessed with an absolute unconcern for the trivia of household order, so that a table to be cleared for dinner (for mere example) was simply brushed of its clutter in one sweeping motion to the edge and over. One did likewise for seating space. Nobody ever had to clear the floor, of course. In this setting, they were raising four small children in the best alternative tradition: without restraint.

I was fairly well exhausted by the time I got there, for I had been under one and another sort of pressure ever since leaving Dresden; and I could feel the push of this environment against my buttons with each cry of assault or demand uttered by one of the four youngsters. In the interest of self-preservation I excused myself for a bit of sight-seeing in the neighborhood, my real agenda being the search for some cafe retreat where I could reconstitute my sanity. Even at this I was frustrated, for Kassel virtually shuts down at the close of the working day. Nor was it even a pleasant walk to find this out. This is another city rebuilt completely after the war, and the result is a sterile modernism that has left it feeling like a city without a soul.

I finally came to a tiny eatery, closed and being cleaned for the night, but able to sell me a sandwich. It hadn't the relaxing atmosphere I sought, but I was somewhat compensated by the gift of a free second sandwich, wrapped to go, from a proprietor who perhaps took my look of utter resignation as the down-and-out misery of a homeless transient – and he was not far off the truth of it.

Had I not a very good reason for remaining awhile in Kassel I'd have left the next morning. But I was here on a quest: the third and last of my needle-in-a-haystack searches, and by a long margin the most likely to fail. Finding Jim Hall's sister in small-town Scotland took no more skill than playing Blindman's Buff. Finding the *Boulevard of Broken Dreams* music in Amsterdam was a relatively simple matter of tracking down its creator. But this time the quest was in search of someone more than two hundred years dead – or of what he may have left behind, to be more precise.

I was put to it by a young Michigan friend, Glenn Rouse, a writer I'd met in the mid-'80s, drawn to him by his passion for Thoreau. Glenn had once carried out, for an entire year, a daily morning reading of each entry for that date in the full 24-year journal Thoreau had kept – so that he could frame his own day in Thoreau's nature-focused perception of it. Glenn had since become interested in an early 18th Century German mechanic and inventor, Johann Bessler, who claimed to have built a perpetual motion machine.

This, of course, is a heresy in the orthodoxy of science and it was no less so then. But the record indicates that Bessler built a large scale model of his device that apparently worked. Careful to shield its mechanism, he demonstrated it convincingly to critically qualified observers who were suitably impressed, though still unwilling to take it at face value. His object was simply to sell the secret rather than reveal it for nothing; but he could find no one interested enough to pay his price, so he eventually destroyed the machine.

Glenn became convinced of the man's sincerity when he learned of a series of 141 woodcut engravings prepared by Bessler, or for him – a thorough survey of the likely approaches to perpetual motion for a book that he, Bessler, was writing on the subject. No simple charlatan would go to such lengths, was Glenn's reasoning. All the further he knew of it was that these engravings were "kept in the Kassel library." He wanted me to find them, if possible, or whatever else about them I could turn up, and he was willing to stand a cost of up to $200 for my time.

I didn't see much chance for success. Not reading German at all, therefore not able to play around in the library on my own terms, I couldn't quite see how a grey-bearded, somewhat unkempt and not very scholarly-looking old goat with a pack on his back was going to get into the requisite archives to find what was wanted. If it was even to be found, in a city that had been rebuilt from the ground up. But Glenn was a friend and he seemed to have some inexplicable confidence in me.

Exactly what was meant by the "Kassel library," I wasn't even sure. But the obvious place to begin the search was at a local science museum, the *Hessisches Landesmuseum*. I walked out there on Friday morning and encountered, first, someone who spoke no English at all. He turned me over to someone who spoke a little English – enough to grasp the nature of my inquiry. And he, in turn, called someone on an internal phone system, turning the telephone over to me when they answered. I realized at once that this was a qualifying hurdle, for the fellow on the phone – besides speaking excellent English – knew of Bessler and was putting questions to me that seemed intended to discover how much I knew about him. So I put on my best scholarly act, and hoped I wouldn't put my foot into it. Fortunately, Glenn had sent me good briefing material.

It worked. At least, to the extent of getting me past the telephone barrier. I was taken up an elevator and through a series of doors beyond the working laboratories of the museum's inner sanctum, and finally into the office of Professor Dr. Ludolf von Mackensen, in charge of the astronomy and physics section – or kabinet, as it said on the door – the one I'd been speaking with. A man of middle maturity with glasses and a well-trimmed beard, he greeted me with some congenial reflection on time spent, years earlier, at the University of California in Berkeley, and then asked what part of the country I was from. I managed to roll off the names of a few professors from the University of Washington, where he'd fortunately never been, and it served to establish my credentials. When I showed him the documentation Glenn had provided, Dr. von Mackensen went at once to a glass-enclosed bookcase and pulled out a 1719 volume with a long Latin title – the very book from which one of Glenn's copied pages had come! By what seemed sheer Grace, I had found the one man with enough instant background on Bessler to give me the help I needed.

He was puzzled, however, by the reference to 141 wood engravings. He didn't know of any such. He put through a call to a colleague in the library nearby – telling me, almost as a confidential aside as he waited for the connection, that he was calling the only person in the archives section with the imagination to know where any such material might be hidden. But it went nowhere; the man was away for a full month. I would just have to search the archives myself, he said, and then gave me the library catalog number of the Bessler papers that he, himself, had gone through at some prior time – but which, he assured me, contained no such engravings as those I sought.

The *Murhardsche Bibliothek* was practically next door to the museum. My English was understood at the reception desk, from where I was escorted upstairs to the manuscript room and turned over to a large, stolid-looking guardian of its treasures, who brought out for me a huge and ancient bound volume of papers, easily five inches in thickness and maybe twelve by eighteen inches in flat measure. It held hundreds of hand-written pages – separate documents of diverse size, almost all of them in German, a few in French. All equally obscure to me. I could tell a bit by the format: many were letters, some were inventories and others appeared to be legal documents. The dates I saw ranged from 1712 to 1746 and a good many were signed by Bessler himself, but in the curious affectation of an anagram he used: *Orffyreus*. I couldn't immediately see how any of it could possibly be of use to Glenn. I might arrange to have a few copied and sent to him – though on what basis of selection I wasn't at all sure. Nevertheless, I stayed there patiently for an hour or more, going carefully through them page by page.

I was about done with it, hurriedly flipping pages toward the back binding, when I reached what certainly looked to be the engravings! Their smaller page format was almost tucked under the larger material above and might have thus been missed by Dr. von Mackensen. It had to be what I came for, for they counted out to 141 exactly, annotated extensively, perhaps by Bessler himself, and their subject matter was quite clearly what Glenn had expected. Hardly able to contain my excitement, I had now to deal with the language problem, to discover whether, and how, I might get copies of the entire batch.

The amazing Grace that hovered over me that day hadn't yet run dry: the woman in charge of document reproduction was a transplanted American! I was able to arrange, with complete confidence in the details, for a full set of photo-negatives to be sent and billed to Glenn . . . at the surprisingly low cost of about fifteen cents each.

I felt light as a feather when I walked out of the Bibliothek and crossed the avenue to reward myself with soup and salad. Nearby was a woman playing the flute, and a vaguely familiar melody piped up from her skilled fingerwork: *Que sera, sera* . . . I tossed her a deutschemark and headed toward the restaurant. But just before I got there I was waylaid by the display in a bookstore window: a German translation of one of my favorite *I Ching* resources, an insight-packed commentary by Carol Anthony on the sixty-four hexagrams. Here it was in German, the perfect gift for someone back in Dresden – if only I could afford $25. But I was sure I had already overspent for the week.

It was a good moment, in the restaurant, to bring my accounts up to date and see where I actually stood, as I savored my victory feast. When I drew the balance for this seventh week on the continent it came in just under the budget line: $99.68. My average still held nicely at $89.94. But it hardly warranted starting a new week with a $25 deficit, much as I was tempted by that book. Still . . .

That was when I remembered Glenn's offer to pay for my archival detective work. I'd had no intention of taking anything at all for it, but $25 seemed a fair price and it was the key to a win/win/win triple-header: engravings for Glenn, a book for Simone . . . and for me, the satisfaction of making the gift without compromising my budget. Que sera, sera.

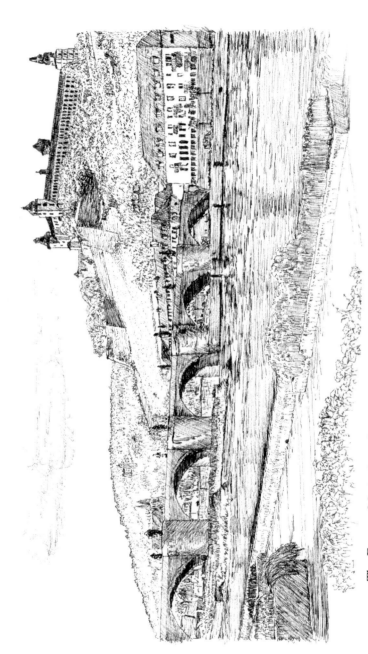

The Festung Marienberg fortress, on a Wurzburg hillside overlooking the Main River. The scene is almost identical in renderings made 150 years apart.

The perils of high summer (I)

Kassel, Germany: July 27, 1991...

Life has taught me to be wary of high summer, the time from late July through mid-August when the year's energy is at peak, pulling me along with the swift and turbulent intensity of a river narrowing. It can be quite as high, in fact, as raft-riding a rock-strewn rapids. But, oh . . . the hell it can wreak if it gets out of hand! There's not much help from expecting it, but I'm at least left with consoling explanations for strange events otherwise shrouded in mystery. Of which this week certainly had its share.

On the last Saturday morning in July I made my way to a south-bound autobahn service area on Kassel's fringe, feeling an urge to get back on the open road. I was only slightly dismayed that someone was there ahead of me, an Ethiopian Black. It made little difference, as it turned out, for no vehicle entering the freeway paused at all – not for two full hours! The longest wait of my entire summer. By the time one pulled over, there were three more hitchers lined up and waiting in-cluding a young red-haired woman traveling alone – who may very well have been the effective bait. But the ride was mine by the rules of the road, the Ethiopian having elected to wait for someone who could take him all the way to Munich.

This one was going only half the 125-mile distance to Wurzburg, my own destination, but it was good enough for me. He was a young physicist who spoke good English and drove with such a relaxed air that I seem to recall him with a leg thrown over the dashboard, which was hardly likely. It was easy conversation all the way to where he left the autobahn, and I had a half-hour wait in the sun, there, for the next stage in my journey.

A van with a couple in it, the woman driving, pulled up. The man, a bearded fellow near my own age, hopped out to engage me in a barrage of German, a one-sided discussion that I presumed had to do with where they were going, for he took the map book out of my hand, flipping pages as he continued his soliloquy. He couldn't find what he was looking for. I took it back, but didn't quickly find the page I wanted, either, and he grabbed it again for another try – all the while of which we were both now talking an increasing fury of words in our respective tongues. It was an utterly senseless scene and I thought sure I'd lose the ride, until the woman got out in some disgust and just made room in the van for me and my stuff.

Having already reached our linguistic threshold with one another we rode in complete silence. I was seated between them, unfortunately, and they couldn't very well talk across me. In desperation, I pulled out the small 14-language phrasebook I hardly ever made use of to see if I could kindle anything at all. With its help I learned the bearded one was 61 and had lived his entire life in Wurzburg. He told me with his hands of the wartime bombing. But of the woman, much younger than he, I learned nothing. She stayed distantly silent through the entire ride, which she drove at a miserably slow pace that eventually reduced me to a state of drowsiness.

In Wurzburg at last, barely off the autobahn, I was unceremoniously dropped at a noisy wayside spot. For a moment of bleary-eyed *deja vu* I was in Portland, Oregon. Only after they rolled on did I realize my 14-language phrasebook was still in the van. It was an exact year, come to think of it – within a day or two – since I'd toppled over a

Portland curbstone, running the rapids of that earlier summer. It should have warned me.

I had been looking forward to Wurzburg for a long time, for there was a friend here whom I hadn't seen in almost ten years. When I met Wuni he was in his 30s, doing graduate work in Theology at one of the satellite colleges close by the University of California in Berkeley. Somehow, between my impious, adventurous spiritual quest of those years and his solid grounding as a Catholic, an unlikely but refreshing mutual respect had emerged. I didn't, and still don't know enough about the varieties of Catholic experience to put Wuni into any pigeonhole, but I found his searching and open mind a stimulus to refreshing discussion, and he seemed to feel the same about me. After his return to Germany to pursue a ministry we had exchanged letters just often enough to remain in touch.

Wuni knew I was coming, but I had been no more specific about timing than a vague reference to "sometime around the first of August." I should have telephoned ahead, but it just never occurred to me that mid-summer could be as relentless in his world as it was in mine. By the late afternoon hour that my calls finally connected I heard surprise and dismay in his voice, not delight; but I had no idea how bad it was until he drove out to pick me up. I had arrived on the very weekend that they were celebrating his wife's 40th birthday, and Ilse's parents were there from out of town for the weekend. That meant his time and head were fully occupied, and his guest space as well. He had excused himself for awhile to greet me but now he was preoccupied, as I could clearly see, with the problem of what to do with me.

We drove east out of Wurzburg maybe a dozen miles to a huge Benedictine monastery that Wuni had some connection with and where he hoped to find retreat quarters for me. He explained little of this; I could only grasp the sense of it as I followed him around, listening to the unintelligible dialogue and watching his expressive features shift from expectancy to downcast disappointment. We had arrived just too late for the last available space. He drove on, then, looking for a bed-and-breakfast vacancy. Had he left it to me, I could as easily have found a Good Neighbors host in my usual way. But Wuni took it as his own responsibility and kept assuring me he'd find a spot – and eventually he did: a tiny skylight room at a small B & B, and his whole body sagged in grateful relief. Then he treated me to a salad feast and I finally glimpsed something of the Wuni I had known.

A decade's time could be expected to leave its mark. A few more pounds, but Wuni's large frame carried them easily. Patches of gray, but his hair still tossed freely in the wind, a youthful touch he hadn't lost. The remnant that really flashed me back, however, was a captivating boyish grin that emerged as we dined. The infrequency of it was less the fault – it was clear, from our talk – of his momentary anxiety over my arrival than the twin burdens he carried, of family life and pastoral responsibilities. Wuni had become a counselor to the clergy, which carries another kind of responsibility, a lonelier sort perhaps, than that of a parish priest.

As we finished the meal I laid out a hastily revised agenda for myself. I'd stay the weekend in the small B & B, as he insisted, then take a side-trip to Darmstadt and return toward the week's end, so that we could have our reunion at a more leisurely time and pace. This made Wuni about as happy as anything in the moment could, and he said he'd be back for breakfast on Monday and take me to the train.

In the circumstance, I probably got a far better weekend rest than I would have had I stayed with Wuni. Sunday was a sparkling-bright day and the gently flowing Main River, close by, offered some wonderful hiking paths along its banks. In a pair of short red pants that I had brought for just such an occasion I crossed to the sunnier opposite side and hiked three easy miles to the village of Dettelbach, to discover there a charming relic of Medieval Germany, all the more exciting for the fact that I came on it entirely by surprise. Dettelbach is an old walled town, like Conwy in Wales but much smaller. Everything, in fact, seemed miniaturized. The village had hardly grown since feudal times, and a circuit of the entire fortification could be made in barely more than twenty minutes. The buttress was largely intact and more than a dozen quaint post towers remained, some in use as private shelters, none with any sign of commercial exploitation.

The walk out to Dettelbach, free of backpack and excess clothing, was a rare experience. I had the path almost entirely to myself, and my pocket radio tuned to some German marching music that I could set a pace by – not just a pace, but drum-major gyrations as fancy as I could contrive on an instant's notice. With nobody there to see or inhibit me, I hit a stride straight out of *Music Man* – wheeling, strutting and twisting up the bank of the River Main in blazing red shorts and a floppy-brim hat, like John Philip Sousa's worst nightmare.

That evening I made a writing desk in the tiny room by propping a wardrobe shelf atop the porcelain sink, pulling the bed lamp over and using the toilet seat for my carcass, and wrote a few letters. In the morning Wuni relieved my minor but real concern about the cost of the weekend lodging by covering it entirely; and then he whisked me off toward an early train to Darmstadt, some three hours to the west.

Had my timing been better at Wurzburg I'd never have taken this side trip, which was a mixed blessing if ever there was. I picked Darmstadt because it was the location of the world famous *Bauhaus School,* and a seminal source of Jugendstil art and architecture. The city had also suffered postwar modernizing, however, and its reputed abundance of old architecture had, for the most part, disappeared. But that was the least of my problems in Darmstadt.

With surprising ease, I found GN hospitality with a pair of fellows in their mid-20s – engineering students at the Technical University who shared an apartment in the northwest part of town, a good mile or more from the railway station. Because of the distance, I had the bright idea of strolling around the inner city before going out there. I left my pack in a rail station locker, taking only a few hand-held folders and notebooks with me, as I often did. But this time they included an envelope containing some of my most important papers: financial records from London and the entire list of British and European addresses I had collected up to now. The risk of loss actually flashed through my mind, in a curious bit of premonition. But for a reason I'll never know, I discounted it, slammed the locker door shut and took the envelope with me.

M

It was not until almost eleven o'clock in the evening, long after I'd done my walking tour, collected my baggage, gone to meet the fellows and had dinner with them, and was now arranging my gear for the night, that I realized the envelope was gone. My head raced back along the day's trail, sorting among the several possibilities, and I was almost positive I'd left it on the counter of the pub-like eatery in the station, just before returning to the locker for my pack.

I looked for Bernhardt, the one of my two hosts who had an automobile; but he had gone out for the evening. Jurgen, the other of the pair, had an old bicycle he said I could use, and in the time it took me to tuck my trouser legs into my socks I was pedaling madly through darkened streets, over tracks and around parked vehicles, caution tossed aside, hoping to get there before the place closed for the night. But that had already happened an hour earlier and all my effort gave me was a weary ride back, to pass a miserable half-sleepless night trying to remember – and trying to forget about – everything that was in the lost envelope.

By mid-morning when the eatery opened, I was back at the station, only to meet with the worst sort of resistance trying to get myself understood. I think they felt I was accusing someone of theft. I cursed myself for not having left a counter tip because I hadn't been very happy with their service – quite sure I'd never be back. For all my pleas, even with a note in German from the stationmaster, I got only head-shaking denial that they had ever seen the envelope. After peering fruitlessly into every crack and crevice around the lockers, every trash bin – which had of course been emptied the night before – I reluctantly gave it up. I retraced my course around town, equally to no avail. The envelope was gone ... finally and irrevocably, *Gone.*

The loss was a harsh one and it would reverberate for many weeks as I tried to understand it – for I don't at all believe in accidents – and as I worked at recovering the lost addresses, such as I could. Some of the more important I still had on letters, either with me or awaiting me in Munich. Most Good Neighbors addresses I could get again, for all the names were in my journal notes. But there were others, people I had met along the way who wanted to stay in touch or offered faraway shelter if I should pass their way. And many of the casual friends I had made in London. It cast a gray shadow over my visit to Darmstadt, despite the city's basic charm and appeal.

The *Hesse Landesmuseum,* alone, justified the sidetrip with an exquisite display of Art Nouveau jewelry, possibly the finest assemblage to be found anywhere. And it was here that I ran into the best assortment of art books I had yet come across – Jugendstil, of course. They were not cheap in western Germany, and I ended up spending far beyond my budget limit in order to acquire a few. I passed it off with the rationale that I was entitled to consolation after such a great loss a fresh take on the old thesis that 'living well is the best revenge.' Healing comes high when life turns contrary; and I'd hardly be surprised if it's misery that really drives our market economy, more than pleasure and need, or plain greed, ever did.

I stayed three nights with Bernhardt and Jurgen, who were great hosts in the easy-going fashion of college students everywhere. When I departed for my return to Wurzburg, it was by rail again and by way of Frankfurt, a short distance to the north, for the sake of visiting a photography museum that Bernhardt had cued me to. Like most else of this ill-starred week, it brought both reward and grief.

The reward was in a picture postcard. Long years ago, when I lived in California, I was entranced by the image of a woman captured on film by the Scottish photographer James Craig Annan, in the early part of the century. I knew little more of her than the name in the photo caption: *Frau Muthesius.* Only that she was German, and a distinctively beautiful woman. Browsing in one of the Darmstadt bookstores, I came across a second photo of her by yet another noted photographer. But all the further information it gave me was a first name: Anna. That this singularly captivating woman had been a portrait study for two notable photographers and then all but vanished in the mist of history suddenly piqued my interest. For she appeared to be a woman of some substance and achievement.

I had asked Bernhardt if there was a photo archive or museum in Darmstadt. He knew only of the *Fotografie Forum* in Frankfurt, which proved to be hardly more than a small gallery. I expected nothing there at all, but glancing through their stock of postcards for sale, I came across a third portrait of Anna Muthesius – this one by still another photographer, Jacob Hillsdorf. Realizing it must have represented a showing there, I hastened to the shelves of the gallery bookshop and, sure enough, there were a couple volumes on Hillsdorf's life and work, and in one of them I finally learned a bit about this mystery woman.

Anna Muthesius was an early-day feminist, author of several works on women's clothing styles, and children's books as well, and she had been a performing vocalist before marriage to a noted architect. She lived to 91 years of age, dying in 1961 in Berlin.

It would have made an exciting fourth quest in Berlin, had I the time to return there – but I had already given it more time than I could spare. The half-day spent in chase of it cost me the last likelihood of a satisfying reunion with Wuni. Or maybe it was lost regardless; the recapture of postponed pleasures may simply be one of life's lesser delusions. Whatever the case, we got our wires crossed once more.

Wuni had been expecting my early Thursday return, and waited all afternoon for me – and I cannot be sure I didn't promise it. By the time I found my way through twisting streets to the newly built house in their hilltop suburban section of Wurzburg and rang the doorbell, it was well past their 6:30 dining hour. I was served a re-heated dinner, with all the forced cheer of such an occasion, and we sat together as I ate, engaging in the make-believe conversation that happens when people can't reveal their feelings. Had Ilse any disposition to regard this road-weary guest of Wuni's with anything more than simple charity, it certainly ended with the *faux pas* of my tardy return. She spoke no English at all, so I can only judge from her very proper politeness and Wuni's own evident discomfort.

In the remaining light of day, Wuni took me to survey the sights worth seeing. It was the tour he intended had I returned at an earlier hour, but in the circumstances it seemed almost designed to cover the scars of an unpleasant passage. At any rate, nothing of the tour, not even a stop for ice cream, managed to spark the old rapport we'd once had, and I'm sure Wuni was as painfully aware of it as I.

Ilse was a strikingly attractive woman – blue-eyed, blond with an abbreviated hair style that did the most for her strong neckline – yet, attractive in a self-possessed, cool way that suggested high standards of excellence in her world. It was apparent in their home, allowing for the likely limits of clergy income: furnishing that was spare but comfortable, a house run with orderly precision – meals on schedule, everything planned. I could easily see Ilse's appeal for Wuni, and that their home life was geared to his professional needs. But the up-scale style contrasted with the Wuni of student days that I recalled, and I wondered if he, himself, had changed or if his world was pushing him into ways he wasn't entirely easy with.

Their guest room was an open half-level above his study, and he could surely have been under a strain, being displaced from his private retreat for the better part of a week, at least, first by Ilse's family and now by me. But there was a weariness about him, or a want of joy that seemed to go deeper. The sunshine burst through whenever he played with little Dorothea or her tiny brother, but it only made the general overcast more apparent by contrast.

Four-year-old Dorothea was a delight, my only unalloyed pleasure in the household. Even at the ungodly morning hour, long before their 7:30 breakfast time, that she dragged me back into the world with a steady, soft babble of German at my bedside. It was amazing how beautifully we got on with each other without a single understood word between us.

Friday, I was on my own and I used it to explore a great old fortress on a high hill, the Festung Marienberg. An ancient stone bridge with statuary figures of saints atop its massive piers took me across the Main River, and I climbed successive levels of long stairways, moats, and high walls, seemingly without end, before reaching the ramparts of this redoubt – itself many tiers high and the size of a small village. The city of Wurzburg spread below like a fiefdom reinforced the glory of this high prominence. Later, on a postcard, I found a painting of the fortress done in 1835, a riverside view with the multi-arched bridge in the foreground, hardly any different than the scene looks today. Where, in America, is there a place so readily in touch with its past?

I made damn sure of getting back to Wuni's before 6:30 on this night, though it didn't much change the feeling of *pro forma* hospitality; and I couldn't help but reflect on the contrast with a Good Neighbors household, where one is not merely a guest for a night or two, but – even on the shortest of notice – a cause for enthused conversation often lasting long into the evening. Here, sad to say, I felt almost like an intruder except for the joyful attentions of little Dorothea. The really sad part is that I know they were working at hospitality – Ilse even did a wash of clothing for me. But the heart knows what the head refuses to acknowledge . . . and actively denies.

A day later, on the train to Nürnberg, I reviewed the whole business – everything that had happened during the week, though most of my concern still focused on the lost envelope of addresses. As I looked at the messy jumble of events an oddly consistent pattern began to emerge. Even given summer's madness, when chaos strikes in a life that relies on the grace of the Universe there is a pretty clear implication that something has been done wrong: a path not taken or one mistakenly taken, or some cue missed along the way. What I suddenly saw threw some illumination on what might have been happening all week long.

The loss of the address list could easily be a metaphoric statement that I really didn't need the baggage I carry from the past. It was certainly true: I have a tendency to 'collect,' in ways that are not always material but can be just as burdensome, maybe even more so. I collect friends, and I hate to see friendship's path split and diverge so greatly that a friend is lost. But friends follow separate trails, and once-touching worlds lose their points of congruence – in which event neither one's life is enhanced by maintaining the connection.

When I came into Wurzburg, the ill-timed 'accident' of it should have told me as much – for there are no accidents. Instead, I colluded with Wuni to try and salvage something not really there any longer. Then in Darmstadt, my guiding spirit alerted me to the particular difficulty I have with loss of friendships, even as they begin! The twinned phenomena, on both ends of the friendship spectrum, made the point so sharply that I hardly wanted to look at it – yet could hardly avoid it.

Other ways of seeing it would come to me, in time, for truth is like a cut jewel: it shines anew as it is turned this way and that. But this was good enough for now. Friendship should neither die nor be dismissed. But it shouldn't always be pursued, either, for it lingers most richly in memory when its embers are not raked. I salute you, Wuni, dear friend of other times, and wish you well on your life's course ... and I apologize for attempting to impose the past on your present world.

The cost of my indiscretions, in purchased 'consolation' (more books), pretty much blew the budget credit I had accumulated up to this point. My Jugendstil indulgence took the week's expenditures up to $150.58, and my weekly average was now very near the borderline, at $97.52. The rapids had yet a week or two to run. I could only hope that their worst had been done.

Yet to come, on my journey, a better look at Prague. This is one of her prime jewels, the Art Nouveau Municipal House and the ancient Gunpowder Gate Tower alongside.

The perils of high summer (II)

en route to Nürnberg, Germany: August 3, 1991...

I had to suffer a crowded compartment in the smoking section for the hour it took to reach Nürnberg. It might have been simpler had I hit the highway and headed straight for Munich. But Wuni advised me to see Nürnberg for its historic interest, and so had Bernhardt. Anyway, I wasn't ready for Munich just yet. That promised to be another challenging experience – a first-time meeting with a longtime pen-pal, young and feminine. I needed a lull between Wuni and Rachel.

I made the opening mistake of taking tea in the station, at Nürnberg, because the panelled dining room was impossible to resist – for which I paid three dollars! And then it required six phone calls to find a host. But things got better from there on. I took a local bus, following instructions, to a mixed residential and retailing neighborhood, spotted the sporty yellow convertible I was told to look for and went upstairs to a second-floor apartment.

Quite unimpressive from the outside, it had the sensitive, comfortable feeling, inside, of a woman's touch. But Klaus, almost fifty though he looked much younger, lived there alone. He was a freelance computer engineer – as unimpressive from the outside, himself, as the apartment he lived in, but I soon saw there was much more going on inside than one might suppose from his terminally rational profession. He had been raised in Indonesia, of German parentage, and his cross-cultural outlook was flavored with subtleties of awareness not generally found among westerners.

All of this and much more came out over a pizza dinner, that evening, when he took me out to see the town. We discovered almost at once a shared interest in the right/left hemisphere relationship by which the brain coordinates body activity . . . and in some mysterious way seems to ride herd on one's life as well. Klaus had much the same view of this, and the same respect for it, as I did. While much has been written on it, no one really knows the full extent of the right hemisphere's contribution to our lives. Its activity is screened from consciousness. Yet, there is evidence at every hand of some shaping influence, once we begin to watch for it, with implications that challenge our insistence on a completely rational world.

We sparked one another with our observations on it. Klaus spoke of left-handed tennis players who seem, by nature, more agile, better coordinated in their footwork than right-handers. And I recalled for him precious moments when life had forced me to act instantly, without time for thought to interfere – and I had always done exactly the right thing. I told him of my left-hand portrait experiments, intended to open a channel for right-hemisphere expression, and how they seemed to put me in more conscious touch with that inner mystery.

Any such discussion of reality and the extent of its rational content has nuances that call for absolute clarity, and the fluency that Klaus had, with English, helped a lot. He made one point in a humorous way that would have been lost on me without the full rapport we had.

"The difficult part, here, you know, is that every time we start thinking about the limits of rationality we lose the benefit of an open mind."

"How do you mean?" I asked, not sure what he was getting at.

"Well . . . imagine that we've scheduled a debate, and we invite a speaker from the left hemisphere to prove the world is essentially rational."

"Of course," I replied. "That's its natural province; the left brain would make the best possible case for rationalism."

"So it would," Klaus shot back. "The same air-tight case made by philosophers of mind and nature down through history."

I waited for him to proceed. But he sat there with a smug smile until I finally took the bait. "So then the right-hemisphere, I suppose, would take the other side of the issue, and argue against a rational world?"

"And there you have it."

"Have what?" I asked. "I'm waiting for your point."

Klaus chuckled softly, almost to himself. "You've made it yourself. The right hemisphere has no way of speaking directly to us, no voice to speak with. All of our conscious thought comes from the left hemisphere; and if such a debate were to take place – as it supposedly does, whenever we consider the question – the only speaker present would be the voice for the affirmative."

Klaus took me, that evening, on a native's guided tour through the historic heart of Nürnberg. Up alley passages, down stone stairways, between ancient walls and into charming courts – I only realized how well he knew the place when I tried to retrace some of our trail the following day, and couldn't do it, even with a map in my hands. One particularly fascinating item was a half-timbered two-story structure, its beams intricately 'keyed' to each other in such a way that they locked securely into place with no use of nails or pins! The building had been slated for demolition, he told me, until a last minute x-ray probe revealed the old structure beneath an outer facing that had covered its ingenious craftsmanship for as long as local tradition or record could recall.

We ended up in the northwest corner of the old section at the Tiergarten Platz, an open area of intimate size in the shadow of a great gate tower that pierces the old city wall here. A quiet gathering spot for evening crowds who sit and stand around as if something were about to happen – but they, themselves, are the happening. As the soft amber lighting of outdoor beer and 'eis' gardens (ice cream) took over from the deepening twilight, it was a lovely scene: people in chatting/laughing/singing clusters, a pair of young women doing a juggling routine, an organ grinder and his monkey ... and back-dropping all of it, lit by yellow floodlight, the looming Imperial Castle and its grandiose stable house – now Bavaria's most popular youth hostel – its high sloped roof raked by successive tiers of dormer windows thirstily open to the evening breeze. Altogether, a summer's evening ambience that was hard to leave, even though I was exhausted from the long day.

The rest of that weekend provided the temporary respite from travel and summer intensity that I sorely needed.

Over a sendoff breakfast on Monday morning, Klaus told me of the *Wanderjahre* tradition: the wandering year of a young apprentice who has learned his art and goes out to share his skills among the people he meets along the way, for sustenance and shelter. He can go anywhere during his wander, but cannot return home until the year is done. I thought about the circumstance that my own year abroad would reach fullness in just a little more than a month. But what had been my apprenticeship ... the rarified art of living in innocence? Had I really become a journeyman at it?

Klaus cleared the dishes away and then took me in his zippy yellow roadster for what seemed a long ride out the highway toward Munich, finally arriving at a busy service stop on the autobahn, the perfect place from which to resume my *Wanderjahre*.

It was an unusually bright morning and I felt singularly alive and high as I walked to the far end of the service area, picked my spot and unhitched the pack on my back to set myself for another go at the road – when a sudden momentary catch between my chest and throat alerted me to something all too familiar; but I was too busy untangling myself from the pack to make the instant response it called for. For those few seconds of delay ... I blew it.

A tachycardia attack had taken hold! My heart was speeding off like Klaus' yellow roadster, in a race with itself, and I had lost the moment to apply the brakes.

I can't recall how long I've been dealing with tachycardia. I do remember some scary times it has put me through, going back at least twenty years. It takes over the body with a sudden flush and weakness, and one can barely keep going at minimal energy level. It might take a half-hour or the whole day to run its course – I've never had the fear-free patience to wait and see. I work at stopping it, for there is no other choice. It takes the spine out of one's being, and the mind can be turned to nothing else while it's happening.

Over the years, I've learned a few methods for snapping the heart-beat back to normal, but like a bacterium that develops a drug-resistant strain, each has run its course of effectiveness and no longer works for me. The only consistently reliable counter-measure has been a response in the first few moments of fluttering pulse: to stop everything and breathe deliberately and deeply, holding the first lung-full of air for a moment and then slowly and evenly letting it out all the way, doing a mental count at the proper rhythm. But the deep and slow breathing must begin immediately – before the tachycardia gains a momentum that is far more difficult to break.

The moment I realized it had gotten away from me I knew I was in trouble. With traffic pounding all around me, people looking at me from every direction (the idiotic things we worry about!), nowhere to hide, no place to go for help – as if I even knew what help to seek, miles out on the autobahn from Nürnberg . . . *What to do?!*

In dizziness and uncertainty, free of panic only because I hadn't the energy for it, I sat down cross-legged beside the onrushing traffic, put my earplugs into place and tried to find the calm for a return to deep-breathing. But it was impossible, trapped between that maelstrom out there and the one going on inside my head.

I looked desperately around for a way out of the maddening high-way situation. A restaurant stood nearby, but the last thing I wanted was a social setting that required any effort at normalcy. I wanted to be alone somewhere. I saw a path to the side of the restaurant going through the trees, and I followed it – into a sheltered, rustic garden area curiously graced with a small stone Celtic cross, and no one in sight. A narrow bench faced the cross, a seating for one, as if it had been or-dered for the very moment. I sat down to figure out what next in this situation of no options.

I tried again to meditate there, but it just wasn't happening. I tried one of the tricks I learned years ago when an attack had once driven me to a Berkeley emergency ward: holding a deep breath as tightly as possible while trying at the same time, with all available force, to exhale it. It had worked for me then, and maybe once or twice since. But it only resulted now in profuse sweating.

I considered getting someone to call for medical assistance . . . but that brought a whole other range of problems into prospect. No insurance, for one thing, and I was not quite ready to trade off my shallow funds for the riddance of my shallow heartbeat. Every avenue seemed hopeless. Must I get out on the road in this condition and try for a ride? How would I even handle it if I got one?

I'd once read a believable interview with a woman who led a hitch-hiking life, who said she'd continue to thumb when she became ill, and a doctor would pick her up. It sounds far-fetched, I know, but one rule of innocence is that the answer to any serious problem is to be found somewhere in one's immediate world. And it had always worked that way for me. I could hardly fault it even now, for this secluded glen at least gave me a measure of peace – however small the consolation. But what else was here for me?

After maybe an hour of this debilitated agonizing – which might have been a form of prayer, sitting there in front of a mystic cross, though I had no such conscious intent – a strange idea popped into my head. I recalled how medical attendants, in the case of a suddenly failed heart, would beat on a victim's chest . . . massively, with solid blows. Ready to try anything, I fisted my right hand and hit my chest over the heart as solidly as I could.

Nothing changed. But I had pulled my punch, I thought. It's not easy to pound yourself that way with full abandon. I closed my eyes, tried to release myself to a total effort and did it again. Still nothing.

Once more, and a roundhouse swing, doing my damnedest this time to forget it was my own body I was slamming . . .

I rammed myself so hard that for a dazed moment I thought something was different . . . but it WAS different – I was breathing easily. I quickly grabbed a wrist to check my pulse and felt it steady and strong. The tachycardia was gone!

I sat there in an indescribable moment of relief, hardly daring to move lest it undo the results of that marvelous inspiration. I shall probably never know where it came from, whether out of left brain or right. Nor how I knew enough to keep trying until that successful third slam.

Back on the highway again, my spirits soared as only on a spring day. It felt like I'd been let free after standing on a gallows, or magically become a stripling despite my sixty-four years. It put me into a care-free, singing space, and when another hitch-hiker turned up not more than a few minutes later, a tall and gangly young fellow dressed in short pants and tank top with a big floppy-brim hat, I was quickly into conversation with him. From Hamburg, way to the north, and heading for Innsbruck, Austria, he spoke English easily and was a good deal curious as to how I found the hitching "at my age." (Ha! ... If he but knew.) The implication, of course, was that drivers would hardly be stopping for an old man. And even as I pointed out, in reply, that all kinds of people sit behind the wheel, one actually – then and there – pulled over for me.

For the two of us, as it turned out. A middle-aged fellow going to Munich, and he spoke only German; but the gods, now working smoothly for me, had provided a translator in my sudden roadside friend. I saw to it that he took the front seat, while I sat in the rear. It wasn't long before we stopped so they could switch places up front – our driver apparently weary at the wheel from a long morning on the road. I silently gave it my blessing (for wasn't I now precisely at the center of Grace?).

Munich was hardly more than an hour away; and once there, we pulled into a parking area by a satellite rail station on the east side. I helped my Innsbruck-bound companion find his routing, through the transit maze on the station's wall map – I was getting good enough at this game to give assistance to a native! For me, the next stop would have to be a bank, via the subway downstairs. In good banana-peel form, I had once more let my pocket cash drop below the ten-dollar level.

I came out of the underground station literally agasp at the sudden surround of ornate and colorful old architecture. I was in the Marienplatz, the heart of Munich's downtown, with the *Rathaus* – the city hall – towering in front of me; yet the entire mid-day scene of lunchtime shoppers and browsers was as peaceful as if their world stood still. An incredible contrast with Berlin's hectic midtown pace.

In the span of an hour I found the only bank in town providing Visa cash, and then the American Express agency where a small bundle of letters awaited. Not among them, however – and it gave me a momentary jolt – the expected packet from London that should bring my last batch of maps and GN host lists for the countries I had yet to travel through. Well, I'd be here until week's end, and it would surely arrive by then.

After taking time to indulge in the lately rare privilege of reading mail over a cup of tea, I set out for the suburb of Grafelfing, where lived Rachel and Andreas with several other college students. I'd been looking forward to this since well before my departure from Seattle, for I had never met Rachel though we had been corresponding for some ten years – ever since she was a grade-schooler in small-town Texas.

It's an interesting and somewhat unusual tale that goes back to my California years, when I was a resource person on Simple Living for the *Holyearth Foundation,* from which the Earthstewards later emerged. Rachel was given my name by a teacher as part of a class project to familiarize students with groups working toward a planetary consciousness. She wrote to me, initiating an occasional exchange that continued as she progressed through school, and on to college in Iowa. She was now in Munich doing graduate work toward a language doctorate. In all that time I'd received only one photo, a high school graduation picture of an engaging young teen-ager – no longer a schoolgirl. So now, at last, I was going to meet Rachel, a co-ed well into life's stream.

Grafelfing felt comfortable, like an older, well-settled American suburb. Large homes stood on quiet streets shielded by shrubbery and picket fences; a few residents worked at lawn and house maintenance

... the usual buzz of mowers and such, but very little auto traffic. I was expected, having phoned ahead, and received a broad grin from the fellow at the door, who called behind him for Rachel.

She was smaller, it seemed to me, and slimmer than the image that remained from that photo seen so long ago ... more engaging, actually. Especially when her hair was let loose and allowed to flow free, from the severe way it was tied back for that first glimpse. I saw a serious young woman not quite grown into her studied self-image of the mature professional, for it gave way often enough to a charming laugh and smile. Her big fellow, Andreas, had also his serious side but was even more often light and playful. No longer in school, himself, he worked as a cartographer.

The experience of getting to know Rachel in this abbreviated week, after we had known each other by mail for practically half her lifetime, was rare and unique – something to be treasured not just for its own sake, but for the inter-generational element. There had been just enough substance in our correspondence that I had felt at times like a mentor – if not, indeed, like a wayward grandfather. But I don't think Rachel saw me in either light, for she treated me like an old friend, which was really what I wanted. She and Andreas had the attic portion of the house to themselves, a pair of fairly large rooms, and I was given sleeping space in one of them. Their three housemates occupied the lower two floors. Meals were shared or not, as convenient, though they made a point of trying to eat dinner together, with a system of rotational responsibility for it. I asked to have Friday night for my contribution.

Rachel and Andreas were taking off at week's end for a holiday in Spain, which is why I had to get to Munich when I did. Amazingly, I had arrived on schedule – the unintended schedule that had been pushing me, week by week, ever since Paris. The whole five days became an idyllic retreat from rigors of the road. I soaked it in like a thirsty sponge, sometimes going sightseeing into town with Rachel, sometimes on my own, but spending most of the early evenings and late mornings just lazing my time away at the homestead. August at this point was refreshingly free of intensity or hassle – almost to the point where I wondered how I could have gotten such notions. But there was still the matter of the missing packet from London. Day by day, as often as I went into town, I'd check for it . . . and day after day it wasn't there yet.

On the other hand, there was an indication, in a very lucky break on the local bus taking me back to Grafelfing one afternoon, that my August woes were finally over. I was trying to stretch my bus ticket beyond its legal limit – either as to distance or time, I no longer recall which – and just as I was about to exit, a quite ordinary looking passenger revealed herself as an inspector, asking the person ahead of me in line to show her ticket. I scooted by and out the door as they were involved. Rachel later told me that I had barely escaped a heavy fine.

My mail packet had included a letter from Evelyne, my first Parisian host, whose address had been among those lost in Darmstadt. It was a reminder of her August translation assignment here, and contained a Munich phone number. She answered my call and on Thursday afternoon we got together to re-convene our rambling-everywhere conversation, while we strolled and lolled the Isar River's grassy banks near the huge *Deutsches Museum* where her services had been engaged. I had to 'shape my hearing' all over again, to the strange rhythm of her accented English.

Evelyne always had a look of quiet amusement about her, not residing in a smile but in her features as a whole, as if she secretly knew that the world was nothing more serious than a place to enjoy . . . and was content to keep the secret of it to herself. She knew of a modest, not very crowded cafe and we went there for dinner and more talk, late into the evening, mainly about the adventures I had come through. She still thought it possible to pay me a winter or early spring visit if I found sufficiently roomy quarters for myself on some sunny Greek isle.

I finally had to accept that the expected packet of onward travel resources was not going to arrive. Whether by error or outright loss, it had just vanished, like my addresses in Darmstadt. And maybe for similar reasons in the scheme of things – something I had better take into account. A second piece of awaited mail hadn't come, either, which fit right into the picture. One of the lost addresses had seemed critical: that of Georghe in Romania, for he was practically the key to my easy passage through the Balkans, getting ever more significant as the Yugo-slavian conflict continued to roil and boil. So I had written immediately for it to Tom, in Amsterdam, whose address I had on a booklet he'd given me. But no reply from Tom ever arrived.

The circumstances seemed to present a clear pattern. It was August, the year's energy was at peak, and I was getting the prompt that my journey was just about done. Or should be, at any rate, for I could not much longer ride nature's own energy crest. Like a surfer who has lost his wave, I'd just be struggling to stay afloat. Never mind that my plan was to search out a winter's haven in Greece. Never mind that Evelyne might even join me there for a week or two – something for fantasy to play with – or my promise to Georghe. Or that another longtime correspondence friend awaited me in Budapest.

I couldn't help wishing that Klaus was there to talk with. It was a clear contest between the urgings of left brain and right. My conscious side had an agenda too rich in promise and potential to set aside; but the right brain, in its characteristically silent but insistent way, was telling me to let it go.

Well, there is beauty in living by innocence – taking the measure of things as they come and adapting to their requirements. There is also beauty in taking one's own reins in life and charging through obstacles. I have strong convictions about which is the better way to live, but I am not without the urges to glory and love and plain old self-gratification that from time to time can overpower the most dedicated convictions.

In retrospect, I might have paid more heed to those messages – which I'm sure I correctly understood – but ... I chose to ignore them. Even as Freud is said to have once observed, "sometimes a cigar is just a cigar," pointedly ignoring the `Freudian' implications of his habit (but neglecting to add that one *chooses* the left-brain perspective). I sent an urgently worded letter to Europe's top coordinator of Good Neighbors, in Denmark, asking her to send the host lists for Romania, Bulgaria and Greece, as well as Austria – to mail them to me in Vienna, in time for my arrival there.

For Friday evening, I prepared a favorite eggplant dish in a sim-mering veggie-rich tomato sauce and completed the dinner with a special dessert known only to me (up to now, at any rate). I call it a Black Hawaiian: chocolate ice cream topped by chunk pineapple in its own syrup and finessed with a touch of cream sherry or marsala. These folks in Munich could not know it, but I was celebrating a twentieth re-birthday, though the proper occasion for it was yet several days away.

Refreshed completely, by Saturday morning's departure time, I bid my two young friends a happy holiday, had a brief last rendezvous with Evelyne, and resumed my own further journey – heading this time northeast toward Czechoslovakia. I had originally intended to go south into Austria, but the lack of a host list argued against it. Besides, I had promised myself another visit to Prague after that flawed first time with Albert. If I went directly, however, I'd be back in a weekend situation there, so I decided to linger awhile in Regensberg, an hour by rail from Munich.

There wasn't much of a host list there, and I ran entirely through it, connecting on the very last one – a couple living a few miles out of town. Roland, a teacher in his mid-30s, came out to the station for me, and we were quickly back at their cool, white-walled villa-style home high on a hill. Ute, a journalist, greeted me there with an immediate spread of tea and cookies, but warned me that her time was mostly taken up by work on a doctoral thesis. It had to do with women's support of Germany during the first World War – a subject I naturally knew nothing about, yet our brief exchange somehow led me into a conversational entanglement over general feminist issues, and I found myself unaccountably cast as a male apologist. It wasn't in any real sense a confrontational discussion, yet it felt like each of us was defend-ing territory and somewhat barbing the tips of the points we made.

I didn't see much of Ute after that except for dinnertime and its considerably more subdued conversation, and I was a bit concerned that I might have been more offensive than defensive in the afternoon's lightweight joust. As I turned in that evening, in a very comfortable upstairs room, I wondered why some feminists seem to draw that sort of response from me while others do not. Some claim their ground by making an issue of it, even if only in tone of voice. While others – and

I thought of Evelyne once more, and Simone, too – are simply being themselves, in some easy, sure sense of who they are.

Sunday morning, up before anyone in the house, I set out on foot to retrace the route Roland had driven and to see what I could of the town. Like a rabbit warren, it was ribbed and crossed by narrow stone-paved streets, each hemmed between tall pastel-tinted walls, so similar in general appearance that it called for constant attention to a map, to avoid going in circles. I had my first glimpse of the Danube River here, too, marking the old town's north boundary and split by lenticular islands, here, into several channels. One of the bridges I walked across that morning was a narrow stone structure dating from 1135 – said to be the oldest original bridge still in use north of the Alps.

Off to the right, just before reaching this crossing as I came toward town, was a narrow path bordered with greenery and sheltered by natural arbors. Unable to resist its pull, I hiked up to a poster-perfect Bavarian setting: a little hilltop church that stood alone in a meadow, edged with bright flowers and etched against a deep blue sky. At right angle from my own path to it was another, much steeper, coming directly from town and bordered by a hewn-rail fence. On alternate fence posts were small wood-carved scenes of the stations of the cross. Church-goers, some of whom labored up this path with all their aged energy, completed the picture. In a parking lot near the church were automobiles that had come by some other access road; but a few of these villagers seemed to prefer the long, difficult pathway to the top.

That evening, as I sat outside with Roland in the still warm air, both of us silently watching stars blink into view in the deepening purple of an unusually peaceful twilight, I thought about the interesting conjunction of perspectives at that little church on the hill. For some people the automobile is just transportation. For many more it's the most present-able way to get to church. For still others – and maybe most – it's sufficient power not to even need a church. But there are yet a few who choose the strenuous walk over the easy ride. They radiate a strange aura of contentment, even cheer, though they tend to say very little of such things as these.

Roland drove me into town early Monday morning. I drew a week's worth of Visa cash: two hundred deutschemarks that I could exchange as I went, taking my chances as always that I'd find another Visa-honoring bank the next time I needed one – a little the more risky in the unpredictabilities of eastern Europe. My sheltered time in Munich had been easy on the budget, the week's expenses amounting to only $83.88. It took me a bit back from the brink, to a nine-week average of exactly $96.

I wasn't sure until the last minute, which of two possible train routes I'd take. The schedule decided it and I went for a pleasing little village called Furth-im-Wald, three miles shy of the Czech border. I deliberately spent the last of my German coin there, somehow making it clear to the woman behind the pastry counter that I wanted as much as it would buy. It bought cherry cheesecake with tea, savored at an outdoor table while I wrote a postcard to Terry. Then I set out along the meadowed, rolling countryside at a good stride toward Czechoslovakia and eastern Europe, once again.

OM

Dating from 1270, this is the towered gate at one end of the long public square in Domazlice. Taken from a watercolor rendering by Jan Paroubek, long ago mentor to a youthful Jan Prokop Holy.

My Holy experience in Domazlice

Czech border near Furth-im-Wald, Germany: August 12, 1991...

The tingling promise of adventure surged through me once more as I neared the country that could practically call oppression a birthright. Czechoslovakia, a child of the First World War, had been under Soviet or Nazi domination for more than two thirds of its political existence. By any odds, they were a strong people merely to have survived with a modicum of national integrity. In my book, they were heroic.

That personal assessment goes back long before the 'Prague Spring' of 1968, Alexander Dubcek's effort at liberalization under Soviet rule. I can recall sharing an elevator in San Francisco, during the founding days of the United Nations, with Jan Masaryk, the son of Thomas Masaryk who was regarded as the father of his country. Not many months later the younger Masaryk mysteriously 'jumped to his death,' coincident with the end of Czechoslovakia's brief postwar renewal of sovereignty.

Reflecting on all of this, and the fascinating postscript that they had still the imagination to select a poet – Vaclav Havel – as their head of state when self-rule finally returned, I walked across a border with little

more to mark it than the change from a well-paved and graded roadway to a pitted and dusty one that lurched steeply upward. But I no
longer felt the shock of contrast, as once before on the road to Leipzig.
Something unarguably exotic took precedence, now, about these lands
of the past: tense, and the present: imperfect.

Nothing was here at this minor border crossing but a patrol station, and inside, a change bureau where I took my first portion of
Czech kronen. The area looked like an abandoned construction project
– not a cheery spot from which to hitch. But with the steep hill in
prospect I saw no point in walking further. The traffic was sparse.
Family-filled vehicles for the most part, zooming past me to gain momentum for the climb. Nobody paid me much heed. After an hour of it,
with the skies curdling into a possibility of rain, I started wondering if it
might make more sense to return to Furth-im-Wald and take the next
train.

But a better option came along in the form of a local bus, easily
fifty years ancient. When it swung around and opened its door for
several waiting people at the border station, I was ready to go wherever
they were headed. I took a hard seat by a window, after paying what
amounted to twenty cents for passage, and we were underway at once,
bouncing along at a fair speed given the age of the bus. We went by a
resort called Babylon, a simple rustic lake-front place with a holiday
crowd of bathers. No gaudy billboards and no traffic jams . . . fun
without hassle or hype, and a sudden rush of awareness that the communist years had preserved something more than bleakness from the
past. It was woods and farmland, from there, for six or seven miles until
we came to the town of Domazlice, the end of the line, and I followed
everyone off the bus.

The immediate view was anything but promising. A general dreari-
ness in sidewalks bordered by grey walls and somber, featureless buildings . . . I followed the others along a side street that narrowed toward
an opening up ahead, perhaps a market square. Everyone seemed intent on getting there. It took me by surprise – a tremendous open
court, longer by far than any market square I'd seen, as if a typical
square had been stretched in one direction, stretched until its ends were

too far apart for hailing distance. At one far end stood a magnificent Medieval gate tower, half the width of the court itself and rising six floors ... with its high-angle roof line almost doubling the height. But my view was stolen at once by a structure just as wonderful right alongside my avenue of entry – a circular tower that rose twelve to fifteen stories, capped and spired with delicate architectural care.

The court, like a spacious avenue, was flanked solidly on each side by a long arcade of shops set back beneath sheltering arches supporting the overhang of three and four-story buildings. People stood around in casual groups or strolled at such an idle pace that the setting took on a dreamlike quality, the entire effect suggesting not only a journey back in time, but to another kind of planet.

I sat for a long moment on a stone bench taking it in, and I thought about the backdrop of conditioning that made this scene seem so unreal – my reflex ideas of what a marketplace should be: crowded, bustling, competitive ... in short, a style that seemed from this perspective a little insane. Here, community was at least as important as commerce; and even this with an easy grace, a consideration for life's full measure: taking the sun, breaking the day to chat a bit, browse a bit ... maybe even get a bit of shopping done. None of it with any hurry or tension. I was gazing at the social equivalent of an endangered species, already extinct in the West.

I wanted to see more of this place I had stumbled across in such fortuitous surprise. I strolled down to the tower portal at the far end, and at a little kiosk on its other side I purchased a map of the town for fifty cents, an artful production graced with superb watercolors of local scenes. To my further surprise it was done in three languages including English. Back to the arcade, then, to shop for the makings of an impromptu lunch: a quarter-loaf of fresh hard-crust bread, a half-pound of butter (the smallest amount I could get) and a large, warm cola drink – all for ninety cents. Dining in the sun on the stone bench, ignored by most but regarded with curiosity by a few, I pored over the map. Every useful bit of information imaginable was in it. Even a 'tourist dormitory!' Maybe I should stay the night in Domazlice.

Off I went, to find the tourist dormitory – whatever it might be.

But it was not so easily done. The map wasn't the problem, it was the town itself. Streets had no indication of names and were in various stages of repair, so that I couldn't quite tell if a lengthy ditch was a street or just a hole in the ground. At one point I was sure I had come to a certain intersection, but the map didn't quite match what I saw. I was puzzling over it when a short, greying man with a shopping bag came along and I took a stab at asking him where the tourist dormitory was. To my surprise, he spoke a little English. Not enough to give me a clear answer, but he kept pointing in the direction I was headed. So I continued on my path . . . to where it should have been, but wasn't. I circled back, returning to the point of puzzlement, and . . . here came the little man again, his shopping bag now full. This time, seeing my plight, he insisted on leading me to the tourist dormitory, himself.

When we got there – beyond where I had thought it was – it looked like part of a recreation complex, a section gated off from the rest of town. I followed my newfound guide inside to the desk of a stern-faced, dark haired woman with whom he engaged in some sort of negotiation – an absolute blessing, for there was no English spoken here. After a good deal of energized, head-shaking talk between them he finally received for me a key and an armful of linen – after I had paid $3.20 for the night's privilege – and led me across to the dormitory building. As near as I could make out from his uncertain English, I'd gotten the only available room for the night, and it was only because two Russian soldiers had unexpectedly departed that morning (though in fact, I never saw more than a few people in the entire place while I was there).

His impromptu services extended to helping me with the bed linen. When we were done tucking in sheets he told me his name, Jan Prokop Holy, and said he was the town's high school music teacher. I felt I should offer something in return for the gracious, unstinting assistance of this angel, but all I could think of was to ask if I might buy him a beer. He nodded his head and led me away in search of a beer parlor. When we found one, Jan Prokop took me inside, ordered what turned out to be a single beer and then excused himself, saying he'd be back in an hour. He had apparently understood me to mean I wanted it for myself.

Well, I neither wanted a beer nor did I feel like waiting there for him, so I took just a few sips until he left and then I headed off in another direction to resume my exploration of the town. I didn't bother to return on time, either, figuring he would merely shrug it off and go happily about his affairs. But I was wrong. When I found my way back to the tourist dormitory, two hours later, there was Jan Prokop Holy standing by the gate in the tree-filtered light of a setting sun, waiting for me with a big grin. He was a bit better dressed now, with a smart little cap over his thinning grey hair.

"You come, now. You to see house . . . for me . . . where to live."

What else could I do at this point? Off we went, to the house he occupied with his 80-year old mother – the house where she had given birth to him 54 years before, as he labored to tell me. He took care of her now. It was just the pair of them together and a sorry little dog with the absolutely untrue name of Spark.

His withered and slightly crippled mother stood in the kitchen with the smile of a pleased hostess while Jan Prokop served me tea and some sort of prune pastry. She spoke no English at all. I hadn't quite realized it, but Jan had a much harder time with my English, himself, than I had with his. He never indicated directly that he had trouble understanding, he would just nod happily at anything I offered, even at my questions, and continue with whatever he had been trying to tell me. I started being much more careful about my choice of words.

It took me awhile to realize that he wanted to show me the entire house. Only as I was about to leave, after what seemed a decent time for visiting over tea, did he insist upon taking me on a thorough and quite amazing tour.

Jan Prokop was not just a music teacher, he was surely the town's archivist, and his home the local museum! He had been collecting odds and ends all his life, and every bit of it – three entire floors worth, filling each room plus the hallways – was presented for my inspection: photos, paintings, antiques, pottery, archaeological artifacts, musical instruments, books, sports gear, even urns holding the ash remains of his forebears. Level on level, room by room, each door was opened with a flourish, lights switched off behind and on ahead of us in ritual fashion as if to celebrate each room's special significance . . . and each, in fact, held a different range of collectibles.

When I thought it was finally done I was wrong again. Now he brought out four huge scrapbooks, each filled to brim with a fantastic assortment of treasured mementoes: letters, poems, drawings, testimonials, portraits – most of this material personalized, given to him by people he had known or been in some contact with, apparently over the full course of his life: teachers, students, perhaps visitors to the town, and not a few accomplished artists among them. He apparently had known at one time or another a good many Czech luminaries in the art world. Lovely pen-and-ink sketches had been given to him by Jan Paroubek, the watercolorist whose work adorned my town map. When I remarked on this he went to another drawer and made me a gift of one of his personalized bookplates, created for him many years before by Paroubek. It had been sketched when the artist was seventy-seven, and Jan Prokop at that time a young man of seventeen.

At long last, after he had persuaded me to leave a few words of my own in his scrapbook, and after a private performance for me, a composition of his own, on what was probably the most costly treasure he'd ever bought for himself: an electronic organ, he finally accompanied me all the way back to my dorm. It was sometime after 11 p.m. when he bid me an almost reluctant goodnight and farewell.

Of all the people met on my summer's journey, Jan Prokop Holy made the deepest impression, for the simple charity of his being and the wonderful energy he had for life despite its obvious constraints on him. I wish I had managed to learn something from him about the lovely woman whose photograph – taken perhaps thirty years ago or more – I saw in two places among the dozens that were up on his hallway walls. I tried, with several intentionally offhand inquiries, but he resolutely refused to take my bait. I'm curious, too, about a passage I've just noticed for the first time in the historical notes that accompany the map of Domazlice: " . . . the Hussite armies under *Prokop Holy* quickly defeated the crusaders . . . in 1431."

I was half afraid he'd be waiting for me by the gate in the morning, for I would not have known how to make a gentle escape. But he was not, and I walked through the town one last time toward the rail station at its far end, where I bought a $1.50 ticket for the hundred-odd miles to Prague.

It wasn't quite so easy as just getting on a train. Barely a dozen miles out of Domazlice we all had to get off at a small station. I had no idea what it was all about, or what everyone, including the train staff, was milling around and waiting for. Until five old buses pulled in, and we all piled aboard – including the train staff. I found myself sitting next to a bearded old gentleman who managed to convey, with a bit of difficulty, that it was a short haul to the next station, where the rail trip would resume. I never did learn why. My twinkle-eyed informant had once represented Lionel Trains in Czechoslovakia. He was eighty-one and suddenly thrilled over this brief chance to renew his seldom used and nearly forgotten English.

I continued to sit and talk with him all the way to Pilzen, where I impulsively hopped off the train, prompted by the briefest glimpse, as we slowed coming into the city, of panels of tile artwork set into ordinary brick building fronts. I'd never seen anything like it. It was old and tattered, but nevertheless stunning and worth a brief layover to see if I could find more of it. And I did: a block-long row of tile-trimmed buildings just off the town's Masaryk Square – an array of epic scenes hand-crafted in that lovely Art Nouveau style. From close up I could see the inlay of small tiles, tightly patterned like the very best of stained glass design.

Had I not felt urgently drawn on to Prague, I could easily have spent more time in Pilzen. This was no sleepy village like Domazlice. For a brief couple hours I was energized in its strong pulse, captivated at the same time by that earthy simplicity that seemed to be every-where in the old east bloc – an ever-haunting reminder of times and places long gone from my life. I made my way back to the station along a grassy footpath near the rails, walking through weeds and feeling like I belonged there.

The final hour and a half of rail ride that took me into Prague that day was spent at the passageway window, not entirely to soak in the passing scenery but to be by myself for some reflection. For this was the day, the thirteenth of August, on which I had walked away from my old world twenty years before – abandoned it entirely for as uncertain a future as ever any newborn faced.

I wasn't dwelling on the event, but on how unforeseeably and uniquely different my world had become as the result of it. The fellow who took his desperate chances on that day in 1971, at forty-four and all too sure he was over the hill, could never have imagined he'd be vagabonding like this at sixty-four, free and easy and tremendously alive. He was a rationalist through and through, dedicated to logic and reason like the computers he worked with; at least he had tried to be, up to that moment. He hadn't ever heard of the *I Ching,* nor could he likely have imagined a life attuned to the seasons. The one was superstitious, and the other much too primitive – hardly useful ideas in a rational world. His greatest fear, in taking that irrevocable step, was the hazard of living without a regular income … the likelihood of ending up homeless and friendless. Providence was just a place in Rhode Island, or otherwise a Biblical fiction to comfort the forlorn. Not in his wildest speculation could he have seen himself roaming Europe for a summer on $100 per week, or whatever was its 1971 equivalent.

It should seem that a person is fairly stable by his mid-40s – at least as to knowing who he is, and what's real in life. But a signature is about all that would now suggest a shared identity between us. That old Irv Thomas simply couldn't have given credence to the world this one lives in. I would seem to him either an alien or a madman. And he, if I met him today, would be a poor fool confined in the world of his own limiting beliefs. Not entirely, perhaps, for he had the daring to walk away from them. If ever I could capture the secret of that moment when reason lapsed and faith took over … I think I'd have the elixir of life itself; the magic key to all its possibilities.

Late in the afternoon I reached Prague and found the intensities of my August re-kindled. From dozens of possibilities, the only host I could locate, this late in the day, was a single-night prospect. They lived on the city's fringe, and I nearly got lost in a sea of identical high-rise apartment houses, getting out there. I was watching for a particular bus stop – difficult enough when the signs are unreadable and the bus is racing to maintain a schedule . . . I didn't need the passenger with his head bobbing back and forth between me and the window. I was afraid I had missed the stop; and the driver – when I managed to get the question across to him – seemed to think so, too. An angel suddenly spoke up at the last possible moment, a woman about to get off at the very stop I wanted. She even lived in the same high-rise as my host.

Inside, she had to rescue me again. I was four flights up a windowless stairwell when the interior lights went out, plunging me into pitch black and sudden panic. I yelled out in desperation, thinking someone, somewhere, had switched them off – and my angel heard me, and turned back to come to my assistance from the hallway she had taken. The switches worked on a timing principle and had to be clicked again, on each floor, if continuous light was required.

Somewhat shaken, I arrived at the yuppie-furnished apartment of Milena and Radomir, immediately startled by the elegance of their world. I had already adjusted to a 'backward' land. But here in this condo-style apartment they had it all: starkly modern furniture, stacked stereo equipment – expensive luxuries in the east. I had to make an instant readjustment. It was Milena who greeted me and accounted for their up-scale circumstances. She was the one who spoke English and spoke it quite perfectly, for she taught it at a university. Radomir, she explained, had recently started a thriving new magazine on the pop music scene, and they were soaring with its sudden success.

It prompted a long conversation, next morning over breakfast, about Milena's concerns for what money might do to their lives. I was amazed at her awareness of its hazards, considering the shift to instant capitalism already underway here, and the near universal urge to instant wealth. I'm sure, in fact, that she must have been as surprised at discovering an American with a positive perspective on poverty, as I was at finding yuppie life already alive and thriving in Czechoslovakia. But our worlds were so far apart, in so many ways, that I could only encourage her to

282 | IRV THOMAS

keep an open mind and stay sensitive to inner reactions, for her most reliable guidance.

I needed another host for that night and Milena let me use their phone to find one. It took awhile, and all I could manage was another one-nighter – more centrally located, but he'd be away at work for the day, which meant I'd be burdened with my pack while exploring Prague, unless I could find a place to leave it. The railroad station provided the solution, with what surely must be the all-time best storage bargain: coin-operated lockers that allowed a full day's use for three cents! I could even set my own 3-digit-code for the combination lock.

For most of the rest of the day I was in Paradise. Without question, without challenge – and for me, sadly, without camera – Prague was the city I had been seeking all through Europe: the Mecca for anyone who loves Art Nouveau style. It is much more, of course – a city with a thousand years of architectural history still standing. In fact, they hardly boast their Art Nouveau heritage ... but it is all there, in structure after structure, detail upon detail – the most ravishing embellishment and artistry that one might ever hope to see. For my money (little though it may be) this is the Queen city of eastern Europe, in a class shared by Paris alone.

In some ways I found Prague even more engaging than Paris. Its central core is a city grown slowly through time, with striking examples of Medieval architecture spotted, here and there, as if by whim or impulse. Avenues and narrow byways intersect in a charming and irregular crazy-quilt of surprises, so that a wandering path is pulled left and then right, and its track is quickly lost – which made it all the more remarkable that I was able to retrace my trail when I had to.

My eyes were not only cast upward at the facades, but down at shop windows, for the prices were incredibly low; and the antiquarian bookstores, especially, were too tempting to resist. In one of them I found two old volumes filled with wonderful art – unreadable, of course, but the artwork unobtainable in the States, and a magnificent bargain at $2.40 for the pair. I had them tightly wrapped for later mailing, and walked on with the treasure under my arm.

Many twists and turns later, as I was browsing in another bookshop perhaps an hour from where the purchase had been made, I suddenly realized I no longer had the big wrapped package with me! A pure disaster. I raced out and back-tracked as well as I could, goading memory to spot every corner turned, every place I had seen. The little card shop, and that crowded waffle stand I hadn't the patience to wait at . . . that other bookstore over there, and the little churchside table with lithographs . . . remarkably, I recovered my entire zig-zag trail back to where the books had been bought, going into every place where I spent time and might have laid it down . . . asking at the counters where I had stood . . . pounding on the door of one book shop that had just locked up for the day . . . taking every detour that I had along the way. But not anywhere was the package found, though I traversed the entire long route and then did it again.

I went back over it, now, in memory, seeking any overlooked possibility. It finally came down to one tobacco shop where a Mucha card in the window had drawn me in to see their stock. I recalled it clearly, but I hadn't encountered it along my retraced path. Was I crazy? The little shop could not have vanished . . . or could it? I do live in a sometimes strange world. Again, for the third time, I walked the entire route looking specifically for the tobacco shop, but it just wasn't there. One possibility remained. I spotted a solid metal draw-gate that had been pulled down over one shop along the way, covering everything – no visible name, nothing. It was a last lingering hope, though admittedly remote. But I couldn't check it out until the following morning.

Made late by the whole sorry event and trying to put it out of mind, I got my pack from the locker and waited streetside for the number nine tram that would take me to my second one-night host. And waited. And waited. Every other tram using the stop had come by several times, but no number nine. I briefly considered that it might have vanished to wherever the tobacco shop went. I'm not sure what made me eventually take a chance on the tram marked 'X' except that there was no provision for it on the posted schedule. It made about as much sense as everything else that was happening. And senselessly enough, it turned out to be the right move. Petr, the host whose apartment I presently reached, could give me no explanation for it.

Petr was a 40-year old computer programmer whose wife was out of town. He had picked up English entirely on his own by reading Agatha Christie novels, puzzling his way through them with the help of a dictionary. By the third one, he said, it was more than just words and sentences, he was able to get a sense of the story as he read it.

Petr had to leave early the next morning, which meant that I did, too. Back to the railway station and the three-penny locker, at 6:00 a.m. This one-night business was becoming a drag, and I decided I'd take it just one more time if it happened again. It wasn't just the hassle; I had already learned that something more than a single night was required to retain a clear fix on my host, and there was not much point in making friends I'd soon be unable to remember. But it was far too early in the day for any phoning, so I walked in toward town and came to the great old structure called the *Powder Tower.* Prague has perhaps a half-dozen of these wonderful old Medieval giants – massive, spire-topped stone gate towers that dwarf everything around them. This one dated to 1475, and alongside of it was possibly the best preserved Art Nouveau structure, both inside and out, to be found anywhere: Prague's *Municipal Hall.* It is kept in pristine condition for theater productions and concerts.

Walking around the far side of this jewel I came to what certainly had to be the ritziest hotel in town, the *Interhotel Pariz,* somewhat matching in verve (if not taste) the style of its elegant neighbor across the street. Feeling high, amidst this abundant display of extravagance, and possibly not yet fully awake, I had a sudden extravagant impulse of my own: to fully indulge myself at these cheap Prague prices by taking breakfast in the dining room of the Pariz!

It was innocence in its worst aspect. I should have been alerted by the fact that the menu had no prices. It did stir a bit of caution, but only to the point of ordering a prudently simple breakfast. How could I be so crude as to ask the price in advance, amid such finery? Eggs with just toast and tea – and they were exquisitely prepared in a creamed, scrambled style that I had never before tasted.

I figured it would set me back some high Czech price – a few dollars perhaps, but ... well ... live it up while the living is cheap! I luxuriated on a refill of tea and didn't look at the bill until the waiter had left.

Seven dollars!

I felt weak as I paid it, and guilt-tripped myself for the rest of the morning. It suggested to me why I might have lost the books the day before. Splashing around in a gusher of suddenly discovered affluence, I had become like every other profligate American. Have it, spend it! Never mind whether you've any need for what you're buying, just throw the money around like you're God's gift to the economy. It brought home why I choose to live in poverty: because it puts a mea sure of healthy restraint into my life. It teaches me to spend with discretion, not abandon.

I was still berating myself thus when I came to the iron-gated mystery spot, now revealed in the morning sun – and sure enough, it was the tobacco shop with the Mucha card in the window. The young woman smiled as I asked about a package of books, and she fetched them from the back room. Suddenly my dalliance with the perils of affluence felt a bit better ... and I promptly found another bookstore, where – God help me – I could not resist three brand new books of art and photography, adding $5.50 to the day's already overblown expenses ... and it was hardly past ten in the morning.

The time had come to see if I could locate another host, so I found a telephone and pulled out my list. I was working now with a short list abstracted from the full one, to make it easier for phoning – just the name and number of only those hosts who were receptive to short-notice guests. And I was about to be swept up once more in the strange ways of fate, synchronicity and unintended error. Without realizing it, I had linked the *name* of one such host with the phone number of an *adjacent* one who had specified seven days advance notice. So it was a rather strange conversation that took place on this first call I was making.

"Hello," I said, to a male voice, "Could I speak with Jana?"

"This is no Jana here," he replied, in a near variant of English.

"Uhh ... is Jana home?" The momentary silence on the other end prompted a full disclosure. "I'm a Good Neighbors traveler looking for a place to stay tonight."

"No Jana here, but I'm Good Neighbor."

"Oh ... " this set me back for an instant, but I quickly figured he must be a guest who had gotten there first. " ... you're visiting Jana, yourself?"

"No Jana here. This is Daniel, and I'm Good Neighbor, too, and maybe is okay if you come for tonight."

He was a *guest*? ... inviting a second guest on his own? I didn't think that was going to work at all. "How do you know she'd want another guest?"

"No, I try to explain. This is my place now and you can come tonight."

It still made no sense to me, but he was definite about the invitation. Perhaps Jana had gone out of town and left him there. So I simply said okay, I'd be there early in the evening. Fortunately, when I turned to the main list for an address, there was the name Daniel below Jana's, and I quickly figured out what had happened. It was a wonderful break for what ultimately came of it.

I found his place up a cluttered, uncertain stairway in a massive old multi-unit structure badly in need of maintenance. It looked as if it had been converted, long ago, from a warehouse – sometime, say, in the 19th Century. His own quarters, however, did not seem so blighted, though a bit cramped: basically, a two-room apartment with a loft bed. A half-room bath and water closet was separated from the living room by the kitchen. Daniel lived there with a wife and child who were away, to my good fortune, or else I'm sure there wouldn't have been room for me. But he, himself, alas, was leaving on the following afternoon for the weekend. It looked like another one-nighter, after all.

Daniel proved to have a better grasp of English than our phone exchange had at first suggested. In fact, he was a freelance translator of texts and playscripts, from English into Czech. He had recently been to San Francisco, where, by pure chance, he met the people who publish the *Course in Miracles* and had returned home with a contract to make a Czech translation of it. We talked for a couple hours and then he went out for the evening, leaving me there to my own devices. Quite exhausted from rat-racing around Prague for the past two nights, and knowing further that I'd have to be on my way again on the morrow, I did very little more than lay out my sleeping bag and crash for the night, right there on the floor.

In the morning, possibly on the clear evidence of my wasted condition, Daniel said he saw no reason why I couldn't remain there through the weekend while he was away. So here it was again: a restful gift of solitary retreat – all the more remarkable in this instance for the accidental way it had come about.

We had a wonderful conversation that morning. Daniel loved photography, especially the soft, subtle early century work that I, too, had always found appealing. We talked of California, of religion and reality – prompted by the *Course in Miracles* assignment. Daniel didn't really believe any of it, but his curiosity had been prodded and he wondered how I felt about it. I thought it was a pretty fair miracle that had put us in connection and given me a weekend of 'private lodging' in this great old city, just when I most needed it. I told him, simply, that I believe what I experience and try to stay uncertain about everything else.

Before leaving, he gave me the packaging materials I needed to get my books in the mail, and directed me to a nearby post office. That was my final economic jolt of the week: the five books that had cost me less than $8 required almost $17 in postage to mail home. But all else was so cheap this week that I had spent only $90.30 – even with the indulgent breakfast at the *Interhotel Pariz* – edging my ten-week average down, once again, to $95.43.

St. Stephens' tiled rooftop and steeple, in the heart of Vienna.

Abandoned on Freud's doorstep

Prague: August 18, 1991...

I took my final day as a Prague resident entirely in the leisure of Daniel's quiet apartment, playing stereo music, writing letters, pursuing the rare indulgence of my own cookery. Now beyond mid-August and lulled by the ambience of this mellow Sunday, I hadn't any doubt that I had come through summer's worst rigors. I could see myself tripping lightly down the slope from here to Greece, all my hassles behind me. It was a nice dream.

I had written to Geza in Budapest, weeks earlier, that I'd be there close on the 20th, which left me just enough time to squeeze in a taste of Vienna. My only problem was how best to get there – both quickly and cheaply. The railroad fare from Prague was a horrid $15.40, which I didn't understand at all. It was ten times the cost of the rail-ride from Domazlice, but only three times as far. The only possible explanation – and the correct one, as it turned out – was a several-fold increase in the rate structure when international borders are crossed. The rail fare to Bratislava, nine-tenths of the way to Vienna but still in Czechoslovakia, was only two dollars!

But breaking off at Bratislava would merely shift the problem: the day's only train, according to the big board in the cavernous station, was an afternoon departure that wouldn't get there until 9 p.m., too late for either going on to Vienna or finding a stopover host. And a night of paid lodging would wipe out more than the rail savings. Seeking some way through this catch-22, I started playing with the public service computer in the waiting area. I had to fiddle with it awhile, because I couldn't understand the Czech instructions; but when I finally got into it there was a choice of languages – and from there on it was easy. I learned that a secondary rail station at Holovice, just a few subway stops away, had trains leaving for Bratislava all day long.

I was out of Holovice at 9:10 that morning – a five-hour rail ride, uneventful except for the enjoyment of Czech countryside from my favorite passageway window post. The schedule proved just too tight for a quick Vienna connection, however. I was faced with a four-hour wait in Bratislava for the next train, and hardly a chance of making it to Vienna before the American Express agency closed for the day. I'd be unable to retrieve the host list that should be there waiting for me. Another option suggested itself: to head for the nearby border on foot – it was only a mile or two distant – and hitch the forty miles to Vienna from there.

Outside the station I found myself amid traffic rushing in all directions. My way toward the border was blocked by the Danube, crossed by a bridge that had no provision for pedestrians. I hopped quickly on a bus headed that way, not at all sure it would even cross the bridge. But it did, and even took a turn on the other side to my advantage. I stayed with it for a half mile, and from there it was a straight walk in open country. I crossed into Austria at four o'clock and had my ride thirty minutes later with a middle-aged couple who spoke no English at all. We rode in silence, for the most part, but managed a bit of exchange . . . as when I registered amazement at a massive tower structure straddling the road, going into a small town, and they told me it was "tausend jahre" – a thousand years old. Uppermost in my mind, however, was the tightness of time: was I going to get my host list, or not?

On reaching Vienna, I used my universal word: "centrum," and showed them the American Express address that I had. They took me practically to the door . . . only minutes after it had been locked. I got absolutely nowhere with my frustrated waving at the people inside. They just smiled and went on about the business of shutting down for the night, leaving me with the familiar old question: What next?

In my haste at the border, I hadn't even paused to get any Austrian money, so that was obviously next. I was right in the heart of town, by the Stephensplatz, a great mall area where automobiles creep along in complete deference to the pedestrians milling around them – a strange sight. But every change bureau was closed. It took me half an hour to find a machine that returned Austrian schillings for deutschemarks, probably at a vile rate of exchange. Later, I would get a full infusion of Visa currency – but I had now a bit of working capital for buses and phone calls. Definitely not a hotel, however. Nor a hostel, either – not in high-priced Vienna.

What to do? Without my usual host-list grab-bag, was I back down to the basics – a night under the stars? I found a bench in the shadow of St. Stephen's Cathedral and sat down to consider the matter. St. Stephen's, standing prominently in the center of its large 'platz', is a startling surprise, with its brilliantly colored zig-zag pattern of roof tiling. A cheerful flash of almost impious levity, that softens the cathedral's sermonizing severity. Gazing up at it, I was suddenly struck by the thought that there must be a GN regional coordinator, here in Vienna, and I dug for my master address list. Sure enough . . . there was one.

I quickly reached her on the phone, told her my dilemma and asked if I could get a local list from her. I got a moment of silence, and then a note of disquietude in her voice, as though I might have upset some protocol. "Well . . . it's inconvenient, but I guess you can come by for it . . . if you have your letter of identification with you."

Getting out there was difficult, for I had no street map as yet. I found a bus to the right part of town, but the driver provided little further guidance. I got directions from people I passed, stumbling through the language difficulties and that momentary apprehension that suddenly grips people approached by a stranger, on big city streets. When finally I reached Greta's address and climbed three levels to her apartment, I was met by a thin and rather nervous woman in her middle years, who seemed uncomfortable with my very presence. She invited me to put my pack on the floor – but not to sit down anywhere – and went to find the list that I came for.

I couldn't imagine what must be going through her mind, encountering this roadweary traveler backpacking it in his sixties and seeking only a friendly host in this city of strangers, with darkness hardly an hour away. It was so unlike the GN people elsewhere . . . she didn't even offer use of her phone. But I got a clue as to what might be lurking, there, when I considered her response to a final question, asked as I headed back down the stairs. I wondered if there was any certain host she might recommend to me, thinking there could be someone particularly easy with such short notice. She thought but a moment and gave me a name that I looked for on the list after I was out on the street. I saw, then, that he was merely a daytime host – one offering local assistance, but unable to provide overnight shelter – which she should have known. It puzzled me until I saw that he was in his seventies. Nothing else but my age, it seems, had gotten through to Greta!

With a host list in my hands, the world of possibilities opened anew, though I had only the leavings of daylight, now – a very late hour at which to request lodging. On my second phone call I reached a rather hesitant fellow who eventually submitted to the urgency in my voice and said I could come over after 8:30, as he'd be out for awhile before then. Hardly two hours had passed, since I sat in the Stephensplatz, in a city entirely unfamiliar to me, sure that I was destined for a night in the rough. In ten continental weeks, I hadn't once had to sleep in the open, as I did a half-dozen times in Britain.

But as the evening progressed I began to wonder if that might not have been the more satisfying course. He was very taciturn at my arrival, and didn't even read through my letter of introduction to get some idea of who I was – nor did he reveal much of himself. All I ever found out was what I could see: a dark-haired serious fellow in his early forties, with self-importance written in his features, who chain-smoked and had neither the sense nor courtesy to open a window and let some air into the room. Some hope arose that the interaction might change when a young woman stopped by and I was invited out with them for a pizza dinner. But they spent the entire time of it privately conversing in Italian, though they both spoke perfect English. I wasn't even offered an explanation for the strange event.

He let me have the smoke-filled room, when the time came to turn in, and the first thing I did was to open both windows as wide as I could. And I left them that way when I departed quietly, very early in the morning – early enough so as not to trap him in a reluctant farewell, for I felt no reluctance myself. This might seem a bit ungrateful for the free lodging received, but it felt, for the first time, like I was merely being hosted from a sense of obligation to some commitment or principle, rather than as a welcome guest.

Downtown again, I managed to find a free city map, and then I returned to the American Express office for the packet of host lists that I wasn't able to get the night before. They covered the rest of my journey, and I could move on in confidence now. I wondered, in fact, if I wanted to linger any longer in this city of strangely unsociable people. Vienna had always been high on my list of places worth seeing, and I hadn't really seen any of it yet – but was it worth the cold chill I was getting? I'd make one more attempt at finding a welcome mat.

This time I came up with a winner. It was a city residence number that I called, but it was pure luck that anyone answered, for the family had removed to a summer lodge in the nearby mountains. Gertrude had returned that morning, by pure chance, for some belongings. Helmut worked in the city as a computer engineer and she gave me his number so I could arrange to be whisked away to their mountain aerie when his day's work was done.

Their summer place was fifteen miles out of Vienna in a rustic Alpine settlement – it wasn't even a village, really, but a cluster of neighborly log homes, so perfectly Tyrolean that the setting could have come right out of a travel brochure. Absolutely lovely! With a welcome that was just as heartening, and conversation to round it out. Soviet politics was the day's hot topic, for this was the moment that Gorbachev had been put under arrest in the ill-starred putsch that tried to unseat him. But these folks were alive to the wide world, quite fluent in their

English, and our talk touched many other bases. A pair of youngsters made a family affair of it, and the ambience felt good enough for me to remain with them a second night.

The evening air was no longer warm at this altitude – a potent reminder that time calls back its gifts and makes no undying friendships. For it wasn't just the altitude, but the imminent change of seasons and all that one could read from it. I am quite familiar with this late August moment of transition, when the energy of time quits and things do not complete . . . like the blackberries that fail to ripen at summer's end. Those who wanted to depose Gorbachev had picked the year's worst moment for it.

I was feeling this urgency of time, next morning, as I rode into town with Helmut to see Vienna, as I might, while he was at work. I suppose I was hampered, too, by preconceptions of Vienna. I went looking for the sort of charm I had always read about, or seen in Hollywood images. Ah, yes . . . magical Vienna: inspirational source of the great romantic music, heartland of Europe's late 19th Century lilt and flair. Vienna, in a class by itself as the embodiment of Europe's fin de siècle era. It was all gone, of course . . . if it had ever been more, indeed, than a memory elaborated by time. I found only the tiniest courtyard remnant, barely enough to satisfy the vision, in a junction of narrow streets at odd angles, with overhead arches buttressing the low buildings against one another. I indulged in a big delicious bowl of creamed spinach soup at an outdoor cafe, there, and tried not to think about the four dollars it was costing me.

For the rest of my day I had to be satisfied with a very vital, very cosmopolitan city – not at all disappointing in its own right, but not the city I wanted to find. It has not even remained very well in memory, except for the political demonstration in the Stephensplatz urging a continuation of the Soviet move toward democracy. That, and the one place I won't ever forget: the building where Sigmund Freud once carried on his work. Though its meaning for me may be slightly askew from the psychoanalytic.

I hadn't even been all that interested in seeing it; but Helmut knew the locale and said there was a small cafe across the street where we could meet for our return ride into the mountains that evening. The time we set was 7:30. Helmut worked at a pace of his own on the job, and often put in overtime.

I was there ahead of time, supposing there might be something worth lingering over, but there wasn't. It was just a commonplace stone building rising many stories, in an area of trade shops, with nothing of related consequence except a small plaque to mark the great man's association with the place. I wasn't really surprised, that Freud had no better personal style than to inhabit such a building.

It left me with an annoying amount of time on my hands, to wait around for Helmut. There was no cafe directly across the street, but one halfway up the block and one halfway down, so that I couldn't confidently have waited in one or the other. But I probably wouldn't have, anyway, so it was no problem. The problem was that Helmut wasn't there by 7:30. Nor by 8:00. Nor by 8:30 – by which time the problem had begun to assume disquieting dimensions.

I didn't have the vaguest idea where their country home was located, not even which way from town. Every bit of my belongings was out there. Dumb me! . . . alone in the middle of Europe, and I hadn't even the common sense to take their phone number with me. I had no choice but to stay where I was, and if Helmut didn't show, I was stranded and adrift for the night.

The measure of my desperation, by the time it took hold, was such that I made a phone call to Greta on the vague chance that she, as coordinator, might know how to reach them at their country home, or be otherwise resourceful enough to suggest some recourse. She reacted to the recognition of my name with something markedly less than enthusiasm. When I explained what was happening, she said there wasn't anything she could do for me, her voice sounding a bit strained – at which point my exasperation suddenly swung from Helmut to her, and I started itemizing things she very well might do for me: come and pick me up, find me an emergency host, call the police for me . . . I suggested just about everything that crossed my mind except that she might put me up for the night, herself – waiting for her to think of that one, but she never did. She just got more and more frantic, saying it wasn't her problem, she wasn't being paid anything for this, people have no right to impose … and no, No, NO, she couldn't do a thing.

Halfway into it I could tell that I was just goading her out of pure meanness. I wanted somehow to shock her out of that self-centered focus. Of course she wasn't obligated to do anything for me, and I knew it – but I still had a charge from the insensitivity she had shown at our earlier encounter and this was the perfect occasion to let it out. It was a wonderful release. I hated myself for it as soon as I hung up … and laughed quite shamelessly, all the same. I'm sure Freud would have had a few things to say about it.

But none of this was solving the problem. I thought about calling the police, myself, simply in the prospect of getting into a cell for the night. But they'd likely find the £680 in travelers checks stashed inside a pants-leg and push me toward the nearest hotel. Anyway, it wasn't yet late enough for either desperate measure. I just went back to waiting. Perhaps some other bright idea would pop into my head.

Along about nine o'clock, there came Helmut casually sauntering up the street – with a look of surprise when he caught the exasperation on my face. Oh, yeah … he guessed he was a bit late – but … never to worry, he always picks people up when he promises to. And I admit I felt a little foolish, after having regaled him and Gertrude, the night before, on my *Que sera, sera* way of going through Europe. I made a point, before we went home, of calling Greta back to let her know everything was okay … and felt a little relieved that she was still answering her phone.

They wanted me to remain another night, and I probably should have, if for no other reason than to let that fresh mountain air and sunshine nourish my waning enthusiasm for the journey. But I was already overdue in Budapest. Helmut drove me to the depot on Thursday morning, in good time for an early train that would take me into Hungary. But wiser to the way of rail rates, now, I intended to hop off at the border stop, quickly buy a ticket for the remaining distance to Budapest and board again, all within the fifteen minutes of scheduled station time.

The adventure fizzled at the last minute. I got cold feet when I saw the line of border guards posted trackside the length of the train. Fearing I'd run into passport and baggage hassles and lose the whole thing, I stayed on board. Now it became a gamble to make it as far as Gyor, an hour further, without my ticket being examined. This one worked. A new conductor came through just as we pulled into Gyor, but she smiled and let me go by without bothering to check the passage I had purchased.

Another country, another language, and an hour and a half to wait for the next train to Budapest. Another currency exchange, too and from now on I'd have to be careful with it. Eastern European money is a paper game, and the exchange is simply buying tickets for it – nonrefundable tickets. I wasn't going to get stuck again as I had in Poland, with currency worthless outside its country of origin. With Visa apparently unacceptable in the old East zone, and the travelers checks reserved for absolute emergency, my remaining 1350 Austrian schillings could easily be all the negotiable cash I'd have for the next couple weeks. For right now, I traded a thousand of them – $78 worth – for Hungarian forints … like buying chips in a casino and going out to find the most interesting game. The day was bright, the streets busy but uncrowded, and the morning mood infectiously cheerful.

The game I found in Gyor was at a counter-service refreshment shop, where I stopped for some tempting, inexpensive pastry and decided to ask for a cup of tea with it. The menu board listed KAVE, KAKAO, and TEJ, which pretty obviously meant coffee, cocoa, and tea. So I pointed to TEJ, the counter woman nodded, and I stood aghast as she put a ladle full of cream into the cup before pouring any tea. I had become so used to tea being served black, all through Europe, it never occurred to me that I might be in another country that drinks its tea with cream like the British. Before I could catch her attention, I watched in frozen disbelief as she poured a second ladle of cream into the cup – and then my sanity returned, in a rush of realization that TEJ didn't mean tea at all. I had ordered milk! Tea in Hungarian, I later learned, is … TEA.

My day's journey resumed on a slow train making every stop

along the way, taking two and half hours to reach Budapest. The rule of thumb, coming into a great city where everything is strange, is to sit tight until the station where everyone gets off the train. But this time we seemed to be heading out into the countryside again before it ever happened. Responding to my apparently evident concern, the young fellow who had been sitting silently across from me suddenly revealed a fluency in English, telling me that we would circle back in a short while to the main Budapest terminal. Bulgarian, and on his way home, he'd been through here many times. He surprised me, then, by contributing part of the hour until his own journey resumed, to be my escort for a mile of subway passage into the heart of the city. Another angel!

Budapest pummelled me with rapid-fire and contrasting impressions. It was a mix of contradictory moods, more so than any other city I had seen. Vitality, elegance, a settled and sure sense of identity – yet: its wide boulevards ravaged by too much vehicle traffic, with all the attendant noise and fumes, a contrary drab silence in the non-arterial streets, and *everywhere,* the crowds and lines of a recently revived economy.

This was a scheduled mail stop, my first since Munich, and I headed directly for the post office. But the day was hot and I was tired, and anxious to go find Geza. I hadn't the patience for the normal frustrations that attend the postal trip ... the predictable collision of language hassles and long waiting lines, often at the wrong window, and further complicated by the uncertainty of whether my first name and last were both fully searched – the constant predicament of a name like Thomas. The general delivery function – *'poste restante'* in Europe – is invariably the shabbiest of a half-dozen orphan-child services lumped together at the same window, not all of them even postal matters to begin with – but *every one* of the others taking more time to service than the simple retrieval of personal mail.

I might have held my cool if nothing more than the above had complicated this particular inquiry. But there was one more thing, a trick not so rare in Europe. Just as I reached the window, after twenty minutes of line time, somebody else edged in from my left side with 'more urgent' business.

I was primed to explode. Whether from one too many irritations of this sort, or my immediate impatience and general weariness ... or because August still had too much leftover charge. Whatever the fuel, this was the spark and I let go with a blast – at the woman who had intruded on me, at the postal clerk who accepted the intrusion, at the people behind me, at anyone within hearing range – probably raving all the more because I knew nobody could understand any of it. I carried on like John Brown in his abolitionist fury, until finally the woman who had edged in on me (probably a postal worker, herself) turned around, and with a narrowed eye of the sort shown to insignificant underlings, simply said, "Shutup!"

It's funny now, but it wasn't then. It shut me up, alright, though I kept rumbling, half to myself, like some punctured volcano preserving its dignity, as they took care of their business. After all of that, there wasn't even any mail waiting for me.

I recall learning, as a youngster, that Budapest was the joining of two ancient towns on opposite sides of the Danube: *Buda* and *Pest,* and I thought it very funny at the time. The Pest side is the city's commercial portion, its heart a half-circle grid of avenues radiating like ripples from the river-front, and sliced by boulevards into pie-shaped segments of high urban density, both business and residential. Behind the shop fronts that line the avenues are compact apartment structures, in one of which I would find my friend, Geza. He was close to a central boulevard, about midway along its mile-and-a-half stretch between the Danube and the railway station.

For the second time, I was about to meet someone I had known for years through correspondence, with never an opportunity to know him in person. My mail connection with Geza went back even farther than that with Rachel – far enough, so that its origins are a little vague; each of us remembers it a bit differently. I think it was 1977 when Geza contacted me through an alternative newsletter that carried something either by or about me. How that newsletter ever reached Geza, in those Iron Curtain days, I do not know.

He wrote in a curiously florid English, with quaint twists of usage and grammar that made his letters adventurous reading quite in their own right. But being in touch with a socially perceptive, environmentally aware attorney from behind the Soviet shield had been an adventure of a higher order. I relished every letter received from him. They were not frequent – perhaps three or four in a year, at most, and we may have even lapsed for a year at a time. But over that fourteen-year span, the content had shifted from the purely surface cultural curiosity of our earliest exchange to deeper waters of philosophical concern and Geza's personal frustrations in living under the Soviet system. Strong transcendentalist leanings had made the realities of his life exceptionally burdensome, and a spiritual rapport began to grow between us. He was a lawyer, yes ... but forged by heaven as a philosopher and a poet.

It had never seemed possible that we should ever meet in person. Initially, of course, the Iron Curtain formed an absolute barrier; but even with that down, nothing in either of our lives suggested any likelihood of international travel. Least of all in my own. So this walk through rain-freshened streets to finally meet Geza in person had more than the usual high, of excitement in a new city, that by now had become familiar to me. The very atmosphere of Budapest seemed charged with the wonder and uniqueness of the correspondence that had set this occasion up.

I wouldn't have guessed that there were courtyard residences behind the busy shops and office buildings that fronted on these avenues. Living near such a constant thunder of traffic was impossible to visualize; Geza's address was just fifty feet from the roar of a major intersection. Yet, the noise vanished as I entered its inner court and gazed up at three tiers of encircling apartments set back on walkway balconies. This enveloping structure silenced the traffic outside as surely as it eliminated the sight of it. Even from the top balcony, no street noise at all could be heard as I knocked at Geza's apartment.

The man who opened the door caught me entirely off balance. I'd had a photo of Geza, long ago, and had not been much impressed by it. One among a group of people in what amounted to a snapshot, he looked average in height, balding (in my recall), with what I had characterized at the time as a Leninesque growth of beard. But this man at the door was tall and decidedly good-looking with short, greying hair – not at all balding – and a very trim beard that suggested no such personality comparison. In fact, if he put me in mind of anyone at all, it would be an Omar Sharif or a Ronald Colman – albeit with a Slavic flavor ... a certain brooding, regal touch in his features.

We greeted each other like old friends – which of course we were – and I was immediately introduced to his wife, Ancsi, who spoke no English at all, and then his youngest boy, Peter, about 14, whom I suspect knew a bit more English than he could be persuaded to try. Geza's English was perfectly good, far better than I ever sensed from his writing.

Ancsi had a strong yet easy nature, the balance and ballast for Geza's diverse currents. She and I could not talk directly, but she sent revealing glances, flashing with wit and sensitivity, as Geza translated between us. Nothing seemed to ruffle her. She was clearly a stabilizer for Geza's turbulence, and probably tempered his passions. She was lively enough, on the other hand, and attractive enough to feed the healthiest of his passions.

That week was a fine mix of exploring on my own, going places with Geza and his family, then Geza alone, dining with them every evening – occasionally dining out – talking with Peter in the mornings (which became a game, to see what we could get across to one another), watching TV with them in the evenings, browsing Geza's floor-to-ceiling shelves of books, and generally getting a recuperative rest. I could hardly know it, but some of the journey's roughest passages lay yet ahead of me, and the rejuvenation in Budapest may have been vital to my well-being.

It was also a particularly poignant time in Geza's life, for me to be there. That full week was a pageant of upheaval in the Soviet Union, which we watched every night on TV. Gorbachev had returned in victory, and then immediately proceeded to outlaw the Communist Party. Geza's entire life had been dominated by the influence of that party on Hungarian affairs. He was alternately ecstatic and disbelieving, as the news nightly burst forth like a display of fireworks.

"Can you *imagine*, dear Irv ... the Communist Party ... abolished!"

He left no room for a response from me, but went right on ... comparing the event, for my appreciation, to an inconceivable outlawing of democracy in America, or the sudden nullification of our Bill of Rights. All of which would hardly equate, for me, to the psychological burden suddenly lifted from Geza's world – which he well knew, but there was nothing else of such impact and magnitude with which to frame an appropriate comparison.

Geza had lived through devastating and traumatic events arising out of their proximity to the Soviet Union. He took me to see the streets where house-to-house fighting had taken place during the 1956 uprising. Geza was a grown teen-ager at that time, a young man, and it stays with him in terrible detail, the block-by-block defeat of Hungarian hopes. Earlier, he had seen his mother wounded by deliberate rifle fire and then been forced, each morning at school, to honor the goodness of the Soviet regime and pledge his allegiance to the puppet government.

He studied law as a practical matter, but his heart was never in it. Choosing to learn English, reading Thoreau and Emerson, he was regarded as a pariah among his professional peers. He found his relief in ferreting out obscure American periodicals that dwelt on the more timeless elements of human life. But his career suffered in consequence of his rebellious ways, and he was hard put to keep his family at better than the barest economic level. His letters to me had often been testimonials to frustration, mournful agonies over what must be and what could never be. I always wondered if the reflections I sent on my own free life might not have been more hurtful to him than helpful.

Then came the changes. Suddenly, a lawyer who could read and speak English was in demand. He found himself with more work on his hands than he could keep up with – though in an economy now in continual danger of foundering. As yet, very little of real benefit from it had filtered into Geza's personal world, and he still had to contend with a profession that was not personally fulfilling. But at least he could now speak out on matters that no one had wanted to think about or dared

INNOCENCE ABROAD | 303

to, before. People turned to Geza, now, on environmental issues and he had even become a local resource for bio-regional thinking.

In fact, he made positive use of my presence there by setting up a half-hour local radio interview with me. We sat before a vintage microphone – the two of us and Mrs. Maruka, the young woman doing the interview, with Geza acting as translator – and talked about how and why I had come all the way from west coast America to eastern Europe. For Geza, it was an opportunity to spread some light on the values inherent in a deliberately simple lifestyle, relating it to environmental concerns. I doubt if it made much registration in a country striving for a toe-hold of economic sufficiency, but Geza was pleased and I had my moment of celebrity in Hungary.

Geza is not a stranger to lonely causes, nor does he discourage easily at such a prospect. That much is obvious from a wonderful poster over his desk in the little office/study/library that served as my quarters, in their five-room apartment. It is a cartoon filled with thousands of sheep, as far as the eye can see, coming forward en masse, only to plunge like lemmings over a cliff, headlong and heedless into disaster. A single sheep, however, heads in the other direction, patiently working his way against the multitude, saying: *"Excusez moi … excusez moi … excusez moi … "*

Thanks largely to Geza's and Ancsi's hospitality, and a bit to my juggling of railroad fares, I came in with a very low-cost week, spending only $80.56, to bring my eleven-week average down to $94.08. But some unexpected cash demands were about to be made on my resources.

Geza lived in a quiet apartment just down the street to the left of this busy Budapest intersection. If the sketch looks odd, it was taken from a unique two-sided postcard, the left side photo 100 years older than the right.

"Hey, Irv!" . . .
Recognized in deepest Romania

Budapest: August 27, 1991...

Considering Geza's rich humanitarian spirit, I was thoroughly surprised when he cautioned me on the dangers of my upcoming swing
through Romania – referring, of course, to the people themselves. It
wasn't the first hint I'd had of such sentiments between the two countries. Mrs. Maruka at the radio station had volunteered similar warnings. For that matter, a student friend in Seattle, a recent Romanian
emigré, had once told me quite earnestly that she never wanted to
return to her native land, not even for a visit.

How seriously should I regard it? Georghe had seemed a remarkably gentle man when I met him in Holland, but how representative
was he? Geza hadn't even been to Romania, yet he assured me that the
danger there of theft or worse was common knowledge. But his certainty, sincerity aside, had the self-invalidating ring of my host in Norwich who assured me that Ipswich wasn't worth seeing – never having
gone there, herself.

Still, I recalled Georghe's own reflections, a year earlier, on his fear of revealing his affiliation with Good Neighbors. But that was political, a completely different sort of hazard. Anyway, I had no other reasonable way to get from Hungary to Greece, now that Yugoslavia had become a battleground. Airfare was out of the question.

My unease over the whole business contributed to a fortunate impulse to re-check the visa situation at our Embassy, two days before my intended departure from Budapest. The American Embassy in Berlin had assured me that anything necessary for entry could be taken care of at the Romanian border. Now I learned otherwise.

Cold War was still the operational reality at the American Embassy: a fortress mentality, with armed guards both inside and out and two locked doors that I had to pass through. I was told now that the visa for Romania had to be arranged right here in Budapest, and its $30 fee would be accepted in *American currency only.* How was I going to find thirty dollars in greenbacks?

American Express came first to mind, since I had their travelers checks. I went to the smaller of their two Budapest bureaus, but they had no dollars for trade; they suggested I try the city's prime tourist facility, the Intercontinental Hotel. That would likely mean a stiff fee. I went instead to the larger American Express agency – and there they could do it! They wanted, however, a 12% surcharge, since I had taken my travelers checks in British pounds, not American dollars. At that rate I'd have to cash £30 worth – much more than I needed, with a consequent increase in the rapacious penalty-fee. I turned it down and continued the search. At the Intercontinental Hotel, I was told they don't even make exchanges for a non-guest. They brushed off my pleas with a confidant assurance that the Romanian Embassy would certainly take travelers checks.

I consulted with Geza that evening, and he felt sure that some less pretentious hotel nearby would make the transaction, so we went out together to find one. Three out of four suggested the National Bank near the American Embassy. The fourth advised me to make a purchase at a duty-free store and insist on change in dollars. Fat chance, thought I, with dollars apparently more precious here than gold, itself. One day down, one to go, and a 12% ace – just in case – in the hole.

Reality is so fluid in Budapest that I had been given three different office-hour schedules for the Romanian Embassy. Wednesday was the only day common to all three, so the Embassy had to be my morning's first stop – just to clear the slight possibility that there might be an alternative to cash. It was a twenty-minute bus ride up a tree-lined avenue, heading away from the center of town. But I couldn't even get in. An iron wall shielding the half-block complex from view had the only entry and it was locked. But the sign beside it made everything perfectly clear: *Cash, in dollars, and no substitute.* And then my spirits took a ski-slope when I saw the posted hours. Closed tomorrow, and open today only until noon! I had exactly three hours to get the cash and get back here with it, or I'd likely be stuck in Budapest through the weekend.

It looked like the 12% tribute was my fate. But I headed first for the National Bank, in one last effort to avoid the galling penalty. By pure chance on my way there, I spotted another small bank that had also been mentioned as a remote possibility.

Wonder of wonders! I went in and discovered they would do it for only 6%. That meant I could slide by on a smaller exchange, cashing only £20 and paying only two dollars for the privilege. Done! I'm not sure what Geza thought of my expending so much effort just to save four dollars, but for me it was another great victory over the vicissitudes of improvisational tourism. Celebration, however, was premature; the day's vicissitudes had hardly begun.

I raced back to the Romanian Embassy, cash in hand, only to find a small crowd now gathered around the locked door, perhaps twenty people of assorted nationalities. It wasn't even a queue-line, and there was no way of knowing when the door would open, though it was now well into their morning hours at half past ten. But I had no other option than to wait there with the rest.

Maybe twenty minutes into this uncertainty the door in the iron wall opened and out stepped a pleasant, mustachioed man who began calling names from a list for entry. He clearly wasn't about to call mine, so I kept looking at him intently until he finally returned a quizzical look to me. I said I needed a visa. He established that I was an American, took my passport and the thirty dollars from me, and shut the door. In fifteen minutes he was back with my visa-stamped passport. The crowd looked at me with wonder and envy as I turned and went on my way ... foolishly imagining that I had overcome the last of the vicissitudes.

The next one turned up at the railway station on my way back to Geza's, where I tried to arrange a Thursday morning passage to Timisoara. The only direct train was a six a.m. departure from the Buda station on the other side of the river, an ungodly hour for warm farewells and a dismal one for getting across town. As an alternative, I purchased a late morning departure from this station, with a train change just across the Romanian border at Arad. It all seemed nicely resolved ... until I checked the details on the big schedule board and saw that my Arad train was headed for Belgrade. It seemed odd that a Belgrade train should be routed via Romania at all, and especially without going through Timisoara. Geza thought so, too, and returned later with me to check it out, only to have another ticket agent tell him exactly what I had been told.

It puzzled Geza enough to set him poring over an atlas at home, and what he saw didn't satisfy him at all. He put his expert assistant on it. Ancsi got on the phone, and somehow managed to ferret through levels of information hierarchy to learn that the Arad connection was available from a Bucharest train leaving *two hours earlier*. The train I almost took by mistake was going directly into Yugoslavia, just as we had supposed.

In view of the whole mixup, and everyone's warnings about Romania, I seriously wondered whether I needed more cash with me than the 640 Austrian schillings that constituted my remaining liquidity. It was hardly more than fifty dollars, and maybe I should have gotten more hard currency while I had the opportunity. But the momentary apprehension went nowhere; I was used to traveling on the financial edge, by this time, and reluctant to cash more travelers checks than I really needed. They seemed, after all, a sufficient wellspring of security unconverted. The gods of mischief laughed at the poor innocent fool, but I couldn't hear them.

Peter saw me to the station early the next morning – he demanded the privilege. I tried to press my last hundred-forint note on him, a bit more than a dollar, assuring him I'd have no further use for it; but he insisted that I keep it . . . "for memory," as he put it. He waited with me in the train until it was ready to pull out.

The moment he left, I was conscious of a strange sense of foreboding hovering about this train. My coach was not the usual compartment style, but an older one with open seating, and I contemplated the shawl-hooded country women who half-filled the car, sitting morbidly silent at their individual windows. It had the eerie feeling of an old Ingmar Bergman scenario. The train itself seemed hesitant about the journey, as it bucked and lugged a few feet, then stopped, repeating the pattern one or two times. Rain starting shortly after we left the depot added its own gloomy note.

Halfway along the Hungarian portion of the journey the train was held for an unusually long delay with no indication of cause. The brooding, dour-faced women were suddenly chatting in animated conversation, like hags over a witches brew, and I wondered what it was all about. Then at the small village of Gyoma, still in Hungary, most of them got off the train – destroying at a clean swipe my image of them as grim Rumanians. I tried, then, to let go of these apprehensions foisted on me and getting tangled in my own vision. I wanted only to receive Romania for whatever it was.

At the border, it was a picket-posted line of sentries in camouflage-dappled gear and side-arms, standing along the track with rifles at the ready. Immigration officers boarded and made their way through the cars. But it was a polite and cheerful routine of inspection. Outside, the soldiers were soon bantering among themselves like soldiers do everywhere, with none of the grimness of a military stereotype. To Peter, in the train, I had said that people were just people, everywhere. The only troublesome ones were those whose eyes were glazed with the self-importance of authority. I told Peter it was always visible in their eyes ... and I didn't see it in their eyes, here at the border.

A soldier was shouting, now, at an aging Romanian who apparently cared not a fig for these border formalities and was trying to get on board with his small grandson. He retreated, fuming at the restraint, his resentment peppered with political references: Ceaucescu ... Gorbachev ... democrazie ... even Stalin got into it somewhere. He got on board a few moments later but it didn't silence him, to the obvious amusement of everyone around, even the soldiers outside. It was finally obvious that he, himself, was enjoying the sport of it.

I had to move to a forward coach so that the rear cars could be left at the border. The Rumanians I was now among were a weather-bronzed peasant stock, recalling to me the earthy immigrants of San Francisco's pre-war ethnic neighborhoods. I had not thought of them in long years – their disappearance after the war had been absorbed, without reflection, as the supposed outcome of America's transition from depression to prosperity; but now I realized another possibility: the Iron Curtain had closed off this source of immigration. Our whole concept of ethnic immigrant minorities has shifted as a result, from peasantry seeking a 'land of opportunity' to castaways trying to crash our barriers and 'steal our jobs'. Yes, the prejudice was always there, but racism gives it a nastier twist.

The rail yard at Arad was chaos. For unknown reasons we stopped short of the platform, and passengers scrambled across rails and gravel, hauling bundles and sacks as they went. Out on the street it was even worse: the pavement almost entirely torn up, with people crossing anywhere in no kind of order, disregarding what was left of the vehicle and tram right-of-way. Here and there, vegetable vendors sat cross-legged beside a box of potatoes or a sack of onions – swarthy, shawled, looking more like beggars hawking pencils, than tradespeople. Or is this simply another foolish distinction reflecting the bias of my own culture?

I had about an hour until my train for Timisoara, and what I had to do in that time was get some Romanian currency. I would have to find a bank somewhere in town, for there was no exchange bureau in the station. To get a measure of how much I'd need in Romanian funds, I checked the price of a rail ticket to Bucharest – 500 lei – and then set out to follow a line of tram rails along the gentle curve of what had once been an avenue but was now a mass of potholes linked by irregular patches of pavement. The sidewalk, too, was torn up; people angled this way and that for level footing. It would seem to account for the jam-packed trams, passengers hanging out of every opening, some hanging in only by literally hanging on to others.

The bulging overflow struck me as both risky and shabby once the novelty of it subsided – like I had come into a land where even the basic utilities can't serve safely for people's needs. And then a shock of sudden recognition threw me back across the decades to old San Francisco, to streetcars embellished, front and rear, with ingenious things called cow-catchers, the delight of every nervy kid in town. When lifted and out of use in the rear, they provided superb outdoor seating for up to three or four of us, shielded from view of the conductor by passengers packed, often to overflow, into the trolley's back platform. Risky? Shabby? I certainly hadn't thought so in those unvarnished days!

The town improved steadily as I came to its center. It was shaping up as a respectable community. But nothing on my way looked like a bank and none of the few people I asked could understand what I wanted. At last I saw the word, *Banco,* across the street ... only to find it closed for the day. But a watchman was on duty for the building above. Using every communicative trick in my bag, I got it across to him that I had to find a place to change money. He pointed up the street, repeating to me what sounded like "Hotel Astoria" – a name I hardly expected to hear in Romania.

Peering into one impressive building, I found myself eye to eye with a guard sitting just inside the door with an automatic rifle in his lap! I quickly asked if he spoke English – as much to cover my sudden alarm, as for wanting to know. He sullenly shook his head. But I had spoken loudly enough to be overheard by a woman at a desk down the hall, who was now waving a finger at me. I checked the impulse to hurry over and carefully made sure it was okay with the gunman.

She had a slight grasp of English, and we were quickly into what could loosely be termed a discussion as to where the Hotel Astoria might be. She took me outside to where a pair of taxis were parked, bringing the two drivers into our talk, and I at once tried to indicate that I had no local money with which to pay a fare – though it was really my knee-jerk mistrust of taxi drivers. But it may have been irrelevant to the situation anyway, for the woman shortly got into one of the cabs and then both taxis took off together, leaving me to wonder what it was all about in the first place.

I walked on, mindful of my time slipping steadily away, and was accosted at the corner by the ever-present do-it-yourself exchange entrepreneur, a hazard for unwary travelers in general and doubly so where such exchange is illegal – such as Romania. I backed away as quickly as possible, looking nervously to my rear toward the building with the man with the rifle.

On the next block, back a bit from the street, I finally spotted the Hotel Astoria, a touch of down-home charm in a light shade of yellow with white trim, attractively graced with a veranda porch. Inside, the lone clerk directed me across the lobby to a small exchange office, where someone soon appeared to assist me. And now I had to make a careful decision ... or, really, a gambler's choice.

The 500-lei railroad fare to Bucharest – a full day's journey – was the equivalent of $2.50. My fifty-plus dollars in schillings was tied up in four bills: a 500, a 100, and two twenties. I could either trade the 500 schilling note ($40), which seemed far more than I'd likely need for a four-day hosted stay and my transportation needs, combined. Or I could exchange the three lesser bills, though their $11.20 value would be a pretty tight fit. If I chose high, anything left over was thrown away. But if I chose low and it was not enough, I'd be forced to change the larger bill anyway, thus losing even more and leaving none of the schillings for Bulgaria.

The safest choice seemed obvious: go for the high figure, and so I traded my 500 schilling note for 8000 lei, in a land where one-sixteenth of it would get me clear across the country and I'd hardly need half the rest. The choice became a ticking time-bomb that would eventually leave me completely without cash resources in Bulgaria – the very development I wanted to forestall – with results that I couldn't possibly foresee. Had I not been so tight about those travelers checks, I might have realized that they offered a third (and best) option: each of the £10 checks was worth 3300 lei, so that one of them could have seen me nicely through Romania and left my schilling liquidity entirely intact.

For now, however, I could afford a taxi back to the depot, which seemed necessary in view of how much time had elapsed. In the tradition of cabbies everywhere, this one asked where my train was going and then offered to take me to Timisoara for only 1500 lei – $7.50 for 32 miles. Not a bad deal for someone with more lei on his hands than he could readily spend; but habits of austerity are not so easily broken. And I'm glad, for I'd have missed a rare and unforgettable experience at the railroad station.

It was hazardously near train time when I got back there – considering that I had yet to figure out how to find the right train to board. I was soon engaged in one of those frustrating semi-conversations with a station employee, asking which of several train-occupied tracks was number 2. He kept pointing dumbly at the ground, when suddenly it struck me that he wasn't being dull, but trying to point out an access tunnel beneath the rails, which had earlier eluded me. I hurried through it, spotting stairway number 2 and surfacing at my track, and . . . sure enough, the train there had a Timisoara placard on its closest coach.

Always on the cautious side, I looked for confirmation somewhere and tried to ask a passenger getting on board. But at my mention of Timisoara, he shook his head in the negative. I pointed to the sign on the coach, but he only replied in a babble of Romanian and shook his head the harder. Was it possible he hadn't understood me? I fumbled for pen and paper to write the name out, when from somewhere in the background I thought I heard my name being called . . .

"Hey, Irv."

I heard it, but it made no sense . . . like a voice filtering into a dream from some other world . . . as if I were being pulled out of sleep. But I wasn't asleep, I was here in a Romanian railway station . . . Wasn't I? It was an eerie moment, and I forced myself back to the issue at hand, as though the call hadn't really happened.

But again, and more insistently, it rang out ... *"Hey, Irv!"*

I looked around, now, in a state of queasy confusion, momentarily uncertain of where I really was – two worlds contending for my attention, for my very reality!

Halfway down the car I was trying to board were two young people hanging out of a coach window and they were clearly waving at ME – waving like old friends, but ... neither face was familiar. They were total strangers!

I walked slowly closer, abandoning the poor fellow I'd been struggling with, to his own undoubted relief. I must have looked as stunned as I felt, for the two fellows I approached were laughing. "You don't know us, Irv ... but Georghe told us all about you."

It was certainly too crazy to be real. These kids – there were three of them, as it turned out, all from Seattle! – had just come from Timisoara, where Georghe had put them up, and he had shown them the GN letter of introduction I had given him at Carty's, in June, with my photo on it. And here they were – spotting me on the platform at a train stop, bent upon boarding their very car in the mistaken impression the train was *going to* Timisoara instead of coming from there.

But if I had the right track, how come it was the wrong train? These guys gave me that answer, too ... I had the wrong time! It was an hour earlier than I thought. I had entered another time zone coming across the border – but I never knew it until now.

By tricks and quirks of mistaken timing and thoughtless error, corners turned and wrong-turned, accidents and misunderstandings, the impossible connection is made. Like running into Albert in Krakow ... or finding myself in the same London office as a woman with whom I had an entirely separate connection, though neither of us at the time knew it ... or plugging into the perfect Berkeley hospitality situation for a two-week stay by dropping in on the only one who knew of it, two hundred miles away.

What does it all mean? The magical intersection happens far too often – in my world, at least – to justify the millions-to-one odds often quoted for such things.

Curiously, the common factor is connections between people, suggesting a vast inter-personal psychic linkage beyond the grasp of reason. Is this what the right-brain and its irrational prompting is all about: a person-to-person communion network, unsuspected until it surfaces in the fashion of synchronicities, angels and benevolent flashes of Providence ... a function that must be 'explained away' with disclaimer terms like coincidence and the mathematical odds of chance, because we are too intimidated by rationalism to take it at face value? If so, what an incredible gift! And what an incredible forfeiture of well-being if we leave it unrealized.

I finally reached Timişoara, and took a taxi for the second time that day – not for feeling rich, but because the heavens let loose a downpour of truly Biblical proportions shortly after I got there. I was on my way by foot to find Georghe's home, and getting lost at it when the skies opened up and dissolved all further hope of doing it on my own. When a telephone failed to work for me, a pair of 'dangerous Rumanians' passing by took the trouble to hail a taxi for me and tell the driver where I was going. How could Geza have been so woefully wrong about these people?

I hadn't sent Georghe any word of my impending arrival. I wanted to surprise him completely. I even deprived him of his own attempt at surprise – that only the day before, he had been speaking of me with three young Americans. But none of that mattered at all, he was so gleeful at actually seeing me at his door. Georghe's features quite ordinarily radiated contentment and the calm joy of a steady course in life; but when he had reason to be especially happy he fairly beamed, like a cat on a purring spree.

The sharp reduction of street noise when I entered his home seemed magical, for this was not an inner-court apartment like Geza's. It was a ground-floor unit just off the street, old and massive – much like the place I stayed at in Leipzig, with the very same gift of sacrosanct inner space that has vanished from our concept of apartment living. Three great bedrooms edged the street, shielded from its noise by double windows and heavy drapes. These rooms, in turn, were buffers for their central living area allowing not a whisper of street noise into the home's inner sanctum.

I had arrived the day after Moldavia, the Soviet buffer province between the Ukraine and Romania, had declared its independence, and that evening a TV musical spectacular from the Black Sea resort city of Constantia began, and went on for several nights. The sheer number of pop performers featured, all of them Romanian, made a deep impression, for I had come to think that Europe – east and west – was slavishly addicted to American pop. I watched with Georghe, Elena, and their grown daughter, Otilia, while we dined at a linen-spread table for the occasion of my visit.

Elena had prepared eggplant, among other dishes, in a country-style virtually unknown in the U.S. – but familiar to me, for it was exactly how my mother used to prepare it. The eggplant is baked in its own skin – Mom used to do it directly over a very low burner, turning it every ten minutes or so – then separated from the burnt skin, drained of its juice, chopped with onions and olive oil and served chilled as an appetizer or salad. It had been many years since I last tasted it that way. I had always supposed it was a Jewish dish, but now realized that it must be regional, for my family had emigrated from the Ukraine, just a few hundred miles away.

I had to tell Elena these things by translation, for she could speak no English at all. Otilia, on the other hand, was as fluent in English as Georghe, himself. She had a strangely quiet kind of vitality ... an alive-to-life young woman in her early twenties, but yet so different from the hyperactive fashion of American youth. She seemed to epitomize freshly gained maturity, free of marketplace manipulation or the narrowing of consciousness so common in a fad-driven, peer-pressured culture. Talking with her, in fact, set off a remarkable resonance in me, taking me to that time in my own past, and I could feel her awareness of life's infinite possibilities ... as if it were still my very own.

All three of them, for that matter, seemed radiant in a world that might have superficially appeared drab. I became conscious in this household – more than anywhere I had been – that everything is a part of all it touches. I couldn't be sure, for example, that Otilia's personality was not partly a subtle reflection of the peacefulness of their home ... or that this, in turn, wasn't just an extended construct of the contrast immediately sensed on coming in from the busy street outside. Things here seemed to grade into one another, almost like an Escher drawing – each losing a bit of its own substance, each lending substance to everything around it. I had no idea why the effect should be felt so strongly in this particularly simple environment, except maybe for the clarity inherent in simplicity.

I was invited briefly into Otilia's own room, and it left the deepest impression on me of the entire house, for there was an irrepressible sense of some long-ago past in my life not even, so much, of any real place I had known, as of another whole world that I had once lived in. Walking into that room, even gazing in from the doorway, pulled me into a timewarp in the same fashion that old music can sometimes do. It would be useless even to attempt a reconstruction, for description could not capture it. It was a mood ... the mood of a world where time and space have not become issues, for they are endless and given. The mood of inner peace, and a future so immaculate with promise that each day may be taken in wholeness, accepted as complete – busy or idle – without the least concern for anything missed. I don't know if Otilia felt it so, but that's what I saw in her world ... a world that somewhere, some long time ago, was once mine.

I stayed a second and a third night at Georghe's – I simply could not resist the spell of their home, though it was hard upon September and I knew I must be on my way. The town, itself, was very ordinary, its most intriguing downtown attraction a newly opened department store complete with escalators (not yet in operation) and incredible bargains in clothing – like seventy-five cents for two pair of wool socks, and fifty cents for a little red hat that I had no use for but could not resist. I picked up a small bouquet of nine carnations for Elena, for only twenty-five cents.

On the way back, I discovered a colorful orthodox cathedral, a blend of Byzantine and Gothic styles, not very old but quite decorative in its patterned green turrets and steeple. Inside I saw, for the first time, a place of worship with no seating – a startling effect, yet I imagine it may have been the common temple style long centuries ago, when religion was a more humbling experience than today, and the connection between people and the earth much more real and celebrated – even by the simple, oft-forgotten act of sitting directly on it.

Georghe made a tub of soap on the night before my departure. I don't mean a tub of suds – he made his own solid bar soap! That, too, brought back a memory of kid times, when I played at chemistry and had a big formula book with such things in it. Make-it-yourself recipes for everything from toothpaste to rat poison, from glue to fireworks to ... soap. I could almost remember the formula as I watched him: ashes, cooking-fat remains and lye, or some such, stirred mightily until it begins to thicken, and then left overnight to harden and be chopped in the morning into bars. It was a game and a learning when I was young, but for Georghe it was real life. And I looked at this mellow old guy, straining every sinew to swirl the thickening brown mix in the tub, and I thought about those sun-bronzed people on the train, tough and hardy ... and I couldn't help wondering which end of the world's economic imbalance is really closer to living 'the Good Life.'

I asked Georghe how he felt about the Hungarians.

"Strange people," he said, after a moment's reflection. "They leave us alone, and we leave them alone."

To my next question, as to whether he'd hosted any Hungarian GN visitors, he shook his head. "They don't like to come down here."

"And what about you, Georghe? Do you ever travel up there?"

He shook his head again, this time with a sheepish look on his face. He knew what I was getting at. "This is a very tormented part of the world, you know. Distrust runs deep, here, with so much hatred. History has trampled us over and over again, and many resentments have taken root. I had some friends ... in Yugoslavia ... " He left the subject hanging with a helpless shrug of the shoulders. I suddenly felt a sharp, deep pain for him that almost brought tears up; and the aspect of Good Neighbors that I, as an American, could only *understand,* up to now, had become visceral.

On my last exploratory walk through town, that day, I bought my passage on to Bucharest without realizing that they only honor *same-*

day tickets at the station. In mock seriousness, Georghe chided me for wasting money on a ticket that was useless the next day – realizing as well as I that the loss to me was so minimal as to be almost meaningless. It was uncomfortable feeling 'wealthy' in his presence; but he, himself, took the disparity between us with grace. He had just had his salary as an electrical engineer tripled, in response to inflation, from 4000 lei per month to 12,000 – or, from twenty dollars to sixty.

He rose with me at the crack of dawn on Sunday. He wanted to accompany me to the station to make sure I'd have no trouble exchanging the ticket I had mistakenly bought. We walked a bit out of the way, to go by the building where the revolution of 1989 had begun – the revolution that freed the country from Ceaucescu's government. Troops had tried to take a popular Turkish priest who had claimed sanctuary here, and people gathered to protect him. Shots were fired and word traveled quickly across the country – not very different from the famous old Boston Massacre that inflamed our own revolution. And Georghe had been right where it happened.

He waited for the train with me, and my last impression of him, standing there on the platform, was that beaming, magnificent grin.

The week's accounting had begun back in Budapest, midway through my visit with Geza. What with paying $30 for the visa and the $25 fare to Timisoara, my costs had soared past budget all the way to $118.49. My twelve-week average was now up at $96.12. It wasn't crowding me; I felt innocently confident of an easy week ahead of me.

A church in Timisoara, with strong middle eastern influence in its style.

The Great Train Robbery

en route to Bucharest: September 1, 1991...

It was an all-day ride from Timisoara to Bucharest and I remained for most of it inside the compartment, where I had for once a window seat looking out on some of the loveliest verdant mountain country I had yet come through. Then down along a barren stretch of the Danube – that river heartline that strings the fabled cities of east-central Europe like a necklace of classic pearls. Yugoslavia on the opposite shore. Upstream a hundred miles or so was Belgrade . . . and beyond lay Budapest, Bratislava, Vienna and Regensburg, where I had walked over it on an 850-year-old stone bridge, ages ago – three weeks earlier.

My $2.50 passage was first class, a somewhat fictional distinction on this train, but one that held for me as long as I remained in my compartment, which was filled with an unusually genteel assortment of fellow travelers including what appeared to be a ranking military officer. I was even deluded into thinking there might be a dining car worthy of the name, and broke the spell of the compartment when I went in search of it. I quite shattered the spell, for it was never regained after that.

Bucharest! . . . another of the great European cities . . . one whose very name prompts images of romantic intrigue – though it looked very ordinary as the artery of rails took us slowly into its heart. Georghe had suggested a particular host here, and the connection was made easily with a one-cent phone call. I didn't have to figure out bus routes this time; with Romanian lei to throw away, taxis had become an affordable convenience. Several turned me down, however, before I found a cabbie willing to drive out to the residential sector. He took time out on the long ride for a stop where his girlfriend lived, so he could call my host for precise directions. The trip came to $1.50 after adding a generous tip.

I found Violette and Lucia, my mother-and-daughter hosts, living in a modest apartment in a concrete-block complex agreeably set back from the ceaseless roar of city traffic. With little Sabina on hand, it was a household three generations deep. Georghe had psyched me out on this one, for I felt here the most congenial 'American flavor' of all my hosts in eastern Europe, though I cannot say what accounted for it. Violette was a biologist and a university professor with an impressive grasp of world affairs. Lucia, with a short haircut that could have come right out of Seattle, was equally alive to the times, especially their personal potential for her – though for now she was entirely being a mother, indulgently attentive to her five-year-old: a future beauty queen already aware that she could trade on it for almost anything.

I spent Monday at large in mid-city Bucharest, rewarded by a topsy-turvy mix of impressions, from pot-holed and cobblestone streets, to grandiose architecture quite as spectacular as any I had seen elsewhere. Broad boulevards intersecting in great traffic circles gave the city a continental magnificence undiminished by the startling contrast of an occasional horse-drawn wagon clopping alongside the motorized traffic – not carriaging tourists, but doing actual drayage work in the heart of the city ... directly above a modern subway system. But it was a subway strange to Western sensibilities. It was not only free of advertising, but almost dreamlike in its severely subdued lighting. Very nearly depressive, in fact. But a lot could be forgiven, for it cost one cent to ride!

The incredibly low cost of things in Bucharest had its usual head-bending effect on me. Finding shelter in an *"antiquariat"* bookstore from another of those sudden heaven-shattering downpours that were beginning to seem indigenous to Romania, I turned up a pair of irresistible art books costing all of thirty-five cents. There was no provision for having them mailed home; I was told to find a "paper store" to get wrapping paper, and then take care of it at the post office.

At the paper store – the Romanian outlet for anything from note pads to toilet tissue – the most enticing prospect I saw for my purpose was a large calendar poster of a dark-haired, somewhat immodestly clothed young lady, whose full-color charm had a plain white backing suitable for wrapping and addressing. But the shop was crowded with mid-day trade and too few sales clerks to handle it. Watching the action, I could see that each customer first paid a central cashier, gaining a receipt with which to claim their purchase.

I looked for a price on the poster and saw what I took to be 150 lei – seventy-five cents, and twice what the books had cost. But I had 'lei to waste' and really liked the poster, so I stood five minutes in the cashier's line, then spent five more minutes to catch a clerk's eye. Giving her my receipt, I pointed to the poster I wanted; but she had a problem with it. Nothing came across to me until she found a pad and carefully pencilled: 152. A tax increment, perhaps. I tried to give her a two-lei piece, but she insisted I go back to the cashier. So for the sake of another penny to pay, I stood in line five more minutes. When I handed over the new receipt, she opened the showcase and drew out for me . . . seven copies of the poster!

Bucharest was my farthest eastward penetration of Europe, though I may have been a bit closer to the Russian border in Warsaw. It was close enough, however, that I thought about making a one-day sprint up to the new country of Moldavia. I went to check out the possibility at the American Embassy, only to find it closed for the Labor Day holiday – which seemed a bit absurd in Romania. It helps maintain the fiction, I suppose, that the Embassy is a tiny bit of America adrift in an alien world. So was I, in a sense, but more intent on establishing bonds, here, than preserving cultural barriers. At any rate, I had to let the urge go and turn back to my southward journey.

On to Sofia! But only as far as the border in one hop. I would carefully avoid the trans-national rail rates. Giurgiu, a river town on the

Danube, was the crossover point – forty miles and only sixty-seven cents from Bucharest . . . yet it somehow took me all day to get there. I left Violette's apartment early, with plenty of time to catch an 11:30 train, but a hassle erupted at the post office when I tried to send my pair of books by surface mail. The clerk insisted it was "less problem, less problem" to send it airmail – the problem being the task of plastering the package with dozens of stamps because she didn't have the proper denomination. I finally found a clerk who understood English, and had my way; but it cost me the morning train.

Had I caught that train, I would have been out of Bucharest before noon and at the Danube within an hour, possibly changing the whole course of the next couple of days' events. Instead, I had to wait four hours for a local taking a roundabout route that wouldn't get me to Giurgiu until six in the evening.

For consolation, I had an absorbing afternoon spectacle in the parade of peasant life on the outdoor rail platform. There were entire families en route to somewhere, going shoeless often as not with immense sacks and bundles of heaven-knows-what – possibly their entire range of belongings. There were old men stoically proper in tattered old suits under the hot summer sun. There were peddlers who doled out handfuls of seed to chew, barefoot kids foraging for whatever the day might provide, and at one point two under-teen ragamuffins flushed by a brakeman from the hidden reaches of a coach sitting 'empty.' There were Gypsies, too, though not 'working the crowd' here, as they do at the tourist-frequented depots. These are the saddest enigmas of Europe – everybody despises them and it's easy to see why, when confronted by their infuriatingly persistent begging. It does no good at all to try and satisfy them with a coin or two, which merely intensifies their effort and draws in hoards more, like pigeons flocking to a park bench handout.

I watched in amazement, too, at the way people piled into/onto/over and around trains that pulled in to load for departure. Some would actually clamber in through open windows to outwit the crowds packing the more usual avenues of access. I was glad for awhile that I had purchased first-class seating. But the illusion died as soon as my train arrived, for it had no first-class cars. I had to settle for what I could get, in the mad rush that the afternoon's show had at least prepared me for. I managed a side-bench seat in an oddly designed double-deck rear car filled with smokers and other swarthies who kept shutting the window I tried to keep open. Wafting odors from an overflowing water closet that grated even the country-tempered nostrils of those around me finally quelled the resistance to my open window and its small satisfaction.

The ordeal ended with our eventual arrival at Giurgiu, a rather sizable border town. It was too late in the day to head directly for the bridge, which I could see to the east of town. I walked instead toward the central area, passing through a lot of street life on the way, even barbecues cooking on curbside grills. There were no GN hosts in this small town, but perhaps a better prospect: my first affordable hotel room in all of Europe – a reasonable consolation for the day's frustrations. It looked that way in prospect, anyhow.

I am occasionally hooked by the notion that whatever can be had for free, like the rides I get on the open road, or the Good Neighbors accommodations, must ergo be inferior to things that cost money. Isn't there, after all, a piece of folk wisdom that says you get what you pay for? Be it known, once and for all, that the old adage is just another fable. I spent the first hour in my hotel room jousting with mosquitoes scattered on the walls, after shutting the window that was thoughtfully left open for them. I used the second hour piecing together some decent lighting from among the seven partly operational fixtures and two working bulbs in the room. I had hoped to salvage the third hour relaxing in a tub – already stripped down for it – when I discovered there was no hot water in the tap. At $2.50, of course, some might say I was getting what I paid for.

In the morning, I realized it was pointless to walk to the bridge while I still had lei in my pocket – almost 1500, which would be absolutely worthless as soon as I set foot on the other side of the river. So I found a taxi and told the driver to take me as far as he could toward Ruse, the town on the opposite shore. He set off west, instead of east toward the bridge, and I hastily called a halt, took out my map and put the matter to him as clearly as I possibly could, given that we had no common language. I figured he was another sharp taxi driver, counting on the naiveté of an American tourist. Then he put it as clearly as he possibly could that he was taking me to a ferry, just up ahead. It was brilliant, as the British would say. The ferry, for a dollar, plowed the Danube upstream far enough to reach the center of Ruse. Had I insisted on the bridge, I could have been faced with a walk of six or eight miles on the other side.

By dint of hard, extravagant effort – including four taxi rides, one hotel room, and first-class passage all the way (paid for, if not always received) – I had managed to spend 6880 of my 8000 lei, during my six days in Romania . . . the great sum of $34.40. Of course, the remainder was useless. Or so I thought, but I'd get a bit of further value from it down the line.

Ruse was a surprisingly pleasant town with little evidence of the economic deprivation I was by now accustomed to seeing, and a summer-morning ambience very much like that of Dresden's older neighborhoods. But I was now in Cyrillic alphabet territory, the journey's deepest plunge so far, into communicative insecurity. It was a fearsome shock, at the first glimpse of street signs and posters, but it quickly became an interesting game to see how well I could 'decode' it. The word, XOTNL (the N reversed), for instance, identified a hotel. That gave me three letters that were the same in the Latin alphabet and two that were different, and I began a chart that accounted for most of the new phonetics in the short time I was there.

My strongest impression of Ruse, however, was the remarkably friendly, outgoing attitude of its people. A passing stranger directed me to one of the local hotels for my cash exchange, and he even offered to drive me to it. The woman there, who gave me Bulgarian leva for my 100-schilling note, not only told me how to reach the train station, but she phoned to check the price of a ticket to Sofia, without any prod from me. Others actually initiated conversation on the street, an unusual occurrence. And when I asked a bus driver if he was going to the Bahnhof – a more familiar term here than railroad – two passengers who heard the exchange took the initiative to point me on the right way when the bus eventually veered off in another direction. From these first instances of friendly outreach in Ruse, Bulgaria claimed my heart as I would never have imagined it could.

Waiting for the early afternoon train to Sofia, I compared the prices encountered in Ruse with those of Romania, to assure myself that I really had enough in cash to get through the country. The eight-hour train ride ahead of me cost fifty leva – just three dollars! It left me with a bit more than $7.50 in overall liquidity to stave off the use of a travelers check. Sofia would be two-thirds of the way to the Greek border, so I could certainly afford five dollars, there, for cheap lodging – twice as much as it had cost me in Giurgiu. I had checked the room rate in Ruse, and found it was in the same range as the Giurgiu hotel. I would have preferred a GN host, of course, but the scheduled arrival at nine p.m. in Sofia pretty well eliminated any hope of hospitality there. But it was okay, for nothing at all gave me reason to think I might not make it with my $7.50.

Tight figuring, yes, but time was crowding me and I had no reason to stay more than one night in Sofia, nor anything but a hasty meal or two to purchase there. A week or two earlier I might have wanted to linger . . . but now, Bulgaria was just a route of passage. I was anxious to begin my island-hopping search for a place to spend the winter. September's chill was in the evening air, and the journey's accumulating strains had already begun to make it more of a chore than an adventure.

Time was the factor in another way, too: it was now Wednesday, and I had to be in Thessaloniki by Friday to pick up my mail or I'd be stuck the whole weekend waiting for it. And in Thessaloniki, of course, Visa money would once more flow, and all the tightness of this passage would be behind me. I could even go hungry until then, if need be.

That's the way it all seemed to shape up as I quenched on a soft drink and waited for the train in Ruse. The calculating mind has a peculiar kind of innocence all its own. It can see everything . . . except the way things are going to happen.

I found a vacant compartment for myself as quickly as I could get on the train. I'd hardly settled into it by the window, before I was joined by two men, one of them carrying a rather large drum – an oil drum, not an orchestra drum – that effectively kept anyone else out of the compartment. It contained something smelling strongly like turpentine and the window had to be kept open for the mere sake of breathable air. It was too late, by the time all this had transpired, to find any other windowside seating.

He was perhaps my own age, the fellow with the drum – a taciturn guy, not the least bit friendly, not even very talkative with the one who came in with him. The only real communication I got from him was at a midway station where we stopped for an engine change. I was sure of that much because our engine had gone off without us. It seemed safe enough, in fact, to step out on the platform and get a soft drink at one of the kiosks alongside. I was standing there, bottle in hand, waiting for change from the twenty-leva bill I'd handed the woman, but she turned momentarily to take care of another customer. And then all of a sudden, in the side of my vision, I saw MY TRAIN – the one without an engine – moving! It was going backwards ... and sure enough, there was an engine at the other end that had coupled while I had my eye on the empty front part.

I yelled for my change – having, at the same instant, an urge to drop the bottle and run for the train while I still could. But she was counting out my money now ... "three leva, four leva, five leva, six ..."

In frozen, fascinated, confused horror, I stood there while everything I owned was slowly picking up speed. I couldn't bolt for it. Those leva bills going into my palm in slow motion were too important and held me rooted to the spot. The train was not yet going too fast to grab it and swing aboard ... if she would just get the money *all in my hand!*

She fumbled on her count and babbled something, with a slight laugh. *Good God.* Surely she couldn't mistake the anguish in my face! The last car was going by, now, and she was still counting ...

My legs were paralyzed as the moment stretched, like a time-lapse film – until it had stretched beyond the edge of choice. I saw puzzled faces looking back at me from the receding train. But the kiosk woman was trying to tell me something, pointing to another track ... and from others I got a nodding hand-motion, that universal signal: "there, there, take it easy ... " until it finally registered that my train had pulled out of the station only to change tracks and return, to link with another string of cars nearby.

Only then, when I pulled myself back on board with drained-energy relief, did the turpentine drum fellow let himself go: he laughed and laughed and laughed. His words went over my head, but I'm sure it was something like, "Boy, if you could have seen your face ... !"

By early dusk we were rolling through some of the most spectacular mountain scenery of anywhere I'd been – rock formations rivaling any in the western U.S. for grandeur; picturesque, classic Alpine settings, with goats being herded along meadowed roads – all of it the lovelier for its plain, non-tourist, non-exploited naturalness. No billboards, no motels, not a single franchised encroachment on the pristine beauty. I stayed at the window with it for more than an hour, my eyes dry and burning from the wind, until it was too dark to see any longer.

It was well after nine by the time we reached Sofia, and my entire sense of the place was a city already gone to bed. I wanted to, myself, for I was exhausted. But I needed to find a place. There had to be cheap hotels near the railway station, but the area was dark and discouraging, offering no hint of which way to go. The line of taxis outside was tempting, and I recalled being taken halfway across Bucharest for hardly more than a dollar. Surely these guys would know where a really cheap nearby hotel was.

The driver I picked spoke enough English, and he seemed to understand what I wanted. He took me on a zig-zag route that was certainly less than a mile, to a rather seedy looking place above a tavern ... just about what I was looking for. But when he asked for his fare I couldn't believe I had heard him right.

"Forty leva," he said it again. $2.40! It was more than half the leva I had, and almost a third of my total liquidity.

My shocked reaction and immediate reference to prices in Ruse

330 | IRV THOMAS

could leave no doubt that I was seriously outraged. I let him know how little I had and how tight on funds I was – not so much thinking he'd back down, as to vent my sudden panic.

He responded with some explanation about fares going up after nine p.m., but it hardly registered. I had miscalculated badly, and my entire speculative structure was crumbling as I stood there.

Wanting a moment to turn this sudden development over in my head, I said I'd have to go inside and see if I could cash a travelers check.

He'd wait.

Inside, came the second shock. I was told that a room here, in this little dive, would cost 120 leva. And, no, they could not handle a travelers check! I suppose they would have taken my schillings, but there was no point in asking. Between the hotel and the cabbie, I couldn't make it – not without using a travelers check, which could only be done, now, by checking-in at a larger hotel. I was wiped out. Busted.

What to do?

There was only one thing I could possibly do. I went out and silently paid the cabbie off, grabbed my pack, ignored his puzzled look and started walking. It made no particular difference which direction I walked or what corners I turned, and I made no effort to keep track. Somewhere, I'd find a place to lay my sleeping bag; and I offered a silent word of thanks for the tough-guy that emerges from some hidden corner of me when I need him.

Finding a bivouac spot after dark in the congested center of a big city is a risky challenge even where things are familiar. But Sofia, a city of dim lights and brooding shadows, turned cool nerve to chills. The streets were virtually empty, the lighting an eerie yellow glow of street lamps, so shallow that I might as well have been in a thick fog, and the footing an uncertain process of sidestepping holes in the sidewalk, open ditches in the street. It was a kind of nightmare alley that didn't change, appreciably, block upon block. Quiet . . . mysterious . . . threatening in its very sense of isolation – yet a darkness one could feel hidden in, for all its unknown dangers. Foot-falls echoed sharply in the hollow silence of empty streets, and I made an effort to pad my steps as softly as I could, searching like an animal with only instinct for guidance, looking this way and that … into shadow tinted by street lamp, into shadow that was pure black.

I came at last to a large school yard, fenced but open in a couple places. Crossing the street to it, I went in quietly to search for a proper spot and thought I had found it, when some young boys came through from an opposite corner, laughing over some private thing – a jarring contrast to the deserted streets I had come through and the mood they had set. The boys were merely on a shortcut and went on, but it was enough to dissuade me from any idea of staying there. As I was leaving, however, I spotted what could be a perfect situation across the street, one that I might easily have walked right by. The school yard gave me a larger view, sufficient to notice a rise of brush and weeds behind a high fence along the walk.

Sure enough, a little side-passage gave access that took me around some rubble and up onto a knoll quite invisible from the street. I had only to be careful of nearby householders, revealed in silhouette by the light of their second and third floor windows. Here and there, while I laid out my gear, one would emerge onto a porch and I'd have to freeze for a moment to offer no eye-catching motion. But it worked. I could even see a span of stars overhead. It was the perfect spot for a night's sleep, all things considered.

Sometime after I had drifted off to sleep, a sudden urgency pulled me back into the world. Something had gotten to me, intestinally, and I had to crawl out and away from my sleeping bag: *diarrhea!* Twice that night I had to make my peace with nature, shivering in the chill air, wondering why it couldn't rather have happened the night before in the Giurgiu hotel room.

Bleary, barely energized by the night's half-sleep, I was up and out of there just before daybreak – trying now to judge by its earliest light toward which direction the train station might lay. The easiest solution was to follow other early-morning risers, assuming they were headed toward transit facilities. It took me to a main arterial with perhaps a dozen people waiting in the early dawn for trams. Recalling that the French term, *gare,* meant rail station here, I put the one-word question to a young woman. Perceiving my limits of language, she raised seven fingers. I waited for a tram number seven, paid nothing to ride it, and was soon at the depot renewing body and spirit with a sixteen-cent cup of hot coffee. After which, at precisely seven o'clock, the insanely frustrating exercise of trying to purchase passage to Greece with my remaining cash got underway.

At the International ticket window I was told in English what I already suspected – the rail fare to Thessaloniki was out of my range, at $30.54. I was told, also, that the portion of that applying to Bulgarian mileage was $19.05; but having come twice as far, from Ruse, for three dollars, I knew it wasn't the domestic rate. For that, she pointed me across to the Information window.

The woman at Information spoke no English. I used my map, indicating the border, and she shook her head in the negative, pointing back to the International window. I clearly needed the name of a station. I asked for it at the International window, and was told I could only get that information at the Information window.

Puzzling over this strange dilemma, looking at the various 'boards' for some clue, I encountered a Bulgarian teen-ager who spoke some English, and I asked if she could get me the name of the last Bulgarian station on the route to Thessaloniki. She came back with the name of Svilengrad. I thanked her profusely and went back to the Information window for a price figure. The woman looked at me a bit weirdly, now, but gave me an appropriately low figure – long-since forgotten, for I soon discovered, from the schedule board, that Svilengrad was on the way to Istanbul, not Thessaloniki.

Still at square one after an hour of futility, I decided I'd have to find out myself, on a decent map, and headed back into town on the quest. It took another hour, but I finally found it at an automobile club – a fine highway map, given to me free, which indicated a border town named Kulata. Back once more to the Information window. I ignored the withering look reserved for Americans who can't decide where they are going, and requested the fare to Kulata.

She shook her head vigorously, *No!*

With the help of another clerk who spoke a bit of English, I was told that Kulata was just a switching yard, not a station. Having at last someone I could actually discuss it with, I learned which station I really wanted. Just a few miles back from Kulata; it was called General Todorov, and the fare to it was $1.40 – narrowly within the few leva that I still possessed. I'd neither need schillings for it nor a travelers check. Success at last, beyond my wildest earlier-trashed hopes!

But the day was not yet done. Not nearly.

It was ten a.m. It had taken three hours to get a ticket to the border. I had two hours until train time, but this land of pitfalls and quagmires was not going to tempt me any further. I headed directly for the platform, making double-sure I had the right one by questioning a railroad worker who spoke some English. He pointed up ahead on the track to a train sitting at the far end of the platform, and then cheerfully walked out to it with me. I had told him I wanted the Thessaloniki train, merely to make sure I was on the right platform, and now he took me past all the rear cars, up to the one at the very front, which he assured me was the Thessaloniki car. The rest, he said, were only going as far as General Todorov, where they'd be shunted to the junction track. As it turned out, this happenstance development, two hours before train time, was a stroke of pure innocent fortune, and this man clad in overalls was clearly an angel.

He was also a bit of a lush, for he now said something about going for a bottle of Scotch, to celebrate. I didn't know what he was celebrating, nor why I was a party to it, but finding myself already lodged in a border-bound coach was good enough reason to contribute, so I gave him the smallest reasonable thing I had to give: one of my two twenty-schilling notes. He disappeared down the track with it and never came back.

I picked a choice compartment and settled-in for the two-hour wait . . . just in time to receive another railroad functionary – this one in a conductor's dark uniform – who stopped by for a bit of semi-conversation in his somewhat tenuous English. I soon realized he only wanted to exchange some cash, thinking that an American must have loose dollars. I assured him I had none, laying out for his inspection my leftover Romanian lei and schilling note. And then I realized he might be able to put the lei to use, whereas I certainly couldn't. So I simply gave them to him – $5.60 in Romanian currency. After a moment's surprise at my generosity he seemed to realize that I hadn't any Bulgarian leva with me for journey refreshment, so he gave me a ten-leva note – which would serve me in an unexpected way, down the line. In fact, all these chance events were like bit players coming in to set up the scenario that lay ahead.

And they continued to arrive, as passengers boarded just before departure. Amazingly, two men who spoke fairly good English sat down in my compartment. The one alongside of me, whose name was Marchal as I presently learned, said very little. He was only interested in listening to my conversation with Peter, the other, who sat directly across from me. Peter was engaging and articulate, though he had the underlying motive of trying to make a Christian of me. But he was nevertheless quite enjoyable. In fact, we jousted repeatedly over his efforts.

He insisted, for example, on telling me of places along my route where I could get "help for my problems," even as I kept replying that I had none.

"Sure you have problems," he'd say, quite confidently.

"Like what?"

"I don't know. You go see these people, and they tell you your problems."

It was great sport. He'd smile at my heresies and seemed to enjoy the exchange as much as I. When he said something about "those no-good Gypsies," I challenged him on it, asking how he, a good Christian, could say that Gypsies were no good. He forthrightly insisted that the Bible upholds honest labor, and Gypsies refuse to work.

Marchal just sat there, almost deadpan, taking it in. But when the conductor came through to check tickets, Marchal came through for me with a masterful job of translation. The conductor, seeing my ticket was for General Todorov, wanted me to vacate the compartment and move into one of the back cars. But I wanted to go all the way to Kulata if I could – right on the border, even if it wasn't a true station – and since a ten-leva note was now in my pocket, I grandly said I would pay the difference. That was good enough for the conductor; but he said to pay it when the time came. He let me remain in the Thessaloniki car. Marchal left the stage shortly after that. Peter remained just long enough until another conductor came through, checking tickets once more. For some reason, he took Peter's fluent assurance that ours had been checked already, and went on without an actual inspection. He must have been the one who would have taken my further fare, for no one came through again before we reached General Todorov, where the rear cars were disengaged and I remained aboard. As we rolled on toward the border, the compartment on this Thessaloniki-bound coach was in my sole possession.

I'm not sure at what point I was struck by the playful thought that I might just sit tight and see how far this continuity of lucky breaks would take me. I do know it was only a larkish idea at first . . . except that this was barren and hot country at four in the afternoon and I wasn't very anxious to release my shadyside, air-cooled comfort.

We were at the switching yard of Kulata, now, the border stop. Three separate Bulgarian officials came through to check passport and baggage, but none asked to see my passage. Finally, a conductor I hadn't seen before looked in at me and asked in fairly good English, "You're going to . . . ?"

"Thessaloniki," I responded, as a mere statement of fact, and he went right on through the car. I then realized I had committed myself to the bluff, almost without intending it. Could it be that simple? Was the Greek style so casual that I merely had to be on the coach coming through from Sofia?

For the next hour or more the train chugged back and forth in the yard, linking to various cars, changing an engine – and being boarded in the midst of it by border officers from Greece, but still with no request to see my ticket. I argued with myself to take my small gain and leave while I was ahead . . . but Kulata was such an isolated and lonely outpost, the highway nearby virtually empty of traffic, and there was no place here to get the next rail ticket. In the end, I just stayed with the game.

We finally moved off to the Greek border station, not very far distant, and here at last, the conductor came by to check my ticket – the same fellow to whom I lightly had said, "Thessaloniki." I at once started searching for the supposed ticket . . . trying to look as convincingly puzzled as I could, in my failure to locate it.

He left me to the search while he moved on through the compartments. My foot was all the way into it, now, and I had no option left but to play the bluff through.

I was still looking when he returned, and as distraught as I could possibly make it appear. I told him I'd looked everywhere and could only imagine I had accidentally thrown it away. He suggested I'd better at least buy passage from here, so that he could keep his own records straight.

This was perfect – exactly what I'd wanted to do in the first place!

But in the next few moments my victory vanished in the dry, hot summer air. This little station could not cope with either Austrian schillings or travelers checks. I was referred to the bank in the nearby village . . . but also told that it had closed for the day, several hours earlier.

That spelled the end of it. It would have made little difference had the bank been open, for the train was ready to roll now, and there was no way I could delay it. Playing out my little drama, in fact, had already delayed it. I had simply lost the game, and would have to lose an entire day waiting for the next evening's train.

I wearily hauled my backpack and gear off the coach, to the puzzled unconcern of fellow passengers watching it all unfold from their train windows – whatever they might make of it. I had no cause for complaint, having come all the way through the country on ten dollars, but it seemed just a bit sad to stumble on the last gamble. I sat down beside the station to contemplate the wages of my humbuggery and watch the train leave me in the lurch.

But the conductor had gone forward for a brief conference with his engineer. He returned for another with the station-master, and then came to tell me that they had agreed to let me back on . . . taking my word – my extravagantly theatrical word – for the 'lost ticket!'

As we chugged off for Thessaloniki I experienced a wave of guilt, for it had just been a game, with no intent to cheat the Greek railway system. But it had all started with those gouging international rail rates: *fifteen times* the cost of domestic fares for the same passage ... and before long, laughter overcame remorse. Old tunes, rascally tunes, harmonized with the clickety-click on rails, as we rolled and swayed along the eastern Macedonian highland, down toward the Aegean Sea.

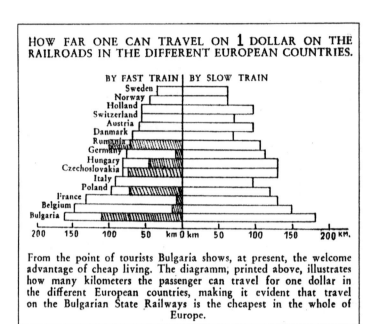

HOW FAR ONE CAN TRAVEL ON **1** DOLLAR ON THE
RAILROADS IN THE DIFFERENT EUROPEAN COUNTRIES.

From the point of tourists Bulgaria shows, at present, the welcome
advantage of cheap living. The diagramm, printed above, illustrates
how many kilometers the passenger can travel for one dollar in
the different European countries, making it evident that travel
on the Bulgarian State Railways is the cheapest in the whole of
Europe.

An interesting graph, straight out of the 1934 *Handbook of Central and East Europe* (typos included), portraying the country-by-country rail rates and the mileage they each obtain. For the countries I went through, I have put an overlay of the rail mileage that I was getting, 57 years later. The difference between east and west Europe in 1991 is at once obvious.

Island hopping
on the Aegean

Thessaloniki, Greece: September 5, 1991...

The diagonal crossing of Europe was done. Thirteen rambling weeks
from the English Channel to the Aegean Sea came to a quiet nighttime
end without ceremony as we rumbled through the sea-level warm air
of Thessaloniki's outskirts. The moment was auspicious, considering
that I did it all within budget, at $96.71 per week, but after the previous
night's fiasco my focus was on the virtual certainty of another one to be
spent outdoors, for it was once again too late to attempt a Good Neighbors connection. But Thessaloniki, I quickly discovered, presented me
with exactly the opposite problem of Sofia: instead of empty, dimly lit
film noir streets, I had to contend with illumination and crowds like a
major holiday occasion. It was perfect, in fact, for my triumphant arrival and I thanked the people of Thessaloniki for welcoming me in
such a blaze, except that ... I was so bone-weary, and hungry, too,
that I really didn't want the honor.

It was my introduction to one of the most charming characteristics
of Greek culture: with the benefit of a mid-day break in their affairs,
they celebrate life on a daily – or rather, nightly – basis, well into the
wee hours. Charming, yes, but not always agreeable to one raised un-

der less extravagant conventions ... especially in the aftermath of the hard-driving few days I had just come through. The fact was, I had to find my way through it and to someplace hospitable to my night's needs.

Lacking two significant pieces of information, I started walking south, just a block or two from the water line. One part of my ignorance, of course, was how late into the night this festive madness would continue. The other part was how far its range extended along the shoreline.

After what seemed an hour of walking, with neither terminus even remotely in sight, I climbed on board one of the frequent local buses that came along, with the reasonable assumption that it would take me out into a quiet residential section. But it never did ... I finally settled for an area with reasonable patches of darkness that should well enough serve my purpose. It was after eleven, now, and I thought that surely, surely this buzz of nightlife would quit by midnight, and I could wait that long at an outdoor cafe near the bus stop, at the same time satisfying the hunger that was by now clamoring for deprivational attention right alongside my exhaustion.

A Greek salad took the edge off, and then a second one. Salads at midnight are not my forte, but I was somehow sure that the celebration would cease at the magical stroke of twelve. It didn't, of course – a Greek evening doesn't quit until the roosters are ready to take over. Eventually, I gave up and lumbered off to make the best of it. Once down to the search, I found greenery everywhere and had little trouble picking a place for the repose of my tired body. Nestled up under camouflaging shrubs alongside an abandoned building, I slipped into an easy and peaceful sleep with little concern for the incomplete darkness or the occasional vehicle going by.

The mail that awaited me on Friday was disappointingly slim, but it contained the most important item, a London packet from Marjory with the routing I had laid out for my next and final stage: an island-hopping search for a wintering spot. A good deal of thought and some research had gone into what I'd look for. I wanted an island, but not the sort with white-washed buildings stark against rocks and sea. The sea, yes, but I needed a warmer, more livable texture and especially trees. I intended to work my way down toward Crete, checking out selected islands along the way before making my choice. As with every other instance of pre-planning, it wouldn't happen that way at all; but it felt like I knew what I was doing, which may be the only thing plans are good for.

Lesbos would be my first stop. The overnight ferry ran twice a week, the next one due to sail late on Saturday. That gave me almost two full days to get ready for it, with a lot to take care of: laundry, letters to write, new provisions to consider – for this island-hopping would be a different kind of travel. And I wanted lodging for Friday night. The strain of my pace through southeastern Europe, these past few days – not to mention two successive nights in the rough – had taken its toll of energy and enthusiasm. With the prospect of an overnight ferry up ahead, I really needed a sheltered night's sleep as a bridge. And a shower if I could manage it.

Coming down through eastern Europe, I was struck by how the culture seems to gradually shift toward Levantine ways. I had always thought there was some hard and fast demarcation line, probably because the map suggests it, between Europe and the Orient; but the fact is, each step along the way becomes a little more eastern in its style and ambience. Greece, if it falls to either side, seems more eastern than western, perhaps from many centuries of Turkish occupation that ended only 150 years ago. It could account for Greece having not nearly the Good Neighbors representation I had found throughout the rest of Europe. There were just two hosts in Thessaloniki, one of whom offered only daytime hospitality. I tried to reach the other, calling him several times before noon.

Meanwhile, I walked the streets in fruitless search of a laundromat. As near as I could tell, the concept of a public laundry facility had not yet reached this part of the world. I finally found a small dry-cleaning shop, with a kid there to translate for me, that would do my laundry that afternoon for just fifty cents. But I'd have to get back for it by closing time, for they didn't open at all over the weekend.

By mid-afternoon, still getting no response from the GN number, I tried a call to the daytime host to ask if he'd let me take a shower at his place, which would at least refresh me for another night in the bush. It was okay with him, and I said I'd be right over. But it was two hours before I got there. I couldn't find the shop that I'd left my laundry with! Lacking a map of sufficient detail, I had drawn my own. But these were angular street intersections crowded with small shops and Greek nomenclature, and nothing seemed to match on my second time around. Getting more frantic by the moment, but refusing to settle for the no-win choice between waiting for a later boat or going on without underwear, I finally located the cleaning shop just ten minutes before their closing hour.

By the time I reached Rudi's second-floor apartment – or more correctly, by the time he picked me up from a nearby cafe whose proprietor found it easier to call him than give me directions – the sun was low on the horizon. His shower was the best thing that happened to me all day. Twenty minutes entirely relaxed me, so that I wanted to linger at his place as long as I could. In fact, the thought of going back out in search of a third night's outdoor sleep felt increasingly bleak.

Providentially, Rudi, a freelance journalist with solid English skills, was into tale-spinning and I was a good listener. He had prepared a modest feast while I was in the shower, featuring a Greek soup thick with seafood, and then my first sip of ouzo, which goes down hard but then softens one like magic. I was beginning to wonder if I'd even find the energy to leave, when he told me I'd be welcome to stay the night.

I slept deliciously late into Saturday. Rudi then took me sightseeing around town, and up to a great old castle site on a ridge overlooking Thessaloniki. Then it was more feasting, more ouzo, and good conversation well into the evening until it came time for me to go for the eleven o'clock boat.

It was 10:40 when I raced out the long dock from the street where the bus had dropped me – as well, that is, as a worn-out graybeard can race near midnight with 25 pounds on his back – and no boat was in sight. I quickly found assurance that I was in the right place for the Lesbos ferry. But shrugged shoulders from among the milling mass of people told me no one knew any better than I where it might be. Promptly at eleven, however, in a seemingly magical materialization, *there it was,* freshly in from Lesbos – a massive multi-decker called the Sappho (what else?) hulking its way up to the dock, with a load of people and vehicles to disgorge, lights strung from one end to the other like a cruise vessel on parade.

The situation shortly became a comedy of chaos when the crowd ready to board refused to wait for those trying to debark. People carrying baggage over their heads collided with and bounced off one another on the narrow single gangplank, the thinnest of them making the most effective headway. The overwhelmed vessel and dock staff couldn't cope with it, and I was quickly caught up in the mood, myself, laughing at the idiocy but 'moshing' with the best of them. I never did see what was gained by it all, for there was no shortage of seating aboard. It was simply an instance of the Greek passion for direct involvement, whether functional or not.

It was well that I had gotten a decent sleep at Rudi's, for the ferry offered little in the way of overnight comfort to those without cabin space. Everyone crowded the main passenger area on bench-row seating with immovable side-by-side arm rests that prevented any real comfort. Lights remained on and a TV blared monotonously in Greek. I made for the deck – plagued, too, by overhead lighting, but at least it offered a full length stretch for my sleeping bag and only the sound of the sea in my ears.

The twelve-hour run to Lesbos was split by a daybreak stop at tiny Limnos Island, apparently made for the sake of a single debarking passenger. I watched the docking with him and found out he was the island dentist in a brief exchange that somehow bridged the gap between his limited Italian and my limited Spanish.

An uneventful five hours later, we steamed into a wide strait with coastal Turkey on our left and the huge island of Lesbos to starboard, sentried by what appeared to be a lonely castle ruin atop a barren hill. In another half hour the ship's whistle wailed as we cleared a stone jetty and swung into the calm water of Myteline harbor, the island's main

OM

city. Suddenly, I was in the pages of *National Geographic* ... docking at an exotic Aegean port with bustling mid-day activity, harbor-side bistros and waiting taxi-cabs – maybe even one for me!

I had intended to bus directly for one of the island's outlying towns; but just before we docked I got into some talk with one of the crew, who told me he had a house on the quiet side of Myteline with rooms to let – *domatio,* one of the first Greek words I learned. His price, $10 per day, was about what I expected. The guidebooks had said that island rates started below $5, but a few years of rocketing inflation had happened in the meanwhile. I asked if he'd take $7.50 if I stayed three nights, and he readily agreed.

I enjoyed only twenty minutes of bargainer's smugness before it crashed. As I waited on the dock while the crew finished their work, I was approached by someone who offered me a $6.50 rate. But I stuck with Antonio, who had promised taxi service as part of the deal. The taxi turned out to be a motorbike, the wheelman Antonio himself, careening me through the narrow, people-packed market streets with a fearsome abandon that certified his place on any roster of cab drivers.

He spoke just enough English to rent his rooms out; and his wife, Katerina, even less. But they installed a writing table for me, and the single-window room was restful and clean if not exactly charming. I was a half-block from the rich blue rippling waters of Myteline's original northside harbor, long ago abandoned and left to become a quiet beach with a rambling old fortress ruin at its far end.

By evening, a torrent of wind sweeping down the strait turned the gentle waters into a raging surf – a taste of the suddenness with which island weather can change. My shutters banged all night long. But it mattered little to me; I slept nine hours that night. And again nine hours, the next. These lingering days in Myteline were exactly what I needed, allowing me to let go of my travel urgencies and just fall apart ... and to realize how much I did need that. But three days was about all I wanted of Myteline. Its bazaar fascinations were overwhelmed by the constant whine of motorbikes from morn until dark. With the angry insistence of a locust swarm, they possessed the town like demons and I was anxious to be out of there.

It may have been that hilltop fortress, seen when we entered the strait, that drew me up to Molivos. I couldn't recall the vaguest sign of a town there when we sailed by, but the map indicated a resort and artist's colony on its inside slope, sheltered by the castle promontory. A two-hour, four-dollar bus ride through some unexpectedly attractive country took me out there.

Gentle inlets rising to rugged, pine-clad strongholds that reminded me of California's Sierra foothills, but with olive trees (by the millions) instead of madrone the basic ground cover, and quaint villages scattered along the way. A twisting downgrade to the sea brought us into Petra, named for a knobby rock that stands like a great thumb, with a unique Byzantine chapel at its crest – but it was hard to keep one's eyes on, for the equally compelling attraction of topless bathers along Petra's narrow strip of beach. Out of Petra, we rounded the headland to a sudden view of Molivos, its tile-roofed houses clinging to the steep slope below that dominating old fortress like children huddled in a mother's apron.

Close by where the bus came to its final stop was a tourist office, where the local landladies pooled their resources and visitors were parceled out like fatted pullets for the dinner table. I told the woman in charge of this sensible and simple operation that I was looking for a few days of lodging at $5 per night.

"No, there's nothing that cheap anymore," came the easy but firm reply.

"Please." I pushed on, "I can't afford any more. Maybe a small, out-of-the-way room somewhere?" I was really testing the waters for a possible wintering price.

She looked pained and told me to sit and wait awhile.

Others came and were taken in tow by bored-looking, business-like landladies who trooped out with them, and finally the last young couple from the bus. This pair was given to a grandmotherly, somewhat robust woman, and then the one in charge cast a baleful eye in my direction, saying something in Greek to the sturdy proprietress, who thereupon looked me over as a fisherman might eye a doubtful catch just large enough to get away with, but hardly big enough to bother with. Finally, giving a half shrug of resignation, she nodded an acceptance.

So I went off with them, trailing behind the pair being led up the steep cobbled walkway at what seemed the pace of a forced march, marveling – between gasps for air – at the grey-haired woman's stamina. She led us along an arbor-covered alley, up past souvenir shops, vegetable stalls and cafes, into and through a tiny churchside courtyard that seemed to rest on the roofs of houses down the slope, and out the other end to one of the many old stone buildings, where we were ushered inside to a dining room that doubled as a reception area. She took the young couple, who were from Holland, upstairs and then returned to assign me a small room right off the dining area with one window framing a narrow view of the bay and distant mountains. I couldn't be sure of my rate, as it was posted at $10, the in-season figure, and the summer season had several weeks yet to run. But we three were her only guests.

The room, the entire house, was a funky relic of earlier times when the tourists were fewer and less particular about the 'quality' of their quarters. I didn't yet know this, but in my subsequent search for a possible rental I found out the town had been glamorized by its tourist potential only in the last several years and had been upgrading facilities almost feverishly to a standard entirely without the old charm of this house run by Eleutheria. From an old register and 'memories book' that lay on the dining table, I could see she had been renting rooms here for some thirty years and had a faithful return clientele. Photos of group dinners lined the walls, with notes penned on them indicating that meals had once been part of the arrangement. Glass cabinets held antique table service and other oddments accumulated over the years, part of the harvest of Eleutheria's half-lifetime here.

A small but charming veranda porch jutted just off the big dining room. Sheltered by an overhanging vine, it offered a full view of the crescent beach and bay far below, like some Riviera vista, and became my favorite dining and writing spot. Feta cheese and big calamata olives were cheaply had in local shops, and Eleutheria donated olive oil for the classic Greek salad. A portable burner just inside the veranda door heated water for tea. At dusk, watching the sun drop into the sea, I'd remain in the warm night air to count stars coming out. Even at $10 a day, it seemed an incredible bargain.

Less providentially, there was a thorn in the bouquet – nothing ever comes completely perfect. At about nine in the evening, every night, amplified dance music came bounding up the hillside from one of the tourist facilities down on the beach and continued, hardly diminished, until . . . three in the morning! It was good music, but not so good that I wanted it with such all-night, boom-box regularity.

Eleutheria spoke not a word of English, but it seemed to make no difference to either one of us. We took an instant liking to one another that went quite beyond the mereness of words. She'd greet me with some Greek phrase, and I'd echo it – never quite knowing what we were saying to each other. She let me have refrigerator space, and I thought seriously for awhile about staying right here through the winter, confident that the juke-box-every-night would end soon with the tourist season. I put it to her, in fact, getting it across by using a calendar. But she merely shook her head and replied by an indication that I should take it up with the woman in the tourist office. Was it her way of saying it had to be brokered there, or a polite suggestion that I should find other quarters? I couldn't be sure.

But I went to check it out – for all the good it did me – next morning before the day's adventure of trekking out to a surfside hot spring. I was simply turned over to the next landlady in line, who led me off to her own offering, nodding cheerfully as I tried to tell her what I wanted . . . until I realized she didn't understand a word I was saying. She had the wits, however, to corral a teen-ager named Korina, who did speak passably good English, and she came along as translator. I was shown a living unit with full kitchen, still under construction and far more classy than I had in mind. It wasn't a bad bargain at a full-winter rate of $300 per month, though way out of my range. But the reasonable value of it encouraged the thought that I might yet find something affordable on Lesbos.

I continued on my way down the hour-long trail to the hot spring, going by several outlying resort inns along the waters of the strait, and finally to a building that had once been used for tub baths, now vacant. Alongside was the hot spring housed in a low, white-domed structure and open to anyone . . . free! The pool was only large enough for three or four people at a time, but I had it all to myself now. The water was just within my comfort range and just deep enough to stretch out in for a half-hour of mineralized, skin-tingling relaxation. It was at the very edge of the sea, some of its warmth even seeping into the outside surf.

The shoreside trail continued along a string of linked beaches, each one featuring more daringly exposed bathers, until at the very end I found myself among a fully naked crew, where I divested myself for a skinny-dip in their liberating company. It was like California of the early '70s revisited. Back then, in that brief and passing time of innocence renewed, I'd had my first release from a lifetime burden of conventional shame about my body . . . our obsessive fear of revealing it in public.

All of this, of course, increased the appeal of Molivos as a possible winter locale and I was primed for running into Korina again, who had been waiting for my return up the trail to tell me that her mother, who also rented rooms, might be able to work something out for me. Alas, Korina's mother also had modernized rooms. But she was at least able to offer an affordable long-term rate. Yes, $5 per day for a full winter, starting in October as I specified, if I would take responsibility for electric heating costs. I couldn't imagine they'd be very high at this San Francisco latitude. She promised the use of a hot plate and refrigerator space for minimalist cookery. It really wasn't the accommodation I'd been hoping to find, but it was the first place within my range in Molivos, and thereby definitely up for consideration. I asked Korina to tell her mom (for she was still doing the translation) that I'd let her know, one way or the other, as soon as I could decide – presumably once I reached Crete. It certainly offered one considerable benefit: having someone nearby with whom I could converse in English.

Eleutheria wrote her charge on a slip of paper: $5 per night, and I left it with an extra $2.50 for her kindness when I departed Friday morning. It seemed too soon to leave, but I had my ticket for that afternoon's ferry to Chios, purchased before leaving Myteline. But boarding the boat, I was suddenly overwhelmed with exhaustion. I felt chilled, despite the warm sun, and huddled myself in extra layers of sweater and jacket as we sailed past the jetty into the open sea. It wasn't so bad as to drive me from the deck, but enough to warn me that I was on an energy borderline, notwithstanding the amount of rest I'd had during my five days on Lesbos.

It was the season, of course. My arrival at Lesbos was two days shy of a full year since touching down in London; and once more, as in many Septembers past, I was intent upon getting settled. The three weeks it had taken me in London had very nearly sapped my reserves of energy. Was it to be the same again, with this dogged determination of mine to get to Crete?

Quite suddenly in the midst of these reflections, I saw something unbelievable up near the prow of the boat: a pair of dolphins, skimming in three graceful arcs right across our bow! A few moments later they came back beneath the boat, amidships, to soar in one final, great leap practically in front of me, their slick bodies gleaming in the sun. No one was around me to verify that it really had happened, and in a few moments I wasn't at all sure . . . it was so silent and swift that it began to seem more like a vision. Perhaps something calling me to attention?

Chios is just a few hours to the south of Lesbos, a first stop on the overnight ferry run to Athens – and again, our approach was through a strait, passing this time close to a small and rather barren island called Oinoussai. I could see a small settlement on its hilly slope, already in the lengthening shadow of a swiftly sinking sun. It was so warm as we came into Chios harbor that I made a quick decision to save myself a night's lodging cost by heading for the hills that rimmed the town. But the sun had already set by the time the ship's lines were thrown for our brief docking, and I had very little daylight time to work with.

I dodged my way through the now familiar dockside madness as quickly as I could, making tracks at an urgent pace with the already bright moon as a navigation aid. It was uphill all the way, the light fading steadily. There was barely enough left to see by when I reached some sort of ravine slicing in behind the last street of houses, though I could see a few dwellings on its far side. In the near-darkness, scattered shrubbery gave it a bit of a parklike quality – but park or not, I had no time to be choosy. What I couldn't see, as I headed into it, was that the local kids used it as a gathering place. Consequently it was a bit of a surprise when I suddenly became aware, as I laid out my gear, of several youngsters standing on a low ridge about forty feet away, watching me.

It was a bit like the situation at Mallaig, back in Scotland, and I figured I'd better defuse it. Hoping somebody understood English, I hollered up that it was a nice night for sleeping out. And one of them agreed with me. They stood there a few moments longer, and it was too dark for me to see any expressions or even guess their ages. A mother's voice rang out, then, from somewhere, and they left . . . one of them calling back to me, "Sweet dreams!"

It set the tone for a long relaxed night of intermittent sleep. I'd waken from time to time with the aroma of sagebrush in my nostrils and just lay there looking up at the clear ceiling of stars. Their brilliance was awesome in the wee hours after the moon had set. The increasing rareness of a star-filled night has made them that much more comforting, for every constellation up there is still where I remember it as a young boy – just about the only thing for which that can be said.

In Saturday morning's first light I saw that I was practically surrounded by houses on hillsides, much as if I were in the center of an arena. I hastily got dressed and out of there before anyone was up to see me.

Back at the harbor looking for information, I saw that a Saturday boat went to that little island of Oinoussai and didn't return until Monday morning. Even with a good night's rest I still felt weary at a deep level, and suddenly the idea of an entire weekend on a tiny, out-of-the-way island seemed immensely attractive. Maybe I needed such time to peacefully reflect on what was going on with me. Maybe I didn't want to go on to Crete, after all!

That possibility had been intruding on me ever since I had seen the dolphins, and as we drew close to the dock in Oinoussai's tiny harbor I could actually feel tension dropping off like a heavy topcoat, at the sight of a village with absolutely nothing going on in the streets. No motorbikes, no bazaar, no Saturday noontime market activity at all. I found a single open cafe and went in to see if anyone could tell me where to find a *domatio*. After she first placed a phone call, the woman sent me up the hill toward a hotel, which was not what I had in mind, but with these streets so empty it might be what I'd have to take. I had never seen a town so starkly abandoned, the shutters closed on practically every building in sight.

The hotel, too, looked deserted. A relatively new two-story structure with a groundfloor veranda balcony that gave access to a spacious, low-ceiling reception area, sparely built but attractively decorated in a blend of Mediterranean and Greek styles. Sturdy, dark-stained wood furniture stood on tile flooring and colorfully decorative ceramics lined the exposed wooden beam supports. But nobody was in sight – neither guests nor staff. I waited a decent amount of time and began searching the hallways.

Some noise led me toward a room being cleaned by someone who fortunately spoke English and spoke it as though she were in charge. To her room price of $10 per night, I protested short funds and we came to an agreement on $15 for the two nights. But it was all very strange, for she told me not to lock the door to my small and elegantly furnished room, for there were no keys!

It fed a growing suspicion that the place had closed for the season and the cleanup crew were taking advantage of anyone who turned up. It made little difference to me, however – could even be seen as a blessing, for there were never many people around and I discovered that I could use the small back-bar kitchen behind the reception lobby for making tea when I wished. I could even spike it with their shelved liqueurs!

The town itself struck me as 'closed for the season' when I strolled its full extent on Sunday morning. A spic-and-span spotless little town, sloped up a hillside like Molivos, offering nothing at all to do on Sunday morning except follow the tolling of a bell to the church – where I at least saw some people. But I was not into a Greek church service any more than an English one, and I set out instead on a long walk toward the west end of the island, picking one or two of the ripe pomegranates that grew abundantly along the way. The day was quite lovely, with no traffic to speak of on the roadway.

I came to a little cove beach absolutely out of anyone's sight except for the rarely passing motorist. I hadn't even thought to bring trunks or towel, but it seemed to make no difference here. For over an hour, I frolicked naked in the blue water and then sat in the sun to dry. It was here, in an ambience that heightened my sense of *natural being,* that I finally accepted my need to settle at once, without going on to Crete. The room in Molivos was far from perfect, but it was affordable and available, and I knew at a deep level that I had no energy for continuing onward.

Late that afternoon, the town suddenly and strangely blossomed with people – as though they had been awaiting my decision. Down the street they came, behind a little marching band in black and white, right past the balcony where I sat drinking tea. Something about 'Mary,' I gathered. The Virgin Mary? No, my informant had said *marry.* It was a wedding!

The festivities carried on at the town's single cafe, and I strolled down to watch a bit of it before turning in. Greek dancing at slow tempo with its careful steps and half-steps, both arms high or one held at the back, hips doing half the dance, studied and serious facial expressions . . . no two of them doing it exactly the same, yet each preoccupied with getting it just right. Then a fast tune was played, and two men, whom I supposed were the new fathers-in-law, were out there by themselves joyously swinging to the beat and the rhythmic crescendo of hand-clapping. It was all very marvelous to see.

I hadn't seen anyone – ever – at the hotel desk, and the cleaning woman only once since that first occasion when she gave me the room. So I was in a quandary, early Monday when it came time to leave for the return boat ride. I had nothing smaller than a Greek bill worth $25, and I wasn't about to leave it. I left, instead, a note asking to be billed in care of *poste restante* in Athens, where I was to call for mail around the first of October. (Needless to say – and hardly to any personal surprise – no billing ever arrived for me.)

All that was left, now, was to get back to Lesbos on Monday's boat, and back to Molivos to claim my winter quarters. I could just about see the surprise on Korina's face, and her mother's, at my sudden return. I wasn't wrong about that ... but oooh, the surprise I was about to run into, *myself!*

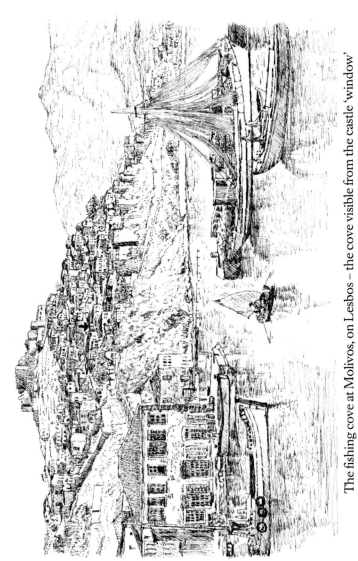

The fishing cove at Molivos, on Lesbos – the cove visible from the castle 'window' in the cover photo. A small arrow on the hillside points to where I stayed the winter.

Becoming a Lesbian

Molivos, on the Isle of Lesbos: September 16, 1991...

"Well, here I am ... back already! I decided I didn't need to go to Crete, after all."

Korina smiled rather weakly, uncertain exactly what to make of my sudden presence on her porch. "Where are you going to stay?"

"Right here. I'm ready to move in."

It should have been obvious. I was lugging a rolled-up foam rubber pad with a brown floral slipcover, purchased that morning before the boat left Chios. A lucky break, to find one there for $20; lucky enough to override the bulky nuisance of hauling it around. Laid out on the floor it would provide, all winter long, the firm bedding I needed for a really good night's sleep.

But I could see, now, the uncomfortable look on Korina's face. There was a hurried exchange with her mother, who had just joined her at the door, and then she told me what it was all about.

"The price you want does not start until October. It is still 'the season' and we cannot give it yet, that cheap."

This was the 16th of September. That meant two full weeks at ... how much? Korina, that doubtful look still shadowing her young features, answered before I could even ask the question.

"Right now the room is still two thousand drachma."

About eleven dollars. It didn't require much consideration on my part. "No. I can't handle that for two weeks. I guess I'll have to stay somewhere else until then."

Another hurried conference.

"Mother says she could give it for 1700 drachma. It is the best we can do."

Now that the initial shock had passed I was beginning to feel put off by their attitude. Here I was, ready to rent for an entire winter, a span of time when rooms sit completely idle on Lesbos, and they could not bend – not even halfway to my level – for the last two weeks of the season.

"I really can't, Korina. I'll stay tonight, but I'll have to look for another place tomorrow."

It took the wind completely out of my day's billowing sails, for I had let myself get carried away by that sweet and comforting sense of 'going home.' Now I'd have to start all over again, looking for a cheap two-week rental. I thought of trying Eleutheria but I didn't imagine she'd want to extend that half-price generosity of two nights to two full weeks. And anyhow, putting up with that all-night dance music for two weeks was an unbearably long prospect.

I couldn't imagine what had gone wrong, for I had followed my instincts, not my head, in coming back here. It was a discouraging moment and the room suddenly looked much drearier than it had seemed in recollection, on the voyage back from Chios. I had to get out of there for awhile and clear my head of this troublesome, unwelcome development. Anyway, I could put the daylight remaining to good use, searching out prospects.

It might be worth scouting the fishing village out on the point, at the far other end of town. It stood a bit aloof from the main part of Molivos, almost a separate little community with something of an Utrillo flavor in the way the buildings seemed to huddle in on one another. A charming place to stay, even if I'd have to pay a bit more.

I took the highside walk to get out there instead of the more direct vehicle route along the rocky cove shore. Molivos in profile is like a prone goose – the crowning castle its high rump, and its stretch-extended head represented by the low headland that shelters the small boat harbor with its mini-village. I had already hiked that land's end of jutting coast, and followed it to a pair of beautifully isolated small beaches, with nothing between them and sunset but the wide, blue sea. Further along, still, was a hermit's rocky outcrop above the bashing surf. Truly, this locale was an expatriate paradise. Even in the tourist season – such as remained of it – a quiet solace was available out there. What would it be like in the reflective deep of winter?

In these musings, as I made my way up disjointed alleyways toward the fortress ruin, the room I was about to commit to seemed more and more a choice hastily made. But it had, after all, brought me back to Molivos; and I'd have all the hours of every day to be elsewhere in the vicinity. Weather permitting, of course – an unknown quantity that I wasn't really giving much thought to, though Korina's mother had fairly warned me with her request that I cover the heating separately.

The castle was a big one, as elaborate as some in Wales, though in worse condition – which is merely to say that thoughts of restoration had not yet struck the local populace. Nor of safety barriers: one could roam the entire battlement, which is quite as it should be for a fortress ruin. There wasn't any admission charge, either, though it had a resident caretaker. The obsession with cost-effectiveness and profit/loss ratios had not yet caught up with this part of the world. And I recalled living in a world once, myself, where it didn't dominate life as it does today.

From the castle prominence, Turkey presented a solid flank of seacoast across the strait to the north, with fabled Troy just 40 miles distant on a crow-line. Legend has it, in fact, that Achilles had conquered this very town, in one of its earlier incarnations. The slope down the other side was more gentle, though still navigated by cobblestone alleys scarcely wide enough for passing motorbikes or burros. A four-wheeler could never make it. Even if it could squeeze through, it would hang up on the stepped ledges that were better than traffic barriers. Vehicle traffic on the slope was restricted to the few slightly wider arteries lined with most of the village shops. People generally walked, of course – it was more practical in the long run.

The clop-clop of a burro sounded here and there, and over it a peddler's high-pitched cry announcing the day's local produce. House-keepers ambled out for an apron-full of fresh vegies and fruit. It fore-shadowed what later became my winter's daily wake-up: the morning garbage horse, a patient-looking old equine soul who'd stand resign-edly still outside my window while being loaded-up. He sometimes gave as much as he took away; yet, the alleys were somehow kept spotlessly clean despite the regular traverse of animals.

And there were cats ... cats everywhere! I've not the least doubt that Molivos has twice as many cats as people. Very territorial animals, maintaining only a testy truce among themselves, intimidating the few dogs in town – and very nearly me, too! I had the strange impression that they entertained a private joke about my feckless pursuit of residence, for I felt the hint of a smirking look as I passed each cluster. But the sneers would vanish in wide-eyed innocence when I turned to look back at them.

I found nothing to encourage me in the fishing village. It was an easy dockside ambience that I could happily have lived with, but I'd have to be content with taking the hike out here when I wanted it. I thought perhaps I was onto something when a heavyset, grey-haired fellow overheard me asking a barkeep about a rental unit upstairs, and he said his daughter had some cheap quarters that were available. I followed him to a nearby notary office, where he called his daughter, speaking to her in English, and relayed to me a two-week price of only $8 per day, a bit cheaper than Korina's last offer. He sat there holding the phone and getting impatient as I turned the bid back and forth in my mind.

"Well, do you want it?"

"Gee, I don't know if I could really manage that ... " I was silently considering a budget stripped down to one meal a day.

"*Do you want it?* Yes or no!"

Pushed, I stiffened. "No."

He slammed the phone down on his poor daughter without so much as saying goodbye to her, and dismissed me just as curtly.

I had come to Lesbos just in time for the close of 'the season.' That was apparent when I returned to the center of town and cast around for a bit of dinner – one or two of the cafes had shut down over the weekend I had been gone. The modest place I selected was empty enough to afford me a window-view table looking out on the wide sea, under a soft but rich sunset, and I felt a bit sheepish ordering the cheapest entree on the menu. But even that cost more than four dollars.

I sat there chewing on chicken and financial concerns, reflecting on how good it had been to be fed as well as sheltered by Good Neighbors hosts, and suddenly had a brilliant inspiration. Why not just go on a two-week roaming and camping trip? Discover the rest of Lesbos on foot. Perhaps an occasional bus ride or even some hitching around the island, and what I save on rent will buy my food. It seemed like a wonderful idea – down-playing the fact that my energy was shredded from four and a half footloose months. I thought I could do it, and the mere thought of it cheered me immensely as I headed back toward my room.

The two-story house owned by Korina's mother stood on the town's very fringe, from where paths headed off across barren hills toward the northside waters of the strait. As I rounded a corner past the last of the eateries on that end of town, I was surprised to see Eleutheria there at an outdoor table with her friend and neighbor, Maria. It was a completely unlikely encounter, for in all the time I was to know Eleutheria she cooked and ate at home, and ventured this far only when she had taken me in tow at the tourist office. But there she was – and quite as surprised as I, for she had every reason to think I was well on my way to Crete by now.

Even more remarkable was Maria's presence, for she spoke excellent English and could easily translate for us. When I reeled out my tale, Eleutheria immediately wanted to know why I had not returned to her *domatio*. So I asked, in response, if she'd have me for two weeks at the same 1000 drachma rate – the $5 per night she had allowed me. Her nodding assent came without a moment's pause. But why, then, wouldn't she take me for the full winter at that rate? She replied, through

Maria, that she closes the house down entirely for the deep winter months and goes off to Athens. Is a Lesbos winter that severe, then? Yes, sometimes it even snows, she told me. I winced at that. But it was too late, now, for any second thoughts about Crete. I promised Eleutheria I'd be there the following day.

When I reached my night's quarters, Korina was waiting for me with the 'good news' that they had talked it over again, she and her mother, and decided I could stay the full two weeks for 1400 drachma per night – about $7.40. If I hadn't encountered Eleutheria, I would either have taken the offer or been gone the next morning on my projected campout – in either case virtually committing myself to a winter in this barely sufficient room. Running into Eleutheria at that last possible moment, in that least likely situation, changed the entire prospect of my winter.

I didn't know that yet. All I had in mind was going to Eleutheria's for two weeks of acceptable economy and then returning to this room. But when I paid the full 2000 drachma, next morning, for the single night, my farewell to Korina had a strong edge of uncertainty. I was already hedging my promise to return, aware that the gates had once more opened wide for fresh possibilities.

It took only two days for opportunity to fulfill itself, and when it fell into place it revealed such an incredible convergence of 'lines of Innocence' that I cannot imagine I should ever have missed it. Yet, it appeared to happen as a completely casual and random development. After a day of thoroughly blissful relaxation in my old quarters off Eleutheria's dining room, and out on the veranda, I began what I expected would be an extended search among the honeycomb of alleys, looking for the weathered red clapboard shutters that marked the older *domatio,* as distinct from the high-varnish hardwood that invariably indicated recent renovation.

Peering down an alley from a triangle junction that had been turned into a tiny plaza, I thought I spotted the quarry and went to check it out. But I was mistaken, and as I pondered whether to continue down this particular path or return to the plaza I heard someone ask in reasonably good English what I was looking for. I turned to see an auburn-haired woman perhaps in her mid-40s, not typically Greek – that is, there was a brightness in her eyes, an easy conversational smile. I had not seen many outgoing, cheerful-looking Greek women.

Caught off guard by the sudden question, I answered flippantly that I was looking for cheap, old-style housing, and she asked what I considered to be cheap. By now, I could see her own 'rooms for rent' sign posted inconspicuously in a window, and also that her large house looked far too substantial for the price I sought. But she beckoned me through the garden gate before I could even frame a reply.

Walking in, I let her have my wishful estimate, " . . . 30,000 drachma a month, for the full winter." I kept thinking of that, in my rule-of-thumb way, as $150, but the going rate of exchange made it more like $160.

"I have a nice little apartment . . . " she began, like a spider sweet-talking a fly, "that is pretty close to that figure. Let's go inside and I'll make us some coffee."

"An apartment!" I sucked in my breath. "Yeah, that's what I'd really like, but I'm having trouble even finding a room, for what I can pay." When I walked in and saw how elegantly her house was furnished I knew she wouldn't come anywhere near my price.

"Well, what do you get, here, for 30,000 drachma?" It was a rhetorical question, and she went right on, " . . . just a little room, and then you find you have to pay extra for the heat all winter, and there is this and that, and before you know, it's costing you 40,000 . . . "

She was calling her shots as if she knew exactly what my bargain had been.

" . . . and I can give you a nice, sunny little apartment with a kitchen and all the heat you want, for a flat price of 40,000. Come on, I show it to you."

Her logic was seductive, but . . . "No, it's a nice thought, but there's just no way I can afford that."

"Well, come on and look at it while our coffee gets ready."

She talked as we walked, a steady stream of hard-sell, punctuated every so often with, "Not that I'm trying to talk you into it, but . . . "

She led me back out the alley gate and around to the other side of the house, where a basement apartment fronted on intersecting alleys. It raised the immediate shadow of another housing taboo: the dark interior of basement apartments. It was only a step below street-level, though, and when we entered I was struck by the loveliness of sunshine streaming in through grill-covered windows to illuminate a Mediterranean interior of simple taste in warm dark woods and colorful fabric patterns. A white-washed backwall and the rough-timber old beams of a low ceiling set the furnishing off to good advantage. To the left of our entry was a small but complete kitchen; and it was one long room to our right, ending in a sturdy brass bed that must have been a century old.

But what my quick scan zeroed in on was the round, dark mahogany writing table by one of the twin windows. It was worn and well-used, but the sunlight slanting across it triggered an image of endless hours in contentment at the task I wanted to begin: making a book. Good writing tables – the sort that invite use, rather than threaten confinement – are terribly rare in rented quarters. This one was the perfect low height for me; and then I saw its companions: padded chairs in a muted green velour that took all the resistance out of me. This was far, far superior to the room I had settled for at Korina's, and very close to the idealized fantasy of a retreative winter that had first engaged me. Somehow, I'd just have to stretch for that $215. It was more than half my monthly income, but with a kitchen to cut the food costs I could make it work – I *would* make it work.

We were back upstairs having the coffee, a bracingly strong brew, and I was telling Betty all the hassles I'd come through, trying to find a place. When I got to the part about the fellow who called his daughter and then hung up on her, she looked at me brightly.

"I thought that was you! That was my Dad you were talking with."

There was hardly time enough to digest this bit of weirdness before a strangely familiar woman came into the kitchen from the garden-side entry ... looking at me as if to say, "What are you doing here?"

Betty said, "Hi, Mom."

... just about when I realized that I was looking at Maria!

She was angry with me, at first, for renting Betty's apartment and 'betraying' my agreement with her friend, Eleutheria ... until Betty assured her that my rental here would not begin until the first of October. I wasn't too clear on anything, by that time, myself. The connections and inter-weaving had left me too dizzy for any further coherence that afternoon.

So I was home, at last. Or would be, as soon as all the preliminaries were done. I stayed the full remainder of September at Eleutheria's, countering the high-volume music by sneaking upstairs each night to one of the vacant bedrooms out of the direct line-of-sound, sleeping on my foam pad on the floor to keep everything tidy. It was no problem since I was Eleutheria's only guest. My days were spent taking tea on the veranda while I watched the last of the season's water sports on the bay and prepared a final journey report for my supportive friends back home – thereby seeding a mid-winter crop of mail for myself.

The pleasures of late September, however, constituted no forecast for the fall and winter that lay ahead of me. To begin with, it took most of October to establish settlement there. In my springtime enthusiasm's reckless contempt for time and energy, I was sure I'd be in Crete by September's end and had scheduled an Athens mail-call for the first of October. That much, at least, I could manage and it became the coda to my larger journey – a week-long sidetrip to mainland Greece, culminating in the Delphi hostel adventure with Matt and David.

I returned from Athens with a pack full of supplies calculated to keep me in livable comfort during my hermitage – cookery ingredients that I feared might be too elusive on the island; teas to serve me better than that intolerably strong Turkish-style coffee served everywhere on Lesbos; a $30 table radio to save me from wearing earphones for hours on end ...

But they were all the wrong purchases. The radio ultimately became an instrument of torment. Try as I might, I could not spin the dial beyond the penetrating, incessantly sing-song tonal style of Middle Eastern music – until I hated the very sound of it. Had I any idea,

OM

though, of what I was in for, I'd have paid and labored for every pound of readable print I could haul back with me; for when I returned to Lesbos the terrible extent of the isolation I had purchased hit me like a brick. Along with the tourists, every last English language periodical – newspaper and magazine alike – had vanished as cleanly as if by edict backed with a flaming sword from on high. Not even among the cluttered kiosks along Myteline's thronging harbor, packed layer on layer with dailies in German, French, Italian, and how many other tongues I can't say, was anything in English to be found.

A stillness had settled over Molivos – not in itself any problem for me, but coupled with this sudden and total dearth of reading matter it felt no longer like a quietude of retreat ahead of me, but more the cheerless pall of exile.

The tone had been set for a winter of withering cross-currents: the truly exquisite freedom from demand and habit offered by an island village, but rip-tided by the most agonizing sense of boundaries and limits and festering isolation likely to be found outside of prison confinement. It would become at one and the same time the sort of winter I had always dreamed of – a writer's idyll, and yet a focusing lens to vivify every frailty that I possess. Touching the poles of contrast can do no more than hint at what I was in for, but I'm afraid that's as far as I can take it, here.

Would I have fared better on Crete, less isolated from mainland Greece and awash in those warmer southern waters? I had time enough over the ensuing months to reflect on that question, along with the vagaries of choice and chance that landed me on Lesbos instead. I had called the turn, myself, of course, when I decided to ignore my August insight in Munich – the realization that summer's energy had been drawn too thin to easily keep my eastern Europe commitments and I should better head immediately south while there was time enough to make a leisurely search for winter options.

It raises interesting issues as to the ultimate value of free agency – or to put a finer point on it, as to the wisdom of exercising free will, when Nature counsels otherwise. The issue is on our doorstep every day, as we move into a future plagued with one piece of 'counsel' from

Nature after another, as our Promethean exercise of power reshapes the world in which our tomorrow will be situated.

This is why, in turn, it's so important to be able to *read* Nature – not just for skills at the classification of her countless organisms, or the heightened pleasure of seeking them out, but for the *message content* that Nature holds for us. The element we have so lost touch with, in our headlong rush toward civilization.

I knew a lot about the ripening pattern of cyclic time when I began the journey this book details; and what I knew provided both help and comfort over the year-and-a-half that had transpired since the impulse that initially set me to it. But I know *more*, as I write this closure, about the awesome depth of the cycle's archetypal influence in our lives.

It would have made little difference had I gone on to Crete, for just as the year's pattern enforced its mandate on my psyche and energy, so did I have to contend with a deeper manifestation of the archetype, as it registers in a seven-year version.

This, you see, is the nature of an archetype. This one is the psychic template that underlies *living time,* and it has a say over the way things happen to us – certainly with respect to our inner experience, and I've found good reason to think that it also has a creative influence on outer experience.

Just as the year, itself, has a winter season with attendant tempers and moods that are readily familiar and quite expectable, so does each round of seven years contain a similar 'seasonal' segment, often manifesting as a retreative undercurrent, even depressive, that tones our lives for a full year and more of calendar time. It particularly intensifies such experience during the annual winters that come along in the course of its passage.

As the fall of that year, 1991, moved into winter, I was moving into such a 'winter' in one of those long cycles, and there wasn't a blessed thing to be done about it, nor any better place to be with it. It was a particularly deep trough for me, because my life, too, was on its way into its 'winter' years – remember, this is an archetype we are dealing with, and it ultimately brings the fully 'ripened' human being into *life's* last season.

But no need to fret your future! – for the seven-year cycle eventually brings its own springtime, even in life's winter, which is what you have to thank (along with me) for this book! I wrote a full first draft of it during that secluded winter on Lesbos, while everything was still fresh in mind. But the final version, along with all the art work and book design, had to await the rejuvenative 'spring' vitality of the next seven-year thrust, a full year down the line.

[And it is interesting to note that the opportunity for a second edition has come along – quite in the natural flow of things – exactly seven years after the first!]

The weary author meditating in the shallow and deserted hot pool, an hour's walk from where I lived, on Lesbos. *(photo by Evelyne Drevet)*

Epilogue: A Septide on

Seven years – what I call a septide – constitutes a significant passage in the lifestream, and parallels are often found to occur. In 1997 I gave in to an overwhelming early-year urge to return to the track of my previous journey and renew some of the friendships I made at that time. At 70, of course, I was not quite as limber, and with a few more dollars at my disposal it was not so rugged or ragged a venture as the earlier occasion. But I tried to keep it so, as I could, just for the remembered fun of it, and did have a few similar adventures.

I wrote up the tale, for personal friends, in a small newsletter I do called Ripening Seasons, and it seems to offer an excellent closure for this new edition of the original book.

You'll find some updating in this final chapter, as well as fresh, new vagabonding in my old style, but most of all you'll find observations on what it's like to try and reprise the one-and-only past. But for all my misgivings, there was a development at the close of it so profound and mysterious that I think about it yet, and wonder what it all means.

Here it is, then...

Seattle: May, 1997...

Why? What reason did I have for going abroad again . . . putting myself through that energy-intensive wringer that any such journey involves? Everybody asked – and frankly it was my own puzzlement, for I had no sufficient answer. To renew old connections, I'd reply. But it seemed a masking response, hardly enough justification for pouring more than a thousand dollars into six weeks of what, to begin with, looked like pure indulgence. Hardly comfortable indulgence, as it turned out, what with the hassles of getting it underway, the endless strain and struggle of pushing it through a stretching winter that simply wouldn't quit . . . I learned one thing, for sure: that I'm not as young as I was in '91. Not that I imagined I was, but I think it was a subtext agenda of mine – to prove to myself that I could still handle such a strenuous challenge to body and spirit.

Well, yes, I managed it . . . but I could never make it through a full season again. And did I really need to learn that?

There were more subtext agendas in this recent adventure than I think I even know about. Rejuvenation, reliving the past, celebrating the attainment of seventy years (in a manner 'proper' to my sense of self), proving again that tight-budget travel abroad is possible (though I faltered on this one – my spending ran closer to $200 per week, this time, than $100), and 'spending down' from a level of gradually accumulated resources that have been crowding the borders of what my subsidized status in life allows . . . it is a strange life, indeed, that urges one to travel abroad in order to remain in a condition of poverty, but such is the fact of it.

But there was no really compelling reason, in the nature of a personal path clearly indicated, for undertaking this journey. Last time, there was; and every major thing I've done over the past twenty years has had that sense of a necessary or advisable direction. The nearest thing I could claim, in that respect, was a recognition that this might be my best moment for such a journey (in personal cyclic terms) for the rest of the decade. But that makes little more sense, as a motivating reason, than looking for a surgical procedure because there's not likely to be a better time for it.

Thoroughly contrary to my accustomed way of life, then, it would seem to have evolved from a lapse in consciousness. I didn't even wait for the fullness of the year's sprouting time, before booking my flight – there was no other choice if I wanted a decent discount. But that's the reasoning of the 'mind in control,' and I really should have known better. It was the first domino in a falling line of them — and the worst of it was that I could *see* these bad moves and their disruptive effects as they fell into place. Transportation plans got kinked like the tangle of a bad fishing cast, and before it was done I was headed into a jumble of lesser bookings and visit commitments that might have earned me a diagnosis of dementia.

Believe me, you will *not* believe the schedule I shaped for myself. You will lose track of it, if I try and portray the entire sequence: London to Chester to Manchester to London to Dresden to Krakow to Gliwice to Prague to London to Bristol to Paris and back to London. Those were the places that my nights were spent, including three addresses in London and an overnight at Heathrow airport. When I further note that the Paris and London finale comprised a full third of my six-week schedule, you'll realize how maddening were the first four weeks of it.

And I should have known better. I had quite enough cues to either pull back from the whole thing, entirely, or else stop trying to plan it free of every insecurity – the characteristic tourist hangup. I should have seen, by the purely perverse way that things were happening, that I was playing the tourist game.

For instance, there was the stunning Web discovery of an outfit called Eurobus that runs a daily scheduled circle-route straight out of London, linking the prime cultural centers of Europe, arranged so that one can book the round-robin (which takes about five days of travel time) over a two or three-week span, choosing points along the route for stays of one or several days, so long as the return to London is done in the allotted time. It was precisely what I wanted, and at half the cost of any rail pass combination I could put together. But at the height of ecstasy, I learned that only late last year they had installed an arbitrary upper age limit of 38 on their passengers.

It so completely infuriated me that I spent a good part of the next few weeks engaged in a running online fusillade, through the travel newsgroups, broadcasting their discriminatory age bias, even as I was pleading (fruitlessly) with them for a personal exemption.

It should certainly have told me that Providence had no red carpet laid out for me on this journey. In the end, I settled for a bargain-rate pair of flights out of London and back, with a tightly limited Continental agenda to fulfill that part of my journey – one hop to Paris, and an earlier one to Leipzig, from where I could take regional rail for a minimal eastern circuit, before returning to London – cheaper, still, than I could do it by rail alone. But no sooner had I booked these flights, irreversibly, than I discovered a new Web site listing *all* of the bargain flights originating in London, and saw that I'd been had again.

By takeoff time, I was at least feeling the spring energy, but already aware that I had an ordeal coming up. The first ten days in Britain were not yet entirely resolved, as to where I'd be. They got further compounded by complications in bus passage (IRA bomb warnings that forced a route detour, and an extended hassle around getting the least expensive fare), plus a feeling that I may have been more under foot than entirely welcome, with one or two of my hosts. They bore it cheerfully, but I could not help feeling somewhat abandoned, at times, to the witless course of a journey that had taken on a life of its own. It was all, by now, frozen in passage certificates, and I was trapped within their unbending timeframes.

Hence, the capstone night spent at Heathrow airport, in order to get a flight at a completely indecent hour to Leipzig. I'd managed to stow my extra piece of luggage, wherein I kept the assortment of books that I knew I'd purchase along the way (. . . and records, and clothing) at the home of a newly-acquainted friend – one of the few instances in which Providence had thus far indicated that I was not entirely left to founder on my own. I'm not sure what I'd have done if Paul Harrison had not turned up on my computer screen, including me in his group of Pantheist devotees gathered for online discussion. Happily, he picked up on my open plea for a night's shelter, which would follow the two weeks in eastern Europe.

Leipzig was not only strategically useful to me, as a direct gateway into the old east, but appropriate in a related way: it had given me my first view, last time, of Europe's eastern face. I stayed this time only a few hours, but long enough to see the tremendous change that has taken place in just six years. It is a totally different city than I saw before: in pace, mood, and the very sense of its being. Leipzig is well on the way to becoming a tourist 'discovery' of some future year. But from my perspective, both better and worse for the change. The quiet, empty market square where I had my small cafe dinner, last time, is now rimmed with upscale shops, its center being ripped wide for new construction. The cafe is no longer there, and I had to settle for something more costly, promoted with more tourist-conscious flair, and far less satisfying.

I went directly on to Dresden, and had to find Simone's place all over again, for she had moved since last time. But I knew where, thanks to an Internet search – a tracking adventure in its own right. Our contact had faded over the years, and I had no response to my announcement of a return visit. So I went on the Web and tapped into the university there – everything in German, but I was able to recognize the Department of English, and within it the American Literature section. I sent off an email message of search to several people in the department; and later found a site for the student newspaper from another avenue entirely. A few responses came back, and ultimately a letter from Simone, herself.

The change of six years was not so apparent in Dresden, as in Leipzig. Yes . . . a bit more activity; and the spanking-new trams were obvious – but also quiet, and they blended easily. One conspicuous eyesore was a flat-sided concrete building that had been allowed to fracture the lovely cityscape seen from the bridge, that I sketched for the book. I missed, also, that idyllic sense of quiet and leisure that had so charmed me in the residential neighborhood. But the streets were still of cobbled stone, and still nightly lit by gas mantles in four-burner clusters, elegant and remarkable to behold, a full century into the electrical age.

I found Simone not far from her old place, living in a divided portion of an old high-ceiling apartment, relic from another age. Imagine, if you will, a gracious old home split in two, with a second bedroom sliced from what had once been a large kitchen. But the old dining room remained intact, trimmed in burnished woods and graced with a wonderful glassed-in sun porch, the combination spacious enough, the ambience rich enough, for the soul to flourish – precisely what Simone required.

. . . When she could find the time for it, for she leads a double life, now: single mom and grant-funded college student majoring in psychology. On both counts, her life has much more promise, now, than it did when I last saw her. Her little Julian, almost five, is a shy kid when it comes to bearded strangers, but he was readily entranced by the three small vehicle replicas Joy had purchased for me to give him.

I stayed five days there, before heading for Poland – a sufficient time for some much needed rest, and to bring a threatening chest cold under control with large doses of vitamin C, which I thankfully had brought along with me. Neither in Britain nor Germany could I find high dosage C tablets anywhere for sale. And the weather was not cooperating at all, so it was up to me, the preventive care.

On the Sunday I was there – and it *was* the only sunny day, though still cold – I went out to make another GN acquaintance, one of only two new Good Neighbors that I was to meet, during the entire journey. Unsure of whether I'd connect with Simone right off, I had written to several prospective hosts in the area. I didn't need any, as it turned out, but it became important to meet with one of them. Klaus was close to my age, and he appeared to be the only GN host in Dresden who had been there during that night of holocaust, more than fifty years ago, that had wiped out the heart of the city. I had to talk with him.

He was hard to find. They had moved into a new suburban development still in process of construction and there was no telephone service yet. Simone pointed me to the right bus, but instead of transferring at the end of its line I decided to walk the remaining distance, several further miles, picking up directional advice along the way. I found the new tract, all right, but it was pure guesswork among its unmarked, unpaved streets, as to which of the scattered homes they occupied. Nevertheless, I managed to find them – and Klaus, who could not be sure that I would even turn up that weekend – gave me a hearty welcome.

I considered myself an ambassador of a sort, from a forgetful but repentant America, carrying a personal and long, long overdue apology for our part in what happened on that terrible night in 1945, and I delivered it with as much gravity as the present situation allowed. Klaus accepted my words with equal solemnity, and then urged me to stop talking and eat lunch while it was still hot. His wife, Rosemarie, had prepared a delicious schnitzel, and I was ignoring my obligation to the present, so wrapped up was I in the past.

Klaus took me on a drive to a magnificent overlook above the Elbe River, surely one of the most picturesque viewpoints in all of Germany, before dropping me back at Simone's, late in the afternoon. Just across the river from Simone's, near the 'Blue Wonder' Bridge, is where Klaus had lived when the bombing took place. He was 13 years old then, and remembers the flames in the night and the refugees afterward. But he only talked of it because I asked, and I only asked because I feel an odd sense of connection with Dresden, almost as if I must personally atone for it. The British usually speak of Coventry, and its destruction by German bombing, when Dresden is brought up; and there is no atrocity, of course, that can stand against the Holocaust of the death camps . . . but there is nothing to gain by one-downmanship in senseless suffering. The world will not become a better place, I think, until we each are ready to accept some responsibility for things evil that have happened in it. Then, and then only, will the cycle stop repeating.

I observed my 70th birthday at Simone's with a very modest celebration, and left early the next morning for the Polish border, planning to walk across at the town of Gorlitz and resume the journey on the other side. At last I had come to fresh, new territory, and by embarking on it in my old style of travel I went through the looking-glass into the land of unplanned adventure: my return, for five brief days, to Innocence Abroad!

I realized it before reaching Gorlitz, with an unwelcome shock. By some fortunate impulse, I went searching for my passport shortly after the train was underway. Fortunate in a kind of goodnews/badnews way: the bad news was that I should have done so before getting on the train; but the good news was that I didn't wait until I was right at the border, which would have lost me some extremely valuable time.

As it was, I spent the first half-hour of the ride to Gorlitz absorbed in the frantic and fruitless search through every vagrant pocket and baggage cranny for the missing blue-jacketed document. I couldn't have left it at Simone's, for I'd had no reason to take it from the zippered inside coat pocket where it should have been. But who could be sure of *anything*, with the increasingly hapless memory that has too often betrayed me?

I had to get back to Dresden – that much was clear. I gave some brief thought to leaving the train at a midway stop, and cut my losses on the return fare; but these were small town stops and I couldn't be sure of bank or money-changing facilities. I was fully back in my old mode of travel, having taken myself down to the last few deutschemarks, and couldn't purchase a return ticket without getting more. So the first order of business arranged itself: on to Gorlitz, get some fresh German money, and then back to Dresden – a $33 setback, and probably only the start of it.

Within an hour of reaching the border town, I was on my way back, catching the Dresden train in time to save myself a two-hour wait for the next one. Very significant time, as it turned out, although it first seemed as though my luck had run dry, when I got there. I pinned my hopes on finding an American Consulate in Dresden, but there wasn't any. I was talking with the Information Booth folks at the Dresden Bahnhof and they spoke no English, so it was a bit spacy, but I was able to get from them the phone number of the American Embassy in Berlin, putting me into the next handicapped stage of the problem.

I found a telephone nearby that not only took credit cards, but had an option for readout instructions in English. It took eight or nine tries to get beyond the busy signal, and then I was rewarded with an endless recorded message ... in German! There was nothing to do but wait for it to end, when it began again – but this time in English, and I was able to copy (hastily) several emergency numbers advised for those who had other than visa problems.

I tried the first of two that seemed to apply to me, but it turned out to be a wrong number – a private residence, where someone spoke English and told me so. The second number, however, gave me the jackpot. The man I spoke with immediately recognized my name and told me they had my passport at the Leipzig Consulate! It had been found by someone – angel circumstances I shall never know – and turned in, there, four days ago.

But I wasn't yet in the clear – there remained the small matter of actually getting it back. He gave me a number to call in Leipzig, and said he hoped I could reach them before the passport was forwarded on to Berlin.

When I tried, now, to call the Leipzig number, the phone would no longer accept my Visa card! The same card that had put me through to Berlin now flashed back "Invalid." Ready for anything, I pulled out my second Visa card, and it worked. Yes, they still had the passport in Leipzig. And by the rarest good fortune, a consulate person would be driving the 65 miles to Dresden that very evening and could deliver it to me!

So this calamity that could have cost me several days out – a trip to Berlin, the added rail fare, and even $65 if I'd had to replace the passport – took a toll of just $33 (plus the $9 in phone calls) and one day off schedule. The return of the precious document was accomplished that evening by an arranged rendezvous at the rail station, the courier spotting me by my passport photo. It all felt very CIA-ish, like some bad movie. And needless to say, Simone was surprised to see me back at her apartment for one more night.

The weather gods intervened overnight and put the rerun trip to Poland on a different footing (literally). In place of Tuesday's cheery sunshine was a leaden-gray sky above a blanket of fresh snow at least a couple inches deep. Walking the half mile through Gorlitz to the river crossing was slippery, and I even lost it once, but good reflexes saved me from anything worse than a slightly pulled calf muscle.

Across the bridge was Zgorzelek . . . small town Poland, as remote and strange as it had been six years ago, 80 miles to the north of here: a new currency to figure out, another language to fumble through, and a railroad station to find. Old and strangely familiar concerns, but the sense of adventure, of living on the edge, was as strong and fresh as ever.

My first move was into a bank. I found no English spoken, quite as expected, but I managed to indicate to a young woman at the teller station that I needed to know the rail fare to Krakow, as a guideline for how much money to exchange. I had brought with me $5 bills for just this occasion. She got the information by calling the rail station: the fare would be about $7.50 (for eight hours of travel!), so I took $15 worth of Polish zlotys. I then got her to draw a crude map to the rail station. I tried to give her a dollar for all this exceptional help, but she reacted as if I had made an indecent proposal, and ended our dialogue forthwith.

Onward, then, to the station, which I might never have found without her map – even *with* it, it was hard to spot . . . the most meager rail terminal imaginable. One station agent, three seedy travelers (?) slouched on a side bench, watching my every move, and a grim silence pervading the entire scene.

I learned, to my chagrin, what the geographic situation should have told me to begin with: there was no traffic flowing from here to the railway hub of Wroclaw, except what originated in Dresden. Preliminary library research back home had indicated the rail link between Dresden and Wroclaw, from where I'd make the connection to Krakow, but I had wrongly supposed there would be more frequent local service than the inconveniently timed, twice daily run out of Dresden, which didn't come through until after midnight, or the alternative option at 8 a.m. It was only noon, now, which meant the unavoidable loss of another day.

Or did it? As I pondered the dilemma, the words of an old song, about loving the woman you've got if you can't have the one you love, flitted unreasonably into mind, along with the irrational prompt to *go where the trains are going!* I was looking at the schedule board, all this while, and saw that there were quite a few departures for someplace called Wegliniec, and so I asked the lady station agent where that might be. It was toward Wroclaw – about a third of the way – and she quickly grasped the drift of my next question. With little difficulty, she worked up a three-train-parlay that would get me to Wroclaw by 7:20 that evening! None of this transpired in English, of course, and I took the tickets as prescribed, wary of losing my gain if I should bring Krakow into the picture. It was enough, for now.

I had a bit more than an hour before train time, and I went back into town for something that might pass for lunch . . . which was just about the measure of what I got: something that passed for lunch. A spit-roasted half chicken served with a dry roll, barren of any salad or vegies. With a glass of tea, it cost only $1.50, however. While eating, I thought about the dumb decision to leave the Polish Good Neighbors list at home (to save weight), which left me without any good recourse if I should have to spend a frigid night in Wroclaw. But I was in Innocence territory, now, and the answer came along in due time.

On the second stage of the triple parlay, from Wegliniec to a larger town called Legnica, I found myself suddenly reprimanded by a fellow passenger for putting my feet upon the seat facing me. He came from across the aisle, well-dressed in the manner of a low level official or a small businessman: clothing that was old but kept as neat as possible – blue serge, of course – and he himself somewhat well-preserved, I'd guess about 50. I didn't understand the scold, but it was clear from his arm movements what he was protesting. Well, far be it from me to deny anyone who cares about the condition of public property (or at least, what had been public property for most of his life), and I readily acceded to his request, dusting off the offended seat to show my sincerity.

He must have had some second thoughts about upbraiding an elderly stranger, for he shortly came back over to my seat to elaborate on something or other, in a more congenial mood. I was cheerful about it, myself, and we continued into one of these 'conversations' in which neither really knows what the other is talking about. But I did get out my map to show him where I was going, upon which he went back to his briefcase and pulled out a rail schedule – a booklet of about 200 pages, actually, covering the southwest corner of Poland in complete detail. And then, to my complete amazement, he made it clear that he wanted me to have it. He was giving it to me, outright!

Well, it didn't take me long to discover – tables being tables, in any language – that I'd have exactly eleven minutes, in Wroclaw, to catch the last train that could get me to Krakow before midnight. In fact, before 3 a.m., which would not be a very good time at all, to arrive. It was precisely the information I needed, with time enough to use it . . . or else end up freezing through a sleepless night, either in Wroclaw or in Krakow.

Of course, there was still the not insignificant matter of whether my train into Wroclaw would be on time, and the more difficult proposition of getting a ticket and finding the right track in eleven minutes. But in Legnica, I had an hour and a half to spare, which was time enough to get the Krakow ticket in advance – if I could manage it. I ate a hearty dinner first, to fortify myself for the challenge. And then I began hunting for a ticket agent, among the dozen there, who spoke some English. No luck at all on that score, and I was making no headway with the intricacies of buying a ticket for use from another station. Nor could I just buy a Krakow ticket from Legnica, because I hadn't enough zlotys left (after my indulgent dinner), and could not use my American cash.

I *had to* find someone who could translate, and so I began canvassing everyone in the station, travelers in particular. But it appeared hopeless. Finally, in one last try, two young women smiled and responded. One of them agreed to help me with the ticket agent . . . and then I found out that I was short by *one zloty* – 33 cents! In absolute desperation, I offered a dollar bill to the helpful young lady for one zloty, and she took it. I was on my way! We got to Wroclaw on time, and I found the right train for the Krakow run, and finally breathed easy again, knowing that I'd be there before the international train out of Dresden, even reached the Polish border.

Despite the icy streets of Krakow, the midnight hour, and my being a day off schedule, Greg and Gorza welcomed me with the gusto of a lifelong friendship – though it had only been a few days, six long years ago. If so many things had changed over the course of time, these two had not, and it was another hour, yet, before we could put our exuberant conversation on hold until the morrow.

Over, and over again, the journey was presenting me with contrasts, which can be very instructive when not idly absorbed and forgotten. This friendship, this very household, had not lost a thing. Yet, the city did not feel the same. It wasn't that worldliness had crept in, as with Leipzig and Dresden, but that everything which before had seemed so expansive was suddenly diminished for me – and I had to chalk it up to the difference between my two impressions, and to a new kind of contrast that the previous day's adventure had suddenly brought home to me: first-time experience is so much more rich because we are totally involved in it, totally alive and present; whereas the repeat – so often done to reclaim the old high – will almost invariably be second-rate. Only when I was going beyond repetition, on this journey, did I experience the highs of the last.

The opportunity approached again when Justyna turned up, the following day. She was my other new GN host, and we were springing a surprise on Greg and Gorza, for they all knew each other. But I had only met Justyna online, when I discovered her email address in the Polish Good Neighbors list. I saw her, now, for the first time – a tall, darkhaired, rather attractive woman in her mid-20s – and I remarked that she *was*, after all, as beautiful as me (referencing my final email message to her). She fired back, just as easily, "A bit more, I think!"

We had a fine early evening meal together, the sort of intercultural festivity that GN generates so well – I prepared my special version of fried matzoh for everyone – and then I took off with Justyna for her home town of Gliwice, not quite half the rail distance back toward Wroclaw, where I was to spend this one night before heading for Prague.

It was much tighter timing than a Good Neighbors visit should have, but filled enough with friendship and shared activity to make up for it.

Justyna is part of a university scene, engaged there in a diversity of activities including computer labs and a quite accomplished choral performance group (which I know, because she gave me one of their tapes). It just happened that this latter group was holding an April birthday party, that night, for several whose natal days were clustered at mid-month. Since my own had just come and gone, it was perfectly fitting that I should be smuggled into the college dorm where it was happening.

What a lark that was! It has been a long time since I last enjoyed a coed party scene, and I'm happy to say that nothing has changed! (Except me, of course – those gyrations are a bit much for me, now, though I was sorely tempted when invited by one cute redhead to the dance floor. It wasn't modesty that stayed me, but an awareness that I had three weeks of travel still ahead.)

In the morning, I had a chance to talk with Justyna's mother – to show her, by my very being, that life may have barely begun, by age 55 – and then Justyna went with me to see that I got the right bus toward the Czech border, and had enough money with me to pay the $3 fare for the two-hour ride. With little necessary luck, she advised, I should be able to cross the border at Cieszyn and get the 1:52 train to Prague.

Oh, yeah? We were just four miles short of destination when the old bus broke down. The situation was obvious, of course, but I had no way of knowing what was going on around it. A bearded fellow sitting up front could speak just enough English to let me know that a replacement bus should pick us up in twenty minutes. But since the driver had to go find a telephone to even try and make this happen, I had my doubts.

A few of the passengers didn't believe it, either – several middle-aged women together managed to hail a passing automobile. It suddenly seemed a very good idea, and I hauled my own baggage up the road a bit and started thumbing. Most of the passengers milling around the bus just looked dumbly at me, but one young fellow – a nerdy type, who had been reading computer magazines across the aisle from me – came up to assist. The Polish don't use their thumb, as I've always done, they give it a whole-arm wave, and my sudden friend succeeded in pulling a car over. And I needed him badly, for though *he* could manage slightly in English, the driver he hailed could understand not a bit of it. It ended with the helpful nerd running back for his own bags, and we all headed on together.

When we came to Cieszyn, I realized how very well Providence was looking out for me, for I could see nothing but hills and traffic, until our driver (at the nerd's behest) pulled up just short of a river bridge, which was precisely where I needed to be. We both got out there, but it was only I who needed to make the crossing, and after a few words of genuine gratitude for this angel who had suddenly taken over (as they always seem to, when needed), I proceeded across on my own, to the town of Cesky Tesin on the other side.

It was something less than a half mile walk, from there to the Czech railway station, and I was guided along the way by an erudite gentleman who spoke English quite well, and had overheard my question about it to the border guard. I'd missed the 1:52 train, by now, but had time enough before the 3:08 to get a quick meal at a nearby hotel dining room, paying with Czech kroney that I had prudently made a trade for before leaving Heathrow. It was $3.90 for the lunch, with tip, and $5.80 for the five hour train ride!

I was an old hand at all this, by now, and only moderately befuddled by the challenges at Prague's central train station. After all, I'd been through here already – twice before. Nevertheless, it did require another angel to refresh me on the subway system – an angel who even paid my 35-cent fare, because I lacked the proper change. But in the end, I had to wrestle with an impossibly monstrous traffic circle in the darkness, where I got off, that totally wiped out my sense of direction. When the rain started, I finally gave up, willing to pay a taxi driver $1.50 for the final few blocks of the journey – and in my utter confusion over the coinage, I left him a shameful seven cent tip.

In a sense, I was making a first-time GN host connection, but I had met Roman on the earlier journey and had about an hour's conversation with him, over some matter that I do not now recall. I regretted, *then* – we both did – that I had no time left to remain in Prague, for we found an instant sense of rapport with each other. So it was a sure thing, this time, that I'd visit him and he'd host me. I met his wife, Iva, this time, and two mischievous children that they didn't yet have, before. And our rapport was still there, as strong as ever.

I stayed five nights with them – longer than Roman would have ordinarily felt comfortable with, for he carried the job responsibility of managing sales personnel for the Czech outlet of Ford Motors. I didn't see much of him on the weekdays, which was okay because I had enough to do on my own in Prague. One entire day, for example, was devoted to mailing a box of purchases home to myself, in a misadventure with the postal system that I'd rather not even recall, let alone recount. But I never did manage to find as many old bookstores, or see as much of the lovely Art Nouveau building decor, as I remember having been there before. Again . . . the contrast. Prague seems twice as thickly filled with tourists as before, and this time I tried to avoid those parts of town.

On the Sunday after I arrived, Roman took me on a drive (in a factory-new Ford) out to the little town of Domazlice, where I had run across that fabulous little man, Jan Prokop Holy, the 'town archivist'. What had then been the entire town, to me – a network of narrow streets centering on a magnificently dimensioned square of Medieval buildings – is still there, intact; but from the perspective of the Ford, it is just the quaint centerpiece of a much larger settlement area, and so has lost a bit of its luster for me. Technology inevitably diminishes enchantment. We were unable to make contact with Jan Prokop, as I had hoped to do – almost as if fate had stepped in to prevent me from tarnishing the heart of that earlier experience.

And by some quixotic bit of Providence, the Ford's 21st-Century, state-of-the-art technology took a funky plunge in Domazlice: the servomechanism controlling my passenger-side window suddenly quit, in the wide open position. I rode the 80 miles back to Prague in a vengefully chill wind that seemed to be saying, "That's what you get, for not being satisfied to let things be."

I'm not so sure that it wasn't the central message of my entire journey! I think we tamper with reruns at a huge risk, and sometimes a terrible cost – and I seem to be especially driven to so tamper with the sanctity of the past gone by. I must either quit this fool's game, or learn to handle it better than I do.

There isn't space, here, to recount everything of the journey. I returned to England by way of Leipzig, and subsequently enjoyed a full relaxing week in Paris, hosted by the GN friend I've come to know best, over the years – Evelyne, who has visited me twice in the States since that earlier journey. That was followed by a week of staying put in one place, in London – the place being Marjory's, my longtime reliable host friend. But it was hard, even there, to recapture the feelings of what London was once like, for me. I had the good sense not to visit Balham, at least, where I'd spent that nitty-gritty winter.

There is a final tale to tell, though, that casts some entirely different illumination on relating to the past. It concerns one of the two incredible synchronicities that marked the passage, from my hopeful job hunting days in London to the hard and barren winter that I had to survive and master. Let me refresh the memory, if it eludes you . . . it had to do with a man named Michael Clarke, whom I simply referred to, earlier in the book, as Clark; but I think it time, now, to revert to his real name.

I met Michael by way of a Good Neighbors host with whom I stayed during my first month abroad, when I was trying to get settled in London. Anthea and Barry were the names of the host couple, and they took me to some sort of alternative Sunday service, back then in late September of 1990, also attended by Michael. He was just about my own age, and we connected like a pair of charged magnets. He was conversant with a wide range of my own interests, motivated by much the same values, and before the afternoon was done he had invited me (on learning of my circumstances) to share his quarters for a few days toward the end of the week.

I needed that, of course, but I was far more interested in his friendship, for it felt the best and richest of any I had encountered since coming to London. And it seemed to get only better in the time I spent with him. But something happened that broke the spell, and I was never sure what. My only clue came about a month later, when I received from him a bundle of mail he thought was mine, together with a letter that, in rather cold terms, said I should never have had mail forwarded to his place without consulting him first.

But it wasn't my mail. What had happened is that within days from the time I left his first floor flat, someone named Thomas Irvin had moved into an upstairs unit, and Michael had been gathering in the poor fellow's mail all this time, thinking it was for me! I finally got it all squared away, but the explanation did not seem to entirely satisfy Michael, and I was never able to get with him again. I tried several times, but he was always too busy for me.

Well, the whole situation had such strange overtones, both in my unusual resonance with Michael and the decidedly unlikely mixup that had transpired, that I have ever since felt an eerie sense of connection with the man, and have even speculated that it may have something to do with the life coming up *next* for me. That might sound like an odd twist on the oft-considered *past* life connection, but I have reason to believe that seeds are planted in the October/November phase of the living cycle, and this was the very portion of my life during which I found myself in London.

Be that as it may, or not, Michael has ever since had a place in my reflections on such things, though we never communicated again. I did send him a copy of the earlier edition, suitably inscribed, but received not a word in response.

I had no intention of attempting a contact, on this return – his silence had made his indisposition toward me perfectly clear. But I did write to Anthea and Barry, who knew nothing at all, of the above – not from me, at least. Theirs was one of the addresses I lost in Darmstadt, and so they merely never heard from me again. But in going through the new GN list for Britain, I saw they were still in it, and I sent word that I'd love to connect again, if even for an afternoon visit. A briefly worded card came back from Anthea, and I was resolved to call them when the time felt right.

The moment came during my last week in London. I had just gone into town, with nothing in particular on my schedule for that Tuesday afternoon, and made the call at 12:30 in hopes of setting up a get-together for a day later in the week.

"I am so glad you called," said Anthea, with some level of real urgency in her voice. "There is going to be a memorial service for Michael Clarke, this afternoon, at St. James Church in Piccadilly. Can you make it?"

I was absolutely stunned, of course. At the news, to begin with, but more profoundly at the fact that almost seven years after I'd last seen Michael, and with that strange course of our brief friendship, I had returned to London, and made the entirely happenstance phone call *just in time* to attend his memorial service! I had two hours to get there.

Listening to the speakers, I realized once again what a remarkable man Michael had been. The interesting thing was that so many had the same perception as I: that he could talk on practically any subject with the expertise and conviction of someone who had been devoted to it all his life. I later had lunch with Anthea and Barry and a couple of their friends, hoping for some further clarification of the strange conjunction between Michael's life and mine, but nothing came of it. Except, perhaps, for the equally strange impression that we were all simply fulfilling bit castings in some unknowable drama. When the lunch was over, it was like the curtain came down.

He died in January, actually – about the time I was tussling with whether or not to make this journey, and just a short few weeks before I plunged for the booking. Was *this* really what I went abroad for? The thought spooks me, but I cannot escape it. I've certainly discovered no better reason.

Ripening Seasons, *by the way, is still being published as a newsletter/journal, ranging into all topics of discussion. You will find current and past issues of it, as well as other writings of mine, at my web site:* http://irv.popco.com/beginning.htm